07-238

D1408641

T
58.5
.D58
2006

Diversity in
information
technology
education.

DATE			

T
58.5
.D58

DEVRY UNIVERSITY
ALPHARETTA, GA
Diversity in Information technology

35214000598033

BAKER & TAYLOR

Diversity in Information Technology Education:
Issues and Controversies

Goran P. Trajkovski
Towson University, USA

 Information Science Publishing

Hershey • London • Melbourne • Singapore

Acquisitions Editor: Michelle Potter
Development Editor: Kristin Roth
Senior Managing Editor: Amanda Appicello
Managing Editor: Jennifer Neidig
Copy Editor: Michael Goldberg
Typesetter: Sara Reed
Cover Design: Lisa Tosheff
Printed at: Yurchak Printing Inc.

Published in the United States of America by
Information Science Publishing (an imprint of Idea Group Inc.)
701 E. Chocolate Avenue
Hershey PA 17033
Tel: 717-533-8845
Fax: 717-533-8661
E-mail: cust@idea-group.com
Web site: http://www.idea-group.com

and in the United Kingdom by
Information Science Publishing (an imprint of Idea Group Inc.)
3 Henrietta Street
Covent Garden
London WC2E 8LU
Tel: 44 20 7240 0856
Fax: 44 20 7379 0609
Web site: http://www.eurospanonline.com

Copyright © 2006 by Idea Group Inc. All rights reserved. No part of this book may be reproduced, stored or distributed in any form or by any means, electronic or mechanical, including photocopying, without written permission from the publisher.

Product or company names used in this book are for identification purposes only. Inclusion of the names of the products or companies does not indicate a claim of ownership by IGI of the trademark or registered trademark.

Library of Congress Cataloging-in-Publication Data

Diversity in information technology education : issues and controversies / Goran Trajkovski, editor.
    p. cm.
  Includes bibliographical references and index.
  Summary: "This book investigates the status of diversity in the field of IT education with research on racial, gender, national origin, disability and other diversity categories"--Provided by publisher.
  ISBN 1-59140-741-9 (hc.) -- ISBN 1-59140-742-7 (pbk.) -- ISBN 1-59140-743-5 (ebook)
  1. Information technology--Study and teaching. 2. Multicultural education--United States. I. Trajkovski, Goran, 1972-
  T58.5.D58 2006
  303.48'34--dc22
                              2005027412

British Cataloguing in Publication Data
A Cataloguing in Publication record for this book is available from the British Library.

All work contributed to this book is new, previously-unpublished material. The views expressed in this book are those of the authors, but not necessarily of the publisher.

Diversity in Information Technology Education:
Issues and Controversies

Table of Contents

Foreword

In our lives as faculty members, nothing comes close to matching the complexity of the task we face in teaching. Unlike the arduous but deeply satisfying and familiar job of disciplinary research, teaching requires skills that were not part of our doctoral training. Most of us discharge that complex responsibility conscientiously and feel satisfied that our students have learned by relying on our grading system as a fair and accurate measure of their learning.

However, if we consider our teaching role as an important part of our professional productivity, one of the most difficult questions we should ask ourselves is whether our grading system actually reflects student learning. Good grades may only be indicators of superficial learning. Success of top students in their ability to secure a place in graduate programs is a measure faculty frequently cite of their own effectiveness. Clearly, for professionals who are trained in critical evaluation of data, this should not be the only measure used to determine our effectiveness in supporting student learning.

It is time to start asking ourselves about the effectiveness of what we do in the classroom and, most importantly, if what we do results in student learning. For instance, if lecturing is the only method of instruction used in the classroom, we should remember that a substantial body of research indicates that little of what we say in the classroom is remembered by our students. Lecturing works well for low-level thinking and is measured accurately by multiple-choice questions. But it has not been shown to work for understanding and lasting learning. A study documenting the importance of active engagement by students in the learning process found that the highest density of material covered in a lecture is recorded in the first 10 minutes of class, as measured by density of information recorded in students' notes. Active processing of the subject matter by students themselves, inside and outside the classroom, has also been shown to be essential in learning. Not surprisingly, active participation of students in class discussions and student collaborations have been shown to be more effective in producing learning and long-term retention than passive note-taking.

It is only recently that American higher education accrediting bodies have instituted student learning into their institutional accreditation process. The responsibility for determining student learning will ultimately fall on faculty shoulders. To facilitate this evaluative process, course design should have the overarching goal of organizing activities that result in student learning. We in higher education now find ourselves in the same place as medicine in the 1930s, when it had to change from an art into a science. Empirical evidence of efficacy was a good place to start in determining treatment, but research was needed to determine why certain drugs or treatments worked. Such research efforts evolved into what we now know as evidence-based medicine.

Continuing our metaphor, we have plenty of evidence of what works in facilitating learning. Reaching the great majority of our students should be our most important goal as teaching professionals. There is an expanding body of work that informs us about the highly complex and demanding job of achieving efficacy in teaching. Unfortunately, very few faculty members have the training, the time or the inclination to explore this literature on their own. Universities that have Teaching/Learning centers are able to support faculty with information and guidance about what works in the classroom. Sorcinelli's recent article in the *Chronicle of Higher Education* (Cook & Sorcinelli, 2002) argues strongly for the necessity of maintaining these centers to provide a support system for faculty in their teaching role.

In order to improve their course delivery, some faculty members viewed technology as a panacea for better teaching. Evidence for this view is shaky at best. The most effective technology-based interventions have proven to be only as effective as lecturing in promoting student learning. Using technology in the classroom should not be confused with teaching innovation. Technology is simply another tool and can only serve to complement or enrich the basic design of a course created by a faculty member with the essential knowledge of the discipline. It is how the technology is used to actively engage students' minds that will stimulate their learning. Excellent examples of creative and effective uses of technology in the classroom are given in several chapters of this book.

What we do in the classroom to motivate and inspire our students matters. Our task is not only to prepare an environment for our students to learn the specifics of our discipline, but also we are implicitly charged with shaping our students behavior to ease their path toward becoming learned and responsible citizens. As part of our American heritage, higher education is an important partner in achieving the overarching goal of bringing all students, not just the wealthy or outstanding, to the common table of knowledge accumulated during human history.

I view diversity as an inclusive and very American exercise, which aims to accomplish this overarching goal of sharing the rich cultural treasure of knowledge that is our common inheritance. Inclusion of all members of our society, regardless of gender, race or sexual orientation is essential if we are going to thrive in the complex, interconnected world we inhabit. Most importantly, the inclusion and retention of women in the sciences is urgent if we are going to succeed in our highly complex global economy. We may no longer rely solely on men to sustain the level of productivity needed to prevent the decline of our scientific and technological edge. Time and again it has been shown that cognitive differences are greater within members of a gender than between genders. The aptitude is there, but educational access is lacking, as are the mechanisms for retaining students in the sciences. Women who leave the pursuit of science education say that the most important reason for doing so is unsatisfactory teaching, especially at the college level, but also in high schools. We know that women benefit greatly from having science taught to them in a societal context, as exemplified by the success of feminist pedagogies in retaining women in science programs. Are we doing this in our classes? If we are not, as research suggests, are we designing courses to study science contextually? Are we requiring collaboration in the classroom, which also helps women and minorities to succeed? Also, it is well known that networking and mentoring opportunities are not optimal for women scientists or science students. Are we involved in mentoring and facilitating these opportunities for such students?

Although race in itself has no biological meaning because DNA variability is higher among people within the same race than it is between members of different races, the idea of race is a social construct, and the barriers it creates for student achievement is still a contentious and important issue that needs to be accounted for in higher education. As in gender differences of aptitude, greater cognitive and achievement differences are observed within members of a single race than between members of different races.

Uri Treisman, working with African Americans and Latino students in California, designed a course to help remedy the low achievement in college mathematics shown by these two groups (Treisman, 1986). Treisman created an honors course called "Calculus for Future Nobel Prize Winners." Students were not required to have a high GPA to be included but had to accept two requirements before being admitted to the course: They had to agree to do homework before class and to work in groups. No calculus problem was solved by Treisman in class unless students had worked with each other outside the classroom. Course grades for minority students improved significantly after the course, in many cases surpassing grades obtained by their Caucasian peers. As this example clearly illustrates, racism, either overt or carefully hidden by social convention, could have very negative impact on students but may be reversed by pedagogical intervention. More importantly, and to me a great source of hope and inspiration, there is abundant evidence that *any* pedagogical intervention will benefit those students with lower achievement indicators.

If our inclusive frame of mind is going to be global and lasting, it is also very important to remember sexual preferences in our course design. Inclusiveness extended to all should include accepting differences in that aspect of human behavior, especially now when theological considerations are obfuscating our secular goals.

There are very few roles as important as ours as teachers. Our university and our department have entrusted the development of our students' minds to help them reach their highest potential.

Luz Mangurian

References

Cook, C., & Sorcinelli, M. (2002, April 26). The value of a teaching center. *The Chronicle of Higher Education.*

Treisman, U. (1986). A study of the mathematical performance of black students at the University of California, Berkeley. Doctoral dissertation. University of California, Berkeley. *Abstracts International,* 47:1641A.

Preface

Introduction: The Wh_ Questions

Why This Book?

Diversity is an omnipresent buzzword in academic circles in the continuing efforts to diversify curriculum. The term itself is hard to define, but everyone seems to understand it as plethora of varieties. We can define it as narrowly or as widely as needed in a given discourse, but the bottom line is that diversity is "being aware of what is there."

When thinking about my personal development in this very field, I am able to pinpoint the time I started thinking about diversity issues as such. In the 1980s there was a huge campaign for tolerance and against xenophobia in several European countries under the motto "All Different – All Equal!" Although the outcomes of that campaign are unknown to me, the developments in different parts of the region (SouthEast Europe) are perhaps witness that it was not too successful overall. Nevertheless, I learned that an awareness that we are surrounded with people different from ourselves in so many ways is perhaps the natural path that one could take when starting to explore the world of differences. Moreover, we all have our personal stories that motivate us on a daily basis to continue our diversity efforts.

Diversity awareness enriches a person. Being exposed to a variety of differences, a person's horizons broaden. Stereotypes and prejudices start to disappear. Once initiated, the process is lengthy and gradual. The global advantages of diversity awareness are more than obvious, especially in the context of current world affairs.

We do not live in perfect academia. At the 2005 Yale Bouchet Conference of Diversity in Graduate Education (Yale School of Graduate Studies, Yale University, New Haven, Connecticut, April 1-2, 2005), a colleague and administrator of a large land grant institution in the Midwest was speaking about his personal experiences in convincing science and engineering faculty of the benefits of diversity as related to their research. He said that there are three groups, green, orange, and red, making a parallel to the colors of a traffic light. Those in the green zone had already understood the benefits of diversity and largely support the efforts of the institution; as such they were his supporters by default. Those in the orange zone were the "swing votes," and open to discussion. After some work, many of them "converted" into the green zone and became his greatest supporters. The red zone, however, composed of people that opposed diversity efforts, even openly, did not show signs of change in size.

Probably all of us have had experiences with colleagues from the red zone. I remember vividly a quite disturbing personal experience with a colleague that was a revelation of the ignorance and close-mindedness of the red zone academia. As we were closing up a meeting, I mentioned that I needed to wrap up quickly as I was getting late for a meeting of the University System of Maryland Faculty Diversity Network. The question I was asked was "What are you going to do there; is not diversity about women and African American only?"

As educators, we hold a great moral responsibility towards our students. We are shaping their minds, helping them grow, molding their lives and helping them to be exemplary members of society. That is a task, a responsibility and a challenge on one hand, but definitely an extraordinary opportunity, pleasure and honor on the other. Being aware of our differences makes us understand each other, solve differences more easily and even avoid them all together.

How This Book Kicked Off

In the beginning of my career in academia, I felt the need for guidance when striving to infuse diversity topics across the course curricula that I was teaching. In search of support, I came across a number of general titles, and especially literature on interventions in the lower segments of education (K-12).

Other books were clearly written for a Humanities audience on very specific topics.

Although there might not be a body of literature termed "studies on diversity issues in IT," that does not mean that there is a lack of it. One can find a body of work by prominent educators that refers to various aspects of the problems. There might not be a sufficient literature on what one would call the diversity theory as it relates to the field of IT, but there have been numerous articles where experiences from diverse Information Technology classrooms have been shared.

The idea for this volume came out of my personal need as educator for a tool of this kind. I used a few general education materials available and thought of transforming them to fit my teaching style and my students. I am glad that this book is being published, as it will save a lot of our successors many efforts that we had to go through when we needed a "one-stop service" volume such as this very one.

In an experimental (and, I might add, highly risky) venture, Yvonne Hardy-Phillips (Director of the Towson University African American Cultural Center) and I (a "diversity enthusiast" and junior faculty at the same institution) chaired the Tenth Annual Multicultural Conference "Dimensions of Diversity" at Towson University in March 2004. We decided to focus on the diversity issues in the sciences. Actually, the working title of the conference was "The Diversity of Science, the Science of Diversity." The conference was nothing short of a success and assured me that there is an audience and researchers even within the natural, computer and mathematical sciences for diversity topics. There is a need for research, a need to know the state-of-the-art issues and share experiences in providing solutions for the problems identified in the process. This revelation was my single most important motivation for starting work on this book.

A serious survey of the literature would reveal that this book is a first of its kind to deal specifically with diversity issues in Information Technology education. In lengthy discussions on these topics with colleagues across disciplines, it seems to me that the common perception of the Information Technology field is that it is, for lack of a better term, "diversity-unfriendly."

At first glance, the Information Technology field does not appear to be a "natural" for infusing diversity topics. Granted, due to the nature of the field, we might not be teaching as many diversity-specific courses as our colleagues in the Humanities (e.g., Women's studies, History, etc.), but we are certainly able to infuse as much diversity into our classrooms by simple transformations of our tools. In a generic and low-level example, when teaching a skill, such as creating table in Microsoft® Word, instead of using generic hiring data from an ACME Tomato Company, we could easily find data on the number of women in the senates (or equivalent governmental structures) in a few countries (especially Scandinavia) and substitute a diverse example for the sterile one the textbook provides. This will initiate a process that builds upon on itself, and is extremely beneficial to both the students and the instructors.

To attempt to satisfy what I assumed would be a widespread curiosity about the diversity issues in Information Technology education, I invited several colleagues to comment, in a brief and personal way, on what they consider to be the greatest challenges in the field. To a degree, my curiosity about the state-of-the-art of diversity in Information Technology education at large has been satisfied. But above all, it has been sharpened: and that must be the greater compliment to the authors. As one would expect with such an array of contributors, the chapters speak with authority and a willingness to venture challenging views.

What is This Book All About?

It is true that the definition of the term diversity varies, based on context. Normally, authors choose a working definition that suits their discourse. These chapters cover a wide range of diversity categories, its various aspects, dimensions and how diversity relates to Information Technology education.

By looking at relevant statistics, or at introspective testimonials given by the authors or those surveyed, the state of the diversity landscape in Information Technology crystallizes. It seems that at present, the predominant, severe issue is the numbers of female and African American students in the classrooms. Studies have investigated environmental and other parameters that might have been the cause of these problems, and propose ways of fixing them. Of special concern are the low numbers of women and minorities enrolled in the Information Technology majors. There *are* and *have been* statistics to document these numbers and analyses have been performed. The situation is not only grave for those most visible (for lack of a better term) "diversity slices." Other "slices" are not as easily identifiable or surveyed. But even with the information we have at hand, we can say that the situation is serious, and that efforts need to be made, not only quickly, but also on a large scale.

In this book, not only gender and racial issues are being discussed. Disability and learning styles issues, for example, are also being raised in some chapters. Diversity (of a different kind) can also emerge in a classroom setting. Within open-ended and autopoietic organizations with their multi-agent human environments, various social phenomena emerge and are observed.

Diversity in the classroom can be accommodated in a myriad of ways. Studies suggest that the way we teach IT, for example, might be better suited for our male students. Different teaching strategies can fix that. For the students with disability, there is a wealth of accessibility options available today. Open-ended projects seem to work better for both the students and faculty.

It would be a natural assumption, if going by the title itself, that this book would treat only issues that concern the student in the classroom. However, it is actually not so. The issues concerning the student and the classroom are dominant in the book, but faculty is not neglected. Tips for faculty development and self-development are given in several chapters. These tips aid instructors who may be confused on how to approach the diversity infusion, how to manage the diversity in his or her classroom and how to prepare to face the challenges of a diverse Information Technology classroom, where not only the technology but the people are diverse as well.

Therefore, the basic idea of the book is to serve as a teacher's tool. When needed, an instructor may not only find relevant information, but be able to use the strategies overviewed in the book, to grow as a diversity-aware and -transfusing educator. The students will love it and so will the instructor. This process, however, does not happen in a one-way fashion. Students enrich teachers as much as the teachers enrich the students. I speak from personal experience.

What are the Issues and Challenges that the Chapters Focus On?

The spectacular specialization of research in Information Technology areas, coupled with a corresponding proliferation of journals, has meant that in many cases it is virtually impossible to keep up with what is happening in research areas adjacent to one's own, let alone those that are far removed. Other areas, however, are just emerging. Interdisciplinary research, coupling the Information Technology disciplines and the social studies, for example, is quickly emerging, producing significant insight into the problems and social phenomena that Information Technology inherently introduced and has continued to produce.

It is a cliché of book reviews that edited volumes are often a curious and idiosyncratic collection of chapters. Note that essential to the personal character of this volume was the need to avoid constraining contributors with rigid guidelines. We ended up with a rich selection of chapters, as diverse in focus as the topic of the book itself, but complementary to each other nonetheless. A brief description of each of the chapters follows. The chapters offer one of the many possible logical orderings that I have considered, and significantly complement each other. The book starts with chapters that may be termed theoretical, as they focus more on the *identification* of diversity dimensions relating to Information Technology education, and identify the present issues. Via chapters that are more *introspective*, contributors share their own and their students' experiences, we stress again, more personally on the gravity of the problem. The last few chapters offer solutions and are presented in the form of best practices—experiments that have worked for our colleagues and thus contribute to piecing together the *solution* mosaic. Therefore, to reiterate, the underlying idea of this book is to state the theory first and, by identifying the issues, provide possible solutions.

In the chapter, "Dimensions of Diversity in the IT Classroom Onground and Online," Bhattacharya and Jorgensen introduce us to the dimensions of diversity in a cultural context with special reference to the development of Information Technology in general, and make a special reference to Information Technology education. They justify that globalization of education in a true sense cannot be achieved only by establishing accessibility and developing cost-effective technologies. The authors debate the influence of Information Technology on diversity and global culture issues via the modes by which technology is currently being used. The authors argue that the ideal is not possible within present Information Technology usage unless the underpinning culture of the Information Technology curriculum is acknowledged, openly discussed and adjusted for. They develop a model in phases to discuss the difficulties in engaging with technology and thus find ways of increasing its usage particularly in the education sector.

As educators, we need to work towards creating a culture and providing an environment in which students are able to express themselves without risk or fear of retribution. In order to promote higher order thinking skills, we must move from the single expert view to a more collaborative and engaging classroom. In Information Technology, there are controversies and different solutions to problems. For example, students need to be helped to understand arguments for different points of view and to see how they relate to each other. The development of technological literacy, as well as life skills, would be accelerated using argumentation skills such as debating, justifying an opinion, weighing up conflicting points of view and analyzing disagreements. These skills are intrinsically linked to problem solving skills, and may be assessed in dynamic and exciting ways, such as observation, interaction, group work and challenge. Arguments can be grounded on common knowledge, personal knowledge, testimony, plausibility and necessary truth. That is the essential message of John R. Daker's chapter titled, "Dialectic Argumentation for Promoting Dialogue in IT Education: An Epistemological Framework for Considering the Social Impacts of IT." These philosophies are essential to understanding both the made world and the new electronic age.

In the third chapter, "Bridging the Digital Divide: A Feminist Perspective on the Project," Mary Kirk examines the problem of power and access gaps in relation to both users and developers of Information Technology and proposes solutions from a feminist perspective. The chapter begins by explaining the importance of cross-disciplinary dialog between the so-called "hard" sciences (such as Computer Science and Information Technology) and the "soft" sciences (such as Psychology and Women's Studies). Next, Kirk attempts to demystify the "F Word" (as in Feminism) by providing a primer on the feminist approach and explaining how social institutions operate to teach values, attitudes and beliefs. The remainder of the chapter examines the impact of three social institutions (mass media, language and education) in relation to science and technology. Kirk explores the influence of mass media by providing examples of how stereotypes are used to teach limited and limiting beliefs that influence perceptions of science and technology. She demonstrates how language operates as a social institution in the male-oriented technology culture to privilege one gender over the other. Lastly, Kirk explores education as a social institution by sharing a brief history of women in science in the United States and explaining how methods of teaching and learning privilege certain groups over others. The chapter concludes by sharing the vision of feminist science-studies scholars for a science and technology for all and encourages us to pledge ourselves to birth a new social revolution on a global scale by bridging the digital divide.

In the chapter that follows, "Gender and Programming: Mixing the Abstract and the Concrete," Peter McKeena provides us with an examination of a theory of gendered styles in (computer) programming. The theory is predicated on the differences between male and female students in using the concepts of abstraction and black boxes. It critically explores the theoretical questions and issues raised and summarized in the design of an empirical, quantitative means of testing gender-based attitudes to black boxes, alongside and triangulated with ethnographic research into the experiences and attitudes of female students in relation to programming. This might be critical in identifying the low enrollment of female students in the Information Technology-related fields and the problems of their retention within related majors once they have decided to pursue a degree in these fields. The paradigm shift represented by object-oriented programming is given particular consideration because of the claims made on its behalf within this debate, and as a special case of abstraction. The chapter concludes that there is no gendered difference in attitudes to black boxes in programming, and that the reasons for female under-representation in computing lie elsewhere, which gives another perspective on the assumed gender stereotypes of the male and female abilities and attitudes towards abstraction.

The fifth chapter, "Dimensions of Sustainable Diversity in IT: Applications to the Information Technology College Major and Career Aspirations Among Underrepresented High School Students of Color" by Stockard, Akbari and Damooei, acknowledges that diversity issues in the Information Technology field go beyond racial and ethnic dimensions to include many more. A finer resolution of the problem is presented in this chapter. Diversity aspects here include disability, age and other factors. While the chapter examines the different forces that affect the career aspirations and opportunities of individuals of color, women, the disabled and the young as they make decisions about relating to the Information Technology field, this chapter is inspired, but not fundamentally driven, by data rather than the need to expand the traditionally investigated aspects of the diversity complex. The authors assert that diversity should be viewed globally with the understanding that the globalization process has begun to change the dynamics of the phenomenon of diversification. In an effort to show the impact of career aspirations and the influences on the development of such aspirations among minority and nontraditional students, they show results from a recent study. This study looks at the career experiences, opportunities, attitudes and aspirations with respect to Mathematics, Science, Computer Science and Information Technology of underrepresented students in the federally funded Upward Bound and Math/Science Upward Bound programs. The chapter concludes with a brief discussion of the role of social and cultural creativity and innovation, arguing that these are essential components of a notion of *sustainable* diversity.

Alfreda Dudley-Sponaugle presents the sixth chapter of the book, "Under-Representation of African American Women Pursuing Higher-Level Degrees in the Computer Science/Technology Fields," with plentiful introspective on the problems of the missing student in the Information Technology classroom—the female African American. Statistical data show the disparity in representation of female students in general and African American women in particular in the Information Technology fields. There are relatively few African-American women represented in the Computer Sciences/Technology areas. The number of African-American women pursuing a higher degree in these areas is almost non-existent. There are many factors, which may contribute to this trend. This chapter focuses on some of the complexities involved in this problem. Using statistical data, the author covers the socioeconomic, educational and cultural barriers, which have an effect on this under-represented populace. In conjunction with this information, Dudley-Sponaugle elaborates on some of her own experiences as a former student and an educator, as well as selected experiences of some of her students.

The situation in the enrollment and retention of students in the Information Technology fields is not different from the corresponding situation in the fields of Mathematics and the other "hard" sciences. In Chapter VII, "Working with Students in Math, Technology, and Sciences for Better Success: One Faculty Member's Experiences," Shah and Miller elaborate on an extensive effort to improve retention rates via specific advising strategies. These efforts span over a long period and have been successful. As a measure of success, the authors have used their own courses in chemistry as case studies. Therefore, with this chapter we present a successful case from another discipline that is completely transferable to the Information Technology field. By strong mentoring and devotion, students can make it. The interventions are done via—amongst other methods—devoted tutoring in basic Mathematics. Once the strong basics are built, the student's understanding of the core is strengthened and they manage to progress more easily through the more challenging upper-level courses. The authors present their efforts and experience in interventions in a vast range of courses for a diverse audience—traditional and nontraditional students in a university setting, as well as students in courses tailored to meet the needs of a specific private sector company.

In the eighth chapter, "Assessing Diversity Issues in Instructional Technology: Strategies that Enhance Student Learning and Generate Outcomes Assessment Data," Virginia Johnson Anderson stresses that the primary focus in higher education today is the assessment of student learning. IT faculties and departments are being asked to document quantitatively what students have learned in relation to goal-oriented expectations. Although that "students will value diversity in the academy and the workplace" is a common course, General Education or institutional goal, we often know little about how well students achieve this goal because we do *not* assess it. This chapter describes how to construct Student Learning Outcomes consistent with valuing diversity, how to design tests/assignments to see if students have achieved those outcomes and how to use that information to inform and enhance student learning in their IT courses, departments or institutions.

Holding up diversity as something that has to be learned as if it is part of the curriculum may sometimes be counterproductive. It is perhaps much more natural and sensitive to allow diversity to become part of the curriculum by the way it is integrated into student learning. The projects that Chapter IX, "The Open Ended Group Project: A Way of Including Diversity in the IT Curriculum," is devoted to, are one such method that can allow educators to tackle the issues surrounding diversity without making it a separate part of the curriculum. In this way, students are able to discover the many issues that a heterogeneous society has as part of its makeup. They see how differences between people operate in the real world and experience for themselves that these differences are a source of much strength and excitement. The OEGP seeks to foster cooperation amongst students by providing a common goal for them to work to and encouraging them to pool their skills. Educators can work definite diversity issues that need to be addressed into the OEGP idea or they may leave it more fluid and tackle issues as and when they arise. By simply putting people together, their differences are bound to surface, and students will necessarily have to face those differences and learn how they might be used to best advantage. In this way, the OEGP provides a natural method of confronting diversity and learning how rich people's differences make social and working life.

Many in Information Technology education—following more than 20 years of multicultural critique and theory—have integrated "diversity" into their curricula. Nevertheless, while this is certainly laudable, there is an irony to the course "multiculturalism" has taken in the sciences generally. By submitting to a canon originating in the humanities and social sciences—no matter how progressive or well-intentioned—much of the transgressive and revolutionary character of multicultural pedagogies is lost in translation, and the insights of radical theorists become, simply, one more module to graft onto existing curricula or, at the very least, another source of authority joining or supplanting existing canons. In this essay, we feel that introducing diversity into Information Technology means generating a body of creative criticism from within Information Technology itself, in the same way multiculturalism originated in the critical, transgressive spaces between literature, cultural studies, anthropology and pedagogy. In Chapter X, "Attack of the Rainbow Bots: Generating Diversity through Multi-Agent Systems," Collins and Trajkovski trace their own efforts to develop isomorphic critiques from recent insights into multi-agent systems using a JAVA-based software agent they have developed called "Izbushka." With Izbushka the authors not only study the diverse learning processes in human subjects, especially learning in context, but in this environment, diversity emerges and is generated.

The eleventh chapter, "Adaptive Technology in a Computing Curriculum," describes how adaptive technology for the disabled can enhance a computing curriculum. Blaise Liffick argues that computer professionals will naturally have an increasing role in the support of adaptive technology because of economic, legal and social pressures, and that consequently, adaptive technology topics should be covered within a standard computing curriculum. Ideas for integrating adaptive technology topics into computing courses are presented, along with an outline of an advanced course on adaptive technology from an Information Technology perspective. A model adaptive technology laboratory for supporting these efforts is described in detail. Liffick hopes that this chapter will encourage Information Technology educators to use adaptive technology topics as examples within their courses, ultimately leading to a computing workforce that is ready, willing and able to provide fundamental adaptive technology services to those with disabilities as well as a workforce that is aware and knowledgeable of the issues of their colleagues with various disabilities, and knows how to accommodate their needs.

Introducing diversity topics in the natural, mathematical and computer sciences is a hard task, since these disciplines are traditionally labeled as "diversity-unfriendly," due to the primary foci of their study. In Chapter XII, "Tessellations: A Tool for Diversity Infusions in the Curriculum," Sarhangi, Meiselwitz and Trajkovski illustrate how tessellations can be used as a tool for the infusion of multicultural topics. The authors give a framework, designed after the Towson University (Towson, Maryland, USA) course "Computers and Creativity," where these concepts have been successfully implemented.

With the last chapter, "Training Faculty for Diversity Infusion in the IT Curriculum," Trajkovski offers a flexible training environment and strategies for diversity infusion in the Information Technology curriculum. The chapter overviews the so-called "My First Diversity Workbook," and how the author uses it in his diversity trainings for faculty. The major part of the workshops consists of four parts. In the first part, the trainer talks abut his or her positive experiences of diversity infusion in the curriculum, and serves as a motivational component of the training. The second and third components provide inspiration for the micro and macro infusion of topics into the curriculum from the outside and the inside. By using external examples and facts, or internal experiences and introspections, the instructors can successfully diversify a unit lesson or the whole curriculum. In the fourth component, the trainer talks about continuing to share classroom experiences after the workshop is done—usually online—within the framework of an e-group. Trajkovski offers a description of how to fit these four components in two different contexts, and describes in detail the schedule and the experiences of the participants from those two workshops, custom-tailored to the needs of the institution that the trainings had been designed for. These workshop patterns are fully replicable. The chapter not only describes the author's strategies in covering the topics, but also provides a selection of sources that the trainer and the participants may use when replicating or modifying this training pattern.

How to Use This Book

This book presents an organized reading on the state of diversity affairs today in the field of Information Technology education. With convincing facts, we now see the actual problems more clearly and are able to identify the critical points that need mending. As for the readers that are professional educators in IT, they will see that they are infusing diversity in their teaching on a daily basis, without realizing it or labeling it so, which will give them a personal motivation to do it even more and better.

This book attempts to shed light on the status of diversity in the field of Information Technology education. As a first book on this very topic (to the best of our knowledge), it identifies a wide range of problems that educators face on daily basis and proposes practical, applicable solutions, mainly by showcasing successful and replicable examples. Chapters present research and introspection on racial, gender, national origin, disability and other diversity categories. The course and training examples, success stories from retention efforts and the strategies in assessment that account for diversity all supplement the topics with practical examples on how to identify, face, act and intervene when an instructor is thinking of infusing diversity topic(s) in the curriculum, whether on a small, unit level, or course-wide or even curriculum-wide level in general.

This book represents a pioneering work in a field that is slowly shaping itself. Despite the other Information Technology fields, this branch is in its very inception. It is a significant repository of relevant statistics teaching strategies and case studies that are easy to replicate.

The foreword of the book calls for education for all. That basically is the motivation of all chapters of the book. We want to be effective, equal opportunity instructors and do the best we can to accommodate all of our students in our classrooms. We as educators—especially in higher education—are not in a position to do miracles when trying to remedy problems that have rooted deep in, say, the socio-economic background of a student. However, we can do something, and that is important. We can work on helping our students broaden their horizons, know diversity and enter a more comfortable and accommodating workforce (and world in general), one that suits them better.

Acknowledgments

Projects of this ambition and size cannot come to completion without the support of literally a whole army of brave, open-minded and knowledgeable people, all of who helped out to the maximum of their available energy. As all of them are academicians, and as this project was going on during the academic year, their contribution is especially appreciated, taking into consideration the other, for lack of better terms, regular, ongoing scholarly, and especially teaching, activities. There was not a single person that refused to help out when asked—I attribute that to the fact that they are top educators and to their realization of the importance of this book and enthusiasm to have it see the light of day. Therefore, preparing this book has been one of the most enjoyable experiences of my academic life.

The quality of an edited volume depends on the constructive input from the reviewers. I would like to acknowledge the help of all involved in the collation and review process of the book, without whose support the project could not have been satisfactorily completed.

Many of the authors of chapters included in this volume also served as referees for articles written by others. Thanks go to all those who provided constructive and comprehensive reviews. However, some of the reviewers must be mentioned as their reviews set the benchmark: Georgi Stojanov of the Computer Science Department, Faculty of Electrical Engineering, "Ss Cyril and Methodius" University, Skopje, Macedonia, and Samuel Collins from the Sociology, Anthropology and Criminal Justice Department, Giovanni Vincenti from the Computer and Information Sciences Department, and Yvonne Hardy-

Phillips from the African American Cultural Center of Towson University, Towson, MD, my home institution for the duration of the project. I believe that thanks are also owed to my home department, the Computer and Information Sciences Department of Towson University.

A further special note of thanks goes also to all the staff at Idea Group Inc., whose contributions and support, in the many ways that one can imagine, throughout the whole process from inception of the initial idea to final publication have been invaluable. With their help, all deadlines were met. From today's perspective that is by no means a small task.

My prerequisite for seamless functioning is the support of my family. I thank them for their encouragement and for letting me use a great chunk of "our" time to devote to this book. I promise to make this time up.

Last, but not least, I wish to thank all of the authors for their insights and excellent contributions to this book. I hope that we have started something very important with this project. Time will tell how influential we will become.

Goran P. Trajkovski, PhD
Baltimore, Maryland
October 2005

Chapter I

Dimensions of Diversity in the IT Classroom Onground and Online

Madhumita Bhattacharya, Massey University, New Zealand

Lone Jorgensen, Massey University, New Zealand

Abstract

This chapter introduces the dimensions of diversity in a cultural context with special reference to IT education. The authors justify that globalization of education in a true sense cannot be achieved only by establishing accessibility and developing cost effective technologies. The debate concerning the influence of IT on the diversity and global culture issues will be colored by how technology is being used. The authors argue that the ideal is not possible within present IT usage unless the underpinning culture of the IT curriculum is acknowledged, openly discussed and adjusted for. They develop a model in phases to discuss the difficulties in engaging the technology and thus finding ways to increase its usage, particularly in the education sector.

Copyright © 2006, Idea Group Inc. Copying or distributing in print or electronic forms without written permission of Idea Group Inc. is prohibited.

Setting the Scene

In this chapter we will try to answer the following questions: What is the relationship between globalization and diversity in the Internet age? Why do we need to know about diversity? What are these diversities? How may learning be enhanced with the knowledge about dimensions of diversity?

With the introduction of the World Wide Web, there is no doubt that mankind is moving towards globalization. We frequently come across the terms such as *distributed learning, virtual communities, learning objects, metadata, adaptive learning systems, texting, blogging,* etc. We need to understand these words in terms of globalization and to recognize diversities in terms of individual needs and interests.

Caine et al. (2004) writes that uniqueness is a fact of life. Race, color, creed and culture all are aspects of individuality, but even within a culture in which all people are overtly similar, immense differences exist. Nature is diverse and, in fact, thrives on diversity.

According to Caine et al. (2004), we are biologically programmed to make sense of our experience. In other words, we are innately motivated to search for meaning. Therefore, with the advent of IT and the creation of the Internet, teachers are no longer required to just transmit information. They are also required to address many other areas, such as helping students to create meaning from newly found information so that it becomes knowledge and learning.

If technology provides metadata, will children ever learn? Is there a risk of technology doing too much for students? Transformative pedagogy is needed to encourage the development of skills such as research, evaluation and analysis skills. This is not possible by just teaching HTML. Sometimes it may be better not to use the computer at all.

Let us compare spelling with critical thinking. Some basic level of spelling is needed. Technology can, however, take care of basic levels of spelling requirements, leaving the opportunity to concentrate on "higher" level cognitive skills such as critical thinking and analysis. In that light technology as such is neither harmful nor useful. It depends on the way we use it.

While teaching either in a traditional classroom (i.e., face-to-face teaching-learning environment) or in an e-learning environment, we need to consider the different type of learners we have. In traditional classrooms we do not consciously think about that, but in fact teachers adapt their lessons to the

Copyright © 2006, Idea Group Inc. Copying or distributing in print or electronic forms without written permission of Idea Group Inc. is prohibited.

learner all the time. There is not just *one* approach. There are differences in approaches within an e-learning versus a classroom-based context. Traditionally, we use off-the-shelf materials for teaching. These follow a pre-determined sequence. Some of these products allow different paths of learning but cannot be described as genuinely adaptive. Adaptive strategies work ideally in a one-to-one fashion. The real world of the classroom is at least 30-to-one. Using the potential of IT, we may capture the learner's profile in a database and approximate the adaptive strategy of the one-to-one approach. More about this will be discussed in the latter part of this chapter.

As we all learn from helping others learn, the degree to which we may be effective is directly related to how much we know about the situation and circumstance of the person we are trying to help. Personalization of the learning experience requires knowing something about the learner. To avoid redundancy, the system must know what the learner already knows. To assemble relevant learning experiences, it must know about the learner's past experiences, learning preferences, career goals and more. Personal profiling enables new approaches to productivity. A profiling system that automatically identifies people's areas of expertise based on the issues they research on the Internet, the ideas in their documents, the e-mail messages they create and the topics they follow in their knowledge bases facilitates creation of virtual workgroups, encourages communication and reduces duplication of effort.

The more a learning system knows about a learner, the greater the opportunity to provide on-target information. At the same time, the learning record should be at least as secure as a credit record and/or medical record.

In e-learning situations there are various options possible. In a typical blended approach, there is content delivery and there are discussion threads. It is possible to analyze students' learning styles to a certain degree in such an e-learning environment. There could be another approach where students are directed in a more open fashion. The main aim is to develop collaboration or to form virtual learning communities where people share their knowledge and bring learning into practice. This might be a very rewarding approach. There are scalability issues though. In the school context you do not have the option to move totally online. In higher education there is that option.

In the past, we had a limited set of tools to teach people. There is evidence that, compared to the use of books, the range of digital devices we may use have a wider range of children responding positively. Many teenagers can do different things at one time such as listening to music, playing electronic games, walking, etc. The question we need to ask is whether multitasking is accelerating critical

Copyright © 2006, Idea Group Inc. Copying or distributing in print or electronic forms without written permission of Idea Group Inc. is prohibited.

thinking skills or whether there is a loss of reflection and loss of coordination due to cognitive overload? How does blogging differ from older forms of note-taking? In blogging one is more likely to be distracted because one has greater opportunity to shift attention outside the immediate environment. According to the theories of psychology, there is a limit to the number of tasks that the central executive nervous system can manage at one time. Maybe there is accelerated evolutionary development here. Again we come across a big difference between present day learners (learning styles, abilities and availability of technology) to that of present day teachers in the classroom or online. Here the teachers not only need to be aware of the learners' diversities and differences but are required to go through continuous professional development to understand the needs of present day learners. We should provide a safe and conducive environment which would enhance learning through various challenges.

Setting the Diversity Parameters

It would be ideal if there were a better and more well-fitted technology suitable for the purpose of teaching. The current process for communicating requirements for educational needs to software developers is very bad, resulting in tools that are inappropriate for teaching practice and difficult to connect together, with some support missing completely. We do, however, expect the tools to improve in the future as technology develops. This will require a better-negotiated process of requirements, gathering rather than just delivering what one party asks with "I want".

There is a realization of a gap in what students expect, or what they have been promised, and the teaching they have received. This is usually due to uneven application of the technology, or the failure of some educators to apply it at all. There seems to be a role gap relating to these expectations—it is not clear where the responsible parties are for some of this support (it tends to fall between libraries, support services, technology services and department staff).

Therefore, the awareness of diversity will not be enough to create an environment where learning for all will take place. Rather, it is that the knowing and understanding of the concept of diversity, and keeping that always in view, will make a better teacher, administrator and curriculum designer.

Copyright © 2006, Idea Group Inc. Copying or distributing in print or electronic forms without written permission of Idea Group Inc. is prohibited.

At national levels, curricula are often designed in a "one size fits all" format. Individuals are expected to be taught according to one set of pedagogical documents designed with a specific, relatively homogenous group in mind. In the field of IT education, teaching occurs across national boundaries and has multiple objectives for work training, education and accessing information. The learner is required to master both the content of the subject and the tool of teaching. Thus, the diversity of potential client groups directs that the IT curriculum be flexible and adaptable. An IT curriculum must be written in such language that it is accessible to a client group both physically and culturally dispersed.

IT curriculum planners need to define the dimensions of the diversity which forms the boundaries of global culture that the technology operates within. The global culture is a mosaic of overlapping subcultures with limits set by the skills, attitudes, expectations and intrinsic knowledge held by each of these sub-groups. *Dimensions of Diversity* implies a relationship in time and space definable by specific group characteristics. Each defined group is delineated by the characteristics chosen. The group, however, is not immutable. Individuals within each group may have more than one diversity characteristic and belong in many groups simultaneously. Previous literature has defined diversity with emphasis on cultural aspects related to age, gender, disability, education, ethnicity and national status (Carnoy, 1999; Roman, 2003). Further consideration clearly indicates that geographic position, as much as national status, creates a diversity dimension in terms of availability of suitable infrastructure. For example, within the same nation rural areas may not have access to the Internet, whereas urban areas will (Tomlinson, 2003). The complexity of the diversity nexus makes it difficult to identify, and to focus on, primary points where action can have huge impact, in terms of improving access to and outcomes of information technology education.

To elaborate further on the dimensions of diversity, we have included the following excerpts from a symposium conducted at the NARE-AARE Conference 2003 (Bhattacharya & Jorgensen, 2003).

Stereotyping: Teachers may have unreasonable expectations of their students depending on the students' cultural backgrounds. An example, might be that Asian students are brighter than others, thus, there is an expectation that Asian children will always excel in mathematics, or that different cultures have preferential learning styles, thus Polynesian children prefer kinetic learning

Copyright © 2006, Idea Group Inc. Copying or distributing in print or electronic forms without written permission of Idea Group Inc. is prohibited.

styles. There may be a presumption that boys don't read, that girls cannot read maps or that old people cannot learn.

Immigrants and the conflicts of interest among teachers and students (this also covers rural/urban migration). The split in home-school environment and reality for students from different cultures to that of the school may arise from conceptual differences rooted in language usage as well as in habits and customs (e.g., the language of science may have no equivalent in the home language, so the student fails to grasp the "reality" of the science concepts). Similarly, a student may have housekeeping duties that prevent him or her from doing expected homework or there may not be access to media or other resources required for lessons in the home.

Teachers' open-mindedness vis-à-vis students' achievements: If teachers expect writing and reporting to be carried out to a certain standard he or she may overlook students' conceptual achievements. For example, a student may express biological terms in the vernacular if these terms are used in the home, and be punished for the language but not recognized for the knowledge. This is similar to problems arising from learning difficulties such as dyslexia.

Teachers' understanding of students' problems arising from cultural contexts: This is similar to other points raised, in that culture is embedded in language and values. Cultural differences may be expressed simply by whether a child meets the eyes of a teacher while speaking, smiles at the "right" times, uses "acceptable" eating habits or uses "please" and "thank you" when expected. Teachers who note these problems can gently guide the students to avoid such problems in the future.

Dilemmas due to differences between value system at home and in school: This may range from religious observation requirements to shared physical education for boys and girls.

Identity crisis: Value conflicts and mismatches between home and school environments may give rise to identity crises that will accentuate normal adolescent identity problems and make school and learning much harder for the international student.

Copyright © 2006, Idea Group Inc. Copying or distributing in print or electronic forms without written permission of Idea Group Inc. is prohibited.

Gender differences, people perception and behavior in face-to-face and in online environments: Online education is the most obvious distributed learning environment. The problems and dilemmas associated with it are not just technical. Language becomes the sole method of communication with no body language to impart meaning or soften the impact. Thus, in one sense online communication removes gender and other cultural barriers, but in another sense allows misunderstandings to develop without recourse to quick correction.

Immersion in the normal classroom. Is this a solution to the problem of multicultural issues? Special education needs students benefit from mainstreaming if the support systems are strong. Thus, multicultural issues may be similarly addressed with mentoring, special support classes, peer support and aware teachers.

The digital divide and the generation gap: The older generation does not have the prerequisite knowledge or even the language associated with digital technology.

Music/visual art and culture: This is an area where much multicultural understanding occurs; for example, youth culture may be approached through their music. Much may be said using visual displays and music that could be misunderstood using other methods.

To simplify the discussion of the dimensions of diversity we will use the term "function" to cover large groups. Each function will have a set of variables within it. These variables determine the extent of the diversity between individuals. To abridge the diversity tangle we create three main functions. Variables are then defined under those functions, and further identified by a grouping index that creates a scoreboard against which the diversity of each client is scored, should that be deemed necessary (Table 1).

Using the scoreboard (Table 1) each person will receive a personal score, which describes their particular combination of needs. As an example, we may consider two potential students. Student one is a 30+ US woman with two children and ten years' education as well as little previous exposure to IT. She lives in a rural area supplied with electricity and phones. Student two is a 25-

Copyright © 2006, Idea Group Inc. Copying or distributing in print or electronic forms without written permission of Idea Group Inc. is prohibited.

Table 1. Dimensions of diversity scoreboard

Number	Function	Variable
1	Socio-economic/ Culture	**Ethnicity:** American Indian, Asian, etc.
		Gender: Male and Female
		Disability and/or Dependent's
		Education Levels of Education, e.g., No schooling, Primary, Secondary, etc.
2	Experience	**Age:** Age groups
		Exposure or Vocation: None, little, some or much
3	Urban Index	**Geographic location:** Urban or Rural
		Infrastructure: None, electricity, electricity + phone or full

year-old Mexican woman with no children, secondary education and some experience with IT. She lives in an urban area with full IT services. The similarities between students may then be estimated for planning purposes. Clients with similar combinations may then be clustered in the same teaching environment, which will have been designed to fulfill those needs. This scoreboard represents an efficient use of resources aimed at the greatest need and a reduction in the frustration that students experience if there is a mismatch between their particular needs and the implementation of the curriculum.

Each function represents different sets of problems that may have to be overcome before the curriculum can be delivered, but only the first two functions are inherent with the client.

Presumably, the aim of all IT curricula is to get the client to engage with the technology. The propensity to engage may be likened to the consumption curve used in economic forecasts: If the price is too high, consumption is low, if the price is too low the manufacturer cannot afford to produce the product. The same qualities apply to the use of IT, if the difficulties are too high, resistance to engage with it will be high, if the difficulties are overcome with money and support, the service becomes too expensive and not offered as widely. This is illustrated by the graph as shown in Figure 1.

Copyright © 2006, Idea Group Inc. Copying or distributing in print or electronic forms without written permission of Idea Group Inc. is prohibited.

Figure 1. Difficulties encountered vs. propensity to engagement graph

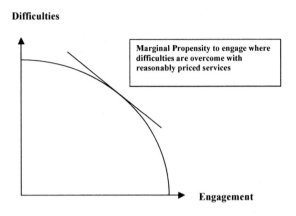

Our Model:
IT Education vis-à-vis IT Cultures

Having borrowed the model from economics (Jacques, 1995; Wisniewski, 1996) it also makes sense to determine what constitute the difficulties to engage with the technology and thus, find ways of increasing its consumerability. IT is often termed "hostile" to access by certain groups and to certain subjects. It is the degree of this hostility and the origins of it that needs to be explored to increase the marginal propensity to engage by the diverse groups defined in the three functions described earlier.

IT itself embodies the particular culture arising from its early development. Computers started as calculators and filing machines developed from a need for data and number crunching. The inventors and developers of these machines, and ultimately the software to drive them, were males (Hofner, 1996; Johnson & Maddux, 2003). The thinking behind them tended to be linear, with an approach that encouraged a conveyor-belt mentality. Time-and-motion studies using information technology seemingly reduce people to machine level, where diversity is not tolerated as it interferes with efficiency. The linear approach further alienates users from cultures where the approach to differing issues traditionally is indirect.

Copyright © 2006, Idea Group Inc. Copying or distributing in print or electronic forms without written permission of Idea Group Inc. is prohibited.

The promise of a more social approach, more inclusive of diversity came later, as computers became the tool for quick communication over large distances. Early e-mail held this promise, but the technology was still rooted in a culture apparently hostile to human needs. The language used was English, that suggested a bias towards the cultures where this language is used. The introduction to the use of icons in IT imposed a new iconic language on consumers of the technology. However, the use of some icons may be offensive and act as a barrier to the marginal propensity to engage with the technology as well. With the Internet and more user-friendly soft- and hardware components, there has been apparently more open access to the technology, offering free exchange of information, with its possibility of open and inclusive education across various cultural divides. However, the user-friendliness may hamper creativity by encouraging digital drawing instead of using proper art tools, composing electronically backed music pieces instead of using traditional instruments and by engaging with a computer screen instead of with real people.

To understand the resistance of the IT environment to the propensity to engage in and its perceived hostility towards gender, disability, social and political issues, it is necessary to understand the underpinning culture of the IT curriculum. In the Western world, IT infused the classroom setting slowly since it was first developed. The technology is implemented both as a tool within other curricula areas, and as a curriculum in its own right. The debate around the influence of IT on the diversity and global culture issue will be colored by how the technology is being used. A simple model can be formulated to embody the old and the new computer cultures as shown in Figure 2.

Figure 2. Positional relationships of "old" and "new" computer cultures

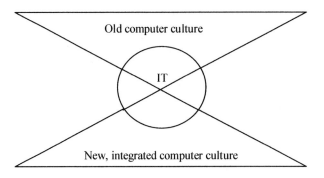

Copyright © 2006, Idea Group Inc. Copying or distributing in print or electronic forms without written permission of Idea Group Inc. is prohibited.

The model illustrates the opposing worldviews regarding computer cultures. The old culture is rooted in the linear, male-dominated thinking mentioned above. The new culture has sprung from a need to integrate and incorporate lateral thinking and "fuzzy" logic. Curricula that do not acknowledge that both of these cultures are integral parts of the technology risk leaving part of their clientele behind. In other words, failure to incorporate both will push the propensity to engage towards the zero position on the difficulties encountered vs. propensity to engage graph (Figure 1).

The sides of each culture triangle represent "skills" and "language" (shown in Figure 3). These are quite different for each group. The "old" culture has a language heavy in symbolism and jargon. The further from the apex, the more extreme this is. The skills are specialized and involve writing and communicating with the computer directly. People operating mostly towards the base of this triangle often carry the label "Computer Nerd." The "new" culture has a more informal language system, allowing communication with the computer in "real" language. The integration and merging with people's life experiences is greatest at the base of this triangle, i.e., there is a connection with the real in virtual reality. This culture also has its own set of skills, which has developed to fulfill the needs of people who would otherwise feel alienated by a "hostile" medium.

The IT curriculum should aim at integrating these two cultures. The areas created by joining the two extreme apices of the skills and language sides represent the areas that the IT curriculum should include (as illustrated in Figure

Figure 3. Language and skills integration between the two IT cultures

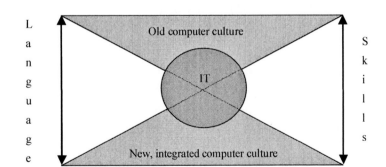

Copyright © 2006, Idea Group Inc. Copying or distributing in print or electronic forms without written permission of Idea Group Inc. is prohibited.

Figure 4. Intrinsic and extrinsic areas of IT education

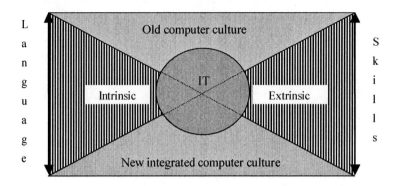

4). The skills area represents the extrinsic factors of this, i.e., the "doing" of IT technology. The language area contains the intrinsic factors, i.e., what lies behind the "doing." Intrinsic factors are much harder both to identify and to change as the learner brings many individual permutations to this area, which are largely invisible.

With the increasing availability of technology at our doorsteps and faster networking, we may find that a teenager in New Zealand and a teenager in the US have more in common with each other than with their respective teachers or parents. Thus, as well as globalizing in the international sense, we are simultaneously becoming more diverse within our homes and in the local communities. Information technology both feeds this process and offers the potential solutions to it. The ability to capture knowlege such that it can be analyzed, reused and shared with others, thus developing a spiral of new knowledge creation, is perhaps the most powerful promise Information technology can provide. The impact on learning of "just-right" information flowing to the right place, person and time cannot be overstated.

Expertise used to demand constant improvement of one's ability to perform the tasks or skills of a profession or trade. However, as multiple professions converge and fuse, as tasks and skills are constantly replaced with new ones at an ever-increasing rate, expertise becomes a matter of steadily renewing one's knowledge base and extending it to new areas. Critical expertise has transformed into the continuous creation and acquisition of knowledge and skills. This lifelong cycle of learning is the new foundation of professional self-worth and that of all teams and organizations. One's primary responsibility, and

Copyright © 2006, Idea Group Inc. Copying or distributing in print or electronic forms without written permission of Idea Group Inc. is prohibited.

perhaps the only sustainable competitive advantage, is to improve one's ability to learn and apply the right things faster.

As the changes and discoveries noted overlap in time, they have obvious synergies and relationships that converge to create the inflection point, or take-off, of the information/ knowledge age. As this occurs, we will also witness a level of revolution equivalent to the agrarian or industrial revolutions in the form of the information, knowledge revolutions and information automation. As with previous revolutionary creations, we will realize order of magnitude increases in productivity and performance, but in the information revolution these will be increased productivity of knowledge and number of service workers. This is not to be confused with merely generative processing of information, just as the factories of the industrial revolution were not merely the automation of previous process and practice. This will involve the invention of entirely new processes for knowledge capture, converting raw data into information and the subsequent creation of new knowledge in an ever-spiraling crescendo. As was the case in the industrial revolution, these changes will, for better or worse, impact people's lives and their cultures.

In a world of constant and increasing rates of change, one of the most prevailing trends and traits is that of convergence. Technologies converge to create new technologies and products; concepts converge to form completely new concepts; people converge into new local, global and virtual communities; and professional skills converge to create new professions. However, these convergences pale in comparison to the implosion of learning, working and capturing knowledge and the management of their sum total. These previously disparate and relatively independent activities are converging to become one, and in so doing will create a completely new existence, a new way of being.

In this chapter we tried to define the dimensions of diversity and how to cope with diversity within the implementation of IT curricula. We have tried to place the diversity conundrum within the development of IT itself, the changes that occurred during this development and what this has meant in terms of the teacher's interaction with the learner. We have signaled that not all change is synonymous with progress, and that the globalization of IT can often mask an internal diversity chasm, which may mean that people within the same communities move further apart in knowledge and access to information.

Our recommendations are that the dimensions of diversity be an integral part of curricula design to encourage the strength of IT in offering meaningful adaptive programs approximating those of one-to-one delivery.

Copyright © 2006, Idea Group Inc. Copying or distributing in print or electronic forms without written permission of Idea Group Inc. is prohibited.

References

Bhattacharya, M., & Jorgensen, L. (2003, November/December). *Distributed Learning Environment in a Multicultural Context*. A Symposium presented at International Education Research Conference AARE — NZARE, Auckland, New Zealand.

Caine, R., Caine, G., McClintic, C., & Klimek, K. (2004). *12 Brain/mind learning principles in action: The fieldbook for making connections, teaching, and the human brain*. CA: Corwin Press.

Carnoy, M. (1999). *Globalization and educational reform: What planners need to know*. Paris: International Institute for educational planning (UNESCO).

Hofner, K. (1996). *Where wizards stay up late: The origins of the Internet*. New York: Simon and Schuster.

Jacques, I. (1995). *Mathematics for economics and business* (2nd ed.). Boston: Addison-Wesley.

Johnson, D.L., & Maddux, C.D. (2003). *Technology in education: a twenty year retrospective*. Binghamton, NY: Roundhouse.

Roman, L. (2003). Education and the contested meanings of "global citizenship." *Journal of Educational Change, 4*, 269-293.

Tomlinson, S. (2003). Globalization, race and education: Continuity and change. *Journal of Educational Change, 4*, 213-230.

Wisniewski, M. (1996). *Introductory mathematical methods in economics* (2nd ed.). New York: McGraw-Hill.

Copyright © 2006, Idea Group Inc. Copying or distributing in print or electronic forms without written permission of Idea Group Inc. is prohibited.

Chapter II

Dialectic Argumentation for Promoting Dialogue in IT Education:
An Epistemological Framework for Considering the Social Impacts of IT

John R. Dakers, University of Glasgow, UK

Abstract

If a deep and meaningful understanding of Information Technology is to flourish, we need, as educators, to create an ethos in which students can express themselves in a risk-free environment. In order to promote higher-order thinking skills, we must move from the single-expert view to a more collaborative classroom. In information technology, there are controversies and different solutions to problems: Students need to be

Copyright © 2006, Idea Group Inc. Copying or distributing in print or electronic forms without written permission of Idea Group Inc. is prohibited.

helped to understand the arguments from different points of view, and to see how they relate to each other. The development of technological literacy, as well as life skills, will be accelerated through the use of argumentation skills such as debating, justifying an opinion, weighing up conflicting points of view and analyzing disagreements. These skills that are inextricably linked to problem-solving skills, may be assessed in dynamic and exciting ways, such as observation, interaction, group work and challenge. Arguments may be grounded on common knowledge, personal knowledge, testimony, plausibility and necessary truth. These philosophies are essential to understanding both the made world and the new electronic age.

Introduction

Jonas (2004) argues that Information Technology has come about as a result of the revolution in the passage from electrical to electronic technology. This, for him, "signifies a new level of abstraction in means and ends" (p. 27). Whilst he concedes that technologies and instruments designed to give us information, or aid cognition (such as tying a knot in a hanky as an *aide memoir*, or using a thermometer to gauge the temperature of some liquid) were around for some time prior to the concept of electronics, these devices did not, with the possible exception of the clock, generate information in an active sense. In the world we now inhabit, however, Information Technology actively shapes and directs our lives. Thus, information delivered through Information Technologies is socio-technological. This has consequences not only for education concerning Information Technology, but also for society in general.

In this chapter I would like to begin by problematizing the prevailing model of learning and teaching within the Information Technology curriculum. (This also resonates strongly with other domains such as technology and science education.) In schools, and also, I will argue, in further and higher education institutions, the Information Technology curriculum makes certain assumptions about the nature of the various Information Technologies in terms of "fitness for function," and that these functions are seen in some narrow instrumental context. By this I mean that Information Technologies are regarded very much as a means to serve specific ends. They assume an epistemology that is more concerned with the processes embedded within the methods of their produc-

Copyright © 2006, Idea Group Inc. Copying or distributing in print or electronic forms without written permission of Idea Group Inc. is prohibited.

tion and manipulation and are less concerned with the social consequences that will ensue as a result of their existence. This narrow functionalist model, I will argue, tends to be the current dominant orthodoxy. Many students, as a result, when faced with a problem, especially in Information Technology, attempt to proceed directly from problem statement to solution. I will argue that as a result of this narrow mastery system, students are unable to engage with the social and political ramifications engendered by the proliferation of Information Technologies. What will follow is an argument that learning in this narrow model is linear and instrumental and, to all intents and purposes, not meaningful learning at all. Moreover, a direct result of this narrowly-focused pedagogy is the creation of Information Technology systems that are also narrowly conceived. This, I will argue, can, and does, have serious implications for the end users of Information Technologies.

I will then go on to explore a learning paradigm in which learning about Information Technology is seen as a social process. I will present an argument, in line with current educational thought, that a need now exists to abandon current behaviorist pedagogies and to move towards a more broad-based learning environment which encourages dialectic and argumentation. This is necessary for the development of more informed attitudes about the impact of Information Technology on individuals, societies and, indeed, the world. This model of learning goes beyond, but encompasses, social constructivist theories of learning in which dialogue plays a central role.

The Transmission Model of Learning

The legacy of behaviorist, teacher centered, whole-class teaching methodologies, with teacher as expert and student as passive recipient of knowledge, continues to assert itself as the dominant orthodoxy in education today. As ever more centralist agendas inform the practice of educators, established hierarchies continue to embed themselves into the very fabric of the education process. As a result, traditional management strategies, founded upon devolved school and university economies, begin to emerge. New discourses, such as, "full economic cost recovery," for example, are surreptitiously entering the world of academe. Thus, the commodification of knowledge transforms teaching and learning into "supplier" and "user," emulating the marketplace of productivity and profit, where profit is based upon a determination of examination passes (Peters, 1995, p. 28). This emphasis on a knowledge economy

Copyright © 2006, Idea Group Inc. Copying or distributing in print or electronic forms without written permission of Idea Group Inc. is prohibited.

results in teachers and lecturers experiencing an increase in pressure to deliver a more centralist and prescribed curriculum for accountability in order to meet the productivity targets demanded. Students, moreover, whether at school or universities, are encouraged to adopt the type of instrumental strategies that will ensure a pass in their chosen subject. Mayor (1992) highlights the dangers of this "learning as a response acquisition" in his analysis of behaviorist methods. This type of teaching style, however, has particularly serious implications for an information technology-dependent population, which, through ignorance and apathy, is becoming increasingly unable to engage in informed debate about the way Information Technology is shaping and dominating society (Head & Dakers, 2005). This recent, but exponential, trend, in which intellectual processes are giving way to a new instrumentality of knowledge acquisition and production, is impacting upon pedagogy at all levels in education. Jardine (1992), moreover, argues that this technical image of educational inquiry leads us collectively away from the matters themselves towards the method alone in order to render the concept of inquiry objectively presentable.

*They are designed to pass on information that is already understood, **given** a certain method or research design and a specific history of inquiry. In such approaches, understanding begins and ends with method and operates in service to such a method. Understanding is thus educationally neutered: It is not designed to educe the possibility of understanding, but **assumes** such a possibility of its ground.* (p. 117, emphasis in original)

Thus, paradoxically, the very ideology that espouses the commodification of education with its emphasis on accountability and efficiency of delivery, serves to devalue knowledge in the current climate. Wells (1999) further suggests that in this model, conflicts arise between teachers' espoused beliefs and perceived external requirements. He sees difficulties arising when teachers try to demonstrate initiative by adopting innovatory practices, when external administrators, and indeed the wider community, are not perceived to be supporting these practices.

Jardine (1992) offers an interesting analogy that might help to explain this paradox:

Animals under various forms of threat—the continuous presence of predators, lack of adequate food, drought, and the like — tend to play less

Copyright © 2006, Idea Group Inc. Copying or distributing in print or electronic forms without written permission of Idea Group Inc. is prohibited.

and less. They tend, quite naturally, to revert to those kinds of activities that will aid them in gaining comparative control over their environment, activities that involve little or no risk. *They revert, so to speak, to what is tried and true, what is most familiar.* (p. 121)

In this analogy, play may be seen as a more free form of expression and inquiry that, by its very nature, requires participants to explore and interpret their word actively and communally, and as a result of novelty, often requires some degree of risk. There is no imposition of behavior in play. Young animals (including humans) are initiated into their particular culture through play (and other methods) and learn about their world together in a community of practice which, for Lave and Wenger (1991), involves progressing from "legitimate peripheral participation," towards central participation. It is through this intersubjectivity that learning takes place (Rogoff, 1990). It is in this respect that Wenger (1998) bases his thesis about "communities of learners" around the following four premises:

1. We are social beings. Far from being trivially true, this fact is a central aspect of learning.

2. Knowledge is a matter of competence with respect to valued enterprises—such as singing in tune, discovering scientific facts, fixing machines, writing poetry, being convivial, growing up as a boy or a girl and so forth.

3. Knowing is a matter of participating in the pursuit of such enterprises, that is, of active engagement in the world.

4. Meaning—our ability to experience the world and our engagement with it is meaningful—is ultimately what learning is to produce. (p. 4)

Using Wenger's model, it becomes clear that the processes surrounding Information Technology cannot be separated from the social context. It is essentially about the communication of information that is considered to have value and significance, requires active participation and involves active engagement in the world. However, if the paradigm is altered from one in which learning is socially constructed to one in which learning about Information Technology is purely instrumental, the result is diminishment. Education about Information Technology then becomes the acquisition of objectively-designed knowledge, which serves to train, or more importantly control, an effective

Copyright © 2006, Idea Group Inc. Copying or distributing in print or electronic forms without written permission of Idea Group Inc. is prohibited.

workforce in order to satisfy the perceived needs of a socio-cultural economy. Learning in this uncritical model conceptualizes knowledge in Information Technology as the simple development of knowledge bases that evolve out of an already established hierarchy of "relevant" subject matter. Students conform to the perceived expectations demanded by the system, which in turn serves to inculcate an identity that is hegemonic in nature. This is "…a form of domination so deeply rooted in social life that it seems natural to those it dominates" (Feenberg, 1998, p. 10). This uncritical and undemocratic form of teaching and learning within Information Technology has, and will continue to have, serious implications for those involved in its future development. Moreover, it forms the basis of what I will call a "hegemonic behaviorist cycle." By this I mean that inculcation into a behaviorist system will serve to shape the learners' actions when setting into practice what has been learned.

An example may help to illustrate this point. Speed cameras are an example of both hegemony and behaviorism. The rationale for the recent proliferation of speed cameras is that they help to reduce accidents and save lives. Statistics, indeed, would seem to support this. This, however, is an imposed rationale that clearly does not accord with the views of a significant number of drivers. If it did, we would not need speed cameras. So why is it that so many drivers do not agree with the imposition of these cameras? It may be that they feel they are able to drive safely at higher speeds than those imposed; it may be that other technologies such as pedestrian crossings, tunnels or bridges are considered to be a more appropriate solution. The issue reverts back to intersubjectivity or, in this example, the lack of it. In a community of drivers, a shared understanding of the problems associated with driving fast in a certain area, together with an exploration of alternative strategies, is more likely to lead to an accepted resolution than the imposition of sanctions. In the current situation, when drivers see the speed camera they slow down, not because they agree that they should, but rather, because they do not want to get caught. On the other hand, a situation where a shared understanding, or intersubjectivity, is evident is in drinking and driving. Evidence suggests (in the UK at least), that where advertisements are behaviorist in nature, there is not a significant decrease in drinking and driving. For example, in the UK there has been a regular campaign every New Year to cut down on drink driving. Advertisements warn that more police will be out on the streets and that will increase your chances of getting caught. However, when the emphasis moved from the subject to the object, where advertisements shifted the emphasis to portrayals of the consequences of drink driving, where families who had lost a significant other as a result of

Copyright © 2006, Idea Group Inc. Copying or distributing in print or electronic forms without written permission of Idea Group Inc. is prohibited.

drink driving told their story, incidences of drink driving reduced. I would argue that this is a result of the development of an intersubjectivity, a shared understanding where drivers choose not to drink and drive, not because they might get caught, but because they see the potential consequences that might ensue should they drive when under the influence of alcohol. In the first case regarding speed traps, behavior is regulated externally and subject to the dominion of others, whereas in the second case, behavior is negotiated and founded upon a moral imperative.

A sinister example of the uncritical use of Information Technology in the not too distant past might serve to illustrate this point. Albert Speer, a German Armament Minister in 1942, delivered the following speech at the Nuremburg trials:

The telephone, the teleprinter and the wireless [Information Technologies] made it possible for orders from the highest levels to be given direct to the lowest levels, where, on account of the absolute authority behind them, they were carried out uncritically; or brought it about that numerous offices and command centers were directly connected with the supreme leadership from which they received their sinister orders without any intermediary; or resulted in widespread surveillance of the citizen, or in a high degree of secrecy surrounding criminal happenings. To the outside observer this governmental apparatus may have resembled the apparently chaotic confusion of lines at a telephone exchange, but like the latter it could be controlled and operated from one central source. Former dictatorships needed collaborators of high quality even in the lower levels of leadership, men who could think and act independently. In the era of modern technique an authoritarian system can do without this. The means of communication alone permit it to mechanize the work of subordinate leadership. As a consequence a new type develops: the uncritical recipient of orders. (Speer, 1942, quoted in Moos, 1997, p. 126)

Therefore, for those engaged in the process of learning and teaching Information Technology there is a clear imperative to develop a new form of pedagogy which will encourage interrogation of the received wisdom of the day. This notion has indeed already received some attention in high places; the U.S. President's Information Technology Advisory Committee in its 1999 report, for example, highlighted the fact that:

Copyright © 2006, Idea Group Inc. Copying or distributing in print or electronic forms without written permission of Idea Group Inc. is prohibited.

*Information Technology will significantly improve the flow of information to all people and institutions in the Nation, and could be a powerful tool for **democratization**. Our National well-being depends on understanding the **potential, social** and economic benefits of on-going advances in Information Technology. However, problems are arising from the increasing pace of information technology-based transformations ... brought about by the integration of Information Technology into our lives.* (PITAC, 1999, p. 5, my emphasis)

Given the deep rooted conservatism inherent within the psyche of Western educational policy makers, however, new ideas about teaching and learning, such as the new standards for various literacies (scientific, technological, computer, etc.), will prove difficult to implement as a model of inquiry and creativity until a break can be made from the current transmission model. This requires Information Technology education to be seen as a necessary imperative and not just a political cause. The standards, in their delivery, must not become a reconstitution of what went before by creating and selling knowledge in a synthetic knowledge economy in which knowledge is neatly packaged to encourage "remembering previously remembered material" (Dakers, 2002, p. 47), and in which students are seen in an empiricist sense as *tabulae rasae,* waiting to be filled up with a prescribed curriculum which considers particular skills in Information Technology imposed by industry to be an economic necessity.

Bergman (1991) reinforces this point in his criticism of the notion of teaching as a form of the transmission of information:

If truth is not theoretic but that which a person must verify through his life and the way he lives it, how can one person be another's teacher? A person cannot transmit his philosophy the way an object is given and received. This kind of transmission is impossible in relation to existential truth. The teacher's reality can only open the possibility for the student to live his own truth, to actualize it through his way of life. Therefore, the teacher must not go beyond the limitations of this possibility. We must prevent the birth of a direct relation in which the student passively receives the doctrine of the teacher. (p. 41)

Copyright © 2006, Idea Group Inc. Copying or distributing in print or electronic forms without written permission of Idea Group Inc. is prohibited.

The Effect of Mediation in a Technologically Mediated World

The transmission model is, by its very nature, a monologue. Any interaction between teacher and student is a one-way process. There is, however, a growing recognition that, in order for human beings to learn, there has to be active involvement in the learning process. Humans construct meaning through the process of interaction and inquiry, and this involves communicative action (see, for example, Cole & Wertsh, n.d.; Engestrom et al., 1999; Lave, 1998; Lemke, 1997; Matusov, 1998; Rogoff, 1990; Vygotsky, 1978; Walkerdine, 1997; Wenger, 1998).

Learning does not take place in a vacuum. Humans do not learn by constructing their own realities that are separate in some way from the cultural, historical and social environment into which they were born. Our development is thus both mediated and shaped by our interaction within the space we occupy in the world.

The nature of learning, or mental processing, according to Vygotsky, involves four areas of development: an evolutionary process (phylogenesis), a sociocultural historical process, individual development (ontogenesis) and development through interaction with specific socio-cultural settings (microgenesis) (Wells, 1999).

Learning is social in that it involves the interaction of others. Even when learning apparently occurs in an isolated way, such as studying for exams, reading a book or interacting with a computer, it is still a social process. It is either mediated through direct experience with others, such as lecturers, teachers, peers and colleagues, etc. or through interaction with the artifacts created by others, such as books, videos, television, buildings, etc., and now, more than ever, learning is mediated through the medium of Information Technologies.

The socio-cultural interaction between developers of Information Technologies and users, however, is not straightforward. The interaction may, therefore, have unforeseen consequences, as when the original conceptualization of the technology becomes subverted by its end users. Feenberg (1998), for example, discusses the evolution of the French communications device, "Minitel." This was designed to give subscribers access to databases that would improve the flow of information in French society, thus bringing France into the information age. The developers' intention was to redefine the social image of the computer by giving it a less businesslike look and a more user-friendly

Copyright © 2006, Idea Group Inc. Copying or distributing in print or electronic forms without written permission of Idea Group Inc. is prohibited.

format, more closely resembling a telephone. "The 'cold' computer became a 'hot' new medium" (p. 10). However, the narrowly conceived function of the 'Minitel' became subverted by "the very nature of the advanced society it made possible" (p. 10). Many within French society redefined the serious function intended into a device for developing anonymous chat rooms in a search for "amusement, companionship and sex" (p. 10). Other examples include the development of new forms of bullying in schools through the sending of cruel text messages on mobile phones and the exponential rise in plagiarism through the Internet, where complete assignments on every subject and even post-graduate degree theses can be purchased on line.

These examples serve to demonstrate the complexity of the mediating role of Information Technologies between the subject, in this case the designers of the Information Technology, and the object, in this case the end user. Whilst the technology remains the same, the user subverts its original intent. It is through the mediation of the human-technology relationship that "the human, material, and practices all undergo dynamic changes" (Idhe, in press). These changes can, moreover, be mediated from an external hierarchy which involves impo-sition, or from within a community which involves collaboration. The develop-ment of an Information Technology and the consequential impact it will have upon a society will be determined by the mediation utilized.

Information Technology can thus be adopted into a cultural system through a process of intersubjectivity, developed from within and adopting community structures which, in turn, give rise to identity; or at the other end of the continuum, adopted as a device which is hierarchical in nature, imposed from above and without, and so designed to shape and control societies. Heidegger (1962), and Feenberg, in his critical theory (2003), suggest, however, that it need not be a case of either one or the other scenario and that a synthesis between these opposing polarities is possible. They argue that in association with the instrumental role a technology may have, we must also give consider-ation to the essence of the technology in terms of its social and cultural implications. Out of this emerges a synthesis that leads to an anamorphosis in Information Technology education. In other words, the technologies that we simply accept as they are presented are often distortions of the truth, much as the lettering used in road markings appears to be elongated and distorted from the point of view of a pedestrian. However, the same markings, when viewed from a driver's point of view, seen head on and from a different perspective, appear, as a result of foreshortening, to be in proportion. This is deliberate on the part of the designers but, significantly, very few of us, drivers or pedestrians, are actually aware of this. It is only by repositioning ourselves that we may begin

Copyright © 2006, Idea Group Inc. Copying or distributing in print or electronic forms without written permission of Idea Group Inc. is prohibited.

to see a different perspective, and this may in turn serve to transform our previously distorted view by illuminating and clarifying the controlling logic of the technologically-mediated world we inhabit (Dakers, 2005). A technological literacy where the dialectics of "calculation versus meditation, objectification versus art, 'world' versus 'earth,' identity versus difference" (Kroker, 2004, p. 38) are explored, is therefore a crucial part of a learner's technological development.

It is thus that a society's cultural identity should be formed through links with its past and present, mediated through forms of discourse and where meaning is co-constructed and reconstituted. As globalization takes hold, and cultures communicate more and more with each other, specific cultural identities are eroded as new globalized multicultural identities become formed within what Baudrillard (in Lane, 2000) refers to as "hyperreal" worlds or virtual worlds. Passive members of societies set within these virtual or hyperreal worlds will lose their local cultural identities as global corporate identities subsume them. The voyeurism associated with reality television serves as an example of this new world order. Information Technologies can therefore be seen to actively shape society; in order to participate in this hyperreal world, we need to engage in new discourses which require active dialogues, face-to-face or electronically.

Dialogue necessarily plays a central mediating role since it is the principle means of arriving at a common understanding of whatever question is at issue" (Wells, 1999, 10). Wells goes on, however, to illustrate that research clearly indicates that there is a dearth of dialogue in the years of schooling and, as I would strongly argue, within higher education also. Whilst the "banking" (Freire, 1970) conception of knowledge prevails, classroom or lecture theater dialogue is not seen as a necessary imperative. Wells, however, rejects the prevailing view in which knowledge is treated as some "thing" that people possess. "Knowledge is created and recreated between people, as they bring their personal experience and information derived from other sources to bear on solving some particular problem. (Wells, 1997, p. 10)

Copyright © 2006, Idea Group Inc. Copying or distributing in print or electronic forms without written permission of Idea Group Inc. is prohibited.

Argumentation

The term argument is often considered to have negative connotations. Thus, argument is commonly regarded as confrontational and often irresolvable. It is perceived to involve raised voices at best and physical violence at worst. Whilst this may be true in some circumstances, the reality is that arguments occur all the time. A discourse on the financial worth of a football team's latest signing, a discussion on the best entry for the Eurovision Song Contest, an enquiry into the existence of God, all involve some form of argument. This may take the form of externalized interaction with others or internalized interaction within oneself. Every thinking human being engages in both forms on a regular basis.

Arguments may be grounded in common knowledge, personal knowledge, testimony, plausibility and necessary truth. They may be simple in their constitution and easily resolved. The postulation that the earth revolves around the sun would be taken as a necessary truth by the proposer, but may be considered as implausible by the opponent. Using the many Information Technologies available in the 21st century, it is very likely that the proposer would be able to convince the opposition of the validity of this argument. Significantly, however, this was not the case several centuries ago when Galileo argued for it. He suffered with his life for his argument that contradicted the received wisdom of the time. But his argument was profound and affected the way we now live our lives. The process of argument indeed brings about many profound changes.

This orientation of communicative action to validity claims admitting of argument and counter argument is precisely what makes possible the learning processes that lead to transformation of world views. (Habermas, 1987, pp. xvi-ii)

To exclude this form of free exchange in a classroom prevents the learner from becoming a person who, through a natural curiosity inherent in all human beings, interacts with his or her environment by interpreting, repudiating or affirming experiences, creating instead one who is reactive, conditioned and, at best, trained. A world without argument is a world without inquiry. It is a passive world of blind acceptance.

Khun illustrates this point by postulating two extreme sociocultural positions:

Copyright © 2006, Idea Group Inc. Copying or distributing in print or electronic forms without written permission of Idea Group Inc. is prohibited.

We have described two very different kinds of knowing, although they are in fact poles of a continuum on which most knowing lies. At one pole, knowing prevails in the comfortable ignorance of the knower's never having considered that things could be otherwise. At the other pole, knowing is an ongoing, effortful process of evaluating possibilities, one that the ever present possibility of new evidence and new arguments leaves never completed. (Khun, 1991, p. 267)

This has important implications for learning about Information Technology, which should, in line with modern educational thought, be a form of inquiry that occurs within a community of learners. This inquiry-based pedagogy, however, involves a clear paradigm shift from the current, conventional form of classroom practice.

Learners bring a variety of beliefs and opinions with them into the Information Technology classroom. These beliefs and opinions are formed through interaction with their fellow human beings as well as with their particular environment. The formation is consequently socio-cultural.

If we were to consider a scenario where a learner had interaction solely with one mature human being, that human being would then be perceived by the learner to have more experience and consequently greater knowledge and expertise. The consequent likelihood is that the learner would adopt the same socio-cultural beliefs and opinions as their mentor. If the learner was informed that the world is flat and no challenge to this perception was experienced, then this social hegemony would eventually become so deep-rooted in the psyche of the learner that it would eventually be totally accepted as fact. However, any alteration to this hitherto shared belief would place the learner into a state of "disequilibrium" (Piaget, 1928). If, for example, the learner had been told that direct interaction with fire would not cause any pain and discovered, through experience, that it did cause pain, the learner would find him or herself in a state of cognitive dissonance. The resolution to this dilemma would involve either an interrogation of the received wisdom of the day, in this case emanating from the mentor, or, alternatively, a passive acceptance of the world as determined by the mentor, despite experiences to the contrary. The most likely consequence of adopting the second option is an ultimate state of distrust, frustration and unhappiness. This kind of experience appears to be increasingly manifest in the growing disaffection of students in school systems across the developed world.

Whilst it is clear that learners entering the Information Technology classroom have had interaction with many other human beings, the teacher or lecturer is

Copyright © 2006, Idea Group Inc. Copying or distributing in print or electronic forms without written permission of Idea Group Inc. is prohibited.

nevertheless still perceived to be an expert. This perception of a teacher, as with any member of a society who occupies an "academic" position, is usually one of respect, or at least one that validates the teacher as having some degree of subject expertise. This perception, together with the badge of authority that a teacher inherits upon entry to the classroom, tends to militate against the likelihood of challenge from the assembled mass — or at least challenge in the academic or thinking sense. (It is acknowledged that other forms student behavior can cause challenge.)

The opposing perceptions of the teacher as either an expert, authoritarian orator delivering knowledge to the assembled masses from on high, or an expert libertarian facilitator who assists in the creation of knowledge, can be resolved in a risk free environment.

It must be recognized, however, that this may be a paradigm too far removed from the current position of most teachers. Kuhn (1991), whilst suggesting that "argumentative dialogue with others externalizes argumentative reasoning and offers the exposure to contrasting ideas and the practice that may facilitate its development" (p. 294), goes on to discuss whether or not school experience does in fact lend itself to this type of exchange. She argues that although schools may provide a social environment where ideas will be tested and challenged, it rarely leads to pupils thinking explicitly about their ideas in a reflective manner. Whereas debate may be encouraged in the classroom, it tends to be very teacher-directed, with the teacher having a predetermined idea of the direction that the argument should take, and tending to direct it to that conclusion. This "teacher-directed" method is contradictory to the Socratic method, which would be "learner directed."

Plato's Socrates wandered the agora (marketplace) of Athens seeking out all that would listen. He adopted a method that challenged the individuals to seek out the truth for themselves. In pre-Socratic times, "philosophy" had been primarily directed towards the natural sciences. Socrates, however, is held to be largely responsible for opening up moral, ethical and political questions of virtue and justice as being of primary interest. His methodology, as recorded by Plato, has become known as the Socratic method,.the dialectic, maieutic method, that leads the mind in an intrinsically motivated way towards self-discovery. This method was in direct opposition to the methods adopted by the badgering Sophists, who preferred to fill their students minds with "pre recorded data" (Fortunoff, 1992).

Socratic inquiry makes use of questioning as a strategy to encourage the student, or interlocutor, to review their stated positions or assertions in more

Copyright © 2006, Idea Group Inc. Copying or distributing in print or electronic forms without written permission of Idea Group Inc. is prohibited.

detail than they might otherwise, Socrates would thus listen and ask contradictory questions necessitating a continual defense of the position until the participant reached a state where the inconsistencies of the original assertions were obvious and the requirement to rethink the original position became clear. Socrates referred to this form of pedagogy as "elenchus," which means "to contradict." This method of inquiry gave rise to dialectic—the idea that by modifying a person's viewpoint through the use of contradictory questioning and ideas, a closer approach to the truth might be attained.

Socratic inquiry can thus be inferred to be the obverse of transmission models of teaching. Fisher (1998) indeed defines it as: "scholarly ignorance, in which the teacher poses as someone who does not know in order to provide, motivate and facilitate the thinking of students. It is characterized by the teacher showing a self-conscious display of curiosity and puzzlement rather than as the person who knows the 'right' answer" (pp. 146-147).

Although adoption of the Socratic method would resolve Khun's problem with "teacher directed" pedagogy, research carried out by Lampert et al. (1996), suggests that this may in fact be too sophisticated a method for most children.

Lampert's study demonstrated that encouraging children in a fifth year mathematics class to defend a position through argument was too sophisticated a procedure for some and that this was dependent upon their stage of social development. Self-consciousness about disagreement, coupled with differing cultural beliefs about how to interact in public, were found to hinder the use of argument as a useful tool in developing cognition.

The study suggests that most children in this age group are eager to maintain social relationships in preference to adversarial ones. The potential of damaged ego and feelings that would occur when a child stood alone in defending a position, which subsequently turned out to be wrong, was too inhibiting for most to engage. This was true even in the risk-free environment created in the study. The notion of reasoned argument as a form of mediation in resolving matters, moreover, is no more widely accepted in adult Western civilization.

We all know of situations where everyone agrees to play by the rules to avoid confrontation or embarrassment even when the rules are meaningless. How many people have ever participated in discussion in which they have listened to, responded to, and questioned the teacher or one other? Or tried to convince themselves and others of the validity of their representations, solutions, conjectures or answers? ... Although we imagine that these practices should happen with some frequency in

Copyright © 2006, Idea Group Inc. Copying or distributing in print or electronic forms without written permission of Idea Group Inc. is prohibited.

academic research, they are not ordinary practices for working out public disagreements. They are not the activities that most people think of when they imagine trying to learn something. (ibid, p. 758)

Clearly, in order to accomplish an ethos of inquiry, we need to invoke a change in the culture of what learning is. This requires a pedagogical shift in which the teacher's role changes from that of a subject-specific expert to that of an expert in creating effective learning environments. The teacher's role in this model is to question and challenge the learners and to encourage the learners to do likewise (Dakers, 2005).

To achieve this, the notion of argumentation must move away from the current adversarial model that is entirely based upon winning or losing. The process of justification for a point of view in this current model involves deference to an expert model. "It is considered appropriate to call upon authorities like teachers or parents or bosses to sanction the validity of our approaches to problems" (Lampert et al., 1996, p. 758). This attitude is inherited from the orthodox, positivistic worldview, which is seen as a very linear and objective process. It requires quantitative solutions to all problems, which are ultimately reducible to right or wrong answers.

To disagree, especially with someone in authority, is seen as aggressive and even antisocial behavior. Until a major paradigm shift occurs in cultural norms, the promotion of argumentation as a process to enhance cognitive development within the classroom is likely to remain problematic. Even the use of Socratic questioning will leave a significant proportion of children feeling vulnerable.

That this effect may be cultural rather than inherent or developmental, however, may be demonstrated by considering the role of argument in eastern cultures such as China. Here, "the preferred mode of rhetoric was exposition rather than argument. The aim was to 'enlighten an inquirer,' not to 'overwhelm an opponent.' And the preferred style reflected 'the earnestness of investigation' rather than the 'fervor of conviction'" (Oliver, 1971).

Popper, moreover, despite the evident cultural barriers, gives support to the idea that learners (and, I would argue that we are all learners) should be encouraged, as part of the learning process, to constantly challenge the received wisdom of the day.

The proper answer to my question: 'How can we hope to detect and eliminate error?' is, I believe, 'By criticizing the theories or guesses of

Copyright © 2006, Idea Group Inc. Copying or distributing in print or electronic forms without written permission of Idea Group Inc. is prohibited.

others and – if we can train ourselves to do so—by criticizing our own theories or guesses. '(Popper, 1972, p. 26)

Dialectic

Children develop theories of mind (Olson & Bruner, 1996). These arise not through quantitative changes in development but through qualitative changes resulting from integration into society. Vygotsky describes this process as the result of "revolutionary" shifts rather than incremental hierarchical steps. He saw these major transition points in development in terms of changes in the form of the mediation utilized. Development, furthermore, is not limited to the ontogenetic domain. For Vygotsky, the phylogenetic and sociohistorical domains also contribute to development (Wertsch, 1985). Given that truths, whether based on cultural heritage or new thinking, are accepted or rejected on the basis of evidence, argument and construction and not by dint of authority, then I would argue that education must become "dialectical, more concerned with interpretation and understanding, than in the achievement of factual knowledge or skilled performance" (Olson & Bruner, 1996, p. 19).

Reason (1994) cites Hampden-Turner's interesting use of an ancient Greek myth to illustrate the essence of dialectic as distinct from dualism or opposing views.

In early Greek mythology those sailors who tried to navigate the straits of Messina were said to encounter a rock and a whirlpool. If you were too intent upon avoiding the rock you would be sucked into the whirlpool. If you skirted the whirlpool by too wide a margin you would strike the rock. These twin perils had markedly contrasting natures: the first was hard, solid, static, visible, definite, asymmetrical and an object; the second was soft, liquid, dynamic, hidden, indefinite, symmetrical and a process. (Hampden-Turner, 1990, p. 24, quoted in Reason, 1994, p. 31)

Clearly, an apparently irresolvable dynamic of oppositions faces the captain of the ship. "The 'correct' course to steer is not predetermined, but rather continually adjusts to the wind and waves" (Reason, 1994, p. 31). Constant adjustment between two opposing polarities will be required. "Steering the ship

Copyright © 2006, Idea Group Inc. Copying or distributing in print or electronic forms without written permission of Idea Group Inc. is prohibited.

involves leading in order to learn and learning in order to lead; the ship is erring so that it must be corrected, and steering the ship involves maintaining continuity in the midst of change" (Hampden-Turner, 1990, pp. 16-17, quoted in Reason, 1994, p. 31).

Steering the ship would involve a number of factors. For example, a combination of natural, intuitive responses would be evident. Constant adjustment and readjustment is required in direct response to constantly changing stimuli; in this case, the effect of the waves and the wind. The process is iterative.

Why Dialectical Argumentation?

Dialectic argumentation involves the recognition that opposing views exist. Take, for example, the computer. It is ever more accepted that the computer has made one of the biggest, if not *the* biggest, contributions towards globalization. We live in a world where information can be accessed almost instantaneously, almost anywhere. Whilst this is accepted, students of Information Technology are not generally able, I would argue, to discuss the impact that this has had upon societies around the world. Indeed, I would further argue that they are not able to fully realize the impact even upon and within their own culture. Dialectic argumentation can help to redress this. As I have argued earlier, students tend to concern themselves with the processes embedded within the methods of production and manipulation in Information Technologies, and are less concerned with the social consequences that will ensue as a result of the existence of these processes. Many students, when faced with a problem, attempt to proceed directly from problem statement to solution. By using dialectic argumentation, the community of Information Technology teachers and students together can explore some oppositions in order to better understand the impact some technological solution might have.

Again, some examples may serve as illustration. In order to explore and better understand the concept of "freedom of information" resulting from the creation of the Internet, a dialectic argument would wish to consider first the concept of "freedom *from* information." In order to understand the former, an understanding of the latter is essential, since one is constituted in the other. Just as the concept of "dark" cannot exist without the contradictory concept of "light," freedom of information cannot be fully understood without considering freedom from information. Issues arising from this might include debates concerning the right of governments to withhold information *from* the public and the right of

Copyright © 2006, Idea Group Inc. Copying or distributing in print or electronic forms without written permission of Idea Group Inc. is prohibited.

individuals to have freedom *from* unsolicited e-mails. There are, moreover, countless counterarguments that serve to illuminate the social implications surrounding the design and use of Information Technologies. Other examples might include consideration of the societal impact of a world where a virus shut down all computers for a month. (This was a real fear before the millennium.) What would happen if the entire cellphone network stopped working for six months? What would be the implications for business? These dialectical arguments serve to reveal aspects of Information Technology not previously considered.

By incorporating dialectical argumentation into the learning and teaching process, students may be encouraged to become active participants in their own learning. Furthermore, through the creation of such risk-free learning environments, students may be encouraged to feel less inhibited in questioning the viewpoints of others. Whilst this may not necessarily lead to a synthesis or resolution of arguments, it should help to develop individuals who will begin to be able to accept that conflict may not always be resolved and that contradictions are a basic feature of thought (Reigel, 1973). Hampden-Turner (1971) argues that a tolerance for paradox and dialectic is indeed essential to full psychosocial development: "The test of a first rate intelligence (sic) is the ability to hold two opposed ideas in the mind at the same time and still retain the ability to function" (Fitzgerald, S., cited in Hamden-Turner, 1971, p. 39).

Why Incorporate Dialectic Argumentation into the Classroom?

The currently prevailing model of the learner as a passive object in a learning environment stultifies creativity and enquiry.

Those who study Information Technology at school level and beyond, and particularly those who will embark on a career in some aspect relating to Information Technology, must therefore go beyond the present acquisition of a set of narrow instrumental mastery skills. They must be encouraged to learn to behave in a more ethical and responsible manner. They must understand, through active engagement, the social implications, good and bad, positive and negative, that occur as a result of Information Technologies. Therefore, as educators, whether in schools or universities, we need to introduce students to the kinds of moral dilemmas they will face in everyday life as a direct result of Information Technology.

Copyright © 2006, Idea Group Inc. Copying or distributing in print or electronic forms without written permission of Idea Group Inc. is prohibited.

Many of today's computer science undergraduates will go on to create systems that will have major impacts upon people, organizations, and society in general. If those systems are to be successful economically and socially, graduates will need to know the lessons from the computerization story so far, the ethical and social issues involved, and the range of choices available to computer professionals (Forester & Morrison, 2000, p. 273).

A learning environment that will enable the technologist of the future to shape our world for the better will be one in which risk-taking and creativity are encouraged. This can occur, I would argue, only when the current authoritarian transmission model of instruction has been replaced with one in which dialectical argumentation can flourish.

References

Bergman, S. (1991). *Dialogical philosophy from Kierkegaard to Buber.* (A.Gerstein, Trans.). New York: SUNY Press.

Cole, M., & Wertsch, J. V. (n.d.). *Beyond the individual-social antimony in discussions of Piaget and Vygotsky.* Retrieved Septemberr 22, 2004, from www.prometheus.org.uk/Files/ColeAndWertschOn PiagetAndVygotsky.pdf

Dakers, J. (2002). Dialectical methodology: The impact of incorporating a neo-vygotskian approach to design and technology. In E. Norman (Ed.), *DATA international research and UK education conference* (pp. 45-50).

Dakers, J. (2005). Technology education as solo activity or socially constructed learning. *International Journal of Technology and Design Education* (in press).

Engeström, Y., Miettinen, R., & Punamäki, R. (1999). *Perspectives on activity theory.* New York: Cambridge University Press.

Feenberg, A. (1998). Subversive rationalisation: Technology, power and democracy. In A. Feenberg & A. Hannay (Eds.), *Technology and the politics of knowledge.* Bloomington: Indiana University Press.

Fisher, R. (1998). *Teaching thinking: Philosophical enquiry in the classroom.* New York: Continuum.

Copyright © 2006, Idea Group Inc. Copying or distributing in print or electronic forms without written permission of Idea Group Inc. is prohibited.

Forester, T., & Morrison, P. (2000). Computer ethics. In A.Teich (Ed.), *Technology and the future*. Boston: Bedford/St Martins.

Habermas, J. (1987). *The philosophical discourse of modernity*. Cambridge: Polity Press.

Hampden-Turner, C. (1971). *Radical man*. New York: Doubleday.

Head, G., & Dakers, J. (2005). Vérillon's trio and Wenger's community: Learning in technology education. In J. Dakers & M. de Vries (Eds.), Creating communities in technology education: Special edition. *The International Journal of Technology and Design Education* (in press).

Heidegger, M. (1962). *Being and Time*. (J. Macquarrie, & E. Robinson, Trans.). San Francisco: Harper and Row.

Ihde, D. (in press). The designer fallacy and technological imagination. In J. Dakers (Ed.), *Defining technological literacy: Towards an epistemological framework*. New York: Palgrave MacMillan.

Jardine, D. (1992). Reflections on education, hermeneutics, and ambiguity: Hermeneutics as a restoring of life to its original difficulty. In W. Pinar & W. Reynolds (Eds.), *Understanding curriculum as phenomenological and deconstructed text*. New York: Teachers College Press.

Kroker, A. (2004). *The will of technology and the culture of nihilism*. Toronto: University of Toronto Press.

Kuhn, D. (1991). *The skills of argument*. New York: Cambridge University Press.

Lampert, M., Rittenhouse, P., & Crumbaugh, C. (1996). *Agreeing to disagree: Developing sociable mathematical discourse*. In O. Olson & N. Torrance (Eds.), *The handbook of education and human development*. Blackwell.

Lave, J. (1988). *Cognition in practice: Mind, mathematics and culture in everyday life*. Cambridge: Cambridge University Press.

Lave, J., & Wenger, E. (1991). *Situated learning: legitimate peripheral participation*. Cambridge: Cambridge University Press.

Lemke, J. (1997). Cognition, context and learning: A social semiotic perspective. In D. Krishner & J. Whitson (Eds.), *Situated cognition, social, semiotic, and psychological perspectives* (pp. 37-56). NJ: Lawrence Erlbaum Associates.

Matusov, E. (1998). When solo activity is not privileged: Participation and internalisation models of development. *Human Development,* Karger, *41*, 326-349.

Copyright © 2006, Idea Group Inc. Copying or distributing in print or electronic forms without written permission of Idea Group Inc. is prohibited.

Mayor, R. (1992). Cognition and instruction: Their historic meaning within educational psychology. *Journal of Educational Psychology, 84,* 405-12. In Ashman, A., & Conway, R. (1997). *An introduction to cognitive education.* New York: Routledge.

Moos, M. (1997). *Marshall McLuhan essays: Media research: Technology, art, communication.* Amsterdam: Overseas Publishers Association.

Olson, D., & Bruner, J. (1996). Folk psychology and folk pedagogy. In O. Olson & N. Torrance (Eds.), *The handbook of education and human development.* US: Blackwell.

Peters, M. (2002). National education policy constructions of the 'knowledge economy': Towards a critique. *Journal of Educational Enquiry, 2*(1), 2001.

Piaget, J. (1928). *The language and thought of the child.* New York: Harcourt.

PITAC. (1999). Information technology research: Investing in our future. *Report to the President.* Retrieved December 16, 2004, from http://www.itrd.gov/pitac/report/

Popper, K. (1972). *Conjectures and refutations: The growth of scientific knowledge.* London: Routledge.

Reason, P. (1994). *Participation in human inquiry.* London: SAGE.

Reigel, K. (1973). Dialectical operations: The final period of cognitive development. *Research Bulletin.* Princeton, NJ: Educational Testing Service. In M. Grumet (1992). Existential and phenomenological foundations of autobiographical methods. In W. Pinar & W. Reynolds (Eds.), *Understanding curriculum as phenomenological and deconstructed text* (pp. 28-43). New York: Teachers College Press.

Rogoff, B. (1990). *Apprenticeship in thinking: Cognitive development in a social context.* New York: Oxford University Press.

Vygotsky, L. (1978). *Mind in society: The development of higher psychological processes.* Cambridge: Harvard University Press.

Walkerdine, V. (1997). Redefining the subject in situated cognition theory. In D. Krishner & J. Whitson (Eds.), *Situated cognition, social, semiotic, and psychological perspectives* (pp. 57-70). NJ: Lawrence Erlbaum Associates.

Copyright © 2006, Idea Group Inc. Copying or distributing in print or electronic forms without written permission of Idea Group Inc. is prohibited.

Wells, G. (1999). *Dialogic inquiry: Towards a sociocultural practice and theory of education.* Cambridge: Cambridge University Press.

Wenger, E. (1998). *Communities of practice: Learning, meaning and identity.* New York: Cambridge University Press.

Copyright © 2006, Idea Group Inc. Copying or distributing in print or electronic forms without written permission of Idea Group Inc. is prohibited.

Chapter III

Bridging the Digital Divide:
A Feminist Perspective on the Project

Mary Kirk, Metropolitan State University, USA

Abstract

Dale Spender compares the contemporary growth of digital information (due to computer technology) with the centuries-old growth of written information (due to the printing press), which inspired a tremendous social revolution. Today, digital information has the potential to inspire a similar social revolution, if we all have access as users and creators of information technology. Some have described the gap between those with power to use and create digital information and those who do not as a "digital divide." How can we use the potential of information technology to birth a new social revolution on a global scale? How can we bridge the digital divide? The answers lie in a reevaluation of science and technology to include us all. This chapter explores the problem from a feminist perspective and proposes a variety of solutions.

Copyright © 2006, Idea Group Inc. Copying or distributing in print or electronic forms without written permission of Idea Group Inc. is prohibited.

Introduction

The exponential growth of technology today is fostering a concurrent growth in information, but it is digital information — primarily accessible only to those with certain privileges. Dale Spender (1995) describes how the contemporary growth of digital information as a result of computer technology parallels the growth of written information as a result of the printing press hundreds of years ago. Both events inspired tremendous social revolutions, and Spender (1995) underlines that it is not the technology itself that is the substance of today's revolution, "it is the change in society — the shifts in power, wealth, influence, organization, and the environmental consequences — that matters to us all as individuals, and as communities" (p. xiv). Without question, this issue of power, and of who holds the power, and of how they exercise that power, is one of the most significant issues we face as a global technology community. Unfortunately, the power is not equally shared. In fact, we are suffering from a growing digital divide both within the US and between the technologically-advanced nations and others world-wide. I use the term "digital divide" broadly in this chapter to refer to power and access gaps in relation to both users and developers of technology.

The digital divide is a well-documented phenomenon and the divide has grown wider in recent years. Several recent studies (one by the National Science Foundation and another by Federal Reserve Bank economists) continue to show how race, family income and educational attainment influence computer usage in the US. For example, one study showed that while 46.6% of White families own home computers, only 23.2% of African-American families do (Cooper & Weaver, 2003, p. 4). Another study showed that "while 61.2% of whites and 62.7% of Asians use computers at home, only 35.7% of Blacks and 31.6% of Hispanics do" (Valletta & MacDonald, 2003, p. 2). Family income is another powerful determinant of computer ownership and usage. One study showed that "2.7% of families with incomes under $15,000 own computers compared to 77.7% of families with incomes over $75,000; and among all families with incomes under $35,000 computer ownership of white families was three times that of African-American families and four times that of Hispanic families" (Kirk & Zander, 2004, p. 171). Another study showed that the "usage rate is 21.1% for individuals with family income under $15,000 per year and 79.6% for individuals with family income of at least $75,000 per year" (Valletta & MacDonald, 2003, p. 1). Educational attainment even more dramatically influences home computer use. One study showed that "home computer use

Copyright © 2006, Idea Group Inc. Copying or distributing in print or electronic forms without written permission of Idea Group Inc. is prohibited.

ranges from 18.9% for those with no high school degree to 81.9% for those holding graduate degrees" (Valletta & MacDonald, 2003, p. 1). Clearly, better access to education narrows the digital divide in relation to computer usage, but who belongs to the exclusive club that develops technology?

Since this is a professional field that increasingly requires formal academic training, one way to understand the demographics of those who develop technology is to look at the data on higher education. One of the best sources for this data in relation to information technology is the Taulbee Survey that is annually reported in *Computing Research News*. The most recent report showed:

that while the numbers of computer science majors at all levels of higher education has increased overall, there has also been a decline in the percentage of women and students of color at all levels. Of all computer science majors in the U.S., only 18.8% are women, 3.4% are African American, 3.6% are Hispanic, 21.7% are Asian/Pacific Islander (although this population is overrepresented, their percentage has still declined), and 0.4% are Native American. (Kirk & Zander, 2004, p. 169)

If there is this much inequity in the US, then how large is the digital divide on a global scale? The results are about what one might expect. Geographer Joni Seagar (2003) reports that more "than 80 percent of Internet users are in the industrialized countries; Africa is the least wired" (p. 82). Given the deep-rooted causes of the digital divide, how can we begin to bridge the gap?

The following sections of this chapter explore the problem and propose solutions from a feminist perspective. "Reclaiming the 'F' Word: Demystifying Feminism" provides a brief primer on "feminism" and defines the manifestations of a patriarchal social system. "Stereotypes 'R Us: Mass Media as Social Institution" describes how mass media use stereotypes as a marketing tool to teach limited and limiting beliefs that influence our perception of science and technology. "Science is Male, Nature is Female: Understanding Dualisms" explores the historical influence of the philosophy of science on science and technology today. "No Girls Allowed: Understanding Male-Oriented Technology Culture and Language" demonstrates how the technology world privileges one gender over the other in its daily discourse. "Barriers to Education and Employment: Understanding Her-Story" shares the history of women in science in the US and explains how methods of teaching and learning privilege certain groups over others. Finally, "A Concluding Pledge: With Technology

Copyright © 2006, Idea Group Inc. Copying or distributing in print or electronic forms without written permission of Idea Group Inc. is prohibited.

and Justice for All" proposes a feminist vision of a new kind of science and technology.

Reclaiming the "F" Word: Demystifying Feminism

One important first step towards bridging the digital divide is to close the disciplinary gap between the social sciences (such as women's studies, ethnic studies, psychology and sociology) and the "hard" sciences (such as math, engineering and computer science); these two discourses rarely intersect, either theoretically or practically. This is the primary reason that, although many scholars have recognized that there is a problem, few have fully identified the real problem and its origins. In a 2002 paper, computer science educator Carol Zander and I issued the following "call to action" to computer science educators:

Our task is also to bridge the intellectual divide between those who "do" science and women's studies...When all of us better understand the challenges we face in recreating a more inclusive learning environment, we can collaborate towards even richer solutions together. (p. 123)

In a 2004 paper, we again attempted to narrow the disciplinary divide by reviewing two new books in the context of the question "Which book might be most valuable to a computer science educator in higher education who is seeking a map to mend the gap created by the digital divide?" (Kirk & Zander, p. 169). *Unlocking the Clubhouse: Women and Computing*, written by a computer scientist and a social scientist, had already received a great deal of recognition. However, *Gender and Computers: Understanding the Digital Divide*, written by two social psychologists, was little known in the computer science community. Although the first book provides a good overview of the problem and proposes some solutions, the second book provides evidence of the deeper, and often poorly understood, influences of gender, race and socioeconomic factors in terms of the negative impact of stereotyping—especially on the psychology of learning. If computer scientists better understood the work of social scientists, they would not need to spend energy conducting further research to document the problem, but could be more creatively engaged in solving it. Rushing to "solve" the problem without a richer knowledge of its social causes will only ever lead us to partial solutions.

Copyright © 2006, Idea Group Inc. Copying or distributing in print or electronic forms without written permission of Idea Group Inc. is prohibited.

One barrier to more scientists understanding the work of social scientists is a fallacious view of "feminism" that has transformed an entire area of scholarship into the "F" word. Most people's knowledge of feminism comes to them third-hand through popular culture and other mass media images of "angry, man-hating femi-Nazis." However, "feminism is for everybody" since it is engaged in scrutinizing social systems with the express goal of ending all forms of institutionalized oppression, of which gender discrimination is only one (Hooks, 2000). Feminist scholars have spent decades asking and answering questions about how our social systems function, and feminist science scholars have focused on these questions in specific relation to science and technology. Unfortunately, feminist "perspectives are often charged with being biased, because they are overtly political" (they are about social change), but this charge ignores the fact that all knowledge creation is socially situated; meanwhile, most of those in the sciences worship the "cult of objectivity," which allows them to deny "social, cultural, and economic influences" on the production of scientific knowledge (Spanier, 2001, p. 370). To claim that science and technology are created in a social context that influences their creation is tantamount to saying "The emperor has no clothes," which accounts for the "outsider" status of feminist thought in relation to science.

There is no need to fear the "F" word, because the work of feminism is at once incredibly complex and astonishingly simple. For the purposes of this chapter, I offer the following simple definition of the feminist project. We live in a patriarchal society—a hierarchical society constructed around power and who holds it. Allan Johnson (1997) defines "patriarchy" as a society that is "male-dominated, male-identified, and male-centered" (p. 5). Individuals learn a sense of identity that is defined by their social location—a series of factors inclusive of gender, race, socioeconomic class, physical ability, sexual identity, religion, age, etc. This social location determines our "rightful" place in the hierarchy. We learn this sense of our identity, our social location, through social institutions such as law, medicine, business, language, education and media. All of our social institutions (including education and the information technology industry) are organized this way, and gender (specifically the privileging of maleness over femaleness) is one of three primary organizing principles; race is another, and socio-economic class is another (Kirk & Okazawa-Rey, 2004). These social institutions teach the values of the dominant culture, and we all learn the rules of the game from them. Since the game is organized around power and who holds it, we all learn to compete for power and to value winning.

This social system has predominated in Western Europe and the US for about 2,000 years, and, yes, the more recent influences of feminism in the US have

Copyright © 2006, Idea Group Inc. Copying or distributing in print or electronic forms without written permission of Idea Group Inc. is prohibited.

given some women more social authority. However, the historical effect of centuries of patriarchy is that "it has retarded [women from] coming into consciousness as a collective entity and has literally aborted and distorted the intellectual talents of women for thousands of years" (Lerner, 1986, p. 10). Patriarchy has also marginalized people according to race, class, physical ability and many other "outsider" characteristics. As a social group, men still hold the "power to define," and in contemporary industrialized societies, that power is often exerted via the mass media and via information technology.

In the US, men are still the primary owners of media/communications and technology companies. In the latest *Forbes* report, "The 400 Richest Americans" (which ranks people by their net worth), 11 of the top 25 own media/communication or technology companies (Armstrong, 2004). Ranked 1, 3, 9, 10 and 11, respectively, are Microsoft founder Bill Gates ($48 billion), Microsoft co-founder Paul Allen ($20 billion), Dell computer founder Michael Dell ($39 billion), Oracle's Larry Ellison ($13.7 billion), and another Microsoft executive, Steve Ballmer ($12.6 billion). Ranked 6 through 10 are various members of the Walton family, owners of Wal-Mart. Ranked 13, 13 (tie), 15, 20, 23 and 25 (respectively) are Barbara Cox Anthony ($11.3 billion) and Anne Cox Chambers ($11.3 billion), owners of Cox Enterprises, Metromedia owner John Kluge ($11 billion), Viacom owner Sumner Redstone ($8.1 billion), Echostar's Charles Ergen ($7.3 billion) and Newhouse owner Donald Newhouse ($7 billion). It is safe to say that in a capitalist economy, those with the money are also those who influence the information. And, when those with the money literally own the sources of information (both print and digital), they own the power to define reality.

Stereotypes 'R Us: Understanding Media as Social Institution

Mass media is one of the most powerful social institutions in the US, especially in terms of purveying the values of the dominant culture via stereotypes. Stereotypes define the boundaries around where we "belong" and what is "possible" for us in our lives. They are more powerful than they may at first seem, and this has been well documented. We learn both about how to view each other (which teaches us to "discriminate by category) and how to view ourselves (which teaches us to internalize views of being "less" in relation to gender, race, class, etc.). However, the internalized "isms" may be one of the

Copyright © 2006, Idea Group Inc. Copying or distributing in print or electronic forms without written permission of Idea Group Inc. is prohibited.

most deadly effects of stereotypes, because individuals learn to place internal limits on themselves. For example, in *Gender and Computers: Understanding the Digital Divide*, Cooper and Weaver share the results of numerous studies that document the negative effect of gender and race stereotypes on attitudes and perceived ability in relation to computer technology.

Another poignant example of the power of media (and stereotypes) to limit our perceptions lies in the media coverage of several women Nobel Prize winners in science. In 1966, headlines announcing Maria Goeppart Meyer's Nobel Prize reflected the stereotypical expectations placed on women: "The first woman to win a Nobel Prize in science is *a scientist and a wife*," and "British *Grandmother* Wins the Prize" [italics mine]. In 1977, when Rosalyn Yalow won the Nobel Prize in medicine, the coverage wasn't much better: "She Cooks, She Cleans, She Wins the Nobel Prize." And, in 1983, when corn geneticist Barbara McClintock won the Nobel Prize, "*Newsweek* called her 'the Greta Garbo of genetics. At 81 she has never married, always preferring to be alone'" (Nelkin, 1995, pp. 18-19). In all cases, their marital status and roles as child bearers are highlighted, and "Oh, by the way" they're also smart.

More contemporary examples of negative stereotypes are readily available. Today, the stereotypes perpetuated in technology magazines influence how women and people of color are perceived by others as well as the possibilities they perceive for themselves. Stereotypes project limitations in terms of perceived access to, interest in and capability in technology, both as users and developers of the technology (Ware & Stuck, 1985). *Wired* magazine serves as an interesting contemporary example of how stereotypes are purveyed in technology. At its inception, *Wired* claimed to be the voice of the digital revolution and attempted to be the first computer magazine to place technology in a cultural context. Unfortunately, the "culture" tended to be a white, male, educated and economically advantaged subculture, and the images of women and people of color in *Wired* were dubious. In *Cracking the Gender Code: Who Rules the Wired World?*, Melanie Stewart Millar (1998) comprehensively names the rich diversity of issues in relation to women, computing and culture that were missing from *Wired* magazine:

Wired...*negates difference by excluding positive images of women and minorities and denying that digital culture is the creation of a particular dominant elite. In so doing, it presents a particular set of gender, race and class constructions that reflect an underlying ideology characterized by a strong belief in technological progress and the conservation of hegemonic*

Copyright © 2006, Idea Group Inc. Copying or distributing in print or electronic forms without written permission of Idea Group Inc. is prohibited.

power relations. Whether Wired *is excluding, reconstructing or eliminating difference, women and minorities continue to be subordinated in the digital world it creates. Thus, although* Wired *comes wrapped in a dazzling, novel package, like much of the discourse of digital culture, it continues to sell a very old, all-too-familiar ideology: one that serves to perpetuate inequality.* (p. 112)

Millar (1998) elaborates on how *Wired*'s approach not only excludes and masks difference, but redefines "white masculinity in a new, quintessentially hypermodern form . . . [that] combines the mainstays of the emerging digital culture with very traditional constructions of masculine power, frontier mythology and technological transcendence" (p. 113). Thus, *Wired* echoes the historical attitude that science is male by defining computer culture in male terms.

My own research on the magazine's front covers showed a predominance of male images and of "power-over," domination-oriented values in the sex, death and war language used on the headlines. Only nine women were pictured on the front covers of over six years of issues from January/February 1993 through April 1999. Of these, eight were apparently white or light skinned (one was a cartoon) and one was racially ambiguous. There were two additional images that may have been female, but were pictured in such a way that distinguishing their gender would have been difficult or impossible to determine. Language that emphasized sex, war and/or death was used in the headings on the covers of 41 issues out of 71, sometimes multiple headings in one issue. One notable example of death language and imagery exclaimed, "Buy this magazine, or we fry this magician" on a cover with an image of a white man, in his 30s, sitting with legs spread in an electric chair, wearing a black, all-leather outfit and smiling down at the reader (September 1994). Other examples of sexually-oriented headlines are the painfully obvious "Sex Sells!" (December, 1997), and the insulting "Sex vs. Equity? Are you kidding?" (September, 1998). *Wired*'s attempt to discuss computer technology in the context of culture is male-centered and money-motivated with little or no real social context. The dominance of male images and of sex, death and war language contributes to what Millar describes as the "building of the hypermacho man" (Millar, 1998, p. 113). This implicitly and explicitly casts the actors and their actions in the digital world as *Wired* defines it—they are male, they are white and they are dominators.

Copyright © 2006, Idea Group Inc. Copying or distributing in print or electronic forms without written permission of Idea Group Inc. is prohibited.

These examples of the stereotypes conveyed by stories on Nobel Prize-winning women in science and by recent portrayals in computing magazines are classic representations of the gender stereotypes used at large in mass media: "women's place is in the home; women are dependent upon men; women do not make independent and important decisions; women are shown in few occupational roles; [and] women view themselves and are viewed by others as sex objects" (Lazier & Kendrick, 1993, p. 202). The stereotypes of women scientists and technologists are virtually the same. Women are dependent on others (especially men), incompetent and incapable of action (men are the actors), primary caregivers (men are the breadwinners) and victims and sex objects (men are the sexual aggressors) (Wood, 1999, pp. 304-315).

These data may partly explain why one of the most persistent stereotypes in relation to science and technology is the stereotypical image of a "scientist" as male. Forty years of "draw a scientist" data shows that students from the 50s through the 90s have repeatedly imaged "a scientist as a middle-aged or older man wearing glasses and a white coat and working alone in a lab" (Sadker & Sadker, 1994, p. 123). This starts to influence girls' attitudes about science and technology at very early ages. Dale Spender (1995) explains that what girls turn away from isn't the technology; what "they turn away from is the image of the scientist or the computer hacker" (p. 173). In comparison to boys, this leads to many girls being underprepared in math and science by the time they're ready for college. Multiple scholars have documented the predictable self-esteem slide that occurs in many girls as they enter adolescence and begin to feel increasing social pressure to be "feminine" (Brumberg, 1997; Pipher, 1994; Sadker & Sadker, 1995). Since girls shy away from the image of "scientist" as "unfeminine" in those pivotal adolescent years, this leads them to take fewer advanced math and science courses in junior high and high school (Sadker & Sadker, 1995). In addition, "girls are significantly underrepresented in after-school computer clubs, as computer participants, at free-access times using the computers and in advanced computer electives" (Rosser, 1995, p. 147). This leads even fewer girls to make successful transitions from high school to college in terms of being either users or developers of technology.

Media stereotypes in relation to race are just as limiting. For example, a recent study of news coverage in urban areas where racial minorities range between 23% and 26% of the total population, showed that "photographic coverage of minorities was limited almost exclusively to African Americans (who were not the largest racial minority in their communities)" (Gist, 1993, p. 106). In addition, when members of minorities are pictured, they are almost exclusively

Copyright © 2006, Idea Group Inc. Copying or distributing in print or electronic forms without written permission of Idea Group Inc. is prohibited.

associated with negative events. In "neutral stories, ranging from politics to weather to housing . . . it was rare that professional or working class minorities were mainstreamed into the coverage in the way nonminorities are" (Gist, 1993, p. 107). People of color are rarely included, and when they are, they are represented by negative stereotypes.

Although mass media continues to purvey racist and sexist stereotypes, one might expect that education as a social institution could do better. If education exists to help serve our society, and if most of us would agree that we want a just society, education should serve as a counterpoint to the inaccurate popular culture messages. Unfortunately, as a social institution in patriarchal society, education has been at best a schizophrenic site for social change—sometimes making progress, sometimes impeding it. The remaining sections of this chapter focus on several ways in which education and language have operated as social institutions that erect barriers to limit participation in science and technology. These barriers take the form of deeply-embedded institutional practices that privilege maleness, whiteness and being middle- or upper-class. As you read the rest of this essay, keep this thought in mind: Access is not just literal, it is also attitudinal. In relation to information technology, it's not enough to simply have access to the machine. You must also have been taught the attitude that you belong in the digital world and that it has something to offer you.

Science is Male, Nature is Female: Understanding Dualisms

Though one could identify any number of points in previous centuries of patriarchal thought that explicitly and implicitly excluded women from the knowledge tradition, in relation to science and technology one historic moment takes on a particular significance due to its emphasis on dualistic, either/or thinking, of which gender is just one manifestation. Francis Bacon (1561-1626) is often referred to as the father of modern science, as "the originator of the concept of the modern research institute, a philosopher of industrial science, ... and as the founder of the inductive method" (Merchant, 2001, p. 68). Bacon's thinking helped reify the definition of science as male, and nature as female. Many feminist science studies scholars have discussed the ways in which this particular dualism has influenced the perception of science in society, and of who participates in the world of science and technology (Bleier, 1991; Merchant, 1980; Schiebinger, 1993; Wajcman, 1995). In her now classic

Copyright © 2006, Idea Group Inc. Copying or distributing in print or electronic forms without written permission of Idea Group Inc. is prohibited.

book, *The Death of Nature: Women, Ecology and the Scientific Revolution*, Carolyn Merchant (1980) recounts the history of the Scientific Revolution and outlines ideas that have contributed to shaping science into a domain that privileges social definitions of "maleness": the notion of science gaining increasing domination over nature, the rise of mechanistic thinking and power as the "mechanism." Historically, one of the most influential ways in which this split has been communicated is through artistic and literary imagery. As an example of this process in action, Merchant (1980) describes the way in which visual images fostered the view of science dominating nature:

The new image of nature as a female to be controlled and dissected through experiment legitimated the exploitation of natural resources...[T]he image of the nurturing earth popular in the Renaissance...was superseded by new controlling imagery...Natura no longer complains that her garments of modestry [sic] are being torn by the wrongful thrusts of man. She is portrayed in statues ...coyly removing her own veil and exposing herself to science. From an active teacher and parent, she has become a mindless, submissive body. (p. 190)

These ideas alone may not have led to the development of science as a male domain. However, Merchant (1980) describes how coupling these attitudes (the domination of "female" nature) with the growing emphasis on mechanistic thought established a more gender-exclusive framework. Merchant (1980) explains how 17th century French and English scientists and philosophers developed a "new concept of the self as a rational master of the passions housed in a machinelike body" and how this concept began to "replace the concept of the self as an integral part of a close-knit harmony of organic parts united to the cosmos and society" (p. 214). The third piece of Merchant's (1980) puzzle is that "mechanism" as a world view reorganized reality around order and power: "Order was attained through an emphasis on the motion of indivisible parts subject to mathematical laws and the rejection of unpredictable animistic sources of change. Power was achieved through immediate active intervention in a secularized world" (p. 216). These two fundamental elements of mechanistic thought, order and power, informed Western politics, religion and science (as well as most other aspects of society) from this period forward and led science to develop as a domain that increasingly excluded women.

Copyright © 2006, Idea Group Inc. Copying or distributing in print or electronic forms without written permission of Idea Group Inc. is prohibited.

Science was associated with a machine, scientists were the power and nature was the entity to be dominated. Concurrent with the development of these ideas, women were more closely identified with the nature over which scientists sought to gain power. Another scholar of the history and philosophy of science, Ruth Bleier (1991), examines the ways in which 17th century Baconian dualism "elaborated the metaphors of science in sexual and gendered terms, with science as male and nature as female, a mystery to be unveiled and penetrated" (p. 6). This is also an example of how language serves as a social institution to teach values. Bleier explains that according to Bacon, woman was embodied in "the natural, the disordered, the emotional, the irrational," and man, "as a thinker epitomized objectivity, rationality, culture, and control" (p. 6). This view of gender certainly doesn't leave much room for women to participate in science.

Another limiting factor in terms of women's participation in science is the myth of scientific objectivity. The problem, according to Bleier (1991), is that the unacknowledged biases that scientists hold "become part of a stifling science-culture, while scientists firmly believe that as long as they are not *conscious* of any bias or political agenda, they are neutral and objective, when in fact they are only unconscious" (p. 29). These unconscious biases influence the ways in which data are analyzed as well as the research questions themselves, and, in sometimes not so subtle ways, exclude diverse perspectives and experiences from consideration—effectively leaving women (and other marginalized groups) out of the discussion. Sandra Harding (1998) offers a cure for this persistent blindness by proposing a "strong objectivity," which "draws on standpoint epistemologies." To arrive at her definition, Harding first describes how the "demand for objectivity . . . becomes the demand for separation of thinking from feeling," which promotes moral detachment (p. 129). This moral detachment leads one to be blind to historical, political, and economic factors that may profoundly influence the selection of scientific problems and the resources that are committed to answering them. Further, Harding points out how even relying on the "scientific method" of verifying results through experiment won't necessarily help scientists escape this blindness: "When a scientific community shares assumptions, there is little chance that more careful application of existing scientific methods will detect them" (p. 135). If the shared assumptions are that science is male, nature is female, and that science's goal is to conquer nature, this creates severe limits around women's participation.

Copyright © 2006, Idea Group Inc. Copying or distributing in print or electronic forms without written permission of Idea Group Inc. is prohibited.

No Girls Allowed: Understanding Male-Oriented Technology Culture and Language

Another persistent barrier to the participation of women in technology is a computer culture and a computer language that privilege maleness as the metaphor. The legacy of Baconian science was an emphasis on science dominating nature. Since power and dominance are key themes in patriarchy, it is no accident that computer culture tacitly condones power and dominance—often expressed through implicit violence. Computer video games provide one example of how themes of violence and domination pervade computer culture. Most video games feature war, violence and often the abuse of women. Eugene Provenzo (1995), author of *Video Kids: Making Sense of Nintendo*, reported that 13 of the 47 most popular video games featured the rape or abduction of a female character. Although it may seem obvious that this type of violence would not appeal to girls, scholars have documented the fact that video game violence does indeed alienate girls (Cooper, Hall & Huff, 1990; Subrahmanyam, 1998). This explains why "75 to 85 percent of the sales and revenues generated by the $10 billion game industry are derived from male consumers" (Cassell & Jenkins, 1998, p. 11). And, since video games are one of the early entreés to the world of technology, this is one more factor that disadvantages many girls at an early age.

Language as social institution has also had a powerful impact. Since the historical legacy of oppression has meant that most scientists have been men, male-identified language and dominance metaphors are pervasive in science and technology. Computer jargon, such as "boot," "crash," "abort," and "kill," implicitly supports themes of violence (Spender, 1995, p. 200). This is the language of the daily discourse in technology—a language that was obviously influenced by the earlier domination-oriented attitudes in science. Language as social institution both reflects our values as a society and shapes how we view things. Keller (1992) makes a potent argument about the influence that metaphors cast on how we interpret science:

Different metaphors of mind, nature, and the relation between them, reflect different psychological stances of observer to observed; these, in turn, give rise to different cognitive perspectives—to different aims, questions, and even to different methodological and explanatory preferences. (p. 31)

Copyright © 2006, Idea Group Inc. Copying or distributing in print or electronic forms without written permission of Idea Group Inc. is prohibited.

The language of science and technology reflects a male-centered perspective. Using the classic example of the male-defined metaphors that dominate contemporary quantum physics, Sue Rosser (1995) points out how different it *could* be:

With a sense of human agency incorporated into scientific theories, perhaps physicists will no longer find it necessary to speak of elementary particles having attributes such as charm, beauty, and strangeness, or to give seminars with topless, naked bottom, and exotic hermaphrodite states in the titles. (p. 71)

The ways in which maleness is privileged in computer culture are not limited to language itself; they also include styles of communication. Ruth Bleier (1991) documents the ways in which communication about science has been gendered according to maleness in terms of the "public demeanor of scientists." She says that "the patterns of words they choose . . . almost invariably project an image of impersonal authority and absolute confidence in the accuracy, objectivity, and importance of their observations" (Bleier, 1991, p. 23). However, women scientists, who have been gender-socialized not to "brag," exhibit very different behavior when delivering scientific papers. They tend to "call attention to the limitations of their data, to potential flaws in their experimental design, to control experiments that remain to be done," all of which certainly casts doubt on the credibility of their work in the male-identified scientific community (Bleier, 1991, p. 23).

There are other ways in which gender socialization influences communication. Male conversational style is typically characterized by focusing on a goal in a conversation (which is to win) and talking in terms of abstract ideas and rational argument. Women's conversational style is typically characterized by talking in terms of personal story and emotions, and their goal is not to win but to connect (Wood, 1999, pp. 123-129). In mixed sex conversation, men talk more, interrupt more (especially women), direct the topic of conversation more, and define what qualifies as a "worthwhile" topic (Spender, 1985; Van Fossen, 1996). This is the conversational style that dominates in technology, which makes it difficult for women to fully participate without repercussions for stepping outside of socially-accepted gender boundaries.

Dale Spender (1995) describes how this conversational style has dominated on the Internet as well: "Despite the enormous potential of the net to be a

Copyright © 2006, Idea Group Inc. Copying or distributing in print or electronic forms without written permission of Idea Group Inc. is prohibited.

network—to promote egalitarian, cooperative communication exchanges—the virtual reality is one where aggression, intimidation and plain macho-mode prevail" (p. 198). In "Gender and Democracy in Computer-Mediated Communication," Susan Herring reports having studied this so-called "more democratic" form of communication online. Supporters claim that computer-mediated communication is more democratic because it provides more people with access to information, removes the social context within which stereotypical judgments can be made and there is little overt censorship of ideas (Herring, 1998, p. 2). However, Herring's (1998) study of male and female participants in two electronic lists demonstrated gendered patterns of communication similar to traditional research, and showed the dominance of male conversational style online. Women's online messages were characterized by a more personal orientation, supportive language and questions or apologies. Men's messages were characterized by a more authoritative orientation, challenging language and self promotion (Herring, 1998, p. 7). One of the more troubling findings in Herring's data was the pressure to conform to the "male" conversational style. As with earlier data about mixed-sex conversation, Herring's study showed that when "women's rate of posting increased gradually to where it equaled 50% . . . men wrote in to decry the discussion, and several threatened to cancel their subscription to the list." Their objections said that the tone of the messages had become too "vituperative" and that the topics were "inappropriate" (Herring, 1998, p. 5). Far from being the "democratic" world it's depicted to be, online conversation appears subject to the same gendered communication patterns that are evidenced elsewhere.

Barriers to Education and Employment: Understanding Her-story

Without knowing their history, each generation of women believes that they are the "first" and that they face their numerous obstacles to success alone, without literal or historical mentors to lead the way. However, every generation has had its heroes, those who have gained access to education and employment when no one else could, and overcame systemic barriers to success. What these inspirational stories don't tell us is how many others who might have had the talent to make it did not simply because they weren't brave enough to do it alone. In the US, white men know their history, but few other groups do. Margaret Rossiter's landmark volumes on the history of women in science, *Women scientists in america: Struggles and strategies to 1940* (1982) and

Copyright © 2006, Idea Group Inc. Copying or distributing in print or electronic forms without written permission of Idea Group Inc. is prohibited.

Women scientists in america: Before affirmative action 1940–1972 (1995), have filled a huge knowledge gap. Rossiter (1982) details the "series of limited stereotypes, double binds, resistant barriers" and other "no-win situations" that women historically faced (p. xvii). With this knowledge, we can better understand why women remain underrepresented in science and technology today.

Women in the US had extremely limited access to higher education until the late 1800s, when a few of the now nationally renowned women's colleges improved access for some: notably, Smith College (1871), Wellesley College (1875) and Bryn Mawr College (1885) (Rossiter, 1982, p. 10). But, the existence of these colleges did not provide access for all women. For example, due to the historical legacy of slavery and racism, African-American women were often limited to studying at segregated colleges and universities (now called Historically Black Colleges and Universities or HBCUs).

Although some women had begun to gain some access to undergraduate degrees in the 1800s, they did not gain full access to doctoral degrees in the US until as late as the 1960s at some institutions, notably Princeton. Christine Ladd-Franklin's story surely reflects the experience of many women who went ahead and completed doctoral work in spite of the fact that their institutions would not award them a degree. Ladd-Franklin completed her doctoral studies at Johns Hopkins in 1882 at a time when the university did not grant PhDs to women. "Finally, in 1926, at its fiftieth anniversary celebration, The Johns Hopkins University awarded a long overdue doctorate... . Christine Ladd-Franklin... now a sprightly seventy-nine-year-old, made it a point to attend the ceremonies and collect her degree forty-four years late" (Rossiter, 1982, p. 46).

For African-American women, access to any type of doctoral degree was difficult, but it took many decades longer for women to begin to earn doctorates in math and science. According to Scott W. Williams (1999), professor of mathematics at the State University of New York in Buffalo: "The *first American woman* to earn a Ph.D. in Mathematics was Winifred Edgerton Merrill (Columbia U. 1886)... however, it was not until 1949, 25 years after *the first African American [man]* earned a Ph.D. in mathematics that a Black *woman* reached that level [italics mine]." That woman was Evelyn Boyd Granville. Other sciences, such as physics, were even harder to gain entry to; the first Black woman to earn a doctorate in physics was Shirley Ann Jackson in 1973. These notable women are two of only ten doctoral "firsts" among African-American women in science and medicine between 1933 and 1973

Copyright © 2006, Idea Group Inc. Copying or distributing in print or electronic forms without written permission of Idea Group Inc. is prohibited.

(Rossiter, 1995, p. 83). Of the few who managed to hurdle all of the barriers to doctoral education, most of these "pioneers spent their entire career teaching at black colleges." There is no question that racism and segregation limited career options for African-American women in a way that it did not for European-American women. Rossiter speculates that this may have been the reason that many of these pioneers taught at black colleges, but it may also have been out of a desire to serve their communities and mentor other black women (Rossiter, 1995, p. 82).

For those few women who managed to scale the barriers to education, there were new barriers in terms of access to employment in academics, the private sector and the government. In the 1800s, the primary "career" option for educated women was teaching. Even in teaching, women were already experiencing the ghettoization of the only real profession that was accessible to them. In New England in the late 1830s, about one-half of all public school teachers were women, and they were being paid only 40 percent of what their male peers earned (Rossiter, 1982, p. 5). For another 50 years, this would remain one of the few professions open to women, but it would provide barely a subsistence living, and that to almost exclusively European-American women and a very few African-American women.

In higher education, women scientists were increasingly hired to teach at the newly forming public universities, but those women rarely rose above the rank of associate professor even "after decades of service teaching heavy loads of introductory courses" (Rossiter, 1995, p. 130). Women were channeled into low- (or *no-*) paying research jobs in part due to the anti-nepotism rules that prohibited husbands and wives being employed on the same faculty. There were occasional token women in some of the science programs. Some, such as Nobel Prize winner Maria Goeppart Meyer, even filled the "new category of 'volunteer professor'" and taught without pay (Rossiter, 1995, p. 145). The fact that many women scientists were willing to work without pay in order to do their research is another factor that contributes to the gender differences in salaries and employment in the academy that is still evident today.

World War II created tremendous employment opportunities for women in general, and especially for women scientists. Many were employed at the newly developing government organizations such as the Bureau of Labor Statistics and agricultural research units. But, the government had no qualms about paying women less money than they paid men in equivalent positions. In fact, the government was eager to hire women into certain positions because they *could* pay them less. In 1938, while the average salary for men in one Civil Service category was $3,214, women in the same category earned an average salary of $2,299—almost $1,000, or 40% less (Rossiter, 1982, p. 235).

Copyright © 2006, Idea Group Inc. Copying or distributing in print or electronic forms without written permission of Idea Group Inc. is prohibited.

The Navy WAVES, Army WAACS, and Coast Guard SPARS created some of the best opportunities for women in science because they "could receive the advancement denied to them elsewhere" by becoming veterans and reaping all of the postwar benefits that this implied (especially education and home loans) (Rossiter, 1995, p. 8). However, there was also a quota on the number of women who could be "in the highest ranks of military and naval officers." There were "separate lists for men and women 'eligibles'" that allowed "the appointing officer to specify which sex he (rarely she) preferred for any position." According to Rossiter (1995), "a spot survey...showed that for 94 percent of the jobs at the GS levels 13–15 the requests were for men only" (p. 294).

Women in industry faced far more limiting employment environments than those in the academic or government sectors. They were prey to many of the same sort of limitations we still see today. Women could only advance so far and were channeled into certain positions more than others, such as librarians, technical writers and research assistants. One notable exception is the small group of women with undergraduate degrees in mathematics that were hired as early "computers" to work on developing the first general purpose computer, the ENIAC (Electronic Numerical Integrator and Computer), during the period of 1942-1955 (Fritz, 1996, p. 13).

Ultimately, the tremendous economic growth in the 1940s through the 1960s "that could have made room for more and better-trained scientists of both sexes did not benefit the two equally; in fact, it generally unleashed certain forces that hastened the women's exit and subsequent marginalization and underutilization"(Rossiter, 1995, p. xv). Gradually, due to such factors as post-war displacement and demotion, anti-nepotism rules (especially at universities) and the emphasis on "prestigious research," even at women's colleges, many of the women who had entered the sciences in the first half of the century were forced out and replaced by men in both the academy and in industry (Rossiter, 1995, p. xv).

In spite of the somewhat positive influence of Affirmative Action, this historical legacy of barriers to scientific education and the professions informs the degree to which, and the ways in which, women participate in technology today both as users and developers. In 1994, although women in the United States earned over 50% of the awarded bachelor's degrees, they earned only 28% of the undergraduate degrees in computer science and engineering, and this number has been steadily declining since a high of 37.1% in the early 1980s (Camp, 1997, p. 105). In 1996, the number of women who earned doctoral degrees in computer science and information science was even lower, only 15.1% (Schiebinger, 1999, p. 199). The number of women of color who earned computer science and information

Copyright © 2006, Idea Group Inc. Copying or distributing in print or electronic forms without written permission of Idea Group Inc. is prohibited.

science doctorates in 1996 is so low that percentages have not even been calculated by researchers. The *actual number* of women in the United States who earned doctorates in computer and information science in 1996 (including European Americans for comparative purposes) is as follows: three African Americans, 16 Asian/Pacific Islanders, 61 European Americans, seven Hispanic and two Native American (Schiebinger, 1999, pp. 201-202).

Women's salaries have not improved much either. In a report titled "The Gender Wage Ratio: Women's and Men's Earnings," the Institute for Women's Policy Research reports that women's median annual earnings in relation to men's remained "constant from 1955 through the 1970s" ranging from 63.9 to 58.8 and then began to steadily increase through the 80s, grow modestly through the 90s and reach an "all-time high of 76.6" in 2002, but the ratio fell back to 75.5 in 2003. Data on median annual income in 2003 from the US Census Bureau add to this picture: white men $30,732; white women $17,422; black men $21,986; black women $16,581; Asian men $32,291; Asian women $17,679; Hispanic men $21,053; Hispanic women $13,642 (Historical, 2005). This census report did not include data on other cultural or ethnic groups, such as Native Americans. These data together clearly show that women still earn less than men overall, and that when race is included as a factor, the differences are profound.

If you think that women are doing better in terms of median annual earnings in information technology jobs, you're partially correct. The overall earnings picture for women in technology is much brighter than for the population as a whole, but there is still a gender gap. Some of the overall increase in annual median income is accounted for by education, since income increases in direct correlation with number of years of education. Several recent reports demonstrate that there is still a gender gap in annual salaries. For example, a 1999 survey in *Network World* reported that while men's earnings averaged $67,237 (base salary) and $77,322 (total compensation), women's earnings averaged $51,789 (base salary) and $55,596 (total compensation); men are earning 23% more than women in base salary and 28% more than women overall (Shortchanged, 1999). A 2003 survey of 21,000 technology professionals by Dice, Inc. reports that the average salary for technology professionals is $69,400 and that the gender gap decreased for the first time in this survey's history to 11%. "When segmenting by age, women over 50 had the largest gap, earning 13.5% less than their male counterparts," and the "gender gap remained lowest (8%) in the Mountain region and was highest in the south an mid-Atlantic states (15%)" (Technology, 2004). Education makes a differ-

Copyright © 2006, Idea Group Inc. Copying or distributing in print or electronic forms without written permission of Idea Group Inc. is prohibited.

ence and working in technology makes a difference, but there is still a difference.

This may seem like a bleak history that weighs heavily on possible solutions. However, it seems reasonable to say that the primary reason that we repeat the mistakes of our historical past is that we have only known part of our history. The solution lies in telling all of our history. We need to know about all of the women and people of color who have gone before, who managed to thrive in science and technology in times far more oppressive than these, who managed to study, who managed to do the work that they loved and who managed to invent things in spite of living as second-class citizens in a sexist and racist society. The potential that lies in knowing our true history as a human species is limitless.

Another significant influence of education as a social institution in relation to gender relates to how we teach and how we learn. Since science and technology are considered objective domains that exist apart from any social influence, they are often grounded exclusively in abstract thought and methods rather than including concrete thought and methods. This is a classic example of how powerful cultural context is, because most people would never question the validity of this approach. But, the problem with this approach is founded in the dualistic thinking upon which it is based. Thelma Estrin (1996) explains: "the first term in the following pairs generally correlate with men, and the second with women: abstract/concrete, objectivity/subjectivity, logical/intuitive, mind/body, domination/submission" (p. 44). If "maleness" is associated with abstract, objective, logical, rational and dominator behavior, and "femaleness" is associated with concrete, subjective, intuitive, emotional and submissive behavior, which gender is likely to fit into science and technology as it is currently defined?

In fact, we have created a social system in which women who have been "appropriately" gender socialized will not fit easily into the study of science and technology, but most men will. Many scholars have documented why women may be "less comfortable" with the way science is taught (Estrin, 1996; Greenbaum, 1990; Keller, 1992; Riger, 1992; Turkle, 1990). Others have demonstrated that most women are more likely to be concrete learners while most men are more likely to be abstract learners (Belenky, 1986; Goldberger, 1996; Kramer and Lehman, 1990; Rosser, 1995; Turkle, 1990). Setting the inconclusive brain research on sex differences aside, one must ask about the influence of gender socialization on how women and men learn. For now, at least, most women learn best using concrete approaches that provide opportunities for negotiating connections rather than moving "abstractly and hierarchically from

Copyright © 2006, Idea Group Inc. Copying or distributing in print or electronic forms without written permission of Idea Group Inc. is prohibited.

axiom to theorem to corollary" (Turkle, 1990, p. 136). Sherry Turkle (1990) named these types of learners "bricoleurs" and called for an "epistemological pluralism" that allows for multiple ways of learning about and developing computer systems.

Given all of these obstacles, it is no surprise that many women who do make their way to scientific education and employment today ultimately leave. The studies that have examined why women leave and when they leave the sciences tell a daunting and similar story; there is little debate about the causative factors, which provides further evidence of the significance of the issues I have explored in this chapter (Camp, 1997; Seymour & Hewitt, 1997; Sonnert, 1995).

Some of the well documented reasons that women and students of color state for leaving scientific educations: the exclusive male-centered culture of science; the low number of women role models and mentors; inadequate HS preparation (poor study habits); perceived "hardness" of science; competitive, unsupportive culture; outright discrimination; emphasis on grades over learning; "weed-out" tradition; limited pedagogical approaches; sexual harassment from faculty and teaching assistants; different cultural values that are ignored/unacknowledged; cultural restraints on assertiveness; and internalization of negative stereotypes. (Kirk & Zander, 2002, p. 123)

This is the climate we have created, but we can change it if we work together. As I have explained in this chapter, many feminist scholars have proposed a variety of viable solutions to these problems. However, their work often remains little known to those who are working in science and technology. This has meant that the research efforts of many technology scholars and educators are presently being spent on further documenting the well-known problems instead of finding creative ways to work together to solve them. It is time to reexamine our assumptions about science and technology.

A Concluding Pledge: With Technology and Justice for All

How might we proceed to reexamine our assumptions? What is the task really? Ruth Bleier (1991) defines our task as "criticizing the many damaging and self-defeating features of science (the absolutism, authoritarianism, determinist thinking, cause-effect simplifications, androcentrism, ethnocentrism, pretensions to objectivity and neutrality)" and asking serious questions about the "values, opinions, biases, beliefs, and interests of the scientist" (pp. 1-3). Patricia Hill Collins (1991)

Copyright © 2006, Idea Group Inc. Copying or distributing in print or electronic forms without written permission of Idea Group Inc. is prohibited.

suggests that Black women who gain access to social institutions have a unique "insider-outsider" perspective by virtue of their status inside the system and their racial status as outsider. Gloria Anzaldua (1987) and others have suggested that maybe Chicana women share a similarly unique perspective on how the social system works because they exist on the "borderlands" between two social locations. African-American theorist bell hooks (1984) explains that the view "from the margins" can be a much more complex and comprehensive one than the view from the center. Perhaps part of our task is to engage women and men of color who participate in science and technology to share their "insider-outsider" or "border-lands" perspectives.

Even naming the fact that scientists and technologists have a perspective would be progress. A better understanding of science and technology's social context might profoundly change the kinds of questions that scientists ask; we might also consider the broader social uses to which developing technology is applied. In *Teaching Science for Social Justice*, Angela Calabrese Barton (and others) demonstrate what a redefinition of science to be "science for all" might look like by sharing stories of urban youths living in homeless shelters in Texas and New York. In after-school science clubs at their homeless shelters, these youth use science to solve problems in their lives and the lives of their communities and share the value that science is something that helps "to beautify and change your community, to make it a better place" (Barton 2003, pp. 134-135). This is a far cry from the traditional notion of good research science as existing apart from any social context and often even any social purpose.

We must reevaluate the ways in which we have defined science and technology and reexamine the myth of objectivity as the only way to "do good science." Evelyn Fox Keller (1992) describes how "good science" is set up in opposition to so-called "value-laden science," and she challenges this commonly privileged practice of disassociating science from values:

[S]cientific knowledge is value-laden (and inescapably so) just because it is shaped by our choices—first, of what to seek representations of, and second, of what to seek representations for. Since uses and practices are obviously not value-free, why should we even think of equating "good" science with the notion of "value free"? (p. 5)

In the traditional view, the "scientific method" has been the only valid pathway to "good science," and it includes "making observations, forming hypotheses ... testing the validity of the hypotheses by further observations or experiments"

Copyright © 2006, Idea Group Inc. Copying or distributing in print or electronic forms without written permission of Idea Group Inc. is prohibited.

(Bleier, 1991, p. 3). But, Keller (1992) says that the "[s]cientific 'method' is just the name we give to the assorted techniques that scientists have found effective for assessing, subverting, or exploiting" already agreed upon disciplinary boundaries and "more or less collectively endorsed" goals (p. 5). This is another effect of the narrow philosophical foundation upon which science studies have been built. By its very nature, the claim to be "pure" truth, the "scientific method" eliminates serious consideration and validation of diverse perspectives and their possibly "non-traditional" analyses.

This underlines the importance of expanding the focus beyond just fostering the participation of women and other marginalized groups in science. Science itself must be redefined to reflect the actual pluralism of human views on science and society. In *Anti-Racist Science Teaching*, Dawn Gill and Les Levidow (1987) describe specific ways in which current science teaching in the United Kingdom not only fails to reflect "pure truth," but also is implicitly embedded with racist attitudes. Gill and Levidow (1987) describe how current science teaching:

hides its appropriation of non-Western scientific traditions; often attributes people's subordination or suffering to nature . . . rather than to the way science and nature itself have been subordinated to political priorities; is permeated by an ideology of race . . . perpetuates assumptions about nature and human nature that support inequality; and is an alienating experience for many students. (p. 3)

Sue Rosser (1995) also calls for a redefinition of science that is "reconstructed to include us all" (p. 4). In *Re-Engineering: Female Friendly Science*, Sue Rosser (1997) asked: "What would be the parameters of a feminist or women-centered science?" (p. 15). Rosser (1997) suggests changes that include redefining the learning environment for all by focusing on collaboration rather than competition, guiding rather than challenging, practicing theory instead of just talking about it in the abstract, using combinations of qualitative and quantitative methods and placing computer science in a social context (p. 9). These approaches free us from either/or choices such as objective/subjective, abstract/concrete and propose new conceptions of curricula and classroom methods that allow for both/and. Robert Young, a scholar writing about anti-racist science, also calls for "a historical and social approach to knowledge" that examines "the social forces and connections (or articulations) of scientific and technological disciplines and research problems" (Gill & Levidow, 1987, p. 22). Sandra Harding (1998) and others have proposed that acknowledging the social context in which science is done, taught and learned

Copyright © 2006, Idea Group Inc. Copying or distributing in print or electronic forms without written permission of Idea Group Inc. is prohibited.

actually may allow us to come closer to "objectivity" because we can consciously work to identify the ways in which our standpoint may influence both the questions we ask and the answers we find.

What would a new kind of computer science classroom look like? Rosser (1997) and Bleier (1991) both point to the emphasis on competition in science as problematic in terms of attracting and retaining women and people of color in science and technology learning environments. In our 2002 paper "Bridging the Digital Divide by Co-Creating a Collaborative Computer Science Classroom," Zander and I outlined several strategies for moving from competition to collaboration: "(1) guiding students toward collaborative problem solving in class; (2) supporting students toward success with accessible non-violent examples; and (3) creating a positive climate for student questions in and out of the classroom" (p. 120). The issue of competition rather than collaboration is just one attitude and behavior that influences the ways in which science and technology are taught.

What feminist science scholars are calling for is a fundamental redefinition of the culture of science and technology. However, until more of those who do science actually understand the problem, progress towards change, towards a more inclusive science and technology will remain slow. In *Teaching the Majority: Breaking the Gender Barrier in Science, Mathematics, and Engineering*, Rosser (1995) outlined the six phases necessary for change: (1) absence of women noted; (2) recognition that most scientists are male, and that science may reflect a male perspective; (3) identification of barriers that prevent women from entering science; (4) search for women scientists and their unique contributions; (5) science done by feminists and women; and (6) science redefined and reconstructed to include us all (pp. 4–17). Unfortunately, many computer science educators and information technology professionals have not even reached phase 1 or 2, and those who have tend to get stuck there and not recognize how to move on to examine the ways in which institutionalized values may need to be redefined.

Finally, computer culture that emphasizes violence and domination, male-centered metaphors in language and male conversation styles fosters the culturally-embedded attitude that science is for boys/men, not for girls/women. In this climate, it seems unlikely that large numbers of girls/women would view themselves as users or developers of computers. The solutions here should be obvious. We all need to learn about the power of language (as a social institution) to define. This is why language became one of the first issues addressed by feminists and civil rights activists in the US in the 1960s. Unfortunately, most of these efforts to pay attention to language's power to shape beliefs have now been lumped under the pejorative term "political correctness"—a classic example of backlash. In her

Copyright © 2006, Idea Group Inc. Copying or distributing in print or electronic forms without written permission of Idea Group Inc. is prohibited.

groundbreaking book *Backlash: The Undeclared War Against American Women*, Susan Faludi (1991) explained that a cultural backlash is a common result of social progress. Faludi says that when the voices from the margins begin to be heard, the natural response is for the social system to push back in the direction of the familiar and to reassert the values of the dominant culture. The fact remains that language as a social institution has tremendous power—it can reify ideas or change them. If we want more women and people of color to participate in technology, we need to pay attention to our language and what it really says about our beliefs.

What might this new world of science and technology look like? Rita Arditti (1980) described what this reformed and less exclusive world of science could be like when she said:

Science needs a soul, which would show respect and love for its subjects of study and would stress harmony and communication with the rest of the universe. When science fulfills its potential and becomes a tool for human liberation, we will not have to worry about women "fitting" into it because we will probably be at the forefront of the "new" science. (p. 367)

Sandra Harding (1998) also defines a moral purpose for science and technology reform from a global perspective:

If women, the poor, and racial and ethnic "colonies" are kept illiterate, not permitted or encouraged to speak in public, and excluded from the design of the dominant institutions that shape their lives, they do not have the chance to develop and circulate their own politically and scientifically produced perspectives on nature and social relations. (p. 142)

The 21st century will be dominated by the fast-paced sharing of digitized information via computers, and we have a moral obligation to include the voices and perspectives of all of our global citizens. It is time for us to pledge ourselves to creating a digital world with technology and justice for all.

Copyright © 2006, Idea Group Inc. Copying or distributing in print or electronic forms without written permission of Idea Group Inc. is prohibited.

References

2001-2002 Taulbee Survey. (March 2003). *Computing Research News.* Retrieved March 14, 2004, from http://www.cra.org/statistics

Aires, E. (1996). *Men and women in interaction: Reconsidering the differences.* New York: Oxford.

Ambrose, S. (1997). *Journeys of women in science and engineering: No universal constants.* Philadelphia: Temple.

Anzaldua, G. (1987). *Borderlands, la frontera: The new mestiza.* San Francisco: Aunt Lute.

Arditti, R. (1980). Feminism and science. In R. Arditi et al. (Eds.), *Science and liberation* (pp. 350-368). Boston: South End.

Armstrong, D., & Newcomb, P. (Eds.). (n.d.). *The 400 richest Americans.* Retrieved December 30, 2004, from http://www.forbes.com/400richest

Barton, A., et al. (2003). *Teaching science for social justice.* New York: Teachers College.

Belenky, M., et. al. (1986). *Women's ways of knowing: The development of self, voice, and mind.* New York: Basic.

Bleier, R. (1991). Introduction. In R. Bleier (Ed.), *Feminist approaches to science* (pp. 1-17). New York: Teachers College.

Brumberg, J. (1997). *The body project: An intimate history of American girls.* New York: Random House.

Camp, T. (1997). The incredible shrinking pipeline. *Communications of the ACM, 40*(10), 103-110.

Cassell, J., & Jenkins, H. (Eds.). (1998). *From barbie to mortal kombat: Gender and computer games.* Cambridge, MA: MIT.

Collins, P. (1991) *Black feminist thought: Knowledge, consciousness, and the politics of empowerment.* New York: Routledge.

Cooper, J., et al. (1990). Situational stress as a consequence of sex-stereotyped software. *Personality and Social Psychology Bulletin, 16*, 419-429.

Cooper, J., & Weaver, K. (2003). *Gender and computers: understanding the digital divide.* Mahwah, NJ: Erlbaum.

Copyright © 2006, Idea Group Inc. Copying or distributing in print or electronic forms without written permission of Idea Group Inc. is prohibited.

Donovan, J. (1993). *Feminist theory: The intellectual traditions of american feminism*. New York: Continuum.

Estrin, T. (1996). Women's studies and computer science: Their intersection. *IEEE Annals of the History of Computing, 18*(3), 43-46.

Faludi, S. (1991). *Backlash: The undeclared war against American women*. New York: Crown.

Frissen, V. (1992) Trapped in electronic cages? Gender and new information technologies in the public and private domain: An overview of research. *Media, Culture and Society, 14*, 31-49.

Fritz, W. (1996). The women of ENIAC. *IEEE Annals of the History of Computing, 18*(3), 13-28.

The gender wage ratio: Women's and men's earnings. (October 2004). *The Institute for Women's Policy Research*. (IWPR Publication #C350). Retrieved March 7, 2005, from http://www.iwpr.org

Gill, D., & Levidow, L. (Eds.). (1987). *Anti-racist science teaching*. London: Free Association.

Gist, M. (1993). Through the looking glass: Diversity and reflected appraisals of the self in mass media. In P. Creedon (Ed.), *Women in mass communication* (pp. 104-117). Newbury Park, CA: Sage.

Goldberger, N., et al. (1996). *Knowledge, difference, and power: Essays inspired by women's ways of knowing*. New York: Basic.

Greenbaum, J. (1990). The head and the heart: Using gender analysis to study the social construction of computer systems. *Computers and Society, 20*(2), 9-17.

Hanson, S. (1996). *Lost talent: Women in the sciences*. Philadelphia: Temple.

Harding, S. (1998). *Is science multicultural?: Postcolonialisms, feminisms, and epistemologies*. Bloomington: Indiana Printing and Publishing Co.

Herring, S. (1993). Gender and democracy in computer-mediated communication. *EJC/REC, 3*(2). Retrieved November 12, 1998, from http://dc.smu.edu/dc/classroom/Gender.txt

hooks, b. (1984). *Feminist theory: From margin to center*. Boston: South End.

Copyright © 2006, Idea Group Inc. Copying or distributing in print or electronic forms without written permission of Idea Group Inc. is prohibited.

hooks, b. (2000). *Feminism is for everybody: Passionate politics*. Cambridge: South End.

Johnson, A. (1997). *The gender knot: Unraveling our patriarchal legacy*. Philadelphia: Temple University Press.

Kang, M. (1997). The portrayal of women's images in magazine advertisements: Goffman's gender analysis revisited. *Sex Roles, 37*(11/12), 979-996.

Keller, E. (1992). *Secrets of life, secrets of death: Essays on language, gender and science*. New York: Routledge.

Kirk, G., & Okazawa-Rey, M. (2004). *Women's lives: Multicultural perspectives* (3rd ed.). New York: McGraw-Hill.

Kirk, M., & Zander, C. (2002). Bridging the digital divide by co-creating a collaborative co*mputer science classroom. Journal of Computing in Small Colleges, 18*(2), 117-125.

Kirk, M., & Zander, C. (2004). Narrowing the digital divide: In search of a map to mend the gap. *Journal of Computing in Small Colleges, 20*(2), 168-175.

Kramer, P., & Lehman, S. (1990). Mismeasuring women: A critique of research on computer ability and avoidance. *Signs, 16*(11), 158-172.

Lazier, L., & Kendrick, A. (1993). Women in advertisements: Sizing up the images, roles, and functions. In P. Creedon (Ed.), *Women in mass communication* (pp. 199-219). Newbury Park: Sage.

Lerner, G. (1986). *The creation of patriarchy*. New York: Oxford.

Lerner, G. (1993). *The creation of feminist consciousness: From the middle ages to eighteen-seventy*. New York: Oxford.

Merchant, C. (1980). *The death of nature: Women, ecology and the scientific revolution*. San Francisco: Harper.

Merchant, C. (2001). Dominion over nature. In M. Lederman & I. Barsch (Eds.), *The gender and science reader* (pp. 68-81). New York: Routledge.

Millar, M. (1998). *Cracking the gender code: Who rules the wired world?* Toronto: Second Story.

Nelkin, D. (1995). *Selling science: How the press covers science and technology*. New York: Freeman.

Copyright © 2006, Idea Group Inc. Copying or distributing in print or electronic forms without written permission of Idea Group Inc. is prohibited.

Pipher, M. (1994). *Reviving Ophelia: Saving the selves of adolescent girls.* New York: Putnam.

Provenzo, E. (1995). Interview. *Minerva's Machine.* [Videocassette]. Association for Computing Machinery.

Riger, S. (1992). *Epistemological debates, feminist voices. American Psychologist, 47*(6), 730-740.

Rosser, S. (Ed.). (1995). *Teaching the majority: Breaking the gender barrier in science, mathematics, and engineering.* New York: Teachers College.

Rosser, S. (1997). *Re-engineering female friendly science.* New York: Teachers College.

Rossiter, M. (1982). *Women scientists in America: Struggles and strategies to 1940.* Baltimore: Johns Hopkins.

Rossiter, M. (1995). *Women scientists in America: Before affirmative action 1940–1972.* Baltimore: Johns Hopkins.

Sadker, M., & Sadker, D. (1994). *Failing at fairness: How our schools cheat girls.* New York: Touchstone.

Schiebinger, L. (1993). *Nature's body: Gender in the making of modern science.* Boston: Beacon.

Schiebinger, L. (1999). *Has Feminism Changed Science?* Cambridge, MA: Harvard.

Seagar, J. (Ed.). (2003). *The Penguin Atlas of women in the world.* New York: Penguin.

Seymour, E., & Hewitt, N. (1997). *Talking about leaving: Why undergraduates leave the sciences.* Boulder, CO: Westview.

Sonnert, G. (1995). *Gender differences in science careers: The project access study.* New Brunswick, NJ.

Spanier, B. (2001). From molecules to brains, normal science supports sexist beliefs about differences. In M. Lederman & I. Barsch (Eds.), *The gender and science reader* (pp. 272-288). New York: Routledge.

Spender, D. (1985). *Man made language.* London: Routledge.

Spender, D. (1995). *Nattering on the net: Women, power and cyberspace.* North Melbourne, Australia: Spinifex.

Subrahmanyam, K., & Greenfield, P. (1998). Computer games for girls: What makes them play? In J. Cassell & H. Jenkins (Eds.), *From Barbie to*

Copyright © 2006, Idea Group Inc. Copying or distributing in print or electronic forms without written permission of Idea Group Inc. is prohibited.

Mortal Lombat: Gender and computer games (pp. 46-71). Cambridge, MA: MIT.

Technology salaries recover and gender gap narrows, according to dice annual salary survey of 21,000 technology professionals. Retrieved March 7, 2005, from http://marketing.dice.com/releases/salaryrelease.html

Turkle, S., & Papert, S. (1990). Epistemological pluralism: Styles and voices within the computer culture. *Signs, 16*(1), 128-157.

Valletta, R., & MacDonald, G. (2003). Is there a digital divide? *FRBSF Economic Letter,* (38), 1-3.

Van Fossen, B. (1996). Gender differences in communication. *Institute for Teaching and Research on Women, Towson University.* Retrieved August 5, 1997, from http://midget.towson.edu/itrow

Wajcman, J. (1995). Feminist theories of technology. In S. Jasanoff, et al. (Eds.), *Handbook of science and technology studies* (pp. 189-204). Thousand Oaks, CA: Sage.

Ware, M., & Stuck, M. (1985). Sex-role messages vis-à-vis microcomputer use: A look at the pictures. *Sex Roles, 13*(3/4), 205-214.

The wealthiest of America's wealthy. *The News Times.* Retrieved May 11, 1999, from http://www.newstimes.com/archive98/sep2898/bzd.htm

Weinberg, N. (1999). Shortchanged by sex. *Network World.* Retrieved March 10, 2005, from InfoTrac database.

Williams, S. (1999). *History of black women in the mathematical sciences.* Retrieved October 16, 1999, from http://www.math.buffalo.edu/mad/wohist.html

Wood, J. (1999). *Gendered lives: Communication, gender, and culture* (3rd ed.). Belmont, CA: Wadsworth.

Copyright © 2006, Idea Group Inc. Copying or distributing in print or electronic forms without written permission of Idea Group Inc. is prohibited.

Chapter IV

Gender and Programming:
Mixing the Abstract and the Concrete

Peter McKenna, Manchester Metropolitan University, UK

Abstract

This chapter seeks to examine a theory of gendered styles of programming which is predicated on differences in attitudes toward abstraction and black boxes. It critically explores the theoretical questions and issues raised and summarizes the design of an empirical, quantitative means of testing gender-based attitudes to black boxes, alongside and triangulated with ethnographic research into the experiences and attitudes of female students in relation to programming. The paradigm-shift represented by object-oriented programming is given particular consideration because of the claims made on its behalf within this debate, and as a special case of abstraction. The chapter concludes that there is no gendered difference in attitudes toward black boxes in programming, and that the reasons for female under-representation in computing lie elsewhere.

Copyright © 2006, Idea Group Inc. Copying or distributing in print or electronic forms without written permission of Idea Group Inc. is prohibited.

Introduction

This chapter seeks to deconstruct prevalent gender theories on abstraction in programming, and its possible role in the gendering of computing. Such a deconstruction will be critical, and even perhaps controversial, but is not necessarily a negative process. A too-ready acceptance of the supposedly natural inclinations and disinclinations of women and men when it comes to computers and programming has particularly troubling implications for the role of women in large-scale software development. While one of the conclusions is that positive initiatives should not be premised on stereotyped assumptions of gendered abilities, it was the counter-intuitive aspects—also informed, in a fashion, by stereotype—of Sherry Turkle and Seymour Papert's research (1984b, 1992) that demanded interrogation. Males not wanting to look under the hood; females dismissing the general in favor of the particular, and forming personal relationships with machines? It simply did not compute! As one female programmer said, "Men in general have a greater interest in the background working of equipment and such likes."

And so we undertook to investigate the ways in which gender has been, and may legitimately be, interpreted as a dimension of the computer programming curriculum. It is clearly reasonable to look for problems within the curriculum and to seek to reinvent computing culture and views of academic computing in the light of those problems; but the need for specifics also demands that we question all assumptions and categorizations around gender as well as our assumptions about computing. The differences in the extrinsic representation of women and men in computing do not have to have intrinsic correlatives in nature, or even in differences in their attitudes to computers. Nor do theories from other fields always translate well into the specifics of computing. Even social explanations sometimes base themselves on assumed natural differences. Open-minded research, grounded in the practicalities of programming, will provide a surer footing for action to redress the gender imbalance in computer science. As with debugging, the wrong "fix" can generate more bugs than it solves.

The objective of this chapter is therefore to explore the gender imbalance in computer science degree enrolment by examining the ways in which gender has been and may be interpreted as a dimension of the computer programming curriculum. This exploration focuses on the use of black boxes—prepackaged routines, including objects as well as library procedures. The design of the means to test gendered attitudes to black boxes is summarized along with indicative quantitative data arising from such experiments, and these are further triangulated with ethnographic interview data.

Copyright © 2006, Idea Group Inc. Copying or distributing in print or electronic forms without written permission of Idea Group Inc. is prohibited.

Background

The gender imbalance in computer science degree courses is well documented, but is particularly acute in the United Kingdom. In the USA, the National Science Foundation's published figures (derived from the Department of Education's National Center for Education Statistics) show that on average, 28% of Computer Science (CS) Bachelor's degrees have been awarded to women since 1990—down from the 34% average of the 1980s (National Science Foundation, 1966-2001). Data from the Computing Research Association Taulbee Surveys for North America show that Ph.D.-granting Departments award a considerably lower percentage—consistently below 20% over the past decade—of CS bachelor degrees to women (Computing Research Association, 1992-2003). Yet even these figures are higher than the 13% of applicants for Computer Science degree places in the UK in 2004. This figure indicates that the problem is at the point of application rather than selection (the figure for accepted females is slightly higher); it is also typical of the last decade, with a highpoint in 1999 for female applicants of 18% that carried through into 2000 and 2001, but which has dipped down even lower over the past three years (Figure 1).

The figure for the much smaller Software Engineering Subject Line was 10%, with 23% on "softer" Information Systems degrees (Universities and Colleges Admissions Service, 2003). The idea that the Computer Science gender imbalance results from an association with mathematics and/or actual mathematical content is undermined by the significantly more balanced number of women (38%) offered places on Mathematics degrees (Figure 2).

Figure 1. UK computer science BSc applicants (1997-2004)

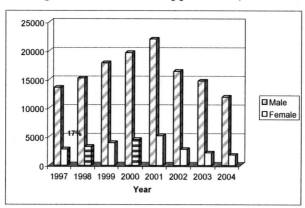

Copyright © 2006, Idea Group Inc. Copying or distributing in print or electronic forms without written permission of Idea Group Inc. is prohibited.

Figure 2. Female applicants in mathematics and computer science in UK from 1997-2004

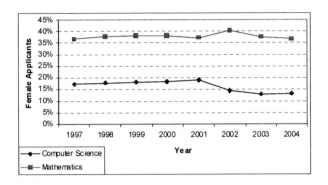

The situation is little better in the computing industry. Ten years ago 29% of the UK's IT workforce was female—a figure which has now fallen to 18% (Bell, 2003). Women are more likely to occupy clerical and lower-paid positions within such figures. These are significant inequities, and as Margolis & Fisher (2002) say, such an imbalance can only be detrimental to the health of computing as a discipline.

The Problem with Programming

Programming—or the translation of specific problems and solutions into sequences of computer operations—is central to the development of software to solve real-world problems, central even to the shaping of the modern world. Programming is important. Yet while it is fundamental to the computing curriculum, programming is at the same time the one major area of that curriculum that appears to discourage would-be students (Krechowiecka, 2002). It is an apparent need for single-minded and obsessive attention to detail (and often equally obsessive working hours) that has led to the popular identification of programming with the autistic spectrum in males. The term "hacker" implies a competitive cleverness that is part of a broader masculine culture, but which gains a particular focus in computer programming. The Oxford English Dictionary (1989) defines "hacker" as "a person with an enthusiasm for programming or using computers as an end in itself," an apparently neutral identity—unless one assumes that programming should really have extrinsic ends.

Copyright © 2006, Idea Group Inc. Copying or distributing in print or electronic forms without written permission of Idea Group Inc. is prohibited.

Although it is this lack of outside points of reference that defines the isolated and unsociable nature of hackers, science sociologist Sherry Turkle has reclaimed hacker culture for women. This may seem paradoxical and obviously flawed—and Turkle does acknowledge that the actual hacker's world is a "male world...peculiarly unfriendly to women" (1984a, p. 216). It would be only with some difficulty that the association might serve to valorize feminine culture (and perhaps incidentally render this particular masculine culture less unfashionable). Yet it seems reasonable to object to the utilitarian assumption about programming: after all, it would be an impoverished perspective that derided the act of writing or painting for its own sake. Turkle—in collaboration with the AI and constructionist learning-technology pioneer Seymour Papert— casts the programmer as an artist rather than as an engineer. The metaphor that underlies programming—that of "writing" in a "language"—perhaps encourages such a view. Turkle identifies a hacking style of programming with "soft mastery" as early as 1980, and by 1984 designates it as the "mastery of the artist" rather than of the engineer (1980, 1984b).

However, while Turkle's Lorraine has dreams about "what a computer feels like inside," (1984a, 1990) and forms relationships with (sometimes named) computers, Margolis and Fisher (2002) make a point of quoting Donna, another female computing undergraduate, who asserts that "I don't dream in code like [the geeks] do." While for Margolis and Fisher the image of "dreaming in code" is a working metaphor for the masculine computer culture, Turkle's women, variously comparing programming to creative and visionary activities such as writing, pottery, painting, and playing the piano, reject mechanistic approaches in favor of imaginative and personal visions that appear to reclaim and reshape the hacker culture.

While some have identified the "tools" approach to computer technology as definitive of a no-nonsense communicative female approach (Frenkel, 1991; Harcourt, 1999; Margolis & Fisher, 2002)—and a patriarchal interpretation might see this approach as a case of girls using things that boys make—a further alternative take is that using a computer as a means is instrumental, with hints of ruthlessness and dictatorial aloofness. A woman, the thinking goes, would communicate with the computer in order to form a relationship (rather than dictate "commands" to it to do things), and write programs in the way that an artist composes a painting. And so we return to the "geek"—someone (according to a prominent member of the "Santa Cruz geek social scene") who "spends time being 'social' on a computer" (Jackson, 1998).

However, are the utilitarian expectations of computer programming really so unreasonable? A poem, song or work of art, after all, communicates in some

Copyright © 2006, Idea Group Inc. Copying or distributing in print or electronic forms without written permission of Idea Group Inc. is prohibited.

way with people—not with the objects or technologies used in their composition. While the software that is born, or *runs*, from it must communicate with users, the primary communication of program *code* is with the computer it runs on. In order to accomplish this, it is with the user and other programmers rather than with the computer that the programmer needs to communicate. If programming is to be a self-contained and private, autonomous activity, it will not be possible to produce software that is either large-scale or usable. These are fundamental as well as practical objections.

In a more focused sense, a hacker's programming style is specifically the inclination to program by personal instinct, using trial and error rather than method. In order to do this, one needs a feel for, and insight into, all the elements of one's program. The hacker will therefore want to write their own subroutines rather than simply use somebody else's. For Turkle and Papert this resonates with feminine psychosocial notions of holism and contact with interior space: while the male—a stranger in the natural world—adopts a style that is "abstract" and distant, the female is engaged with the "concrete," intuitively relating to interiors rather than exteriors. Men are said to want to command from a distance, while women need intimate communication—as with people, so too with programs and computers. Soft masters require transparency, and are said to have "access to a style of reasoning that allowed them to imagine themselves 'inside the system.'" So men, it is postulated, like to work with prepackaged code ("black boxes"), while women prefer to personally go inside them, take them apart or write their own routines instead. Where the masculine style is "abstract," the female is "concrete"; while men pursue "hard mastery," women seek "soft mastery" (Turkle, 1984a; Turkle & Papert, 1992). From Levi-Strauss's concept of concrete and tactile (rather than analytical) science, the term *bricolage* is also reclaimed, to denote the feminized hacker's concrete "negotiation" with computational objects.

The fact that *abstraction* has been set up in opposition to this style possibly owes more to terminological confusion than to any detailed understanding of it as a theoretical or practical programming concept. Programming "abstraction" has been conflated with the mainstream meaning of the word. It is not just that software is "abstract" in the sense of its virtuality, as an essentially intangible set of instructions; the software is a product from which the computer-specific detail of how it works has been removed (abstracted) and replaced by detail that is understandable by people (a user interface). This is the highest level of "abstraction," and the principle also holds true within the code and the coding process: abstraction is the removal of lower-level detail for the purpose of clarity and reusability. Instead of embedding the full detail of how routines are

Copyright © 2006, Idea Group Inc. Copying or distributing in print or electronic forms without written permission of Idea Group Inc. is prohibited.

implemented, these particulars are "black-boxed" into a named routine and then simply called by that name. The programmer needs to know only what it does, not how it does it—therefore its technical detail is "abstracted," or removed from sight. The manner in which programming languages separate interface and implementation varies, but it is usually explicit.

According to Turkle and Papert, however, it is the central role of abstraction in programming curricula that is problematic: it is inimical in general to women's epistemological style and its curricular prominence amounts to "exclusion," to "discrimination in the computer culture" (1990, 1992). Teachers of programming are trained to recognize hard mastery as the only real way to program, whereas it is only a "male mastery" that is inimical to the psychological make-up and preferred learning styles of women. It has therefore been proposed that, in order to attract more women to programming, abstraction should at least be accorded the downgraded status of just one of many different approaches (Turkle, 1992). The gendered styles hypothesis has been particularly influential in the UK: Grundy (1996) reiterates as fact the dislike that women have for black boxes, and Peltu (1993) goes so far as to recommend the removal of abstraction from the curriculum in order to encourage more female participation.

Whether this hypothesis concerning gendered programming styles is true or not is of crucial importance: if such a significant difference between women and men does actually exist, it will have serious implications for the computing curricula and for the teaching and learning of programming. If it does not exist, then there a risk that curricula could be altered to pander to stereotyped views of women, and women would be unjustifiably identified as naturally unsuited to large-scale software development.

Our examination of the theory of gendered programming styles, in conjunction with attempts to test the theory's assumptions by means of exemplifying black boxes in specific programming situations (McKenna, 2000, 2001), raises epistemological and pedagogical issues that are important to gender diversity in computing.

The Further Problem of Gendered Programming Styles

Sherry Turkle's notion of gendered programming styles appears to derive from psychoanalytic theory. A key characteristic of soft masters and their "concrete

Copyright © 2006, Idea Group Inc. Copying or distributing in print or electronic forms without written permission of Idea Group Inc. is prohibited.

style of reasoning" is closeness to, and identification with, what she calls "computational objects." Logic provides "abstract formulae that maintain reason at a distance from its objects" (1992). Girls and boys, according to gendered object relations theory, develop differentially by forming either "a proximal or distant relationship" to objects, and their use of either "the abstract and analytic or concrete and negotiational style of thinking follows." The analysis owes much to Evelyn Fox Keller's (1983) identification of canonical science and objectivity as a separation of scientific objects from everyday life. This separation is said to reflect the "earliest experiences" of men, whereby they are left "with a sense of the fusional as taboo," and an investment "in objective relationships with the world" (Turkle, 1984a, p. 115). Keller (1983) describes Barbara McClintock, a Nobel laureate in biology, relating to chromosomes to such an extent that she "wasn't outside," but became "part of the system." Although Keller comments that this fusional experience is also experienced by male scientists, Turkle hypothesizes that McClintock could more fully exploit such an experience "because she is a woman" (1984a, p. 117), and states that this is "surely the case for the girls in the Austen classrooms"—children (including one named Anne, whom we shall return to) who were observed solving graphical programming problems in creative ways. The transposition of gendered object relations theory onto computer programming produces "computational objects"—similar to transitional comfort objects in childhood—that may be related to "in a way that is not separate from the experience of the self."

A key problem with this analogy is the identity of the relational objects. It is assumed that "communication" with the computer is analogous to (rather than a vehicle for) human communication, and that the programmer who is a "good communicator" will communicate and "negotiate" with their computer and its components. As we have noted, this is a misdirection of communicativeness (feminine or otherwise) to the extent that prioritizing communication with the machine compromises the primary communication that should take place with the users of the software and with other members of the software development team. The role of programming abstraction in this respect is to hide technical detail so that only human-significant detail is visible, and the meaningful whole may be grasped once that detail is removed.

Part of negotiating a relationship with computational objects is getting to know them from the inside. The computer may well feel like one big black box to a beginner, whose desire "to look inside" it merely expresses a desire to understand and/or a desire to not be intimidated. Once the ice is broken and these initial concerns are allayed by a concrete familiarity, it becomes easier to move on to bigger pictures. However, Turkle and Papert explicitly identify the

Copyright © 2006, Idea Group Inc. Copying or distributing in print or electronic forms without written permission of Idea Group Inc. is prohibited.

concrete style as a complete way of knowing how to program, a fully-formed and at least equal "intellectual style" (1992) rather than a stage in a learning cycle that moves onto reflection and conceptualization. To further identify this concrete style as something that is natural to women could make a damaging and stereotyping contribution to the very inequities it seeks to address.

Still, there is much that is constructive to be found in unraveling these overlaps and distinctions between pedagogy and epistemology. Is it possible, for instance, to learn to program in an "abstract" way using (at least initially) concrete learning techniques and styles? On the two introductory programming units which were examined and surveyed, the concrete learning style is seen as serving an educational means rather than an end. Concrete learning styles and methods do not necessarily entail a concrete approach to programming. The "concrete" learning approach of the activities was characterized by the fact that the learner could get immediate visual results in response to their coding activity. This approach may well encourage learners to explore and experiment—but it can exist without any desire to expose or enter the interiors of black boxes. The activities represented not a way of knowing, but a way of learning how to program: the inception of a learning cycle that continues through the processes of reflection and conceptualization, before returning to elaborate on the experimental (Kolb, 1983).

Testing: Exemplifying Black Boxes

The amount of qualitative research in this field reflects the importance of the quality of the student experience. For the relatively narrow hypothesis concerning attitudes to black boxes, quantitative research potentially offers a check-and-balance against the latent subjective vagaries of qualitative research. The central rationale of the field research (McKenna, 2001) was to render concrete what it actually means in practice to want to go inside black boxes, and thereby to examine the hypothesis that such boxes were more inimical to women. The key principle to illustrate was that, in addition to talking to people, it should be possible to test whether women do in practice have more negative attitudes to black boxes than men have, and to situate the question more strongly in actual programming contexts.

This involved identifying some of the different ways in which programming courses make practical use of black boxes, and presenting examples to a sample population in the form of a questionnaire, with the intention of measuring

Copyright © 2006, Idea Group Inc. Copying or distributing in print or electronic forms without written permission of Idea Group Inc. is prohibited.

their attitudes to them—whether they would prefer to look inside or rewrite black boxes at different levels of abstraction.

This experimental survey took place among first year undergraduate student programmers. The choice of student rather than practitioner populations paralleled Turkle and Papert's approach, and provided scope for examining the potential confusion of learning styles with actual programming styles. Two different British higher education institutions were used. In the first—an institution of higher education which specialized in offering subject combinations ("Combined Honors") within a liberal arts education—females were overrepresented, both in the institution and on the programming unit. In the second—a traditional, predominantly male, computer science and mathematics department within the science and engineering faculty of a British new university—females were seriously underrepresented on the unit. The main business of the new university department lay in single honors computer science degrees. Nonetheless, in addition to participating in the institutional combined honors program, it offered a series of pathways that might broadly be described as "contextualized" or "interdisciplinary" (Multimedia Computing, Internet Computing), along with more than one point of entry. The first used an in-house programming environment, while the new university unit used a standard commercial language.

In the first sample group (McKenna, 2000, 2001), there were 17 male and 24 female students, mainly from arts backgrounds, studying Combined Honors. Students used a customized graphical environment to learn to program— sending messages to move an on-screen character around a two-dimensional environment where it could perform specific tasks. In what was a concrete learning approach to programming, output was instantaneous and visual. Students could see immediately what commands did, and combine them in different ways in order to solve given problems.

The second sample group was drawn from an introductory Java unit on the first year of a BSc Combined Honors (CH) degree (in computing and something else) at Manchester Metropolitan University (MMU). The CH intake included more women than the other single honors cohorts who studied only computing. While the choice of combined honors maximized the size of the female cohort, unfortunately it was still too small (11 females against 39 males) to produce results that could reasonably be considered conclusive. However, the principle of testability was plausibly established, and further doubt cast on the hypothesis that women shun black boxes.

Copyright © 2006, Idea Group Inc. Copying or distributing in print or electronic forms without written permission of Idea Group Inc. is prohibited.

Figure 3. Blank questionnaire for second (Java) survey

Questionnaire
This short questionnaire is part of a project to explore different attitudes to programming. Your participation is greatly appreciated.

General information

Personal data
1. Please tick your age-group: 2. Please tick your sex:

18-24	
25-29	
30-35	
36-39	
40-45	
46-49	
50+	

Male	
Female	

3. What (if any) experience of programming did you have before starting the programming course?

None whatsoever	
some self-taught knowledge	
a previous course	
work experience	
other (please specify)	

4. Please tick if you have any of the following qualifications:

GCSE computer studies	
A' Level Computing	
RSA IT qualification	
GNVQ in Computing	
A' Level Mathematics	
Access qualification	

Programming Questions
JAVA ELEMENTS

Bailey & Bailey's *element* package provides easy access to textual input and output facilities.

If time allowed, would you:

a) like to inspect and take apart the code that Bailey & Bailey wrote in implementing the *element* package, so that you could find the detail of how methods such as *readLine* actually work?
Circle one number

```
+---------------+---------------+
1               2               3
no           perhaps          yes
```

b) prefer to write and use your own routines rather than using either *readLine* or another prepackaged method?
Circle one number

```
+---------------+---------------+
1               2               3
no           perhaps          yes
```

c) prefer to use the Java AWT and IO classes directly yourself
Circle one number

```
+---------------+---------------+
1               2               3
no           perhaps          yes
```

And finally:

I am interested in discussing my attitudes to and experience of computer programming. I would be willing to have an informal discussion in more depth at a convenient time
[IF YES - my NAME :-_____]

YES	
NO	

Copyright © 2006, Idea Group Inc. Copying or distributing in print or electronic forms without written permission of Idea Group Inc. is prohibited.

During the previous academic year this unit changed from the academic Modula-2 to a better known and commercially popular language. Java presented an immediate problem that invited a "pre-packaged" solution: basic keyboard input of text is an inordinately complicated task in Java. The level of technical detail required just to read input represents a major distraction from learning the basics of programming. It is a classic example of a means presenting a serious obstacle to accomplishing an end, and it made sense to "abstract" or remove this detail into a simple prepackaged method.

The course book (Bailey & Bailey, 2000) simplified input and output by providing such "prepackaged routines" for immediate use. This was the first example of its emphasis on the elements of programming rather than on the intricacies of Java. In Java a "package" represents a high level of abstraction which "packages up" libraries of related programming components. Clearly the term resonates with Turkle and Papert's notion of "prepackaged procedures" and "opaque containers." One of their students, Lisa, programs her own procedures because she "resents" the "opacity" of "prepackaged ones from a program library" (Turkle & Papert, 1992). In this respect, languages such as Java are fundamentally inimical to her: the standard Java Applications Programming Interface (API) is such a package, as is the Abstract Windowing Toolkit (AWT). Most Java programs—indeed, most common programming languages—begin with statements that import routines from other packages. Experienced programmers will write some of their own library routines, packaging them themselves, but still rely substantially on ones that have been "prepackaged."

The use of packages on this course unit allowed learners to produce meaningful results without having first to wrestle with the internals of Java. Moreover, graphics routines encouraged a "concrete" style of learning. Students generally appreciated being able to call the drawing and coloring routines included in Bailey & Bailey's Elements package and immediately see a graphical result on screen. They experienced a concrete learning environment, yet it was only made possible in programming terms by high levels of abstraction.

The unit as taught used data hiding in a practical way in order to simplify output and input, but as an introductory unit it would not explicitly introduce students to data hiding. This illustrates the dissimilarity between programming abstraction and conceptual "abstraction": using these third-party ("prepackaged") routines represented a "concrete" application of implicit abstraction, while programming in an explicitly object-oriented manner would require an explicit conceptual understanding of abstraction. Even the use of stepwise refinement

Copyright © 2006, Idea Group Inc. Copying or distributing in print or electronic forms without written permission of Idea Group Inc. is prohibited.

for design requires some explicit understanding of abstraction. The pedagogical thinking among the teaching staff was that students needed to experience and understand what calling routines meant in action before they could move to the conceptual understanding needed to make stepwise refinement useful as a design technique.

The unfamiliarity of students with abstraction and black boxes as explicit concepts also helped to reduce the potential impact of such awareness as a variable in the questionnaire. Nor were students aware of the parameters of debate concerning gender in programming, or that gender was a significant part of the research.

In the case of both groups, prepackaged routines were provided specifically to ensure that student effort produced immediate results—routines to move or turn a character, read a line of text, or draw a shape. Questions were designed to evaluate the extent to which students were inclined to find out how these routines worked from the inside, or even to write their own instead—exemplifying particular routines at different levels of abstraction and asking whether they wished either to know how they are implemented, or to write their own version.

Results

Questions in both questionnaires invoked black boxes at different levels of abstraction and the desire to inspect, alter and reinvent them, citing prepackaged routines that were understandable to students and specific to the particular programming environment used on their respective courses. No significant difference was found between female and male attitudes to black boxes in these situated programming scenarios. Due to the sample size—particularly that of females in the second study—these findings were more speculative than conclusive, but they did tend to confirm the theoretical arguments that the hypothesis of gendered programming styles may be flawed. In principle, with sufficient specificity and exemplification, the hypothesis is testable.

Women's Experience

Students were interviewed to obtain qualitative data that could explore the experience of women studying computing and programming—and to serve as

Copyright © 2006, Idea Group Inc. Copying or distributing in print or electronic forms without written permission of Idea Group Inc. is prohibited.

a corollary to Turkle and Papert's student interviews. It was hoped that the process would produce richer qualitative data to triangulate with the more "objective" surveys. Eight women were interviewed at different stages of their computing studies—ranging from Master's level to the second year of the undergraduate Combined Honors degree course at MMU. The two focus areas were the idea of a computer as a psychological machine in general, and as more specifically applied to prepackaged routines or black boxes

Two students had explicit "psychology" connections: Tania came to MMU's MSc conversion course from her previous MSc in Forensic Psychology; and Son-Yong was in the second year of her BSc Combined Honors in Information Systems with Psychology. Two other students were of particular interest: Rupa, a part-time MSc student who worked full-time in a programming job; and Zaida, a pianist as well as a computing undergraduate.

Zaida, a second year, single-honors computing student at MMU was—like Robin, one of Turkle and Papert's second year Harvard students—a highly trained and accomplished pianist. Zaida talked with enthusiasm and clarity about areas of similarity between playing the piano and programming—the mathematics, notation, language, syntax and grammar of music, the absence of an expressive overlay to the notation of programming. Playing the piano, she felt, was a communication process analogous to Java's emphasis on server-client protocols. One had to be insistent and patient to get the best out of both a piano and a computer—yet in neither case did she feel that this constituted a "relationship" with a "psychological machine." The piano player, she indicated, "masters" the piano: the piano is not attributed with any of its own features or agency. Indeed, it was not the piano as such that she played, but a composer's score, which made the piano produce music. When you play Chopin's notation, she said, people say you're playing Chopin—the composer rather than the instrument. One could feel frustrated with both the computer and the piano, but such feelings did not endow the piano with any character or psychological presence.

Unlike Turkle's Robin, Zaida concluded that there is no relationship in the case of either the computer or the piano. Where Robin communicated "*with* her instrument," Zaida communicated *through* her instrument; where Robin felt emotional involvement *with* the piano, Zaida felt emotional while playing it. Zaida spoke of communication, interpretation and style, but did not recognize the "language and models for close relationships *with* music machines" [my emphasis] that Turkle and Papert (1992, p. 28) boldly ascribe to the whole culture of music. It is not the machine or tool that is important. Even the vehicle of Turkle and Papert's metaphor for "highly personal" feminine programming

Copyright © 2006, Idea Group Inc. Copying or distributing in print or electronic forms without written permission of Idea Group Inc. is prohibited.

styles—the "close, sensuous, and relational" encounters with inanimate objects ascribed to artists and musicians—is called into question.

Tania, the student with a Psychology Masters, explained her reasons for undertaking a Master's course in computing in terms that echoed the psychology often negatively ascribed to male hackers. One of the reasons she had been attracted to computers was that it avoided dealing with unpredictable people, and involved no danger: "You are not dealing with any unpredictable people," she said, "you're just sitting in front of a computer, and the worst that could happen is that the system could crash." Where all people are potentially "unpredictable" to the stereotypical hacker, however, Tania's previous job as a prison Psychologist did bring her into risky contact with unpredictable people. This may explain her explicit rejection of the computer as a psychological machine—"because it can't talk back. You're controlling it at the end of the day. All it can do is just respond to your actions, which you've got control of…you're controlling that computer, whereas with a person you can't." She suggested a whiteboard as an approximate point of comparison for a computer.

Son-Yong took a similar view: The computer was "just a machine," and if she ever talked to it, it was as she would to any recalcitrant object. She related the notion to her interest in Artificial Intelligence—one that she felt unable to pursue because the topic appeared to be taught as a technical rather than psychological subject at the University. In terms of the specific issue of prepackaged procedures, Tania initially indicated that she "would prefer to see the overall picture," including the "source code." It emerged, however, that she conceived of this as simply seeing any code that was being talked about, rather than listening to it being discussed "on the abstract level." When asked what seeing the code of writeLn would tell her, she responded: "Well, the syntax, how you write it: write 'L' – 'n,' 'brackets.'" She did not in fact think that she wanted to see any code at a lower level, and would prefer to draw a button in Visual Basic rather than write the code for it herself. Similarly, Son-Yong "wouldn't mind seeing how [the prepackaged Java *elements* procedures] work"— although not if it was "hard," and she would not want to rewrite one herself. That, she said, would be "quite scary." Both Tania and Son-Yong had experience of multimedia authoring software, and both liked the extent to which the automated programming features of these environments made life a lot easier.

It was notable in the interview with Tania how readily the general and pedagogical meaning of the "abstract" was confused with its significance in programming. This observation had implications in terms of the clarity and

Copyright © 2006, Idea Group Inc. Copying or distributing in print or electronic forms without written permission of Idea Group Inc. is prohibited.

precision required of scenarios and questions in any testing of the black box hypothesis: what is meant by "seeing the code" must be unambiguously contextualized.

As a professional programmer, Rupa had considerable experience of using abstraction in the form of library routines. When presented with the idea—new to her—that there might be a difference in the attitudes of women and men to black boxes and abstraction, she indicated that she did not feel that there was a great difference. To the extent that there might be one, she thought that it might be correct "to assume that there would a greater number of men who would be interested the actual working of black boxes and abstractions, than women." In terms of gender and computing generally, Rupa felt that "men in general have a greater interest in the background working of equipment and such likes," and added that "this does include how library routines are constructed and their working."

Rupa explained that "one of the reasons that library routines have been used is to ensure that within the different sections ... that make up an application certain functions work in exactly the same way." For most library routines she had used, she had "just accepted their performance at face value," and there was, in any case, no time to look into them. She had only done so when "the libraries did not perform in the exact manner I expected them to." Even on these occasions, however, she had not amended the libraries, "as this would inflict unnecessary problems onto other users' programs," but had "copied and then amended the necessary areas of the library and then incorporated them into my own program."

Rupa's experience reflected the reality of programming for clients in the real world, and brings out the fundamental need to trust one's colleagues in relation to "prepackaged routines." Her work was essentially defined by the need for egoless programming and team use of library routines. Her expectation was that it would be men rather than women who would waste time tampering with black boxes rather than simply using them.

Future Trends

Turkle and Papert's instantiation of "computational objects" for the "objects" of object relations theory perhaps inevitably led them to identify (1992; Turkle, 1996) object-oriented programming (OOP) as specifically suited to, and

Copyright © 2006, Idea Group Inc. Copying or distributing in print or electronic forms without written permission of Idea Group Inc. is prohibited.

illustrative of, the concrete style. In the 1990s OOP represented the positive face of the future—and the future was therefore more female-friendly.

For Turkle and Papert, OOP offered the fulfillment and "revaluation" of the "concrete" approach (1992, p. 29): it would be, they claimed, "more congenial to those who favor concrete approaches," and "puts an intellectual value on a way of thinking that is resonant with their own" (p. 155). Turkle explicitly suggested that the object-oriented programming paradigm "associated computation with the object-relations tradition in psychoanalytic thought" (1995, p. 296). Grundy, too, has equated object-oriented programming with a concrete (as opposed to abstract) style of programming, interpreting the growing popularity of the object-oriented paradigm as "a surge of interest in a concrete style of programming" (1996, p. 142). By the end of that decade and the beginning of the following century, however, it became clear that OOP was not going to be a silver bullet (a neat masculine metaphor!) for the werewolf of male domination in computing culture. Neither it nor the direct manipulation graphical development environments (typified by Visual Basic) with which it may have been confused, have affected the under-representation of women in computing.

The pioneering OOP language Smalltalk, was developed at Xerox in tandem with the first Graphical User Interface (GUI), and there may have been an understandable confusion with the graphical and direct manipulation aspects of the GUI. A programming object, however, is more than this—it is essentially a black box, and objects are called "objects" because they frequently model real-world objects. Indeed, objects are the ultimate in black boxes—the culmination of the use of abstraction to replicate the real world in the computer, the fulfillment of the potential of abstraction. The programmer knows and works with an object in the way that a customer uses a vending machine: the customer need not know how the machine works, only its state (whether specific drinks and change are available, how much money has been entered), and the actions to be performed by the customer and the machine. The details of the machinery are kept hidden and secure from the customer—to avoid misuse, but also because the customer simply does not need to have access to them. In terms of programming, we are back with abstraction. As Sebesta puts it, "object-oriented programming ... is an outgrowth of the use of data abstraction" (1993, p. 375).

Mendelsohn et al. (1990) suggest empirical research shows that logic "is not how people think" (p. 25). Object-oriented programming is hardly logic-free, however: Green (1980) points out that OOP is far from being "artless." Programming "objects" are very complicated, yet at the same time do not

Copyright © 2006, Idea Group Inc. Copying or distributing in print or electronic forms without written permission of Idea Group Inc. is prohibited.

reflect the intricacies of real world objects. Object-oriented programming is neither natural nor easy. Indeed, various aspects of object-oriented programming render it more difficult to learn than traditional structured programming: in particular, identifying object boundaries and getting objects to communicate with each other are highly challenging aspects of OOP. The Java course book at MMU was chosen partly because it minimized the role of OOP.

In her personal account of life as a software engineer, *Close to the Machine*, Ellen Ullman (1997) tells how object orientation was a test of whether she was "technical": "Object-oriented software: small hunks of code, understandable only if you know a whole hierarchy of logic. Tiny window, fifty-line viewport, to see little blocks in an elaborate pyramid. Murk and confusion" (p. 112).

In traditional imperative or procedural programming, the "unit of thought" is said by Turkle and Papert to be "an instruction to the computer to do something," but "in object-oriented programming the unit of thought is creating and modifying interactive agents within a program, for which the natural metaphors are biological and social rather than algebraic" (1992, p. 31). The language of object-oriented programming does indeed use such metaphors: child, parent, inheritance, message-passing, properties. However, the essence of objects – and it is not just a particular perception—lies in encapsulation. Gorlen et al. (1990, p. 1) refer to data abstraction as the "necessary foundation" of object-oriented programming. Encapsulation in the object-oriented programming paradigm is synonymous with "information hiding" or black-boxing: it provides a "cover,", in Satzinger and Ørvik's words, "that hides the internal structure of the object from the environment outside" (Satzinger & Ørvik, 1996, p. 40). The object-oriented paradigm abstracts data as well as processes, and binds the processes to the data—in a way not dissimilar to the "hard master" who would create her or his own abstract data types in separate modules with a public functional interface and a private, untouchable and often invisible implementation. An "object," normally an abstraction of an entity in the real world, is therefore the ultimate "black box." Its defining characteristic is that no other object needs to be aware of its insides: its internal data structure, and the methods for manipulating instances of it, are all hidden. The maximum amount of detail has been gathered into this black box: "We can then use them simply as black boxes which provide a transformation between input and output. We need not understand or even be aware of their inner working...." (Gorlen et al., 1990, p. 1).

What Turkle and Papert disapprovingly present as the formal, hard master's alternative to the "dazzling" bricolage of Anne, one of their soft masters from

Copyright © 2006, Idea Group Inc. Copying or distributing in print or electronic forms without written permission of Idea Group Inc. is prohibited.

the Austen school (1992, p. 15), actually describes a basic object-oriented strategy:

From their point of view, Anne should design a computational object (e.g., her bird) with all the required qualities built into it. She should specify, in advance, what signals will cause her bird to change color, disappear, reappear, and fly. One could then forget about "how the bird works"; it would be a black box.... (Turkle & Papert, 1990, pp. 139-140)

Instead, Anne hides her birds by using a sky-colored mask: surely a much more unnatural, cumbersome and inflexible procedure that is centered on the programmer and her tools rather than on the problem. Rather than having its own visibility property, the bird would need to have at its disposal every conceivable variation in background.

In object-oriented programming, the class is the major unit of programming. It "represents the abstraction of a number of similar (or identical) objects" (Bell & Parr, 1998, p. 624). The more general the class is, the more abstract it is: for example, the class of mammals is an abstract class because, while specific instances of mammals exist, mammals as such do not exist. In Java, a truly abstract class exists only to serve as a modifiable template, and cannot be instantiated. In order for this to be useful – and, indeed, for classes to be reusable—the characteristics of classes in the hierarchy must be inheritable.

Turkle and Papert also identify "hierarchy" with hard mastery (1990, p. 136), and soft mastery with a "non-hierarchical style" (1992, p. 9). Hierarchy – as the parent-child metaphor might imply—is also a defining characteristic of object orientation. While Gilligan (1982) sees hierarchy as an authoritarian concept based on value ranking, object-oriented hierarchy emphasizes membership and linkage, and could just as well be compared to Gilligan's positive sense of context and association. Inheritance builds on that which is already available: new concepts "inherit" everything known about the previous concept. This may be viewed as antithetical to the "soft master" desire to know everything at once—to break apart rather than reuse that which has already been accomplished and packaged. The family metaphor has a significant communicative layer: interaction with and between objects involves sending "messages" (rather than "commands") back and forth in order to perform one of the actions associated with the object's data. These "object relationships" are most often defined through inheritance. Where a soft master such as Turkle and Papert's Alex insists on literal "repetitions of instructions" (1990, p. 137) to get a feel

Copyright © 2006, Idea Group Inc. Copying or distributing in print or electronic forms without written permission of Idea Group Inc. is prohibited.

for the program, messages obviate the need for duplication of data, and help to keep the detail packaged inside objects discrete.

Hierarchy is broadly analogous to decomposition in structured programming, in that it requires a breakdown of elements according to a structure that represents different levels of abstraction. As with abstraction generally, the higher levels focus on the essentials, and leave the unnecessary detail till later. In object-oriented programming, the filling in of those details—along with any changes or variations—is neatly handled by inheritance. The same methods, inherited from the most abstract class (the parent, or superclass), can be used to manipulate a range of objects of different classes (the child, or subclass); and anything unique to a particular subclass can be kept within that particular subclass.

Meaning is a dynamic process in object as in human communication: the same "message" may be interpreted in different ways by a variety of different receivers. This principle is described in the object-oriented programming paradigm as "polymorphism." A corollary of inheritance-based messaging, polymorphism allows for the same method (message) to be reused and interpreted differently by different types of black-boxed objects. The same command can be sent to different objects, and it is the object that decides what action is appropriate for the command. This cornerstone of authentic object-orientation—message-passing and polymorphism—therefore also falls, as Graham notes (1994, p. 14), "under the general heading of abstraction."

Objects are central also to the trend towards end-user programming. The first end-user programmers were spreadsheet users who wrote their own macros, and modern software applications (spreadsheets, word processors) are becoming increasingly programmable. Within these packages, powerful programming environments use intuitive objects to provide extensibility and adaptability: the beauty of a language such as Visual Basic for Applications is that its central object hierarchy corresponds to the main visible elements of the relevant end-user application. Myers et al. (2002) predict that "end-user programming will be increasingly important in the future" (p. 226). It is envisaged that customized applications will be assembled from prepackaged building blocks by the end-user. Such a scenario carries the prospect of "making every computer user a programmer": the new programmer will not be distracted by complexity, knowing only how to use the available components and tools in order "to solve the problem at hand" (Cox, 1990/1995, p. 385).

Copyright © 2006, Idea Group Inc. Copying or distributing in print or electronic forms without written permission of Idea Group Inc. is prohibited.

Conclusion

We have examined programming abstraction as a possible contributing factor in the underrepresentation of women in programming, and found it wanting. The meanings of abstraction have been deconstructed and clarified in order to distinguish between the more general gendering of the abstract and the concrete and specific senses of these notions in programming. This exploration entailed the need to recognize and establish the empirical testability of the hypothesis that women experience black boxes in a negative way: the means of doing this have to be specifically situated within the subject's experience of programming, and two such tests have been outlined, along with indicative results. This has been triangulated with qualitative data obtained from interviews with women on computing courses. The theoretical analysis, the indicative empirical results and the accounts of women learning to program all suggested that there is no real difference in the attitudes of women and men to black boxes and abstraction.

The readiness to identify suspects such as mathematics and the abstract perhaps reflects an instinct to seek out the "difficult" aspects of computing. This, in itself, may be based on a negative stereotype—although it may certainly be argued that it is the fascination of what's difficult which lies at the heart of the masculine computing culture. We have seen, however, that abstraction serves to render programming more user-friendly—to the extent that it has the potential to blur the distinction between programmer and user. It is black boxes, at varying levels of abstraction, which would facilitate the changes whereby software will be adapted out of reusable software components, and plugged together by end-users to meet their particular needs. Such a situation would represent the use of "prepackaged routines" to facilitate user-friendly programming—two things which Turkle sees as antithetical. The ability to use and reuse black-boxed procedures and objects has therefore, if anything, become more important in the past ten years.

If there is an instrumental and distant approach in computing that disproportionately discourages women, it is more likely to be in terms of pedagogy and the wider computing culture rather than the programming curriculum as such. The negative sense of the term abstraction may lie in the original meaning of the word—where programming is taught and learnt in the abstract, without contexts and results in the real world. Abstraction as a programming technique has been the wrong target: it does not put women off. If anything, because it facilitates contextualization and understanding of bigger pictures as well as teamwork, abstraction has the potential to shift a solipsistic geek wizard culture

Copyright © 2006, Idea Group Inc. Copying or distributing in print or electronic forms without written permission of Idea Group Inc. is prohibited.

towards accessible and open cultures that will encourage a much wider and more diverse range of people to learn programming and computing.

References

Bailey, D., & Bailey, D. (2000). *Java elements: Principles of programming in java*. London: McGraw Hill.

Bell, D., & Parr, M. (1998). *Java for students*. London: Prentice-Hall.

Bell, T. (2003) Group offers help for women in the tech sector. *CNET: TechRepublic*. Retrieved December 15, 2004, from http://techrepublic.com.com/5102-6262-1058108.html

Computing Research Association (1992-2003). *Taulbee Survey*. Retrieved December 15, 2004, from http://www.cra.org/info/taulbee/women.html

Cox, B. (1995). There is a silver bullet. In N. Heap, R. Thomas, G. Einon, R. Mason, & H. Mackay (Eds.), *Information technology and society: A reader* (pp. 377-386). London: Sage.

Frenkel, K. (1990, November). Women and computing. *Communications of the ACM, 33*(11), 34-47.

Gilligan, C. (1982). *In a different voice: Psychological theory and women's development*. Cambridge, MA: Harvard University Press.

Gorlen, K., Plexico, P., & Orlow, S. (1990). *Data abstraction and object-oriented programming in C++*. Chichester, UK: John Wiley & Sons.

Graham, I. (1994). *Object oriented methods*. Wokingham: Addison Wesley.

Green, T. (1980). Programming as a cognitive activity. In H. Smith & T. Green (Eds.), *Human interaction with computers*. New York: Academic Press.

Harcourt, W. (Ed.). (1999). *Women@Internet*. London: Zed Books.

Jackson, C. (1998). *Geek: A definition*. Retrieved December 15, 2004, from http://samsara.circus.com/~omni/geek.html

Keller, E. (1983). *A feeling for the organism: The life and work of Barbara McClintock*. San Francisco: W. H. Freeman.

Kolb, D. (1983). *Experimental learning: Experience as the source of learning and development*. New York: Prentice-Hall.

Copyright © 2006, Idea Group Inc. Copying or distributing in print or electronic forms without written permission of Idea Group Inc. is prohibited.

Krechowiecka, I. (2002). Never mind about maths. *Guardian Education, February 26.*

Margolis, J., & Fisher, M. (2002). Unlocking the clubhouse: The Carnegie Mellon experience. *SIGCSE Bulletin 34.*

McKenna, P. (2000). Transparent and opaque boxes: Do women and men have different computer programming psychologies and styles? *Computers & Education, 35,* 37-49.

McKenna, P. (2001). Programmers: Concrete women and abstract men? *Journal of Computer Assisted Learning, 17*(4), 386-395.

Mendelsohn, P., Green,T., & Brna, P. (1990). Programming languages in education: The search for an easy start. In J. Hoc, T. Green, D. Gilmore, & R. Samurcay (Eds.), *Psychology of programming.* London: Academic Press.

Myers, B., Hudson, S., & Pausch, R. (2002). Past, present, and future of user interface software tools. In J. Carroll (Ed.), *Human-computer interaction in the new millennium* (pp. 213-234). Oxford: ACM Press.

National Science Foundation, Division of Science Resources Statistics (2004). *Science and engineering degrees: 1966-2001* (NSF 04-311), (Project officers). Arlington, VA: S. Hill & J. Johnson.

The Oxford English Dictionary. (2nd ed). (1989). Retrieved December 10, 2004, from http://dictionary.oed.com/cgi/entry/50101136

Peltu, M. (1993). Females in tuition. *Computing, 12*(2).

Satzinger, J., & Ørvik, T. (1996). *The object-oriented approach.* Cambridge: ITP.

Sebesta, R. (1993). *Concepts of programming languages.* Redwood City: Benjamin/Cummings.

Turkle, S. (1980). Computer as Rorschach. *Society, 17,* 15-24.

Turkle, S. (1984a). *The Second Self: Computers and the human spirit.* London: Granada.

Turkle, S. (1984b, November/December). Women and computer programming: A different approach. *Technology Review,* 49-50.

Turkle, S. (1996). *Life on the screen.* London: Phoenix.

Turkle, S., & Papert, S. (1990). Epistemological pluralism: Styles and voices within the computer culture. *Signs: Journal of Women in Culture and Society, 16*(1), 128-157.

Copyright © 2006, Idea Group Inc. Copying or distributing in print or electronic forms without written permission of Idea Group Inc. is prohibited.

Turkle, S., & Papert, S. (1992). Epistemological pluralism and the revaluation of the concrete. *Journal of Mathematical Behavior, 11*, 3-33.

Ullman, E. (1997). *Close to the machine*. San Francisco: City Lights.

Universities and Colleges Admissions Service (2003). *Annual data set*. [Data file]. Retrieved December 5, 2004, from http://www.ucas.ac.uk/figures/ads.html

Copyright © 2006, Idea Group Inc. Copying or distributing in print or electronic forms without written permission of Idea Group Inc. is prohibited.

Chapter V

Dimensions of Sustainable Diversity in IT:
Applications to the IT College Major and Career Aspirations Among Underrepresented High School Students of Color

Russell Stockard, California Lutheran University, USA

Ali Akbari, California Lutheran University, USA

Jamshid Damooei, California Lutheran University, USA

Abstract

This chapter acknowledges that diversity issues in the IT field go beyond racial and ethnic measures to include disability and age, to name but two of the numerous possibilities, and a global playing field. While the chapter examines the different forces that affect the career aspirations and opportunities of individuals of color, women, the disabled and the young

Copyright © 2006, Idea Group Inc. Copying or distributing in print or electronic forms without written permission of Idea Group Inc. is prohibited.

as they make decisions relating to the IT field, it is not fundamentally driven by data, but by a need to develop and expand a definition and the dimensions of diversity. In doing so, we hope to provoke readers to view the issue of diversity and IT from a number of perspectives. We assert that diversity should be viewed globally with the understanding that the globalization process has begun to change the dynamics of the diversification phenomenon. Finally, in an effort to show the impact of career aspirations and what may influence the development of such aspirations among minority and nontraditional students, we report the findings of some studies that have recently been conducted. This study looks at the experiences, opportunities, attitudes and aspirations with respect to mathematics, science, computer science and information technology of underrepresented students in the federally funded Upward Bound and Math/Science Upward Bound programs. We conclude with a brief discussion of the role of social and cultural creativity and innovation, arguing that these are essential components of a notion of sustainable diversity.

Introduction

Information Technology (IT) is at the same time a complex and dynamic field of study and a profession. While populations of color, primarily Latinos and African Americans, are underrepresented among the ranks of professionals in the United States, the dynamics of employment and business development are increasingly influenced by emerging firms operating globally that benefit from profit-minded American companies eager to outsource their employment needs. The following chapter acknowledges that diversity issues in the IT field go beyond racial and ethnic measures of diversity to include disability and age, to name but two of the numerous possibilities, and a global playing field. Knowledge results from the collection, processing and distribution of information. Ultimately, then, our investigation of diversity must include, the diversity of knowledge.

Industry, government, and professional groups have recognized that the IT workforce shortage is a serious problem facing the United States. However, there is a troubling lack of women and underrepresented racial and ethnic minorities in this workforce. In 2001, 135 million people were employed, of

Copyright © 2006, Idea Group Inc. Copying or distributing in print or electronic forms without written permission of Idea Group Inc. is prohibited.

whom women were 46.6%, Blacks, 11.3% and Hispanics, 10.9%. In the Computer and Data processing industry where women and minorities are underrepresented, women made up 30.6%, Blacks, 7.3% and Hispanics, 4.2% (U.S. Census, 2001). The Information Technology Association of America (ITAA) appointed a blue ribbon diversity panel to investigate the problem. In 2003, the panel used the U.S Bureau of Labor Statistics (BLS) to update a 1998 ITAA report. The newer report included findings that the number of women and African Americans in the overall IT workforce actually fell between 1996 and 2002. When administrative positions were removed from the analysis, the proportions of both women and African Americans actually rose slightly, from 25 to 25.3% and 6 to 6.2%, respectively. The authors of the report acknowledged that the small gains made in the number of women and minorities engaged in IT careers did little to correct their gross underrepresentation compared with their participation in the general U.S. workforce (ITAA, 2003).

Despite the presence of useful data and careful analysis in the ITAA report, the authors assume the readers share a definition of the term "diversity." Apparently, they take this understanding of diversity so much for granted, that nowhere in the otherwise comprehensive document do the authors take the trouble to define it.

While the chapter examines the different forces that affect the career aspirations and opportunities of individuals of color, women, the disabled and others as they make decisions relating to the IT field, it is not fundamentally driven by data, but by a need to develop and expand a definition and dimensions of diversity. In doing so, we hope to provoke readers to view the issue of diversity and IT from a number of perspectives. In addition, the chapter goes beyond issues of training and career development to include organizational, community and global dimensions of diversity. The objective of extending the discussion of diversity beyond the customary boundaries of the classroom and the workplace is to bring home the point that diversity is much more than a university or human resources issue. Rather, diversity should be viewed globally with the understanding that the globalization process has begun to change the dynamics of the diversification phenomenon. Implicit in this understanding is the notion that a "glocalization," a linkage of global and local interests is emerging within the larger, transnational phenomenon, resulting in a greater importance on cities and the communities that are contained within them (The Glocal Forum, 2004). The emphasis on sustainability suggests that the cultural differences prized as part of diversity will continue to be a priority among those who understand the

Copyright © 2006, Idea Group Inc. Copying or distributing in print or electronic forms without written permission of Idea Group Inc. is prohibited.

centrality of communities of color, women, youth, the aged, disabled and the other groupings.

Finally, in an effort to show the impact of career aspirations and what may influence the development of such aspirations among minority and nontraditional students, we report the findings of some studies that have recently been conducted. One such study looks at the experiences, opportunities, attitudes, and aspirations with respect to mathematics, science, computer science and information technology of underrepresented students in the federally funded Upward Bound and Math/Science Upward Bound programs. Besides comparing the experiences afforded students by the two versions of Upward Bound, we will compare these experiences and opportunities with those of students not attending Upward Bound programs.

Structure of This Chapter

The structure of the information presented herein may be viewed in the following tables. Following definitions of diversity and related terms (affirmative action, equal opportunity, etc.), the chapter will unfold following the levels of analysis of diversity and information and communication technologies (ICTs) and outcomes of the application of diversity and ICTs. We have chosen this approach because we believe conceptualizing IT as fundamentally consisting of IT professionals and the IT industry is too narrow. We contend that for diversity to be sustainable in IT, it must embrace not only the conventional world of programmers in the United States and the countries of the industrialized North, but also the unconventional, but often innovative, world of the countries of the South. We also have included the notion of equity with respect to information technology and the information/knowledge society. Finally, we have included a description of a study conducted by the authors that illustrates some of the dimensions of diversity discussion in this chapter. The study focuses on the dimensions of gender, race and ethnicity, age, immigration and income as they affect underrepresented high school student aspirations for computer science college majors and careers in Information Technology.

As Table 1 indicates, diversity and IT may be viewed on four different levels or dimensions, starting from the individual and organizational, where much existing analysis has been focused. However, the community networks/ informatics level, where the glocalization phenomenon has emerged, has not

Copyright © 2006, Idea Group Inc. Copying or distributing in print or electronic forms without written permission of Idea Group Inc. is prohibited.

Table 1. Levels of analysis of diversity and information and communication technology

Global	Gender/ Sexual Orientation	Race/ Ethnicity	Age	Disability	Socio-economic Status/ Poverty
Community Network/local	Gender/ Sexual Orientation	Race/ Ethnicity	Age	Disability	Socio-economic Status/ Poverty
Organizational	Gender/ Sexual Orientation	Race/ Ethnicity	Age	Disability	Socio-economic Status/ Poverty
Individual	Gender/ Sexual Orientation	Race/ Ethnicity	Age	Disability	Socio-economic Status/ Poverty

received nearly as much attention. Finally, the global level is the playing field for nation-states that have chosen to commit to neo-liberal economic globalization or to resist it by refusing to commit to trade liberalization and economic integration.

At each of these levels—where gender/sexuality, race/ethnicity, age, disability, and socioeconomic status/poverty are in play—there are operational dimensions of diversity. While the two poles of the diversity discussion in IT have tended to be the under-representation of women and members of so-called racial/ethnic minorities on the one hand, and the so-called digital divide on the other, a more apt conceptualization might include a smoother continuum. The intersections of the geographic and the demographic measures offer useful points of departure for the discussion that follows.

Table 2 refers to the some possible outcomes of ICT applications within the framework of diversity. Using the same geo-organizational levels seen in Table 1, the table includes some of the concerns that under-represented populations and the managers of commercial IT operations alike could voice and seek to implement in planning efforts. Education is one of the continuing battlegrounds over diversity as it has manifested itself in the controversial issue of affirmative action. The recent *Grutter v. Bollinger* case heard by the U.S Supreme Court symbolized the struggle over access to higher education that began with the Bakke case in the 1970s (Edwards, 2004). This relates to IT insofar as the

Copyright © 2006, Idea Group Inc. Copying or distributing in print or electronic forms without written permission of Idea Group Inc. is prohibited.

Table 2. Outcomes of diversity and information and communication technology

Global	Educational	Empowerment	Economic Development	Profit
Community Network/local	Educational	Empowerment	Economic Development	Profit
Organizational	Educational	Empowerment	Economic Development	Profit
Individual	Educational	Empowerment	Economic Development	Profit

conventional computer science pipeline runs through colleges and universities and contributes to a gender, racial and ethnic gap (Camp, 1997; Fisher & Margolis, 2002; Stockard, Akbari, & Klassen, 2004).

The issue we have chosen to characterize as empowerment refers to an outcome in which individuals, members of gendered or racial and ethnic and sexual minorities, and communities seek to use ICTs to gain a sense of confidence or self-esteem needed to bring about social change. The resulting informational power constitutes a tool that transforms its holders.

Economic development refers at the very minimum to the creation or attraction of new job opportunities and the increase in real estate values (Bivins, 2004). It is often associated with the cooperation between business and city and state governments in the United States (Tomljanovich, 2004). "Economic development" is a term associated more with economic growth, while the term "national development" has become linked with less developed countries as a more involved procedure than its growth-oriented counterpart. Cambridge (2002) defines it as a "complex, integrated, participatory process, involving stakeholders and beneficiaries and aimed at improving the overall quality of human life through improvements in a range of social sectors in an environmentally responsible manner." In a very real sense, national development seeks to clear away the residue of colonialism in the countries of the South. ICTs have come to play a vital role in national development. In addition, they are the foundation of the information society that fuels the increasingly globalized economy.

Lastly, profit seeking is a unique objective for the business sector, even though business is involved at every level of analysis discussed so far. Within the scope of its activity, profit-oriented firms rely on the conventional conception of IT professionals, who arrive through the computer science pipeline having a base

Copyright © 2006, Idea Group Inc. Copying or distributing in print or electronic forms without written permission of Idea Group Inc. is prohibited.

of mathematics and programming classes throughout high school and college. However, as will be discussed below, the technologies produced by those professionals may form the bases for unforeseen new innovations by members of communities in the US and abroad. The communities may have rarely sent aspirants for computer programming jobs up the ladder to these companies.

Background and Definitions
of Diversity and Related Terms

Gender, race and ethnicity, age, disability and sexual preference are concepts that are used in discussions of diversity and equal opportunity. According to the Encarta World Dictionary, gender refers to the "sex of a person organism, or of a whole category of people or organisms." Following Woszczynski, et al. (2004), we may use the American Heritage Dictionary (1985, p. 467) to define ethnicity as "having or pertaining to a religious, racial, national, or cultural group."

Broadly speaking, diversity refers to a variety of the objects under discussion. Since the ascendancy of the civil rights movement in the United States, emphasis has grown on the disparity of access to the rights and institutions by White and Black Americans. Diversity is a term that has grown out of the notions of affirmative action and equal opportunity. Affirmative action is a topic that has polarized segments of the population following policy debates over whether the correction of the effects of past racism and slavery in the U.S. may come at the expense of Euro-Americans (Edwards, 2004). The policy dates back to a 1961 executive order in which affirmative action was used to refer to encouraging "by positive steps equal opportunity for all qualified persons within the Government" (Executive Order 10.925, 1977).

The Workforce 2000 Report (Johnston & Parker, 1987) introduced into the discussion of diversity several terms that have grown to be slogans for individuals in both the corporate and nonprofit sectors. Arredondo (1996) provides the following list of much-used words and phrases: diversity, cultural diversity, multiculturalism, workforce diversity and managing diversity. More recently, the catchphrase "valuing diversity" has entered the lexicon (Valuing diversity, 2005; Magazine Publishers of America, 2005).

Copyright © 2006, Idea Group Inc. Copying or distributing in print or electronic forms without written permission of Idea Group Inc. is prohibited.

Controversy Over
Affirmative Action and Diversity

The business case for diversity may be succinctly stated as follows: "to discover how to improve productivity and gain greater competitive advantage and market share" (Magazine Publishers of America, 2005). The MPA Web site goes on to state that it has "become increasingly apparent that focusing on diversity and looking for more ways to be a truly inclusive industry ... and appropriately managing a diverse workforce is crucial for the relevancy and economic vitality of the magazine publishing industry." Finally, the site observes that the U.S. Census Bureau estimates that by 2010, the multicultural population will represent 36% of the U.S. population. The MPA offers its clients the opportunity to keep its risks "at a minimum by understanding what diversity is, why it matters, and how to effectively manage your business in terms of diversity." The lack of ability to manage workplace diversity, it is argued, may cost businesses in the form of negative images in the minds of consumers, loss of advertising revenue, discrimination suits, litigation costs in time and money and high employee turnover rates.

While the acceptance of diversity as a mechanism for competitive advantage may be attractive for business, forces opposing diversity in college admissions have been gathering ideological force and marshalling support in an administration whose party currently controls all three branches of government. In an opinion piece in *The Chronicle of Higher Education*, Clegg (2005) observes those favoring "racial preferences," the term preferred by opponents of affirmative action are in retreat following the U.S. Supreme Court's striking down the University of Michigan's use of race in undergraduate admissions in *Gratz v. Bollinger*. The Court permitted the use of race in law school admissions. Clegg goes on to recount efforts by the National Association of Scholars to determine whether state universities are using "racial and ethnic preferences—particularly in admissions" and, if so, whether they are in compliance with the Michigan decisions.

Clegg reiterates a conservative argument against the affirmative action in college and graduate school admission. Race-based admission is unfair insofar as "it passes over better qualified students, and sets a disturbing legal, political, and moral precedent in allowing racial discrimination" (p. B10). He points out that these remedies "stigmatize the so-called beneficiaries, reinforcing old

Copyright © 2006, Idea Group Inc. Copying or distributing in print or electronic forms without written permission of Idea Group Inc. is prohibited.

stereotypes of black intellectual inferiority." Further, he contends that preferences are actually hurting the supposed beneficiaries. He cites a controversial study by Richard H. Sander (2004, p. B11) stating that by "mismatching students with law schools, the use of preferences results in fewer black lawyers than there would be otherwise."

Another term used interchangeably with diversity is equity. The emphasis in this term is on fairness and justice. Its opposite term, inequity, is often modified by the term "social," pointing out the unjust or unequal distribution of power, status, income and other goods. For the purposes of this chapter, some of the inequality may be observed in the uneven access to computers, the Internet, broadband connections, computer-related professions and education and training related to computers and software.

Community, Social Capital, and Empowerment

Community is an expression of a culture, an interest or set of concerns that may or may not be situated geographically. The identity of a community is at the heart of the concept, but communities extended in physical space require capacity for knowledge, information, creativity and business or economic transactions. According to the Connecticut Assets Network Web site (2003), capacity may be understood as "the potential for sharing assets, resources, gifts and talents." Capacity may be built by mobilizing individual and organizational assets from the community and by combining those assets to build community.

Social capital is a term that has increasingly been applied to society and community. Used recently by Pierre Bourdieu and Robert Putnam, the earliest usage appears in Lyda Judson Hanifan's discussions of rural school community centers (Hanifan, 1916, 1920). He used the term to describe "those tangible substances [that] count for most in the daily lives of people" (1916,130). Social capital reflects the trust engendered by the networks and organizations of people. Putnam's work in the area has come to be associated with the observed decline in civic participation. This decline in turn leads to a loss of "community" (Putnam, 1993, 2000). As will be discussed later, social capital may be restored or increased by the informed application of ICTs.

Copyright © 2006, Idea Group Inc. Copying or distributing in print or electronic forms without written permission of Idea Group Inc. is prohibited.

Empowerment recognizes and utilizes the capacity enjoyed by all people individually and as members of communities. It usually means identifying and mobilizing this power for positive community change. Clearly, civic participation may be a correlate of this empowerment.

The Digital Divide

The digital divide refers to the condition of unequal access to computer-related resources such as computers themselves, the Internet, broadband connections and the training and education needed to operate computers and software. The divide may operate along the demographic dimensions of age, gender, race and ethnicity, education, income and nationality (Kvasny & Trauth, 2002, 2001; Morino Institute, 2002; National Telecommunications and Information Administration, 1995: Spooner & Rainie, 2002; Riba, 2002). The digital divide accompanied the turn from the last century to the new millennium and the rise of the Internet and the dot-com industry. While much of the focus in North America was on the unequal access to personal computers and the Internet by the privileged population segments, women, and the underrepresented communities of color, the global version also included this paradigm at the level of the community of nations.

The digital divide may also be conceptualized as referring to those segments and small and medium enterprises (SMEs) that find themselves outside of the information society. The latter includes those entities and persons who enjoy full connectivity to the Internet and/or who may perform a full range of activities using computers and connectivity to enable participation in e-commerce, e-government and community networking. For the purposes of this chapter, the digital divide was, and continues to be, a measure of diversity—or the lack of it—at the societal level. In other words, inequality in the distribution of the benefits of ICTs carries serious implications for human development. The discussion of community networking examples that follows shows how IT experts and communities have become aware of the problems facing communities and are collaborating to use ICTs to increase community capacity and community building.

Copyright © 2006, Idea Group Inc. Copying or distributing in print or electronic forms without written permission of Idea Group Inc. is prohibited.

IT and Community

Communities of color underrepresented in computing and IT need to be a central dimension of diversity, not just individuals from those communities. The sustainability measure mentioned previously implies that individuals who successfully transit the pipeline must keep in mind the needs of their communities and work to develop solutions to pressing problems facing those communities. While the digital divide captured headlines for the first few years of the new millennium, IT professionals have called for the application of digital technology to such under-publicized issues as Black genealogical research (White, 2001). IT professionals could be a resource for underserved communities and contribute to solving such problems as unequal performance on SAT and AP tests by high school students of color, elevated high school dropout rates among Latinos and high levels of community youth violence.

Community networks, also known as community informatics, may operate at any of the levels of demographic diversity. Much of the importance of community networking lies in the implications for empowerment not found in conceptions of the digital divide that grew out of lack of access to computers or Internet connections. Scholars such as Kvasny and Trauth (2002) and Kvasny (2002) have examined the assumptions behind the digital divide and suggest that careful application of ICTs among underrepresented groups can avoid further stratifying of society and maintaining the information gap. Roach (2003) interviewed Lynnette Kvasny as she studied the digital divide in two Georgia cities. According to Kvasny, basic information literacy only marginally affects the ability of underserved groups to take advantage of the economic opportunity normally associated with IT proficiency. Among her findings are that the most seriously disadvantaged social groups typically receive the briefest technology training and thus suffer from inability to sustain their newfound skills beyond the initial classroom exposure. The outcome is limited benefits for those already lacking in IT skills and possible frustration at technology.

Kvasny points out that people sustain enduring benefits if the technology is integrated into their daily lives and is available where they engage in social networking. For African Americans, these community sites include barbershops, Laundromats, churches and common areas in public housing.

An example of community networking is the Belmont Community-University Partnership in Philadelphia, consisting of the neighborhood and Pennsylvania State University. Despite its official designation by the U.S. Census Bureau as

Copyright © 2006, Idea Group Inc. Copying or distributing in print or electronic forms without written permission of Idea Group Inc. is prohibited.

a "poverty area," the university's partners have sought to utilize "its internal community resources, its cultural and social capital" to substitute for economic capital. Three Pennsylvania State faculty members, Lakshman Yapa, Lynette Kvasny and Ian Baptiste are directing a three-part work plan: enterprise building, information technology and capacity building for community organizations. Projects that are part of the work plan with community partners include the promotion of Internet marketing by the Lancaster Avenue Business Association (LABA). The initial project entails the design and sale of African-American dolls dressed in Muslim-styled clothes. The partners also have continued to update the LABA Web page.

The information technology component encompasses several projects with the Holly Street Garden Literacy Association (HSGLA). BelCUP is working with the HSGLA head Bettye Ferguson to craft a Community Access Center. During the summer, Belmont youth were involved in restoring computers. Another project underway is the creation of a for-profit sector within HSGLA to provide funding for the various activities of the Association.

In 2004 BelCUP worked to collaborate with the Belmont Improvement Association (BIA). One project's focus was the computerization of the BIA office. Current projects include a training program in office management and the development of a newsletter.

The AmeriCorp VISTA program has sponsored BelCUP. As 2004 drew to a close, the partners sought to devise new strategies to sustain the working arrangements as funding was ending.

Communication Rights, Disability: Inclusive Communication

TASH, an organization dedicated to "equity, opportunity and inclusion for people with disabilities," supports communication rights and facilitated communication. They consider communication rights both a "basic human right and the means by which all other rights are realized." Facilitated communication is a means of communication for those persons unable to speak or point reliably. (2005). TASH asserts that the right to communicate is a free speech issue.

Inclusive communication is a concept applied to persons with disabilities affecting their capacity to communicate, such as the deaf.

Copyright © 2006, Idea Group Inc. Copying or distributing in print or electronic forms without written permission of Idea Group Inc. is prohibited.

Communication rights, however, does serve an inclusive function not only for the disabled, but also for all people suffering from unequal access to communication. The People's Communication Charter states that "communication is basic to the life of all individuals and their communities. All people are entitled to participate in communication, and making decisions about communication within and between societies" (2005). The charter goes on to include 18 articles, which encompass freedom, access, literacy, protection of journalists, participation in policy making and cyberspace. For the latter, the charter asserts the right of all people to "universal access" and to "free and open communities" as well as freedom of expression and freedom from surveillance and intrusion.

Related to communication rights is Communication Rights in the Information Society (2005), a campaign to guarantee that communication rights are central to the information society and the upcoming World Summit to the Information Society. Clearly, the concept of communication rights has a place in the notion of diversity and IT developed in this chapter.

Globalization, IT, and Diversity

One way to conceptualize the current version of globalization is social change associated with increased connectivity among societies and their components due to cultural mixing, the volatile growth of transportation and information and communication technologies that facilitate international cultural and economic exchange. Globalization is the new economic system that has come to replace the dangerously polarized world of the Cold War era, when the twin superpowers, the United States and the Soviet Union, dominated politics and economics in their respective spheres of influence (Friedman, 2000). While the hostility level of this period of world history was elevated, the stability of the world system also was high.

Following the fall of the Soviet Union in the last decade of the 20th century, many former Soviet client states were able to make decisions for themselves, increasing the likelihood of smaller conflicts. The bigger change was in another former hierarchy, that of the international economic system. According to Thomas Friedman, that system has been altered irrevocably by a relentless triple democratization. The democratization of technology, the democratization of finance and the democratization of information are the three types of change

Copyright © 2006, Idea Group Inc. Copying or distributing in print or electronic forms without written permission of Idea Group Inc. is prohibited.

hurtling along at ever increasing speed. Falling in their path are tradition, family, leisure, sovereignty and order.

At the same time that Friedman identifies the unsettling aspects of globalization, he also points out that countries can impose filters to "prevent their cultures from being erased by the homogenizing pull and push of global capitalism" (2000, p. 294). He identifies the most important filter as the ability to "glocalize." He defines glocalization as the

ability of a culture, when it encounters other strong cultures, to absorb influences that naturally fit into and can enrich that culture, to resist those things that are truly alien and to compartmentalize those things that, while different, can nevertheless be enjoyed and celebrated as different. (2000, p. 295)

Friedman notes that the glocalization process takes place by trial-and-error. Some countries opt out altogether, preferring not to run the risk of excessive error while others are risking creeping assimilation as they do try out features of the outside culture.

Wikipedia credits British sociologist Roland Robertson with coining the term glocalization by combining the two words, globalization and localization. It refers to the creation of products or services intended for the global market, but customized to suit the local culture. It also addresses the use of ICTs to deliver local services on a global (or potentially global) basis. Examples include Craigslist, the centralized online network of urban communities, offering employment, housing and personal classified ads, and Meetup, the social networking application that facilitates online meetings. The latter organization was associated with the sudden rise of the Howard Dean campaign for president in the U.S.

The filtering or tailoring aspect of glocalization provides an opportunity for users to press their own empowering interests. This capability is another component of diversity and IT. A brief review of two such uses shows another dimension of IT and diversity.

One international example is the global North/South collaboration between Sarai and Waag in India (Surman & Reilly, 2004). Sarai is a Delhi-based new media initiative that encourages people in poor neighborhoods to record and communicate events around them, using the Cybermohalla computer centers. About 15 women and five men have become barefoot journalists and report on

Copyright © 2006, Idea Group Inc. Copying or distributing in print or electronic forms without written permission of Idea Group Inc. is prohibited.

their surroundings that are in perpetual danger of being bulldozed because the settlement is illegal.

The Amsterdam-based Waag Society shares Sarai's interest in seeing media from a multiplicity of viewpoints, performing research, developing software and recognizing the links between technology and culture. The two groups share an interest in open source technology and place software in the public domain for anyone to use. In an article about the collaboration, Michael Hegner (2003) points out: "The main outlet of (the journalists') work is a Hindi newspaper posted on the walls that informs about the things the passers-by may speak about, but about which they never read." The Sarai-Waag partnership forges a new aid model. Instead of the former approach of nation to nation, both institutions work at an equal level.

Another glocalized use of the Internet was by a social movement in Central America to fight the threat of oil exploration at the beginning of this decade. However, that movement had an ancestor a century earlier in the struggle of the immigrant West Indians in Costa Rica to maintain their Protestant English language identity in the face of the surrounding Spanish-language Catholic culture.

Those grievances eventually came to fuel the international movement led by Marcus Garvey, himself a former West Indian employee of the United Fruit Company. The internationalization of the struggle for self-determination of peoples of African descent found a home in Limón, which along with Bocas del Toro in Panama, was a significant focus of the Garvey movement (Harpelle, 2001). The communication dimension of the movement manifested itself through the *Negro World* newspaper, which was distributed through the Caribbean coast of Central America. From the perspective of globalization, the emergence of the *Negro World* represented the advantage of the global over the local. Massey has identified the struggle between elements of global and local culture as an expression of "glocalization." Ultimately, as their culture was increasingly Hispanicized through the acculturating influences of mandatory Costa Rican Spanish language education, West Indians lost their unique newspaper voice. The failure of the Garvey movement stilled the voice of the international Universal Negro Improvement Association and its organ, the *Negro World*. The failure of sojourning West Indians to grow lasting roots of local English language newspapers and other media reflects the confluence of government pressure, banana industry indifference, West Indian factionalism and dependence on Garveyism. Despite its central role in supporting the social movement, Garvey's *Negro World* newspaper was transnational, obviating the growth of a local press serving the West Indians in Costa Rica.

Copyright © 2006, Idea Group Inc. Copying or distributing in print or electronic forms without written permission of Idea Group Inc. is prohibited.

The West Indians attracted to Garveyism enjoyed the organizing benefits of that social movement. The sojourning West Indian migrants perhaps found a psychological "home" and identity in the transnational Garvey movement.

The movement against oil exploration in Limón province is an example of globalization from below, or glocalization. In other words, the same information and communication technology used by transnational corporations to further their capitalist ends may also be utilized by West Indians, indigenous people and their allies to get their message of resistance out to sympathetic organizations outside of Costa Rica and outside of Central America.

ADELA, a front of organizations, has sought to oppose agreements between the Costa Rican government and U.S. oil interests. Organizationally, the movement emerged because members perceived their government failed to protect the interests of Afro-Caribbean, indigenous and Hispanic Costa Rican small tourist businesses and local culture. The movement in Costa Rica soon expanded to the Central American region. By early 2000, North American environmental organizations had begun to ally themselves with ADELA and took the story of the Central American struggle onto the Internet, mobilizing additional support for the movement.

After decades of marginalization, Afro-Costa Ricans of West Indian descent have become agents in a contemporary regional and transnational movement. Grassroots organizations (GROs) and NGOs are effectively using networked information and communication technology in an environmental movement (Stockard, 2002).

Ironically, echoing the Garvey era, identity and agency seem to have emerged as West Indians in Costa Rica have stepped onto a global stage.

In global terms, the digital divide has stimulated responses on a number of fronts. The United Nations Volunteers and NetAid, an organization dedicated to fighting world poverty, collaborated to marshal help from online volunteers. The program recently celebrated five years of operation ("Connected" development: Five years of online volunteering, 2005).

Global NetCorps, NetCorps Canada International and the Trust for the Americas all have as their goal using volunteers to overcome the digital divide and help organizations join the information society. The volunteers not only help communities with issues that can be addressed through computers and connectivity, but they assist small business enterprises computerize their operations and develop capacity for e-commerce. Even the U.S. Peace Corps has begun to send cybervolunteers into the field.

Copyright © 2006, Idea Group Inc. Copying or distributing in print or electronic forms without written permission of Idea Group Inc. is prohibited.

IT, Diversity, and Economic Growth

The IT boom in the late 1990s benefited the U.S economy at large. At the same time, certain urban areas that concentrated on IT products were prepared to take advantage of the opportunity, posting huge job and income gains (Daly & Valetta, 2004). A similar phenomenon in Europe, known as ICT clusters (van Winden et al., 2004) paralleled the U.S. experience.

As in the past, Silicon Valley and the San Francisco economy in general were the IT centers that led this economic expansion. However, the 1990s also saw the rise of several other urban IT centers, including Portland, Seattle and Washington, D.C. While these booming IT centers eventually experienced a decline in their performance during the dot-com crash, Daly and Valetta observed that they stand to benefit from the IT recovery underway at the midpoint of the first decade of the new millennium. The authors do not investigate the role of cultural diversity in the boom-and-bust cycle of urban IT centers, but they do suggest that innovation is key. Van der Meer et al. (2003) in another study of the ICT clusters in Europe, do suggest that images of a particular city may attract labor to that location. Innovation and its midwife, creativity, have been the object of research on IT and economic growth. In the studies discussed next, we will see the linkage between creativity and diversity.

Interest has grown recently in the role of creative persons in economic growth. Richard Florida has identified the presence of a "creative class" as a necessary contributor to regional economic growth (2002, 2001). He recounted recruiters coming to Pittsburgh, a city of considerable cultural clout, to lure young graduates of Carnegie Mellon's top-rated computer science program to Austin, Texas. On inquiring about the attractiveness of Austin, a city smaller than Pittsburgh, without a major airport or professional sports teams, and lacking cultural institutions comparable to its Eastern counterpart, Florida discovered the draw of the rival city for the young man. Besides the lure of the company that recruited him, there is a large community of young people, many activities, a thriving music scene, ethnic and cultural diversity, outdoor recreation and captivating nightlife.

Florida points out that the creative class is "a fast-growing, highly educated, and well-paid segment of the workforce on whose efforts corporate profits and economic growth increasingly depend." Industry categories for this class range from technology and entertainment to journalism, finance, high-end manufacturing and the arts. The members of the class share a common ethos "that values

Copyright © 2006, Idea Group Inc. Copying or distributing in print or electronic forms without written permission of Idea Group Inc. is prohibited.

creativity, individuality, difference, and merit." At the top of the creativity rankings are San Francisco, Austin, San Diego and Boston.

In its most common form, as it too often consumes non-renewable energy sources and gives off greenhouse gases or pollutes water and land, many observers view conventional economic development as unsustainable (Hawken, 1993; International Institute for Sustainable Development, 2005; Robinson, n.d.). A number of alternatives have been posed to enable development, particularly for less developed countries. One such alternative at the heart of the computer software development is FLOSS—Free/Libre Open Source Software—the provision of software not controlled by copyright, operating on the assumption that information technology use and development can be applied to the creation of a society based on co-operation, equality and sharing. The adherents of this movement believe that sharing software promotes progress best if it is free. Software can thus be a means to "the end of a co-operative and ethnically sound society only if it is free in the sense of free speech" (Free as in education, 2002-2003).

Mentoring and IT

Mentoring is acting as an adviser to a junior colleague or student. In the community context discussed above, mentoring may be a seen as a type of social capital and as an asset in empowering individuals as well as the community. In the context of developing and sustaining diversity, mentoring is also a means of valuing diversity. While role models are individuals who appear in the social fields and media landscapes of individuals who resemble them physically, they may not help develop skills, talents and insights in those observing them. Mentors take an active role and may or may not share gender, cultural or ethnic characteristics with their mentees.

The shortage of U.S.-born persons of color and women in computing results from a lack of encouragement of African Americans and Latinos in the K-12 years and distortions of IT career role model images, particularly on television (Taylor, 2000). The typical computer professional is neither a clever lawyer nor a dashing police officer, but a white male geek. Despite the recent addition of crime-solving mathematician to the prime time broadcast schedule (Lloyd, 2005), this cultural and media stereotype is not likely to reverse itself in short order. As a consequence, misunderstanding of careers in computing is rife among potential aspirants for those careers in communities of color. Substantial

Copyright © 2006, Idea Group Inc. Copying or distributing in print or electronic forms without written permission of Idea Group Inc. is prohibited.

numbers of role models and mentors clearly are needed in order to promote sustainable diversity. Despite widespread agreement that mentoring is a needed resource, a number of barriers face those who wish to donate their experience and time to young students, including indifference and even hostility to potential mentors in schools during or following regular school hours (Newcomer, 2001).

Ford, in an article on the demographic changes underway in the IT industry, noted that developing a company workforce that reflects the outside labor market makes the company a more attractive place for diverse outsiders and recruits (2004). At the same time, he notes it is not enough to hire minorities, but "to actively develop their talent" and to create an environment where they can thrive. This may include online and telecommunications-assisted mentoring.

Discussion of Diversity in the Computing Community: Recent Empirical Evidence

In a survey conducted for this chapter, of the first five archived volumes of the Association of Computing Machinery magazine, *Ubiquity,* only one interview concerned the topic of cultural diversity. Thus, not only are images of IT professionals presented on television distorted, the image of diversity by professionals writing about and discussing the subject barely emerges from the background noise. If diversity is to become a sustainable element of the IT world, it should become less rare on the agenda of computing professionals. Rather, diversity should become an essential part of the larger community in order to help sustain the plurality of communities in a world that is increasingly glocalized.

A Brief Survey of Recent Research with Implications for Diversity in IT

Recent research on diversity and IT covers the gamut from investigations to perceptions. It includes IT work based on diversity (Woszczynski et al., 2004)

Copyright © 2006, Idea Group Inc. Copying or distributing in print or electronic forms without written permission of Idea Group Inc. is prohibited.

to the application of IT to transnational social movements (Stockard, 2003) to evaluations of entire international, volunteer-sending organizations (NetCorps Canada International, 2003). We choose to selectively review a few projects rather than attempt an exhaustive literature review.

Woszczynski et al. (2004) attempted to separate factors that specifically influence perceptions of IT work based on diversity. The researchers performed an analysis of such perceptions as they related to diversity in conjunction with factors that influenced the choice of IT as a career. The researchers administered the Diversity Perceptions Inventory (DPI) to a group of 162 undergraduate students at three institutions. A multivariate analysis of variance was used to compare differences in perception based on gender, ethnicity, age and disability status. The researchers did not find any significant differences among men and women, different age groups, work experience or disability status; they did find significant differences in perceptions based on ethnicity, as well differences based on college major. Finally, the researchers failed to find significant interaction effects between gender and any of the other significant variables. The researchers made recommendations for interpretive research to supplement the positivistic approach they used.

Another study that sought to identify factors that influenced choice of IT as a college major and career was undertaken by Stockard, Akbari, Klassen and Damooei (2005). In the following section, we provide a brief summary of the goals, methodology and findings of this study. This provides empirical evidence for some of the arguments presented in the previous sections of this chapter.

Goals and Methodology of the Project

We undertook this project in order to understand the reasons minority group members and women are drastically underrepresented in information technology careers. The lack of minority and female representation that prompted the study has been discussed previously in this chapter. Women and minorities are underrepresented in college IT majors, but that discrepancy begins as early as high school. Anita Borg, founder of the Institute for Women and Technology, asserted in 2000 that if women had been going into IT at the same rate as men since 1984, no shortage of IT workers would currently exist.

This project focused on the information technology higher education pipeline, and why so few male and female African American and Latino and Latina

Copyright © 2006, Idea Group Inc. Copying or distributing in print or electronic forms without written permission of Idea Group Inc. is prohibited.

students are studying computer science at the college level. The study sought to research the experiences, opportunities, attitudes and aspirations with respect to mathematics, science, computer science and information technology of underrepresented students in the federally funded Upward Bound and Math/ Science Upward Bound programs. Besides comparing the experiences afforded students by the two versions of Upward Bound, the research model was synthesized from the pipeline concept, social cognition theory and the status attainment model. First, the pipeline concept focuses on the interplay between high school educational environments (the availability of course offerings, prerequisites, resources, teacher training and mentoring), and the psychological and cultural factors that influence male and female college-bound, underrepresented minority students' interests, motivations and experiences regarding computer science, access and home computing environments, cultural assumptions of who will and will not succeed in computer science, race and gender stereotypes and peer dynamics. We considered the educational environments, cultural assumptions of who will and will not succeed in computer science, race and gender stereotypes and peer dynamics of the respondents. While the research considered the educational environments in high schools attended by these students, greater emphasis was placed on the experiences made available through Upward Bound in addition to those experiences encountered in high school and the educational and vocational aspirations of students. The status attainment model guided the selection of variables and analytic approaches used to study the educational and career aspirations of the target populations and how they are influenced by their pre-college experiences. At the same time that the environments from which the students come were studied, the study also relied on social cognition theory as the third conceptual focus, with its emphasis on self-processes and human agency.

Through a variety of qualitative (focus group and individual interviews) and quantitative (sample survey) methodologies, the educational and vocational aspirations of high school students as they relate to computer science and information technology college majors and, ultimately, to postgraduate careers, were studied.

In addition to the focus on high school experiences and attitudes about computer science and information technology, the authors also have studied graduates of Upward Bound in college and former Upward Bound students who have traveled through the pipeline to graduate from college. These students and former students offered perspectives on decisions to take courses

Copyright © 2006, Idea Group Inc. Copying or distributing in print or electronic forms without written permission of Idea Group Inc. is prohibited.

in computer science and information technology. The sites of this study were schools in the six-county Southern California region, which included Los Angeles, Ventura, Riverside, Orange, Santa Barbara and San Diego Counties.

The research was based on use of surveys, interviews and focus groups with college-bound African American and Latino and Latina students at 12 public high schools in Southern California about their plans to major in computer science in college.

The research was cross-institutional and is based on interdisciplinary perspectives of the computer science pipeline. The researchers worked with cooperating Upward Bound programs, the high schools, colleges and universities with which Upward Bound is affiliated.

Focus groups were conducted with five groups of 10 to 12 current Upward Bound students during their summer residence programs. According to a number of authorities on the methodology, the focus group is useful for gathering data and as a tool to generate new ideas. These focus groups helped the researchers to understand how students were experiencing the math/science pipeline and how they perceived themselves in the context of high school and college computer courses and the information technology workforce.

The focus groups were used appropriately with the 60-student California Lutheran University Upward Bound and 50-student Math/Science Upward Bound groups who spend five to six weeks on the CLU campus taking classes, experiencing cultural enrichment and visiting other colleges. The students were interviewed from several Upward Bound groups other than the ones on the CLU campus in the summer of 2002.

These focus group interviews were used to formulate survey questionnaires that were subsequently administered to 831 current pre-college students in 12 high schools starting in the summer of 2002. For comparison purposes, the authors sought, and were given, access to the UCLA Cooperative Institutional Research Program (CIRP) freshman survey. The CIRP data are collected from a national sample conducted in the fall of each year. Since the majority of the survey respondents were high school juniors and seniors, the researchers understood that it is reasonable to assume that recently enrolled college freshmen are similar to the upper classmen high school students. College students majoring in computer science were interviewed to get a sense of their experiences with the math/science/computer pipeline, their course taking, their educational and vocational aspirations and their sense of resilience, self-efficacy, and self-esteem. The focus group interviews and survey question-

Copyright © 2006, Idea Group Inc. Copying or distributing in print or electronic forms without written permission of Idea Group Inc. is prohibited.

naires were completed in spring, 2003, resulting in the collection of 831 valid, completed questionnaires. Data analysis was conducted, resulting in frequencies and bivariate analyses. The participating programs and percentages of the total sample included in the survey phase included Upward Bound (63.5%) and Math/Science Upward Bound (22.3%), along with other programs, including Educational Talent Search (7.7%), and Young Black Scholars (6.6%).

Geographic Location and Demographic Characteristics of the Respondents

The survey respondents came from a number of Southern California counties. They included Los Angeles County, with slightly over half (50.2%) of the participants in the study. Riverside County was the next largest contributor of respondents with 12.5%. Other counties contributed 17.2% of the respondents.

About three out of five students (60.5% of the respondents) were in the last two years of high school.

The sample tended to reflect the racial and ethnic makeup of the geographical areas where the students resided. When compared to the population, the sample overrepresents female students. Three in five respondents (60%) are female adolescents. Seven hundred fifty-five respondents reported their racial and ethnic backgrounds as follows (Table 3).

Table 3. Racial and ethnic backgrounds of the respondents

	Student	Father	Mother
White/Caucasian	7.8%	5.4%	7.0%
African-American/Black	11.2%	10.6%	8.8%
American Indian/Alaska Native	3.0%	2.2%	2.6%
Asian American /Asian	11.6%	11.0%	11.2%
Native Hawaiian/Pacific Islander	2.4%	2.6%	2.2%
Mexican American/Latino	52.7%	44.5%	46.7%
Puerto Rican	1.8%	1.4%	1.8%
Other Hispanic	11.0%	13.2%	12.8%
Other	6.8%	8.6%	8.2%

Copyright © 2006, Idea Group Inc. Copying or distributing in print or electronic forms without written permission of Idea Group Inc. is prohibited.

To a large extent, the students responding to the survey were children of first generation immigrants. More than two-thirds of the 755 respondents who answered the question about their parents' birthplace reported that their parents were born outside of the United States. As we shall see later in this chapter, this condition was related with consideration of computer science as a college major.

Socioeconomic Status of the Respondents

The majority of the respondents come from families of modest means. Almost half of the respondents (48.2%) reported annual family income of less than $25,000. The mean household size in the sample was 5.14 persons. The median household size was 5.0 persons. As points of reference, according to the Kaiser Family Foundation, the median household income in California was $48,979 over the 2001-03 timeframe. The Federal poverty threshold for a family of three was $14,128 in 2001 and $14,348 in 2002.

In addition to the individual level data, the research team identified socio-demographic data on the school systems from which most of the respondents came in order to provide a context for the survey findings. Income and social status of parents are among the important predictors of high school students' ability to enter a university or other institutions of higher education. There is a body of literature that suggests many low income families are faced with a continuing struggle to make ends meet and are often left with little time or resources to help prepare their children for higher education. They are further stifled by their lack of knowledge and insight to be effective mentors or informed advisors for their children.

A quick look at the existing literature shows that family variables, such as the level of parental education and family income, remain among the strongest indicators of student achievement, accounting for 49% of the variance in math test scores in grades three through five (Darling-Hammond, 1997). The average math test score for students whose mothers have completed college was more than a full standard deviation higher than the comparable math test score for students whose mothers have not completed high school.

Copyright © 2006, Idea Group Inc. Copying or distributing in print or electronic forms without written permission of Idea Group Inc. is prohibited.

A Summary of Some of the Pertinent Findings of the Study

1. Personal Impressions of Upward-Bound Alumni and the Current Generation

Some insight may be gleaned from a brief review of the findings from the qualitative and quantitative portions of the study. The qualitative picture comes from a focus of group of six Upward Bound program "alumni" enrolled in college working as Upward Bound counselors when they were interviewed. When trying to understand the reasons more students aren't taking computer classes, the counselors suggested most students thought that computers are "not for them" and that only certain types of students take computer classes. They also cited misinformation, lack of role models in computers and fear. The students (other than one graphic major alumnus), especially the women, felt that computers aren't needed in their chosen field of study and career. The students also gave the impression that they were either afraid or misinformed, by stating that they liked to spend more time with other humans rather than machines.

By contrast, over 75% of those surveyed agreed or strongly agreed that computers are important for their future professional advancement. Less than 10% of respondents agreed or strongly agreed that having good computer skills is a sign of being a nerd; this shows a high degree of social acceptability of peers with good computers skills. Only seven percent of the respondents either strongly agreed or agreed that being competent with computers is not cool for girls. More than 60% agreed or strongly agreed that they enjoy working with computers. Only seven percent of the respondents still suffer from anxiety when working with computers. The majority of respondents disagreed or strongly disagreed that smart people rarely study computers.

2. Aspirations for College and Computer Science Majors

As described before, the central objective of this study was to understand the role of college and career aspirations with respect to computer science study in college and IT careers following post-secondary education. This aspect falls under the rubric of social cognition, while the occupational mobility aspect is subsumed under the other theoretical construct of the study, the status

Copyright © 2006, Idea Group Inc. Copying or distributing in print or electronic forms without written permission of Idea Group Inc. is prohibited.

Table 4. College and college major decisions

Questions	Yes	No	Don't Know
Do you plan to attend college?	94.6%	1.7%	3.7%
Do you know what your college major will be?	61.4%	39.2%	0%
Would you consider Computer Science as your college major?	36%	64%	0%

attainment model. With respect to the latter, the survey respondents have embarked on a path that could clearly take them beyond their parents' educational attainment, which for the most part reportedly ended before completion of high school. In keeping with the Upward Bound first-generation college status (or income limitation) requirement for eligibility in Upward Bound, only about six percent of respondents reported that their parents had bachelor's degrees.

- More than half of the respondents reported that their parents had not completed high school.
- More than 61% of the respondents indicated that they aspired to education beyond the bachelor's degree.

As indicated in the Table 4, about 95% of the respondents to the survey reported they planned to attend college and more than 60% said they knew their planned college major. More than 35% of survey participants indicated they would consider Computer Science as their college major.

Among students who answered an open-ended question on college majors, nearly 40 different majors were specified. The top ten probable majors emerging in the data were Psychology, Medicine (veterinary science, dentistry), Engineering, Law, Health Technology (medical, dental laboratory), Computer Science, Mathematics, Biology, Education and Business Administration, in this order. Among all fields of study, Computer Science is the seventh most popular "probable" major at 2.5%.

Table 5 shows the gender breakdown of responses to the item asking whether students would consider computer science as their college major.

Copyright © 2006, Idea Group Inc. Copying or distributing in print or electronic forms without written permission of Idea Group Inc. is prohibited.

Table 5. Computer science major by gender

		Would consider Computer Science (CS) or Information Technology (IT) as your college major?		Total
		Yes	No	
What is your gender?	Male	147	149	296
		49.7%	50.3%	100.0%
	Female	126	334	460
		27.4%	72.6%	100.0%
Total		273	483	756
		36.1%	63.9%	100.0%

Table 6. Race and ethnicity by consideration of computer science major

Race/Ethnicity	Would consider Computer Science major?		
	Yes	No	Total
African American /Black	33	97	130
	23.4%	74.6%	15.8%
Asian/Asian American	37	30	67
	55.2%	44.8%	18.0%
Mexican Am /Chicano	138	239	377
	27.4%	72.6%	100.0%
White /Caucasian	16	36	52
	30.8%	69.2%	6.2%

*Respondents could choose multiple categories. *Total column percentage refers to that ethnic group's percentage of the overall total.*

These cross tabs show a significant relationship between gender and the consideration of computer science as a college major. Female participants in the study are significantly less likely to consider computer science as a college major.

Table 6 shows the comparable breakdown by a selection of the larger race and ethnic subsamples and the White subsample. These cross tabs show a relationship between race and ethnicity and the consideration of computer science as a college major. The Asian American participants in the study were more likely, and the African American participants less likely, to consider computer science as a college major. That over 55% of the Asian American students would consider computer science versus less than one-quarter of the

Copyright © 2006, Idea Group Inc. Copying or distributing in print or electronic forms without written permission of Idea Group Inc. is prohibited.

Table 7. Role model and consideration of computer science as college major

| | | Does anyone serve or has anyone served as a role model for you to choose a college major? | | |
		Yes	No	Total
Would consider Computer Science (CS) or Information Technology (IT) as your college major?	Yes	140	127	267
		52.4%	47.6%	100.0%
	No	213	264	477
		44.7%	55.3%	100.0%
Total		353	391	744
		47.4%	52.6%	100.0%

Chi-square 4.156, p=.041

African Americans indicates that perceptions, mentors and role models and experience with computers and computer science may play a role in this consideration. We must caution that the relative small sample size of African Americans and Whites limits the projectibility of the findings.

Mentoring and Computer Science

Over 50% of the students surveyed indicated that having a role model was very important to get them thinking about going to college. Some 37.5% of respondents included their teachers as their role models. Some 26.5% mentioned their mothers among the role models as opposed to 19.3% who included their fathers among the role models. About a quarter (23.5%) of the respondents said that their friends were among the role models they have had in their lives. In choosing a major at college, some 41% of the respondents included their teachers among their mentors. Mothers played a very important role, too, as about one third (36.1%) of the respondents included their mothers as a mentor for the choice of major they are likely to make.

We surmised that having a role model or a mentor in choosing a college major would be linked to the decision of our respondents to major in CS. As Table 7 indicates, the relationship between having a role model for students deciding to go to college and consideration of CS as a college major was significant. The mentor-consideration of CS relationship did not turn out to be significant.

Copyright © 2006, Idea Group Inc. Copying or distributing in print or electronic forms without written permission of Idea Group Inc. is prohibited.

Table 8. Language spoken at home and computer science as college major

| | | Would consider Computer Science (CS) or Information Technology (IT) as your college major? | | |
		Yes	No	Total
Is the primary language spoken at home English?	Yes	133	255	388
		34.3%	65.7%	100.0%
		48.7%	52.7%	51.3%
	No	140	229	369
		37.9%	62.1%	100.0%
		51.3%	47.3%	48.7%
Total		273	484	757
		36.1%	63.9%	100.0%
		100.0%	100.0%	100.0%

In keeping with the significance of globalization, the researchers tried to assess the influence of having foreign-born parents and speaking a language other than English in the home on potential Computer Sciences (CS) students. It was reasoned that students with first generation experience in the United States might have differing attitudes to computer science as a college major. Such students might also have had less exposure to cultural stereotypes about computer-related professions.

Slightly more than half (51.2%) of the participants in the study reported that the primary language spoken at home was English. More than two-thirds of the respondents reported that their parents had been born outside of the U.S. At the same time, nearly three out of four reported that they had been born in this country.

We performed a cross tabulation between the computer science major item and the language spoken at home. As Table 8 indicates, those respondents reporting not speaking English at home had a three percentage-point advantage over their counterparts. However, the difference was not statistically significant.

On the other hand, Table 9 indicates that the birthplace of their parents was more strongly associated with the students' willingness to consider computer science as a college major. The children whose parents were born outside of the United States exhibited a tendency to consider computer science as a college major that was nearly eight percentage points higher than their fellow pre-college students with U.S.-born parents. While this relationship is not highly significant in a statistical sense, it does suggest that further research be

Copyright © 2006, Idea Group Inc. Copying or distributing in print or electronic forms without written permission of Idea Group Inc. is prohibited.

Table 9. Parents' country of birth and computer science as college major

		Would consider Computer Science (CS) or Information Technology (IT) as your college major?		Total
		Yes	No	
Were your parents born in the US?	Yes	74	165	239
		31.0%	69.0%	100.0%
		26.9%	34.2%	31.5%
	No	198	312	510
		38.8%	61.2%	100.0%
		72.0%	64.6%	67.3%
	One was, one was not	3	6	9
		33.3%	66.7%	100.0%
		1.1%	1.2%	1.2%
Total		275	483	758
		36.3%	63.7%	100.0%
		100.0%	100.0%	100.0%

Pearson Chi-Square 4.385, p<0.112

pursued to identify factors in the mainstream U.S. culture that may operate against students' consideration of computer science and IT-related majors. Such additional research may uncover values that could be associated with more robust interest in computer- and IT-related careers.

Conclusion

The notion of diversity as representation of groups at the levels identified previously—individual, organizational, community and global takes into account the dynamic nature of the diversity question. The outcomes associated with this conception of diversity include education, empowerment, economic development and profit. The discussion about the BelCUP collaboration in Philadelphia demonstrates how training, empowerment, economic development and profit outcomes may be addressed in the same project that marries IT and community. The account of the Waag-Sarai exchange represents an innovation in international aid. The ADELA struggle against oil is also an example of a North-South collaboration. These three projects represent four different continents, and the overcoming of barriers of culture and economics and the harnessing of the same forces that set into motion the contemporary

Copyright © 2006, Idea Group Inc. Copying or distributing in print or electronic forms without written permission of Idea Group Inc. is prohibited.

manifestation of globalization. Two of the three projects—the ones in Central America and the Holland-India one—use glocalization in an outbound, grassroots-up direction.

The Southern California study of the aspirations of pre-college high school students for Computer Science majors and IT careers offers a direction for research. While the results were not conclusive for the analysis involving students whose parents were born outside of the U.S., the large proportion of such students in the sample echoes the importance of globalization, with its movement of people as well as information. Further, the importance of role models and mentors was underscored as was the continuing distribution of computer science aspirations among the "usual suspects," young White and Asian-American male students. Further analysis of the data may uncover the decision-making for these aspirations.

In a conference paper on the effects of the Internet on women, Dutton has pointed that the global gender gap involving access to the Internet has narrowed. At the same time, he notes that changes in the fields of computer studies offer new opportunities for women, such as the merging of former schools of library science with computing into new schools of information studies or library and information systems, such as the one at Syracuse University (2004). He points out that further changes, such as new informatics programs, have already attracted more women than the traditional computer science programs. These changes may also attract more students from under-represented groups as well.

The notion of sustainable diversity and IT requires innovation, social capital, empowerment and inclusion of people as individuals, members of organizations and communities. Despite the impressive reach of the Internet, the pre-Internet mass media still control many of the images people hold inside their heads. The development of prime time network TV programs modeled after the successful "C.S.I." franchise could make headway in changing or forming images of computer-related and IT careers. CBS recently added to its schedule a crime-solving mathematician. Can a similar role for an IT professional be far behind, particularly if we pair the old medium of television with the medium of the New Economy, the Internet?

Escobar (1995) has observed that a number of social processes are in motion that together require a significant response by society. These processes include the failure of development, the destruction and protection of the environment, the intervention into biological life by humans and cultural hybridization. Escobar asserts that to confront these processes will require "unprecedented

Copyright © 2006, Idea Group Inc. Copying or distributing in print or electronic forms without written permission of Idea Group Inc. is prohibited.

creativity in all domains of social, economic, and — more importantly perhaps—cultural life." So, reflecting on the earlier discussion of creativity and economic development and the consequences for diversity of communities, we may assume that not only development but also survival itself may be at stake.

As mentioned earlier, the ultimate goal of gathering, storing and processing information is the production of knowledge. Just as cultural diversity should be valued, knowledge should also be honored. If this goal is honored, the knowledge of indigenous peoples, women, the old, the young and various communities will be privileged, not just technoscientific, knowledge. The cognitive justice movement seeks to honor all knowledge. Clearly, the communities holding such knowledge cannot help but be honored in the process. Finally, in the process, the ICTs and the skills to use them will be viewed properly as means to an end, not the end in themselves.

In commenting on Castells' (1996) notion of network society, Visvanathan defines cognitive justice "as the right of many forms of knowledge to exist because all 'knowledges' are seen as partial and complementary and because they contain incommensurable in-sights" (2001). He criticizes Castells for failing to mention a dialogue of knowledges. For a sustainable diversity of people and communities to exist, it is imperative for a truly creative, innovative dialogue of knowledges to begin to characterize the human condition.

Finally, then, diversity and IT are an essential, conjoined component of education. While a vital component of education is critical thinking and analytic skills, to truly value diversity is to recognize the central role of a dialogic creativity. The task of those inside of the IT industry is to realize that those outside of the industry are not necessarily outside of IT. The industry must open its doors wide to include representatives of all who can contribute to the plurality of voices among professionals. This will enable those IT professionals to help sustain the dialog of the rest of society as its members grapple with the large social processes that have emerged.

In an interview, the late Anita Borg, the founder of the Institute for Women and Technology (IWT), stressed the importance of creativity. As she recounted her experience leading a workshop group of 8-13 year-old Australian girls brainstorming about the future, Dr. Borg told how she was energized by the brilliance they exhibited in devising a self-propelled flying-swimming car and describing all the different professions that would be involved in creating it (GirlGeeks, 1999). It is this kind of energizing creativity that will come to the fore if all segments of society can not only participate in information technology but also take part in the valuing of all kinds of knowledge. To do so is to value

Copyright © 2006, Idea Group Inc. Copying or distributing in print or electronic forms without written permission of Idea Group Inc. is prohibited.

a diversity that truly qualifies as sustainable. Cheryl Seals, an African-American faculty member at the Auburn University Computer Science Department, has observed about offshoring computer programming jobs: "one thing I've heard is that you can never outsource creativity" (Parks, 2004).

References

American Heritage dictionary of the English language. (1985). Boston: Houghton-Mifflin.

Arredondo, P. (1996). *Successful diversity management initiatives: A blueprint for planning and implementation.* Thousand Oaks, CA: Sage Publications.

Belmont Community-University Partnership (2004). Retrieved from http://www.community-research.org/BelCUP/index.htm

Bivins, R. (2004, October). Midtown Houston ignites real estate recovery. *National Real Estate Investor.*

Bourdieu, P. (1983). Forms of capital. In J. C. Richards (Ed.), *Handbook of theory and research for the sociology of education* (pp. 241-258). New York: Greenwood Press.

Cambridge, V. (2002). Milestones in communication and national development. In Y. Kamalipour (Ed.), *Global communication* (Chapter 8). Belmont, CA: Wadsworth.

Camp, T. (1997). The incredible shrinking pipeline. *Communications of the ACM, 40,* 103-110.

Castells, M. (1996). *The rise of the network society.* Oxford; Malden, MA: Blackwell Publishers.

Clegg, R. (2005, January 14). Time has not favored racial preferences. *The Chronicle of Higher Education,* B10.

Communication Rights in the Information Society (2005). Retrieved March 15, 2005, from http://crisinfo.org

"Connected" development: Five years of Online Volunteering (2005, January 26). Retrieved February 16, 2005 from http://www.unv.org/infobase/news_releases/2005/05_01_26_DEU_celebration.htm

Copyright © 2006, Idea Group Inc. Copying or distributing in print or electronic forms without written permission of Idea Group Inc. is prohibited.

Connecticut Assets Network Glossary. (2003). Retrieved October 27, 2005, from http://ctassets.org/ctasset_libraryglossary.htm

Daly, M., & Valetta, R.G. (2004). Performance of urban information technology centers: The boom, the bust, and the future. *Economic Review*, 1-13. Federal Reserve Bank of San Francisco.

Dutton, W. (2004, July). *Opening computing studies and professions.* Position paper for The Oxford Internet Institute Policy Forum on Women in Computing Professions: Will the Internet Make a Difference?

Edward, H. T.(2004). The journey from *Brown v. Board of Education* to *Grutter v. Bollinger*: From racial assimilation to diversity. *Michigan Law Review, 102*(5), 944.

Encarta Dictionary. (n.d.). Retrieved March 17, 2005 from www.encarta.com.

Escobar, A. (1995). "Living" in Cyberia. *Organization, 2*(3/4), 533-537.

Executive Order No. 10.925, 26 Federal Register 1977, (1961. March 6)

Fisher, A., & Margolis, J. (2002*). Unlocking the clubhouse: Women in computing.* Cambridge, MA: MIT Press.

Florida, R. (2002, May), The Rise of the creative class. *Washington Monthly.* Retrieved February 16, 2005 from http://www.washingtonmonthly.com/features/2001/0205.florida.html

Florida, R., & Gates, G. (2001, June). *Technology and tolerance: The importance of diversity to high-technology growth.* Survey Series. Brookings Institute.

Ford, M. (2004). Truer colors: Today's IT workforce is mostly white. Tomorrow's may not be. *CIO, 18*(1), 46-48.

Free as in Education: Significance of the Free/Libre and Open Source Software for Developing Countries, 2002-2003. Retrieved March 12, 2005 from http://www.maailma.kaapeli.fi/FLOSSReport1.0.html

GirlGeeks (1999). Chat with Anita Borg. Retrieved March 15, 2005 from http://www.Girlgeeks.org/chat/borg.shtm

The Glocal Forum (2004). Retrieved October 1, 2004 at http://glocalforum.org

Hanifan, L. J. (1916). The rural school community center, *Annals of the American Academy of Political and Social Science, 67*, 130.

Copyright © 2006, Idea Group Inc. Copying or distributing in print or electronic forms without written permission of Idea Group Inc. is prohibited.

Hanifan, L. J. (1920). *The community center*. Boston: Silver Burdett.

Harpelle, R. (2001). *The WestIndians of Costa Rica: Race, class and the integration of an ethnic minority*. Montreal: McGill-Queens University Press.

Hawken, P. (1993). *The ecology of commerce: A declaration of sustainability*. New York: HarperCollins.

Hegner, M. (2003, March). Waag-Sarai exchange exposed. *Sarai Waag Exchange*. Retrieved February 16, 2005 from http://waag.sarai.net/display.php?id=26

International Institute of Sustainable Development (2005). *Business and sustainable development: A global guide*. Retrieved March 22, 2005 from http://www.bsdglobal.com.

ITAA (2003) *Report of the ITAA Blue Ribbon Panel on IT Diversity*. Presented at the National IT Workforce Convocation, May 5, 2003, Arlington, VA.

Kvasny, L. (2002). *Problematizing the digital divide: Cultural and social reproduction in a community technology initiative*. Unpublished Ph.D. Thesis, Department of Computer Information Systems, Robinson College of Business, Georgia State University.

Kvasny, L., & Trauth, E. (2002). The Digital divide at work and home. *The Discourse about power and underrepresented groups in the information society* (pp. 237-291).

Lloyd, R. (2005, January 21). It doesn't add up yet. *Los Angeles Times*, E, 2.

Magazine Publishers of America (2005). Retrieved February 10, 2005, from http://www.magazine.org/diversity

Morino Institute (2002). *From access to outcomes: Raising the aspirations for technology initiatives in low-income communities*. Retrieved February 25, 2005, from http://www.morino.org/divides/execsum_report.htm

National Telecommunications and Information Administration (1995). *Falling through the net: a survey of the "have nots" in rural and urban America*. Retrieved March 15, 2005, from http://www.ntia.doc.gov/ntiahome/fallingthru.html.

Copyright © 2006, Idea Group Inc. Copying or distributing in print or electronic forms without written permission of Idea Group Inc. is prohibited.

Newcomer (2001, March 13), Barriers to mentoring. *Ubiquity, 2, 4.*

Parks, C. (2004). Navigating the 21st century IT marketplace. *Next Wave.* Retrieved March 25, 2005, from http://nextwave.sciencemag.org/cgi/content/full/2004/09/09/4

People's Communication Charter (2005). Retrieved March 15, 2005, from http://www.pccharter.net/charteren.html

Putnam, R. D. (1993). The prosperous community: Social capital and public life. *The American Prospect, 4*(13).

Putnam, R. D.(2000). *Bowling alone. The collapse and revival of american community.* New York: Simon and Schuster.

Riba, E. (2002). *The digital divide.* Retrieved March 12, 2005 from http://www.osmond-riba.org/lis/DigDivide.htm

Roach, R. (2003, January 16) Study analyzes efforts to bring technology to distressed areas. *Black Issues in Higher Education, 19.*

Robinson, S. (n.d.). *Beyond the Twilight Zone: Defining and managing key survival issues for corporate environmental sustainability.* The Environmental Council.

Sander, R. H. (2004). A systemic analysis of affirmative action in american law schools. *Stanford Law Review, 57,* 367.

Stockard, R. (2002, November 21). *Speaking in (Green) tongues: Transnational environmental discourse in resistance against oil exploration in the Costa Rican Caribbean.* Paper presented at the conference of the National Communication Association, New Orleans.

Stockard, R. (2003). Communication dimensions of Afro-Caribbean Caribbean migration, globalization, and a transnational social movement in the Costa Rican Caribbean. *Proceedings of the Socio-Economic and Cultural Impact of West Indian Migration to Costa Rica (1870-1940). Third in Seminar Series on Intra-Regional Migration.* University of the West Indies, Mona.

Stockard, R., Akbari, A., & Klassen, M. (2004). Computer science higher education pipeline. *The Journal of Computing Sciences in Colleges, 20,* 102-113.

Stockard, R., Akbari, A., Klassen, M., & Damooei, J. (2005, December). Stretching horizons: Upward Bound programs in stimulating information technology education and career aspirations among underrepresented minorities. *Final Report to the National Science Foundation.*

Copyright © 2006, Idea Group Inc. Copying or distributing in print or electronic forms without written permission of Idea Group Inc. is prohibited.

Surman, M. & Reilly, K. (2004, Spring). Appropriating the Internet for global activism. *Yes! Magazine.* Retrieved February 16, 2005, from http://www.yesmagazine.org/article.asp?id=732

TASH (2005). *Communication Rights.* Retrieved March 15, 2005, from http://www.tash.org/communication

Taylor, V. (2001, August). Diversity in computing. *Ubiquity, 2.*

Tomljanovich, M. (2004). The Role of state fiscal policy in state economy. *Contemporary Economic Policy, 22*(3), 318-330.

U. S. Census Bureau (2002). *Statistical Abstract of the United States.*

Valuing diversity (2005). Retrieved February 13, 2005, from www.racematters.org/valuingdiversity.htm

Van der Meer, A. Van Winden, W., & Woets, P. (2003, August). *ICT clusters in European cities during the 1990s: Development patterns and policy lessons.* Paper presented at the annual congress of the European Regional Science Association, Jyvaskyla.

Van Winden, W., Van der Meer, A., & Van den Berg, L. (2004). The development of ICT clusters in European cities: Towards a typology. *Journal of Technology Management Geneva, 28,* 356-387.

Visvanathan, S. (2001, July). Knowledge and information in the network society. *Seminar, 503,* 64-85.

White, J. (2001, March 13) Digital technology and its impact on Black genealogical research. *Ubiquity, 2.*

Woszczynski, A., Meyers, M., Beise, C., & Moody, J. (2004). Diversity within the ranks: How ethnicity affects choices in IT. *Tenth Americas Conference on Information Systems (AMCIS),* New York.

Copyright © 2006, Idea Group Inc. Copying or distributing in print or electronic forms without written permission of Idea Group Inc. is prohibited.

Chapter VI

Under-Representation of African American Women Pursuing Higher-Level Degrees in the Computer Science/ Technology Fields

Alfreda Dudley-Sponaugle, Towson University, USA

Abstract

White males have dominated the computer sciences/technology disciplines since inception. Statistical data have shown that representation of female students in the computer sciences/technology fields has been consistently lower than for their male counterparts. Representation of African American students in these areas has been consistently low as well. There are relatively few African American women represented in the computer sciences/technology areas. The number of African American women pursuing a higher degree in these areas is almost non-existent. There are

Copyright © 2006, Idea Group Inc. Copying or distributing in print or electronic forms without written permission of Idea Group Inc. is prohibited.

many factors which may contribute to this trend. This paper will focus on some of the complexities involved in this problem. Using statistical data, the author will also cover the social/economic, educational and cultural barriers which have an effect on one of these underrepresented populations. In conjunction with this information, she will include some of her own experiences as a former student and as an educator.

Introduction

American society prides itself on equal opportunities for all of its citizens. Since the Brown vs. The Board of Education decision in 1950, educational barriers were deemed unconstitutional. However, another piece of legislation, Affirmative Action/Equal Opportunity, was needed to even out the playing field for persons who did not have a fair start in the pursuit of educational and employment opportunities. Of course, these legal decisions have greatly improved the prospects of underrepresented individuals in the pursuit of higher education, but there are still problems. These problems are the result of inequities in educational and social institutions. This paper focuses on an interesting, yet overlooked, situation in higher education: the lack of African AmericanAfrican American/Black females pursuing higher degrees in the computer sciences/technology areas.

What Are the Challenges?

Enrollment

If you look at any degree-granting institution in America, you will see a plethora of students, in numerous educational majors, involved in the pursuit of higher education. Figure 1 shows enrollment statistics for undergraduate students during 1999-2000.

In the computer science/technology areas, males have perpetually outnumbered the females. "According to the National Science Foundation, the number of females receiving bachelor's degrees in computer science dropped from

Copyright © 2006, Idea Group Inc. Copying or distributing in print or electronic forms without written permission of Idea Group Inc. is prohibited.

Figure 1. Where are undergraduates enrolled and what do they study? Field of study profile of undergraduates in U.S. postsecondary education institutions: 1999-2000. (By Laura Horn, Katharin Peter & Kathryn Rooney, MPR Associates, Inc.)

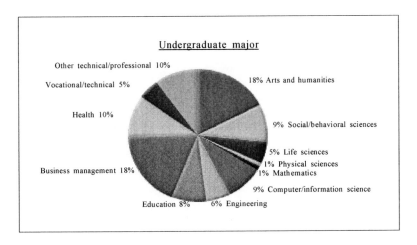

40% to 27.5% between 1984 and 1996" (Radcliff, 1999). The trend of males outnumbering females in the computing areas is continuing to decrease substantially. Figure 2 notes this trend of enrolled males versus enrolled females in the computing major. Males also outnumber females in the engineering majors. However, whereas the number of females is dramatically decreasing in computing majors, it has been documented that the enrollment of females in the engineering majors remains steady.

The explanations to this trend of fewer women and minorities receiving degrees in the computing area are many. "Women and minorities are underrepresented in technology-related careers for many reasons, including lack of access, level of math and science achievement, and emotional and social attitudes about computer capabilities" (Brown, 2001). Looking back on my educational experience, I was not introduced to the computing major until I was in college. Twenty-eight years ago there was no one to advise or encourage me to pursue computing in high school or in college. At the time, my high school did have a data processing course, where we could enter keypunched cards. I was not informed that computing was an option open to me. I was guided to pursue a "safe" major, i.e., business, education, nursing, etc. Figure 3 shows the percentage of undergraduates attending higher education institutions during 1999-2000 based on gender and race/ethnicity.

Copyright © 2006, Idea Group Inc. Copying or distributing in print or electronic forms without written permission of Idea Group Inc. is prohibited.

Figure 2. Profile of undergraduates in U.S. postsecondary education institutions: Field of study 1999-2000. (By Laura Horn, Katharin Peter & Kathryn Rooney, MPR Associates, Inc.)

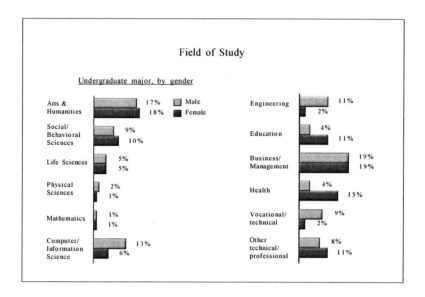

As a student 20 years ago, I can remember only a handful of African American females in the undergraduate computing program of the university I attended,. I find it interesting, as a lecturer in the same field, that the number is still consistently low.

Educational/Institutional Barriers

The consistently low representation of African Americans in this area may be attributed to numerous factors. Some would attribute the lack of representation due to the "hostile environment" of the computing fields for women and minorities. (For the purpose of this paper, "hostile environment" is referring to unwelcoming and/or ambivalent surroundings.) That may be the case, but as the statistics indicate, not all classification of minorities are suffering from this "hostility." For example, statistics show the number of Asian students is growing in this area. It may also be inferred that African American women find this field of study to be abhorrent because of this façade of "hostility." However, it could also be that the lack of African American women in this area

Copyright © 2006, Idea Group Inc. Copying or distributing in print or electronic forms without written permission of Idea Group Inc. is prohibited.

Figure 3. Profile of undergraduates in U.S. postsecondary education institutions: 1999-2000 (By Laura Horn, Katharin Peter & Kathryn Rooney, MPR Associates, Inc.)

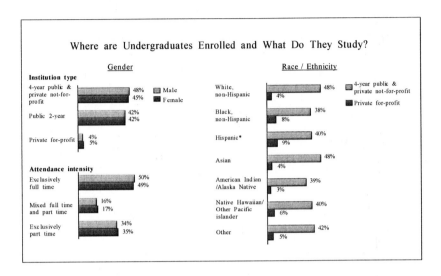

is due to their personal perceptions of this major. In the 20 years that I have been associated with the computing majors as a student or a lecturer, I have noticed consistent favoritism towards the white males. This favoritism is in the form of recruitment, mentorship and acknowledgement of academic scholarship. Females are seldom noticed or encouraged in the continued pursuit in these areas. African American/Black females are mainly ignored or covertly discouraged. A result of this favoritism is indicated by doctoral degrees conferred by degree-granting institutions. The following tables of statistics are from the 2001 Digest of Education Statistics, by the Office of Educational Research and Improvement.

Table 1 represents the number of doctoral degrees awarded in all academic areas during 1976-77 and 1999-2000 (over a 24-year span). In that period, Black men and women show an increase of less than one percent over those 24 years. All other categories show a more substantial increase in the 24-year span.

Table 2 represents doctoral degrees awarded in Computer and Information Sciences at all degree-granting institutions in 2000. In this category, Black men and women made up less than one percent of the total doctoral degrees awarded. [2%]

Copyright © 2006, Idea Group Inc. Copying or distributing in print or electronic forms without written permission of Idea Group Inc. is prohibited.

Table 1. Doctor's degrees conferred by degree-granting institutions, by racial/ethnic group and sex of students: 1976-77 and 1999-2000

				Number of Degrees Conferred			
Year	Total	White, non-Hispanic	Black, non-Hispanic	Hispanic	Asian/Pacific Islander	American Indian/Alaskan Native	Non-resident Alien
Men							
1976-77	25,036	20,032	**766**	383	640	67	3,248
1999-2000	25,028	14,241	**863**	603	1,329	56	7,936
Women							
1976-77	8,090	6,819	**487**	139	118	28	499
1999-2000	19,780	13,279	**1,357**	688	1,051	103	3,302

Copyright © 2003, Congressional Information Service, Inc.
Report Title: Digest of Education Statistics, 2001
Issued By: Office of Educational Research and Improvement
Publication Date: February, 2002

Table 2. Doctor's degrees conferred by degree-granting institutions, by racial/ethnic group, major field of study, and sex of student: 1999-2000

Major field of Study	White, non-Hispanic	Black, non-Hispanic	Hispanic	Asian/Pacific Islander	American Indian/Alaskan Native	Non-resident Alien
Men						
Computer and Information Sciences	246	**10**	11	51	0	328
Women						
Computer and Information Sciences	56	**5**	2	7	0	61

Copyright © 2003, Congressional Information Service, Inc.
Report Title: Digest of Education Statistics, 2001
Issued By: Office of Educational Research and Improvement
Publication Date: February, 2002

Table 3 represents doctoral degrees awarded in Computer and Information Sciences at all degree-granting institutions in 2001. The doctoral degrees awarded decreased in 2001. Black men made up .0015% of total degrees awarded and Black women made up .0006%. [1% & 3%]

Social/Economic Barriers

Another factor that affects the low representation of African American women is the risk factor. This risk may be defined as the numbers of minorities leaving postsecondary education versus other ethnic and racial groups. Statistics indicate the risk factor percentage among each minority group is different. Risk

Copyright © 2006, Idea Group Inc. Copying or distributing in print or electronic forms without written permission of Idea Group Inc. is prohibited.

Table 3. Doctor's degrees conferred by degree-granting institutions, by racial/ethnic group, major field of study and sex of student: 2001

Major field of Study	White, non-Hispanic	Black, non-Hispanic	Hispanic	Asian/ Pacific Islander	American Indian/ Alaskan Native	Non-resident Alien
			Men			
Computer and Information Sciences	253	6	8	44	0	321
			Women			
Computer and Information Sciences	61	4	5	13	1	52

Copyright © 2003, Congressional Information Service, Inc.
Report Title: Digest of Education Statistics, 2001
Issued By: Office of Educational Research and Improvement
Publication Date: February, 2002

factors are defined "…by enrollment patterns: delaying enrollment by a year or more, attending part time, being financially independent (for purposes of determining eligibility for financial aid), having children, being a single parent, working full-time while enrolled, and being a high school dropout or a GED recipient" (Horn, Peter, & Rooney, 2000).

As an undergraduate and graduate student, I had to work full-time and go to school part-time. This was hard because after working a nine-hour day, I had to drive 30 miles (one-way) to school, which means I operated on 15-hour days. I did this for fourteen years while pursuing my degrees. Most African American/Black students experience many types of risk factors, the primary risk factor being finances.

Another major risk factor is the lack of accessibility of information technology to African Americans and the disadvantaged. There is the problem of the digital divide. Most in our society, including our present government, would state that the digital divide is growing smaller. Statistics do not indicate this fact among African American households. "According to the literature, there is a segment of the working population that is disadvantaged by lack of access to IT prior to entering the workforce. This problem, in turn, leads to diminish[ed] ability to acquire IT skills, possible lower hiring rates, and reduced performance potential. Therefore, …positive aspects of IT in relation to pluralism may be negated by the widening gap between the IT 'haves' and 'have nots.' Universities and other parts of society must pay attention to this problem and do whatever is possible to ameliorate it" (Chisholm, Carey, & Hernandez, 2002, p. 58).

As an undergraduate information systems' student, I could not afford a computer. At that time, there was no availability of computers at public

Copyright © 2006, Idea Group Inc. Copying or distributing in print or electronic forms without written permission of Idea Group Inc. is prohibited.

Figure 4. Undergraduate diversity and the risk of leaving postsecondary education. (By Laura Horn, Katharin Peter & Kathryn Rooney, MPR Associates, Inc.)

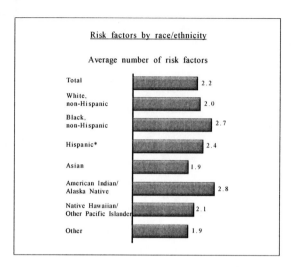

libraries. My only recourse was to use the University's computer lab or the computer at my job. This was a challenge because I was working full time. The accessibility to computing technology is definitely better for minorities and the disadvantaged, but it is amazing that this situation is still prevalent, since my experience took place over 20 years ago.

Cultural Influences

Cultural influences are major factors in the development of a society. Educational institutions have their own cultural environments, which have an impact on the individuals in the society. Lisa Delpit's article, entitled, "The Silenced Dialogue: Power and Pedagogy in Educating Other People's Children" focuses on what skills are necessary for underprivileged children (identified as Black and poor) to survive in a "culture of power." Delpit identifies this "culture of power" as the White authority structure in the educational and social systems. This "culture of power" may be in the form of implicit and explicit communications. The communications concerning the "culture of power" and minority students are based on assumptions, presumptions and interpretations of interactions between the two entities. Delpit states there are rules in order to

Copyright © 2006, Idea Group Inc. Copying or distributing in print or electronic forms without written permission of Idea Group Inc. is prohibited.

succeed in this academic "culture of power." She states that there are codes and rules of how to participate in this power. She explains how these codes and rules are communicated from the teacher to the student (Delpit, 1988).

To indicate how this "culture of power" may affect an African American student in a computing major, the following gives a personal example of how I interpret the codes and rules:

During my student career, all of my instructors and professors were male. Half of them were White males and the other half was Asian or other foreign nationalities. Most of these professors were poor communicators and had a lack of people skills. The majority of computer professors never acknowledged my presence in or out of the classroom. I felt that my academic assessments in computing courses were based rather on my race and gender than my abilities. There were very few African American/ Black students pursuing this major at the time. Almost two-thirds of the enrolled minorities either failed and/or dropped the major. It was my perception that there was implicit communication from the educators and the educational institutions to minorities that the computing major was an unattainable goal. These implicit communications began in high school and as early as grade school. Based on the statistics of enrollment and degrees conferred to African Americans/Blacks in computing majors, I would conclude that these implicit messages are still prevalent in educational institutions.

I recently talked with one of the few African American female students from my class. She indicated that she wanted to focus her study on computer security. I encouraged and supported her decision to pursue this area. I also gave her some contacts in the department to start working within this area. The fact that she did not express her interest, first to the White male professor and the Asian woman professor who teach computer security courses, but to me, indicates that to be able to identify with someone who looks similar an is important factor for minorities interested in pursuing a major. The lack of African American/ Black professors in the computing majors is another implicit communication from educational institutions.

In addition to Delpit's research, there are theories that indicate student empowerment from dominant societies can only be achieved through collaboration with school and community participation. In his article, "Empowering Minority Students: A Framework for Intervention," Jim Cummins reports that

Copyright © 2006, Idea Group Inc. Copying or distributing in print or electronic forms without written permission of Idea Group Inc. is prohibited.

to some researchers, pedagogy is a cause for students at risk. Researchers believe that learning disabilities are pedagogically induced which confines these students to a certain "role." He explains that the major focus of theory and policy aspects is to assess the relationship of success and failure of minority students in educational institutions. Cummins examines the theoretical framework, the primary opinion that students from the dominant society are empowered or immobilized as result of their communications with representatives from the educational institution. These communications are arbitrated by implicit or explicit roles made clear by the educators. He lists three sets of relationships in this framework: *(1) majority/minority societal group relations; (2) school/minority community relations; and, (3) educator/minority student relations* (Cummins, p.105). From these sets of relationships, Cummins examined the patterns of minority students' school failure from an international perspective, the empowerment aspect of students in their school experiences and, the disabling or disempowering aspects of minority students in the educational communities. The results of his research indicated that the performance or participation of minority students is based on the success or failure of the educational framework.

When a segment of the population in the identified society is limited in the pursuit of their goals, it not only affects the individuals but the society as a whole. As statistics indicate, the current trends in the computing majors seems to be geared to the male gender and, in some cases, international students (predominately males). The lack of females, specifically African American females pursuing higher degrees, is the result of these trends in computing majors.

Conclusion

It is my assertion that this is a problem with many complexities. Statistics continually demonstrate that minority student achievement and enrollment in computing majors is still lower than other, empowered groups. I agree with Cummins (1996) that previous frameworks for change only provided a bandaid to the problems surrounding minority students' academic achievement. There have been no changes despite "new and improved" programs and policies. These "new and improved" programs and policies are only an "outward façade" in addressing the problems associated with these issues.

The focus of this paper was to look at a situation that has been documented and researched many times from different perspectives. As an African American

Copyright © 2006, Idea Group Inc. Copying or distributing in print or electronic forms without written permission of Idea Group Inc. is prohibited.

woman, I wanted to look at the statistics and connect them with real-life scenarios. I think personal input in a situation, which affects you and others like you, may lend some answers to a problem that continues to exist or gets worse.

It has been my experience that minority students, especially African American females, are categorized as *outsiders* in the dominant educational society, specifically the computing environment ("the culture of power"). Being classified as outsiders in a "culture of power" puts African American female students at a severe disadvantage. The rules for achievement are made implicit and the interpretations or perceptions can lead to lack of participation or failure.

Future Trends

One program that I am currently involved in is a National Science Foundation Grant at the Community College of Baltimore: Essex Campus. The title of the grant is, *Grace Hopper Scholars Program* (GHSP) *in Mathematics and Computer Science*. The Grace Hopper Scholars Program has a twofold mission: a) to train women to become technicians in computer science and related fields, and b) encourage women to pursue careers in computer science. The project team envisions doing this by providing solutions to the major obstacles faced by women in the community college environment. The project team believes female students will be competitive in the job market if they have a stronger math background and more applied learning opportunities. The program has multiple assessment and exit options to facilitate employment. The GHSP prepares women for success in required math courses, provides an environment that builds their confidence, creates awareness about careers in computer science and emphasizes the impact women can make in this vital field (Leitherer, Hamilton, & Tupper, 2004). It is my belief these types of endeavors can improve the enrollment and retention rates among females, especially African American females, in the computing fields.

References

American Council on Education. (2001, September). *Students of color continue to make enrollment gains in postsecondary education, but the rate of progress is slowing.*

Copyright © 2006, Idea Group Inc. Copying or distributing in print or electronic forms without written permission of Idea Group Inc. is prohibited.

Brown, B. (2001). Women and minorities in high-tech careers. *ERIC Digest, 226.* Retrieved from http://www.ericacve.org/fulltext.asp

Chisholm, I., Carey, J., & Hernandez, A. (2002). Information technology skills for a pluralistic society: Is the playing field level? *Journal of Research on Technology in Education, 35*(1), 58-79.

Cummins, J. (1996). Empowering minority students: A framework for intervention. In T. Beauboeuf-Lafontant & D. Smith Augustine (Eds.), *Facing racism in education* (2nd ed.) (pp. 349-369). Reprint series no. 28. Cambridge: Harvard Educational Review.

Delpit, L. (1988). The silenced dialogue: Power and pedagogy in educating other people's children. *Harvard Educational Review, 3*(58), 280-298.

Digest of Education Statistics (2001, February). Doctor's degrees conferred by degree-granting institutions, by racial/ethnic group, major field of study, and sex of student: 1999-2000.

Digest of Education Statistics (2002, February). Master's degrees conferred by degree-granting institutions, by racial/ethnic group, major field of study, and sex of student: 1999-2000.

Franzinger, K. (Ed.). (2002). Wanted: Women and minorities. *Machine Design, 74*(3), 92.

Hamilton, K. (2001). Historically black colleges strive to bring campus communities up to technological speed. *Black Issues in Higher Education, 18*(2), 30.

Horn, L., Peter, K., & Rooney, K. (n.d.). *Profile of undergraduates in U.S. postsecondary education institutions: 1999-2000.* Retrieved from National Center for Education Statistics Web site: http://nces.ed.gov/das/epubs/2002168/method_npsas.asp

Leitherer, B., Hamilton, P., & Tupper, D. (2004). *The community college of Baltimore Grace Hopper Scholars Program (GHSP) in mathematics and computer science.* National Science Foundation Grant Award, 0302845.

Raddcliff, D. (1999). Champions of women in technology. *ComputerWorld, 33*(3), 46-48.

Copyright © 2006, Idea Group Inc. Copying or distributing in print or electronic forms without written permission of Idea Group Inc. is prohibited.

Chapter VII

Working with Students in Math, Technology, and Sciences for Better Success:
One Faculty Member's Experiences

Shirish Shah, Towson University, USA

Tracy Miller, Towson University, USA

Abstract

One teacher, one mentor, one department…these can make a difference in the success of anyone learning difficult material. This chapter highlights formal academic settings and workplace situations, explaining what one teacher, one company or one department has done to be pro-active in serving its learners.

Copyright © 2006, Idea Group Inc. Copying or distributing in print or electronic forms without written permission of Idea Group Inc. is prohibited.

Introduction

Students majoring in mathematics, computer information technology and the sciences tend to be retained at lower rates than students in other majors (Seymour & Hewitt, 1997). Reasons might include the fact that courses in these disciplines take more time than other courses, and also students might feel disaffected and switch to another major.

Often students, particularly women or students who are from racial minorities, believe they lack the skills necessary to succeed, which is sometimes valid (Allen, 1999). This chapter will focus on successful techniques of planning, advising and mentoring that one faculty member has used in several computer science programs, science programs and in private industry (Bernstein, 1997). We will discuss how he managed his classroom as well as how he worked with the agencies requiring the outcomes.

College students comprise the bulk of the students involved in this study. Dr. Shah also has worked with students in government and industry who needed to learn technical or scientific information. Students from Towson University, the College of Notre Dame of Maryland and Villa Julie College were involved in this study. Towson University is a comprehensive university, Notre Dame is a private, women's parochial college and Villa Julie is a private, co-educational institution, all in or near Baltimore, Maryland.

The same methods that have proved effective to help disadvantaged scholars also help the atypical, occasional student. This chapter shows the steps to success in difficult courses (although science, mathematics and computer science are discussed here) and demonstrates, both anecdotally and by statistical comparisons, the results. The chapter is organized in several sections that overview the steps involved in working with math- or science-phobes. The last section concludes the chapter by discussing the evaluation.

Step 1. Assessing the Level of Knowledge

Before teaching anything, a good teacher must know where to begin. Most colleges now mandate placement testing in verbal and math skills to determine

Copyright © 2006, Idea Group Inc. Copying or distributing in print or electronic forms without written permission of Idea Group Inc. is prohibited.

where to place new students. The theory is that the students' preparation differs widely, even if the same courses appear on the transcript.

Testing, however, can tell us only so much. It can tell us how a student performs on a particular test. It cannot tell us about a student's anxieties, habits or many other factors that play into the eventual outcome in a course. Through listening to the student, a teacher may learn some of the intangible factors and can then adjust to meet the needs.

Students' needs, however, are not the only ones to be considered. The academic program or the sponsoring organization (in the case of government or industry-sponsored courses) also has requirements. The facilitator is expected to satisfy these needs. Companies must be certain that provisions are made to complete work; they need to be certain that the course material, when learned, will benefit them; they need to be assured that the experience will be a positive one for the employees. Most jobs require teamwork, and that also must be incorporated.

In the Academy: For students, we used several academic tests. The Mathematics SAT score can give us a baseline. Any student whose score is under 500 must test to determine if remedial mathematics is necessary. We have used the ACCUPLACER™ test, designed by the College Board™ (Figure 1). Students falling below 82/120 are placed to take two remedial courses. Those students falling below 109/120 must pass one remedial course. This is consistent with guidelines set by the testing company, the mathematics department and other schools in the state of Maryland that use the test. Figure 2 gives an example of an assessment used by a faculty member.

Typically, students who do not perform well on mathematics tests also do not choose majors in the sciences. There are exceptions, however, particularly since Towson University developed several popular programs, such as Forensic Chemistry and Computer Security. Biology has traditionally been a popular major, even among those who do not do well in Mathematics.

For the students interested in the Forensic Chemistry program or any other majors-level chemistry course, the chemistry department developed a course (CHEM 103) that teaches the mathematics and chemistry basics that these students will need in their program. The course bears credit but does not count as a general education course in science. This additional preparation has meant that fewer students have had trouble with the more rigorous General Chemistry.

Copyright © 2006, Idea Group Inc. Copying or distributing in print or electronic forms without written permission of Idea Group Inc. is prohibited.

Figure 1. Development placement test information (from Towson University's Academic Achievement Center)

COMPETENCY TESTING PROGRAM

About the Assessment

Developed ACCUPLACER™The College Board™ Computerized Placement Tests (CPTs), with the help of committees of college faculty, to provide information about [y]our level of skill in reading, writing, and mathematics. Towson University will use the scores you receive and other information that you provide to help determine the English, mathematics, and reading courses most appropriate for you at this time. The tests are given to entering freshmen, transfer students with fewer than 30 credits, and any applicants referred by the Admissions Office. Exemption from testing is based on SAT scores, the possession of 30 or more transfer credits, or the transfer of college-level freshman composition or mathematics courses.

Elementary Algebra Test

This test measures your ability to perform basic algebraic operations and to solve problems that involve elementary algebraic concepts. Before you begin there will be a sample question with the correct answer indicated.

SAMPLE QUESTION

Solve the following problem. You may use the paper you have been given for scratch-work.

$2x + 3x + y =$
A) 6xy
B) 5x + y
C) 5 (x + y)
D) 6x + y

The correct answer is **B) 5x + y.**

Beyond the placement testing, there is another kind of assessment. As mentors listen to their students, they can learn much. Students who trust the advisor or mentoring instructor will discuss their concerns with classroom situations (teaching style, difficulty of work, physical difficulties). The successful advisor is the one who, hearing what is said, helps the student navigate the difficult aspects of a course. The student will learn much more if he or she, once given suggestions, acts upon them, rather than if the advisor does all the work for the student. The mentor may suggest tutoring (and may even help the student work out the difficulties). The mentor, as a member of the department, can share with the department chair, or the whole department, students' concerns if they have been expressed consistently by several students.

In the Work World: In the corporate or government environment, assessing the need takes on a different appearance. First of all, there are two groups who have needs: the employer has one set and the students (employees) have another.

Copyright © 2006, Idea Group Inc. Copying or distributing in print or electronic forms without written permission of Idea Group Inc. is prohibited.

Figure 2. An example of the assessment tool used by one instructor

---

MATHEMATICS REVIEW *Do NOT use your calculator.*
Express in <u>decimal (nonexponential)</u> form. Do not give answers in fraction form. (e.g. $10^3 =$ 1000, $2.0 \times 10^{-2} = 0.020$)

1) $10^4 =$ __   2) $10^1 =$ __   3) $10^0 =$ __   4) $10^{-4} =$ __

5) $\dfrac{1}{10^4} =$ __   6) $\dfrac{1}{10^{-3}} =$ __   7) $10^{-2} \times 10^5 =$ __   8) $\dfrac{10^{-7} \times 10^2 \times 10^{-4}}{10^{-12} \times 10^6} =$ _

9) $\left(10^3\right)^2 =$ __   10) $\left(10^{-2}\right)^3 =$ __   11) $\left(3 \times 10^{-3}\right)^2 =$ __   12) $\left(1+10\right)^2 =$ __

Remember to express your answers to ques.1-12 in <u>non</u>exponential form.
Express in <u>scientific notation</u>. (e.g. $425 = 4.25 \times 10^2$, $35.4 \times 10^{-2} = 3.54 \times 10^{-1}$)

13) $279.3 \times 10^4 =$ __   14) $0.95 \times 10^{-7} =$ __
15) $0.00031 \times 10^3 =$ __   16) $2173 \times 10^{-1} =$ __

ORDER OF OPERATION (*First calculate by hand, then by calculator. If answers differ, decide which is correct. Express answers in decimal form (not as a fraction.)*

17) $2 + 1 \times 4 - 3 =$ __   18) $4 + 8 \div 2 - 3 =$ __   19) $\dfrac{18}{6/3} =$ __   20) $\dfrac{2+4}{2 \times 4} =$ __

21) $\dfrac{1}{1/4} =$ __   22) $3+2-5 \times 3+6+2 \div 2-1 =$ __   23) $5 + 4 \times 3 - 2^4 =$ __

BRIEF REVIEW OF ALGEBRA (Simplify where possible).

24) $\dfrac{x\ y}{x} =$ __   25) $\dfrac{x + y}{x} =$ __   26) $\dfrac{y}{x/y} =$ __   27) $\dfrac{1}{1/x} =$ __

28) $cm^{-1} =$ __   29) $cm \times \dfrac{1}{g/cm} =$ __   30) $cm \times \dfrac{1}{cm/g} =$ __

31) $3\ cm \times 2\ cm =$ __   32) $3\ cm + 2\ cm =$ __   33) $\dfrac{24\ m^3}{6\ m^2} =$ __

34) $2\ cm^{-1} \times 3\ cm^3 =$ __   35) Solve for X. $\dfrac{X + Y}{Z} = X$

SIGNIFICANT FIGURES
 36) How many significant figures are in the following: A) 0.0002? B) 40.0? C) 21.5×10^{-1}?
37) Give the answers to the correct significant figures: A) $152.68 - 21.1$; B) 2.13×3.0.
38) What is the difference between 24 and 24.00 in a Mathematics class? In a science class?
Answer in full sentences on the back of this page.

An employer's needs begin with the information needed to bring the employees up to speed. In addition, financial constraints will dictate the kind of program the contractor can offer. Finally, the employer has time constraints—both in terms of when the project must be finished and how much time the employees will be given to work on the project. Many discussions over several weeks will elicit all this information; the instructor (contractor) will submit his or her proposal. Once the instructor has ascertained the employer information, he or she is ready to work with the students.

Copyright © 2006, Idea Group Inc. Copying or distributing in print or electronic forms without written permission of Idea Group Inc. is prohibited.

Step 2. Working with
Students in the Classroom

For our purposes, students comprise those in elementary schools, community colleges and four-year colleges—both Historically Black Colleges and Universities (HBCU) and predominately White post-secondary schools, factory workers at a medium-sized company in rural Maryland and government workers. Case studies will demonstrate the use of teamwork, problem solving, communicating, nurturing and evaluation.

Elementary school students: In elementary school, students must learn basic skills; they also must gain confidence in the subject matter.

Students were in a church-sponsored, after-school program, needing to learn math. Three of the four faculty members resigned after one month in frustration since the students would not do the work in a traditional setting, forgot the books and pencils, etc. We played math games with them involving money, currencies, etc. Students started coming regularly. We taught addition, multiplication, subtraction and division with matchsticks. Students received rewards for doing well. After they were confident, they began learning by more traditional methods. In three months, they learned four years' work.

In a different program, we went to different elementary schools with an American Chemical Society program to teach chemistry and physics. Students performed the same lab experiments that college students do. After making slime, a third grade student was able to explain the principles behind polymers, and the students claimed to enjoy the program more than recess. There now are approximately 50 volunteers working with the schools.

Community College students: At Chesapeake College (on Maryland's eastern shore) students who were in the new chemistry and physics program visited Calvert Cliffs Nuclear Plant, Philadelphia's Franklin Institute, the Maryland Science Center, farms and the Smithsonian Institute. The field trips supplemented the classroom instruction to demonstrate the real-life applications of principles taught in class. Some of the trips stimulated the development of the first Marine Science and Food Science programs in Maryland at the community college level. Many of those students went on to become doctors,

Copyright © 2006, Idea Group Inc. Copying or distributing in print or electronic forms without written permission of Idea Group Inc. is prohibited.

dentists, medical technicians and attorneys. These were traditional-aged students.

To help the community in general, non-credit courses in food and marine science were offered for adults. This was done in cooperation with the Department of Natural Resources. A fishing clinic every spring attracted fishermen from Virginia to Massachusetts; they learned about sport fishing, salt-water fishing and fresh-water fishing. This appealed to the watermen because it essentially retooled them for different jobs on the water.

At the Community College of Baltimore, Dr. Shah, whose expertise is in the physical sciences, was asked to chair the computer science department because his teaching methods in working with other students had been so successful. The population was largely African American, and these students were trying to learn the skills necessary to succeed in the high-tech fields.

MCI hired some of the graduates of Dr. Shah's program, and they were so impressed that they donated money and technology to the Community College so that more graduates could enter the workforce—with MCI getting first refusal. Other significant grant money came from Hewlett-Packard, who donated $100,000 to build the department.

HBCU students: After assessing need and testing the climate of the class, we determined that, while some students were confident (Grandy, 1998), many students were apprehensive about their abilities. We used different approaches to teach them.

We started by putting a problem on the board; the first students to finish the problem were directed to help their colleagues. When all had finished, a second problem appeared. The process continued until ten increasingly difficult problems had been solved.

We then asked a different student to explain each problem, allowing the once-apprehensive students to gain confidence as they explained to the class their solution to the problems.

Predominately white universities: Minority students, usually African-American, typically are reluctant to take too many courses in the sciences beyond

Copyright © 2006, Idea Group Inc. Copying or distributing in print or electronic forms without written permission of Idea Group Inc. is prohibited.

Figure 3. Comparison of the highest scores in the classes

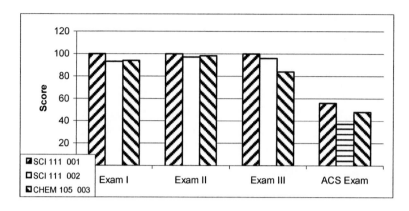

what the university requires (Holmes et al., 2000). The students discussed in this section come from three different colleges.

At Towson University, three different African-American students from an urban area were interested in an allied-health major. In each case, their mathematical and science skills were weak. Members of the chemistry department worked with them after class to assist with their mathematics and science classes. Two of those students currently attend pharmacy school; the third is now a successful senior in forensic chemistry.

Figures 3-5 show the grade distribution for the Fall 2004 chemistry courses between Towson University and Villa Julie College.

Figure 4. Comparison of the lowest scores in the classes

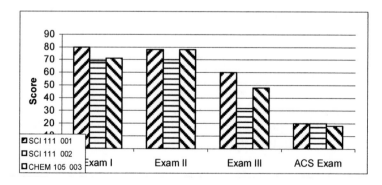

Copyright © 2006, Idea Group Inc. Copying or distributing in print or electronic forms without written permission of Idea Group Inc. is prohibited.

Figure 5. Comparison of the mean scores in the classes

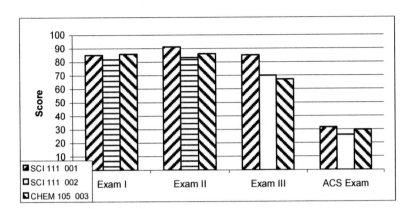

Of 23 students who entered Towson University in Fall 2000 and were assigned to Dr. Shah's advisee group, 12 graduated in four years, half of those 12 majoring in the sciences. Towson's overall four-year graduation rate for that cohort is not available at the time of this writing. For the previous cohort (Fall 1999 entering class) the overall four-year graduation rate was 30.7% (28.6% for African-American students).

Private industry: From training cabinetmakers to developing certificate programs for automotive dealers, we found that flexibility in scheduling met the needs both of the students and of the workplace. We were able to schedule the classes either at night or early in the morning, finding that more students about 50 preferred the morning times and about 20 came in the evening).

Government workers: As an outgrowth of the Community College of Baltimore County program, we devised a training program for three Baltimore city employees to learn Occupational Safety and Health (OSHA). That necessitated the workers' knowing chemistry, biology and mathematics. Those three workers were so successful that we were asked by the mayor to develop training for the workers of the city's water treatment plant and waste water plant. We had only two weeks to plan the program and so called upon the three OSHA workers, who let him know what content was necessary. It necessitated physics, chemistry and biology-based content. The students in that group passed the state certification tests. Of the original three workers, one is now the manager in the Department of Industrial Hygiene, one is a lawyer and the third

Copyright © 2006, Idea Group Inc. Copying or distributing in print or electronic forms without written permission of Idea Group Inc. is prohibited.

is an associate in industrial hygiene. Of the three, one is an orthodox Jew, one is African American and one is a devout Christian woman. They still are in touch with us after more than 25 years.

Step 3. Working with
Students Outside the Classroom

In academia, faculty have the opportunity to mentor the students outside the class. In some cases this is done through a formal advising relationship, while in others it is done through informal coaching. The case studies in this section discuss this relationship.

Showing real-life applicability: For some students, the concepts discussed in class are too abstract. By showing them real life situations that use the sciences, the mentor is encouraging the student to make the abstract concepts concrete. An example of this is a class trip to a water treatment plant, or to a data management center.

Talking with students about classes in which the mentor has no involvement: By finding out where students are having trouble, the mentor can help by explaining troublesome concepts and by determining where the student has had trouble in the past; for example, a student who has had difficulty with geometry very likely will have difficulty understanding molecular structure. The mentor also can get an idea from several students about which teachers work well with students at that level and can convey that information to the department. The department can use the mentor to find out how many students at one level plan to take the next-level course, so that the department can plan enough sections.

Step 4. Responsiveness
of the Department

In all settings: academic, private and government, the department or agency can assist the students/employees in achieving success. Assessing the need and

Copyright © 2006, Idea Group Inc. Copying or distributing in print or electronic forms without written permission of Idea Group Inc. is prohibited.

rising up to meet it are key. Some examples involve development of preparatory courses, sufficiency of courses in a sequence and allowing time from work for completion of classes.

One company on the eastern shore of Maryland worked with us to develop a program that would teach its employees the mathematics skills they would need on their job. Dr. Shah described the amount of time participants would need and arranged that the training be done on work time (and not employee time). That program necessitated the company to arrange substitutes for the employees being trained, and to ensure that work was scheduled in such a way that fewer staff could handle it.

At Towson University, the chemistry department learned from those departments dependant on its courses the approximate number of service courses required, and then the department offered them. The department also surveyed students in courses that usually begin a sequence to determine how many were planning to continue to the next course. In that way, they could reserve spots for those students, while also accommodating other students.

Step 5. Evaluating the Success

In much of the preceding work, results are anecdotal; still, it may be said unequivocally that students can learn difficult material if the teacher listens to their needs, understands how they learn and responds accordingly.

Examples of success rates in all constituencies will be given.

In the government agencies, employee attrition was reduced through apprenticeship training. In the industrial setting, the employee training program improved productivity. In the inner city elementary school, the students learned mathematics successfully when taught using a non-traditional approach. In the collegiate setting, courses such as a chemistry preparatory course, developmental mathematics and reading and developmental geometry and sciences, the confidence of students was improved.

Student advisees' grades have been followed by the author for four years (2001-2004), and those results are included in Figure 6.

Copyright © 2006, Idea Group Inc. Copying or distributing in print or electronic forms without written permission of Idea Group Inc. is prohibited.

Figure 6. Grades of Dr. Shah's advisees in their mathematics and science courses

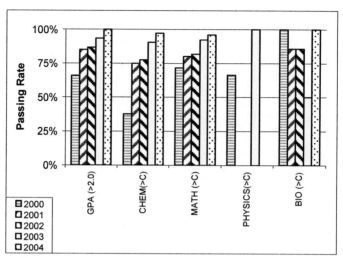

References

Allen, D. (1999). Desire to finish college: An empirical link between motivation and persistence, *Research in Higher Education, 40*(4), 461-485.

Bernstein, D. (1997). Is teaching computer science different from teaching other sciences? In *Proceedings of 13th Eastern Small College Computing Conference* (pp. 137-143). Pomona, NJ.

Grandy, J. (1998). Persistence in science of high-ability minority students. *Journal of Higher Education, 69*(6), 589-620.

Holmes, S., Ebbers, L., Robinson, D., & Mugenda, A. (2000). Validating African-American students at predominantly White institutions. *Journal of College Student Development, 2*(1), 41-58.

Seymour, E., & Hewitt, N. (1997). *Talking about leaving: Why undergraduates leave the sciences.* Boulder, CO: Westview Press.

Copyright © 2006, Idea Group Inc. Copying or distributing in print or electronic forms without written permission of Idea Group Inc. is prohibited.

Chapter VIII

Assessing Diversity Issues in Instructional Technology:
Strategies that Enhance Student Learning and Generate Outcomes Assessment Data

Virginia Johnson Anderson, Towson University, USA

Abstract

Assessment is a major focus is higher education; IT faculties and departments are being asked to document quantitatively what students have learned in relation to goal-oriented expectations. Although "students will value diversity in the academy and the workplace" is a common course, general education or institutional goal, we often know little about

Copyright © 2006, Idea Group Inc. Copying or distributing in print or electronic forms without written permission of Idea Group Inc. is prohibited.

*how well students achieve this goal because we do **not** assess it. This chapter describes how to construct Student Learning Outcomes consistent with valuing diversity, how to design tests/assignments to see if student have achieved those outcomes and how to use that information to inform and enhance student learning in our IT courses, departments or institutions. The chapter reviews key assessment principles and practices. Then, we examine four strategies to document how students' cognitive perceptions, attitudes, values and social actions in regard to diversity issues may be impacted and assessed. Assessment action scenarios elucidate the effective use of rubrics, Primary Trait Analysis, portfolios and affective behavioral checklists.*

Introduction

If you are reading this chapter, you believe that diversity issues are important. You endorse aspects on multiculturalism and undoubtedly model many teaching behaviors that foster a respect for all learners. You work hard to cover the all the Instructional Technology (IT) information, skill sets, concepts, software applications and research protocols inherent to your course. At the same time, you do not ignore related societal, legal and ethical issues in your approach. You endorse global perspectives and discredit ethnic stereotypes. Your faculty engagement is exemplary, but let there be no mistake; the primary focus in higher education today is the ASSESSMENT of STUDENT LEARNING.

Since the mid 1990s, community colleges, colleges and universities, alike, have been reeling from and responding to a paradigm shift. Higher education has changed from a culture of teaching to a culture of learning, from the examination of faculty delivery to the documentation of student performance as chronicled in *Learning from Change: Landmarks in Teaching and Learning from Change Magazine (1969-1999)* (DeZure, 2000). State offices, local governments and accrediting agencies are no longer satisfied with knowing what the curricula and faculty will "cover"; public shareholders are increasingly intent upon seeing tangible evidence of what graduates can know and do (Suskie, 2004). It is the "Age of Accountability" of student learning and assessment (Walvoord & Anderson, 1998).

So, before we address how to assess diversity issues, let's look at assessment in practice. *Academic assessment is the systematic gathering and analyz-*

Copyright © 2006, Idea Group Inc. Copying or distributing in print or electronic forms without written permission of Idea Group Inc. is prohibited.

ing of information (excluding course grades) to inform and improve student learning or programs of learning in light of goal-oriented expectations (American Association of Higher Education [AAHE], 1996).

Goals are broad statements of expectations; they are usually referred to as mission statements by institutions, majors' expectations by departments and course goals by instructors. Goals are "big picture statements," for example in a 100-level "Computers for Business Applications" course, an instructor might list "Learn the value of the computer as a tool of information and technology within a business environment" and "Communicate effectively in a variety of IT-assisted business formats" as two goals for the course.

Goal-oriented expectations are more specific statements of what students will be able to know and do at the end of an experience, i.e., completing the course, completing the major or graduating from the institution. In classroom settings, these kinds of statements are often called behavioral objectives. In assessment circles, statements of what a student may be expected to know and do are called Student Learning Outcomes (SLOs). For example, to better articulate the "communicate effectively in a variety of IT-assisted business formats," the SLOs might be: (1) "The student will be able to compose a literate, content-explicit e-mail to a business superior," (2) "The student will be able to file, send, cc and retrieve the e-mail message" and (3) "The student will demonstrate a willingness to value e-mail business communication by exhibiting prompt and courteous email communication practices."

SLOs may be classified according to their instructional purpose. *Cognitive* SLOs call on students to demonstrate content mastery and mental processing skills such as critical thinking, quantitative reasoning, etc. (SLO # 1). *Psycho-motor* SLOs call on students to demonstrate physical motor tasks (SLO #2). *Affective* SLOs call on students to exhibit behaviors reflective of specific attitudes, feeling and values (SLO #3).

Information (assessment jargon for data, documents, observations, statistics, frequencies, etc.) may be classified as *direct evidence* if it is closely tied to both student performance and goal-oriented expectations. For example, aggregated student scores compiled from a *rubric* (a general grading tool establishing different levels of student performance) for "literate" e-mail would be direct evidence (see Figure 1). These data may be collected by an instructor, a panel of instructors or external reviewers. The percentage of students who could print out a copy of the e-mail in lab the next day would be direct evidence of the students' ability to retrieve their messages. Other examples of direct evidence might be employer evaluations of student performance, subset scores on

Copyright © 2006, Idea Group Inc. Copying or distributing in print or electronic forms without written permission of Idea Group Inc. is prohibited.

Figure 1. Rubric for scoring "literate" e-mail for whole IT class

3: Appears literate
2: Two or less minor errors
1: Constructs distract the reader
Number of students in class: _____
Mean score of class: _____
Number of students at 2 or above: _____

multiple choice items about e-mails on the final, collections of student work or a portfolio of student e-mails produced or collected in a capstone course.

Indirect evidence provides information that indicates students are probably learning, but it is more circumstantial. Examples of indirect evidences include holistic grades (instructor examines the assignment not accompanied by a rubric or detailed scoring guide and assigns letter grades (A-, C, D, etc.), statements about how student felt about the e-mail assignment or students' ratings of what they have learned in a course. In her most recent book, Linda Suskie (2004), past director of the AAHE Assessment Forum and now the Executive Director of the Middle States Accreditation group, lists and categorizes direct evidence, indirect evidence and evidence of support of student learning as viewed by accrediting agencies.

Speaking of accrediting agencies, aren't you wondering why they categorically excluded course grades from assessment data. Was it that they did not trust faculty to grade fairly? Was it that some faculty graded harder than others? Was it that some institutions were less rigorous than others? The answer is to all three questions is NO. Course grades (i.e., A, C, D), were excluded because they do not have the power to yield information that can inform and improve student learning or programs of learning in light of goal-oriented expectations. Quite simply, course grades aggregate too much information into a single unit of evaluation. Look at your grade list from 2002. Can you honestly recall and/or distinguish now those students who made Bs because they had minimal critical thinking skills and outstanding IT skills from those who made Bs because they had outstanding critical thinking skills and minimal IT skills?

Although teachers' course grades could not be used for assessment, as early as 1994 Barbara Walvoord, a national Writing Across the Curriculum leader,

Copyright © 2006, Idea Group Inc. Copying or distributing in print or electronic forms without written permission of Idea Group Inc. is prohibited.

hypothesized that teachers' grading processes had the potential to generate quantitative data that could meet academic assessment needs (Walvoord & Anderson, 1998). Walvoord proposed that Primary Trait Analysis (PTA), a particularly thorough process of constructing a set of assignment-specific, task-explicit rubrics, could provide the rigor and specificity needed to conduct course-embedded assessment (collection of data within an on-going course as opposed to competency measures administered outside the classroom experience). Walvoord and Anderson have led hundreds of effective grading and assessment workshops at community colleges, colleges and universities across the country. They have helped faculty design assignments, construct PTAs, team score student work, aggregate class scores and analyze and act on the data to enhance student learning. Far removed from the "add standardized test and stir" assessments of the early and mid-1990s, these course-embedded assessment data are particularly effective in assessing student learning for Gen Ed (general education), departmental and programmatic assessment plans. However, Walvoord also coordinated a faculty-driven model institutional assessment plan at Raymond Walters College, a two-year autonomous branch of the University of Cincinnati. Over 90% of the faculty constructed PTAs and used them to assess critical thinking/quantitative reasoning in their classes. In 1999, the North Central Association awarded Raymond Walters College an unprecedented 10-year accreditation. Examples of their PTAs, institutional protocols, faculty perspectives and administrative suggestions are available on their homepage www.rwc.uc.edu at the present time.

Now, let's focus on assessing diversity issues in the IT classroom. The first principle in "AAHE's Principles of Good Practice of Student Learning" is "The assessment of student learning begins with educational values" (AAHE, 1996). As you look at each course you are going to teach, you must ask yourself what you value most. What are your non-negotiable, "walk-away" demands in IT content, operational skills, knowledge of IT culture and communications and integration of diversity, ethics and legal issues? Think about cognitive, affective and psychomotor outcomes for these goals. Since we are specifically concerned with diversity issues, you may find it quite helpful to review the six major teaching goals that serve to foster an acceptance and appreciation of cultural diversity as described by Bennett (2003) in her 5th edition of *Multicultural Education: Theory and Practice:*

1.   To develop multiple historical perspectives;

2.   To strengthen cultural consciousness;

Copyright © 2006, Idea Group Inc. Copying or distributing in print or electronic forms without written permission of Idea Group Inc. is prohibited.

3.   To strengthen intercultural competence;

4.   To combat racism, sexism, and all forms of prejudice and discrimination;

5.   To increase awareness of the state of the planet and global dynamics; and

6.   To develop social action skills.

Before you construct some Student Learning Outcomes (SLOs) for diversity issues, why not spend a few minutes in an activity that Bennett (2003) suggests in her academic best-seller. Rank the six goals above from 1, as most important, to 6, as least important, for the course you have in mind. Think about how you would explain your rank order choices to an IT colleague. Then, select another course you teach and reconsider. Would the nature of the new course, the college standing of the students or its position in the IT curriculum change your ranking?

At this point for simplicity, let's assume that you are teaching a 100-level IT course, "Computers for Business Applications." The first step is to identify your major goals. Here are some examples: Students will be able to:

1.   Learn and appreciate the value of the computer as a tool of information and technology within a business environment;

2.   Work effectively in groups to complete IT projects; and

3.   Identify and combat racism and sexism in the actual and/or virtual workplace. (This is what you chose to emphasize from goal number 4 above for the l00-level class.)

The second step is to structure Student Learning Outcomes (SLOs) that will clearly describe to your students what you want them to be able to know and do. Try to avoid words like "know," "understand" and "learn about" when constructing SLOs. Students cannot envision from those terms what it is that you want them to know and do (Walvoord & Anderson, 1998). Here are some SLOs for our goals above:

1.   Identify in theory, or practice, five basic ways computers may be used as tools of information and technology within that business environment;

2.   Work effectively in a group to produce a task-specific, electronically signed document that will receive one grade; and

Copyright © 2006, Idea Group Inc. Copying or distributing in print or electronic forms without written permission of Idea Group Inc. is prohibited.

3.   Identify and describe overt examples of racism and sexism occurring in the workplace and/or the institution and reflectively explain actions that could have enhanced the situation and created a more productive environment.

The next task is to develop a competency measure (some type of test, technology product, written composition, mechanical devise, demonstration or performance) that will enable you and your student to determine to what degree they have achieved mastery of the SLOs. Consider each of these competency measures and how, or if, they can asses each SLO.

A.   Given a scenario description of a small business, its personnel, products, distribution systems, office operations, and physical plant, the student will list and discuss five ways computers can be used as tools of information and technology within that business environment. (Addresses SLO #1)

B.   The student will answer 20 multiple-choice test questions. (Well-structured items can address aspects SLO #1 and/or #3, but not #2)

C.   Working in groups of three, students will observe the university bowling alley and submit a two-page online report explaining how computers are helping this business be more efficient and/or profitable. (Addresses SLO #2 if electronic signatures are required)

D.   The student will submit a three-page Diversity Issues portfolio (a collection of written evidence and reflective statements) that identifies and describes one campus example of racism and one of sexism (instruct students to omit proper names) and reflectively explain why he or she was sensitive to this event and discuss one action that could have enhanced each situation. (Addresses SLO #3)

The next step is *the systematic gathering and analyzing of information to inform and improve student learning or programs of learning in light of goal-oriented expectations.* To examine the portfolio, you will want to construct a PTA to evaluate it (see example in Figure 2). Then design a points plan; place the most value on the skills and content you want your students to demonstrate in the assignment. The essential elements of the assignment are to identify racism and sexism in context and to identify possible actions on the basis of the text, lectures and course discussion. Let's have the three primary trait items count 24 points each. Since you are spending your valuable grading time evaluating this portfolio assignment, you will want to attend to other

Copyright © 2006, Idea Group Inc. Copying or distributing in print or electronic forms without written permission of Idea Group Inc. is prohibited.

Figure 2. Primary trait analysis for evaluating diversity issues portfolios in 100-level computers for business application course

Identifying racism
3: Student identifies appropriate example, reports direct observations, uses key terms, includes relevant situational detail and justifies selection of event with facts and/or objective statements.
2: Student identifies appropriate example, reports direct observations, uses key terms, includes some situational detail but justifies selection of event with opinions and/or overgeneralizations.
1: Student cannot identify appropriate example articulately.
Identifying sexism
3: Student identifies appropriate example, reports direct observations, uses key terms, includes relevant situational detail and justifies selection of event with facts and/or objective statements.
2: Student identifies appropriate example, reports direct observations, uses key terms, includes some situational detail but justifies selection of event with opinions and/or overgeneralizations.
1: Student cannot identify appropriate example articulately.

Combating racism and sexism through situational awareness
3: Student identifies two sets of actions that are more positive alternatives; supportive statements reflect greater knowledge of diversity and self.
2: Student identifies one action that is a more positive alternative; support of accepted choice is reflective of greater knowledge of diversity and self.
1: Student does not identify any actions or selects ones that are overtly reflective of stereotypes, prejudice or cultural insensitivity.

aspects of the performance as well: the student's explanation of sensitivity, meeting format demands, evidence of an appropriate vocabulary, and effective communication skills. Let each of these factors count seven points each since 72 and 28 add up to 100! Read and grade each student's work. Attach the PTA score sheet with the grades and comments to the student's work. Return. That's good TEACHING!

Although grades are paramount to the students (an understatement!) and rewarding or disappointing to faculty, course grades as artifacts (A, B-, C, etc.) are not accepted in assessment, and assignment-given letter grades for the whole task are, at best, indirect evidence. *Are you willing to take the key step in course-embedded assessment?* After you have scored the papers, tally up the total number of students performing at each level of your PTA; see Table 1 for hypothetical results from 50 students in two sections.

Looking at the total class results, you can see that your students have "a good handle" on sexism in the academic workplace; 98% of them can recognize it and over 70% of them can describe its occurrence objectively. Good job! Racism was different. Only 76% of the students could identify an example of racism in context. And what was more problematic is that 66% of the entire class could not articulate and describe that event objectively. At this point, what would you do? Probably, you would decide that your IT students needed more structure

Copyright © 2006, Idea Group Inc. Copying or distributing in print or electronic forms without written permission of Idea Group Inc. is prohibited.

Table 1. Sample class tally (%) of students (N=50) performing at various levels on the primary trait analysis of the diversity issues portfolio with 3 representing highest level of performance

Level of task performance on PTA scale for Diversity Issues	Identifying racism	Identifying sexism	Combating racism and sexism
3	10%	72%	8 %
2	66%	26%	52 %
1	24%	2%	40 %
Mean scores (3.00 ideal score)	1.86	2.70	1.68

in describing racism in context. Perhaps you could show a videotaped scenario depicting overt and subtle examples of racism in the workforce in class and then lead a guided discussion. As for the 1.68 score out of 3.00 for selecting action, you might as well conclude that there is not much point in working on that right now. Reasoned action entries in the portfolio will probably not improve until the students are more informed and articulate about how to recognize racism. As you make these decisions, you are systematically *gathering and analyzing information to inform and improve student learning or programs of learning in light of goal-oriented expectations.* That's good ASSESS-MENT!

Course-embedded assessments are particularly effective outcomes assessment (processes that measure the degree to which course, majors' or programmatic goals have been met) because of their potential for "closing the loop," doing something with your data to enhance student learning (Walvoord, Bardes, & Denton, 1998). Faculty-driven assessment strategies enable the people who need to know to be the first to know. Faculty can rethink their course strategies for the next test or the next semester just as you would have done in the racism example. Department chairs can see that this year's IT graduates in the capstone course are not writing as well as expected and can focus departmental energies on new strategies for rising seniors. In contrast, results of standardized tests and student services inventories may take months, even years, to be re-routed into the hands of the right person to effect an instructional change.

We have just outlined how Primary Trait Analysis may be used to collect important quantitative data to inform and improve student learning or programs

Copyright © 2006, Idea Group Inc. Copying or distributing in print or electronic forms without written permission of Idea Group Inc. is prohibited.

of learning; another strategy that has a tremendous potential to collect quantitative data about diversity outcomes is the Affective Behavioral Checklist (continue reading and then see Figure 3). When we discussed student learning outcomes, we pointed out that some things we want students to walk away with from our courses have to do with attitudes, feelings and values. If we survey students and ask them if they value computer security, confidentiality, courtesy, cultural diversity or lifelong learning, we may get some interesting answers, but it is NOT assessment data. These surveys, like those that ask students if their learning needs have been met, are what the North Central Accreditation Commission calls "non-measures" of assessment (Lopez, 1997). However, when we ask students to self-report behaviors—not feelings, but overt behaviors—we have a valid, valuable source of indirect data.

To demonstrate how the Affective Behavioral Checklist is constructed and used to measure goal-oriented outcomes for specific class, program or departmental purposes, let's begin with two broad affective goals that are characteristic of IT departmental outcomes assessments:

1.   Students will demonstrate a willingness to value lifelong learning by engaging in behaviors representative of, or congruent with, this value (a little assessment jargon).

2.   Students will demonstrate a willingness to value diversity by engaging in selected behaviors representative of, or congruent with, this value.

A departmental committee or the whole group would discuss and agree on some specific behaviors that students who held these values might be expected to exhibit as they completed their required experiences. Figure 3 gives an abbreviated sample of tasks.

The number of checks for each entry (1 through 13) and for each set of responses (values lifelong learning and values diversity) would be tallied for each student and for the class. In this case items numbered 1, 4, 6, 7, 9 and 13 are indicators of lifelong learning and items 2, 3, 5, 8, 11 and 12 are indicative of behaviors for valuing diversity. Item 10 should be included in both sets, making seven out of seven indicators the best student performance possible for each value. After collecting pilot data to improve and norm the checklist, a department might want to set an assessment goal. For example, "Over the next two years, we would like to see that 80% of the seniors surveyed at the end of the capstone course will have an average score of 4.0 or more for each set of

Copyright © 2006, Idea Group Inc. Copying or distributing in print or electronic forms without written permission of Idea Group Inc. is prohibited.

Figure 3. Majors' behavioral checklist

Check each activity or experience you have completed as an IT major:
_____1.   Attended one or more seminars presented by departmental faculty or graduate students.
_____2.   Used multicultural clipart to develop concepts in PowerPoints for a required course.
_____3.   Worked on one or more IT group projects with ethnically diverse coworkers.
_____4.   Attended a hardware or software demonstration presented by an outside expert.
_____5.   Included multicultural perspectives and/or images on my own homepage.
_____6.   Read one IT-related journal article on my own (not assigned) in past 60 days.
_____7.   Continued to apply course strategies to reduce prejudice in my own social thinking.
_____8.   Worked on one or more IT group projects in which we selected a female leader.
_____9.   Attended a career fair or mock interview session to practice interview skills.
_____10. Attended a computer applications activity hosted by a multicultural organization.
_____11. Initiated the inclusion of an international student in an IT project or study group.
_____12. Rejected purchasing item from a Web site because of its blatant use of stereotypes.
_____13. Held office in, or served on, an active committee of student-run IT organization.

values." Ordinarily, departments use an Affective Behavioral Checklist to measure at least three to six value sets and make the whole checklist contain between 24 to 42 items. This way 6 to 10 desired behaviors may be found in each set.

In addition to departmental applications, this process can provide valuable quantitative data for measuring individual course affective objectives, quantifying "needs assessments" for granting agencies and documenting changes in affective changes in students' behaviors as the result of externally-funded projects. This was illustrated in Towson University's Biology Department when they examined behaviors directly related to a goal-oriented expectation that successful biology graduates would "value research as an integral part of science" (Anderson, 2004). In a 35-item checklist, seven of the items were research-oriented behaviors. The item "Worked with a faculty member on research project" was checked by less than 5% of the students (N=90+) and only 30% of the students had engaged in more than three of the research

Copyright © 2006, Idea Group Inc. Copying or distributing in print or electronic forms without written permission of Idea Group Inc. is prohibited.

indicator behaviors. These data were used to demonstrate to the National Science Foundation that there was a critical need for a Research Experience for Undergraduates (REU) grant on the Towson campus. The REU project was funded for two years and then renewed for a third. This occurred because, in part, the behavioral checklist supplied valuable, documented indirect evidence of changes in students' attitudes about the importance of research.

Self-reported data on affective behavioral checklists may also serve as an important source of indirect data about the degree to which students value technology and the acquisition of technology skills. For example, survey your students early in the course to determine how many use PowerPoint, maintain a Web site, use Excel spreadsheets, construct computer graphics, use the Internet to retrieve informative data, design computer programs, adapt or construct assistive technologies or crate and test robotics applications. Re-administer these checklists at the end of the course. Gain scores provide valuable indirect evidence of the importance of quality IT instruction and adequate equipment expenditures (Suskie, 2004).

As you plan for assessment, think back to your best lecture. The cognitive concepts were crystal clear, the PowerPoints were pristine, your voice was animated, and your insights were brilliant! As the students listened intently, one of them eagerly asked, "Will this be on the test?"

Well, that is the question we have to answer about diversity issues! Will they be measured, tested and assessed in our IT courses? Will students be expected to complete assignments that require them to acquire and demonstrate enhanced cultural understandings and sensitivities? Will students be expected to develop more inclusive Web sites as described in *Diversity Inc.* (Meadows, 2005) or compile a working file of multicultural images? Will students be asked to document that they are developing a wider range of communication skills and diversity perspectives? Will IT faculties and departments commit to student assessment in action?

References

American Association of Higher Education (AAHE). (1996). *AAHE's principles of good practice for assessing student learning.* Washingon, DC.

Copyright © 2006, Idea Group Inc. Copying or distributing in print or electronic forms without written permission of Idea Group Inc. is prohibited.

Anderson, V. (2004, Winter). Streak plate strategies for classroom assessment, *Focus onMicrobiology Education.*

Bennett, C. (1999). *Multicultural education: Theory and practice* (5th ed.). Boston: Allyn and Bacon.

DeZure, D. (Ed.). (2000). *Learning from change: Landmarks in teaching and learning from Change Magazine (1969-1999).*

Lopez, C. (1997). Opportunities for improvement: advice from consultant-evaluators to assess student learning. In *North Central Accreditation Commission on Institutions.* Chicago: Higher Education.

Meadows, A. (2005, December/January). Do Lucent, Avon, and Time Warner prove diversity success on Web sites? *Diversity Inc,* 113-114.

Middle States Commission of Higher Education (2003). *Student learning assessment: Options and resources.* Middle States Commission of Higher Education, Philadelphia.

Suskie, L. (2004). *Assessing student learning: A common sense guide.* Bolton, MA: Anker Publishing.

Walvoord, B., & Anderson, V. (1998). *Effective grading: A tool for learning and assessment.* San Francisco: Jossey-Bass.

Walvoord, B., Bardes, B., & Denton, J. (1998). Closing the feedback loop in classroom-based assessment. *Assessment Update: Progress, Trends, and Practices in Higher Education, 10*(5), 10-11.

Copyright © 2006, Idea Group Inc. Copying or distributing in print or electronic forms without written permission of Idea Group Inc. is prohibited.

Chapter IX

The Open Ended Group Project:
A Way of Including Diversity in the IT Curriculum

Xristine Faulkner, London South Bank University, UK

Mats Daniels, Uppsala University, Sweden

Ian Newman, Loughborough University, UK

Abstract

Modern societies are now beginning to accept that their citizens are diverse but, arguably, have not yet faced up to the challenges of diversity. Schools and universities thus have a role to play in equipping students for the diverse society in which they will live and work. IT students in particular need to appreciate the diversity of society as they specify, design, build and evaluate systems for a wide range of people. This chapter examines the concept of the Open Ended Group Project (OEGP)

Copyright © 2006, Idea Group Inc. Copying or distributing in print or electronic forms without written permission of Idea Group Inc. is prohibited.

and uses examples to demonstrate that OEGP forms an effective technique for encouraging students to work together in diverse teams. The appropriateness of OEGP as a means of addressing diversity in the curriculum is examined, and it is concluded that OEGP offers a suitable means of enabling students to develop strategies for accommodating diversity in both their future working life and the wider society.

Introduction

Diversity is a very important topic in the education of IT students since they, more than most others, will need to be concerned with considering, and accommodating, a wide range of diversity (cultural, social, physical, cognitive) in possible users when specifying, building and evaluating IT systems. As more and more people use computers in their work and for pleasure, this aspect of IT will inevitably increase. Students may also be expected to work with very diverse groups of people in teams which can span continents and cultures as well as include people with physical disabilities. However, of its nature, "diversity" is difficult to "teach" and cannot be fully covered in a normal curriculum (in both cases because it comes in so many different guises).

This chapter proposes the use of open ended group projects (OEGP) as a means of both introducing aspects of diversity and of providing a way of integrating students from diverse backgrounds. It also examines some misconceptions about the use of OEGP and shows how they can be overcome. The discussion is illustrated with examples drawn from the experiences of the three authors in using OEGP successfully at the university level over many years as a vehicle to reinforce more conventional teaching and introduce new ideas (Daniels & Asplund, 2000; Daniels, Faulkner, & Newman, 2002; Last, Almstrum, Erickson, Klein, & Daniels, 2000; Newman, Dawson, & Parks, 2000). Since the authors all work in different institutions, two in the UK and one in Sweden, they each bring a different perspective and have different tales to tell, but they are united in reporting that the OEGP method is very effective in making students consider issues that they would otherwise not think about, in motivating them to do well and in offering excellent learning opportunities, i.e., it is ideal for both introducing diversity issues and for accommodating diversity among the students.

Copyright © 2006, Idea Group Inc. Copying or distributing in print or electronic forms without written permission of Idea Group Inc. is prohibited.

All three of the authors are lecturers in university information technology/ computing departments and they perceive their primary task as encouraging students to learn how to use computers effectively. However, to do this well they must also help the students identify, and be prepared to overcome, potential problems, such as diversity. Although none of the authors has focused specifically on diversity as a topic for students to study, all three have had to accommodate considerable diversity amongst the students whom they have helped to learn and who have reviewed the effectiveness of their teaching with respect to various diversity issues. The two authors from the UK universities have cohorts of students with a very diverse ethnic/racial/color mix and have needed to demonstrate that these issues do not reduce the effectiveness of the students' learning experiences. The other author has focused on the effects of cultural differences when working in groups with members located in different continents, requiring the students to accommodate different time zones and different languages (Daniels, Berglund, Pears, & Fincher, 2004). One of the authors has organized both the composition and the management structures of teams to encourage female students to improve their performance (Faulkner & Culwin, 1999), and all three authors have experience assisting students with a wide range of disabilities (e.g., partial and total blindness, profound deafness, cerebral palsy, paraplegic) become fully involved and integrated into the learning process (which has also, of course, assisted the students' teammates become more aware of these issues).

The next section of the chapter discusses the breadth and multi-faceted nature of the diversity "issue" and examines the problems of addressing this within any university computing curriculum. It then explains why OEGP is, potentially, an appropriate approach for achieving this objective, discussing the ideas under-lying OEGP and relating them to the more general concepts of constructivism and Problem Based Learning (PBL). A number of examples based on real experiences are then presented to show how the technique has been used in practice to overcome potential diversity issues amongst the students. Examples will also be used to show how specific diversity issues could be, and have been, explicitly addressed and assessed. The chapter concludes by examining the appropriateness of the OEGP technique, and by recommending that all university educators should consider it as an effective way both of introducing diversity issues into the curriculum and also of accommodating diversity within the student body.

Copyright © 2006, Idea Group Inc. Copying or distributing in print or electronic forms without written permission of Idea Group Inc. is prohibited.

Background for the Chapter:
The Challenge of Putting Diversity
into the IT Curriculum

This section commences by examining the task of including diversity issues in the IT curriculum at a university. It outlines some possible dimensions of diversity and discusses the interaction between diversity issues and computer applications, concluding that it would be impractical to include more than a small fraction of the possible subject matter in any university degree program. The section continues by discussing educational constructivism and problem based learning, suggesting that these may offer a much more effective way of getting students to appreciate, and be able to accommodate, diversity issues. The section also explains the relationship between constructivism, problem based learning and the Open Ended Group Project (OEGP) approach. Arguments for using the OEGP approach for diversity education in a university IT curriculum are included throughout the section.

Diversity in the IT Curriculum: Dimensions of Diversity

As stated in the introduction, the authors believe that diversity is a particularly important issue for students studying computing to consider whilst at university. Such an education should help society accommodate the increasing diversity of its citizens. However, this is not just an altruistic viewpoint, since work by Gurin, Nagda and Lopez (2004) has shown that students involved in programs which address diversity also secure positive benefits for themselves.

The importance of diversity education has increased, and will continue to increase, as legislation against "discrimination" is introduced (e.g., in the UK, as in other countries, there has been legislation against discrimination on the grounds of color and of gender for many years but this has recently been augmented by legislation against discrimination on the basis of disability—the Disability Discrimination Act: http://www.disability.gov.uk/dda/). However, this means that "diversity" is very diverse. At the very least it would ideally be necessary to consider:

- disability, which itself is multi-faceted with each disability, and each degree of severity of a particular disability, posing different challenges for

Copyright © 2006, Idea Group Inc. Copying or distributing in print or electronic forms without written permission of Idea Group Inc. is prohibited.

the sufferer and the people who wish to interact with them (this is exemplified by the much larger number of events in the Paralympics in Athens in 2004, when compared with the Olympics a few years before);

- gender;
- ethnicity;
- race;
- color;
- sexual orientation/preference;
- socio-economic status;
- religion; and
- cultural background.

These "dimensions" are not, of course, discrete. Ethnicity, color, race, religion and cultural background are often perceived as closely interlinked and, in addition, the different aspects can be combined, with each combination potentially introducing new issues. This does, of course, mean that "diversity" cannot conceivably be addressed as a single, teachable subject.

As noted, different aspects of diversity are frequently regarded as being closely interlinked (e.g., the Muslim=Arab=terrorist misconception which has apparently been prevalent in the Western Hemisphere following September 11, 2001). This is an example of people's underlying assumptions (prejudices), which are often unrecognised, and which make it more difficult to address diversity within the curriculum. As is the case for most sections of "civilized society," most students (in European universities at least) do not want to acknowledge their prejudices and will tend to avoid any discussion that questions, or even brings out, their underlying beliefs. Sometimes they aren't even aware that the views they express are indeed prejudices, so ingrained in their culture has the prejudice become. This poses a very substantial problem for conventional lecture-based teaching, since it is likely that students will not "hear" ideas that challenge these prejudices and that different teaching techniques need to be sought. Any amount of telling students that a prejudice is indeed just that and, at the very least, misguided, will not have the impact that forcing them to confront the prejudice will have. Likewise, for minority groups, or individual students who have coped with a particular disability or cultural difference, it may sometimes seem too great an effort to overcome the prejudices of the majority. However, when working in small teams, and

Copyright © 2006, Idea Group Inc. Copying or distributing in print or electronic forms without written permission of Idea Group Inc. is prohibited.

particularly when the team is tackling an open ended problem, as is the case in the OEGP approach advocated in this chapter, diversity has to be accommodated or the team will fail. As an example, if a deaf or blind student joins a team, there is a significant communication challenge which would not occur (for the other students) if each individual was working on their own, since the deaf or blind student has to be communicated with by the remainder of the team and vice versa. As the authors may report from personal experience, all of the team exhibit both pleasure and pride when they have managed to overcome the problems and deliver a successful solution to the task that has been set. This is, of course, rewarding, not just for the teams concerned but also for their teacher. Furthermore, the other teams see that these difficulties are not insuperable and are, therefore, helped to consider diversity issues. The educational effect is enhanced if the team containing the person with disabilities out-performs both expectations and some of the other teams. As will be discussed in later examples, unexpectedly good performances from teams which face "diversity" issues does happen more often than would be expected by chance in the OEGP setting. Research reported by Gurin, Nagda, and Lopez (2004) confirms this observation, showing that confronting diversity issues, and encouraging the formation of diverse groups, provide a significant advantage to students and prepares them for a world which is not homogenous and for cultures which increasingly are having to recognize they are not homogenous.

The challenge of including diversity in any curriculum is further compounded with IT because the subject is, in itself, ultimately diverse, reaching virtually all fields of human activity, and this coverage is still in the process of expanding. Logically, this means that there is a matrix (probably multi-dimensional) covering all of the dimensions of diversity and all of the different applications of IT to be considered if diversity is to be fully "covered," using a conventional teaching approach.

Of course, no curriculum ever attempts to cover more than a small subset of the possible issues in, and applications of, IT and, similarly, it would not be possible to address all of the possible diversity issues. This would apparently mean that a (very small) selection of the possible issues/dimensions related to diversity would be all that would be covered within the curriculum, which raises two questions:

- Which of the aspects (dimensions/issues) within "diversity" should be covered?

Copyright © 2006, Idea Group Inc. Copying or distributing in print or electronic forms without written permission of Idea Group Inc. is prohibited.

- What expectations can there be for "transferability" of knowledge and understanding if the students subsequently encounter a different aspect of diversity or even if they encounter the same aspect but in a different context?

In pedagogic discussions, the issue of transferability occurs more frequently in connection with skills than with knowledge but, in IT, the important thing for the workplace is the ability to apply knowledge effectively to the particular situation that is being addressed. It is the authors' opinion that, like the ability to display a particular skill, this ability to apply knowledge is closely related to self-belief/self-confidence (knowing that "you" can do something because you have done the same thing, or something very similar, before). As will be illustrated by examples, the advantage of the OEGP approach is that students may try out their solutions and approaches in a realistic, but actually protected and safe, environment. Their successes give them confidence and they learn how to adjust their failures so that future attempts can turn these into successes too. With an OEGP approach, responsibility for both successes and failures is focused on the group rather than the educator, but are shared by the members of the group who are encouraged to reflect on the processes they used as well as their output and results. Since an OEGP is a joint effort, it is much easier to survey critically what was positive about it and where things went wrong because the group can do that as a whole and can support one another. It is much harder for a single student working on their own to be self-critical because the "blame" would be all their own. Thus, it is much easier for the individual to find excuses (and other people to blame). The OEGP approach, by sharing responsibility within the group and with the teacher, encourages a self-evaluative approach which aids learning. This is much more typical and realistic in terms of human endeavour in the real world. Very few people work in complete isolation. They are usually part of a team; thus, learning skills that will help them to work in a team and manage teams is a useful experience for undergraduates. The open-ended nature of the tasks is also beneficial in this respect, so the groups are not trying to find the "right answer." Instead, they are trying to identify both important issues and possible ways to address these issues.

Copyright © 2006, Idea Group Inc. Copying or distributing in print or electronic forms without written permission of Idea Group Inc. is prohibited.

Problem Based Learning and Constructivism

Problem Based Learning (PBL) is a well-established approach designed to encourage students to acquire skills in deploying and reinforcing their existing knowledge while simultaneously learning and integrating new material (Kolb, 1984; Kolmos & Algreen-Ussing, 2001). PBL may be seen as a form of constructivism: learning as an active acquisition of ideas and an assimilation of those ideas into a framework that the learner either already possesses or forms as a result of their experiences. It is not the accumulation of facts; rather constructivism requires learners to be active in their relationship with the material to be learned, and seeks to bring about the modification of learner behavior (and thereby to overcome existing prejudices). Setting problems and asking the learner to solve them is perceived to be an effective way to achieve goals of this type, which provides the link between PBL and constructivism.

Brooks and Brooks (1999) recognized that the constructive approach presupposes the existence of a good problem that needs solving by the learner. They define a good problem as one that:

- requires students to make and test at least one prediction;
- can be solved using only equipment and facilities that are available;
- is realistically complex;
- benefits from a group effort; and
- is seen as relevant and interesting by students.

The questions associated with designing problems that are suitable for encouraging learning in particular topics will be discussed in more detail using examples that relate to diversity.

Another way of viewing the constructivist learning environment is to see it as one that encourages sharing between students and between educators and students. The educator ceases to be the source of all wisdom and knowledge and, instead takes on more the role of mentor than instructor. Also the success of the outcome moves from being the responsibility of the educator to being a shared responsibility between the students and the educator. In this context, Copley (1992) suggested that constructivism expects the teacher to act as a facilitator "whose main function is to help students become active participants in their learning and make meaningful connections between prior knowledge,

Copyright © 2006, Idea Group Inc. Copying or distributing in print or electronic forms without written permission of Idea Group Inc. is prohibited.

new knowledge, and the processes involved in learning." This also has the effect of changing the learning experience for the teacher from one of treading a single, well-known path to, at the very least, that of helping each group find a suitable route to the destination and, sometimes (such as when a specific diversity issue affects the group), it may require a new path to be created (i.e., research). In conventional teaching/learning environments, although much of the material students meet is new to them, this is not (usually) the case for the teacher. An OEGP, as advocated in this chapter, may often be a way of creating a much more exciting and fulfilling environment for the teacher too. With an OEGP, both students and teacher are carrying out a piece of work, the result of which may be wholly or partially unknown. Even with an educationally and culturally homogeneous cohort of students, the differing prior life experiences and personalities of the students will inevitably mean that each group will tackle the task in differing ways, focusing on different aspects at any one moment. As the groups become more diverse, or as diversity issues are explicitly introduced, the approach taken by the groups is likely to diverge further, increasing the interest for the staff and students alike, and encouraging each group to find their own way of tackling the task (plagiarism, which is typically a serious concern for coursework exercises, has not been a problem for any of the authors when using the OEGP approach).

As noted in the list above, Brooks and Brooks (1999) identified the need to utilize group working as an important aspect of choosing a suitable problem. The following sub-section amplifies the discussion of the concepts underlying the OEGP approach. In the context of this sub-section, an OEGP offers a form of constructivist/problem-based education that uses group project work as a primary catalyst for learning, which should be particularly suitable for encouraging students to think about diversity issues.

Open Ended Group Projects

The authors have been using a development of the constructivist/PBL method, that they call the OEGP (Open Ended Group Project) approach, in their separate universities for a considerable time (in one case the 2003/4 academic year marked the 25th anniversary of its original introduction into the curriculum). The approach has proved extremely successful in each of the institutions and is credited by students and by industrial contacts alike as being a major factor in ensuring that students can be "up and running" quickly when they join an employer, either on an internship while they are at university, or after they have

Copyright © 2006, Idea Group Inc. Copying or distributing in print or electronic forms without written permission of Idea Group Inc. is prohibited.

completed their degree. The perceived value of the approach is illustrated by the fact that major employers (e.g., Accenture, Citigroup, IBM) offer prizes for the most successful group performances, since this gives them the opportunity to come and talk with all the students and encourage them to consider employment at their organizations as interns or full employees. The details of the OEGP approach vary considerably, not just between the authors/institutions, but also from year to year within an institution, since they are dependent on many factors, the most important of which are:

1. Position within the academic program—which year and, possibly, where within the year (e.g., first or second semester);

2. Size of the student cohort—a cohort of 25 may offer opportunities which are very different from a cohort of 250 (however, the approach has been used successfully at both these levels);

3. Length of time the OEGP will run—this can be anything from one or two weeks to a full academic year—and the number of simultaneous activities (is the OEGP the only thing the students will be doing or is it just a "part time" occupation);

4. Academic credit offered for the work (e.g., as a fraction of the credit required to pass the year)—although the amount of credit is generally related to the amount of time and effort the students are expected to spend, there have been occasions when the approach has been used successfully with no credit at all being offered (the students are expected, and do, use it to gain feedback and as an opportunity for very low risk experimentation) and, quite frequently, the students have to be actively discouraged from putting in a disproportionate amount of effort compared to the credit involved;

5. Method by which groups are formed and managed—in some cases both the composition of the student groups and the management structures that are to be used will be prescribed by the educators, in others, it may be advantageous to allow the students to form their own groups and decide how to manage the process for themselves (in part, this depends on the educational objectives but also, asking students to form their own groups and decide on their own management structures transfers the responsibility for the success of the group to the students themselves, which may increase motivation and group cohesion);

Copyright © 2006, Idea Group Inc. Copying or distributing in print or electronic forms without written permission of Idea Group Inc. is prohibited.

6.   Type of task chosen as the problem—as implied by the name given to the approach, the task has to be open ended (i.e., to have several different aspects which the students might choose to focus on, with no obvious, clear, single, solution) but this still leaves a very large number of possibilities even when combined with the need, in this case, for it to be related to IT (e.g., it may vary from evaluating existing systems to designing and/or constructing new systems, and the systems could be almost anything—robot footballers playing as a team, support systems for improving patient care in hospitals, project management support systems);

7.   Interrelationship between the groups—this can be collaborative or competitive since in some cases the groups are all asked to work together to achieve the task that has been set, while in others every group is set the same basic task (because the tasks are open ended, this does not mean that they all do the same thing; each group forms its own perception of what is needed); the groups "compete" to achieve the best outcome, in at least one case it has been both collaborative within the groups at the institution and competitive with groups working at different institutions; and

8.   Educational "objectives" or "intended learning outcomes"—the focus may be quite restricted, such as reinforcing a particular aspect of previously taught material, to very broad, such as: gaining confidence, encouraging reflection and forming frameworks to integrate existing knowledge. However, there are usually multiple objectives which include elements of both the narrow and the broad and the acquisition of new knowledge and skills.

Of course, all of the factors are closely interrelated, although any one of them could be preeminent in a particular case. If, for example, it was decided to use the OEGP approach to introduce a particular diversity issue (say user interfaces for the blind and partially sighted) to a cohort of first year students where only a fortnight of time was available for the exercise, the educational objectives would probably be more limited and more strictly drawn, than if the task were to get final year students to think about a range of diversity issues and a full academic year was available. Similarly, given the same educational objective, the task is likely to be specific to the chosen issue (e.g., design or evaluate interfaces to assist a person with a specific disability to accomplish something).

This section has identified the challenge of including diversity in the curriculum and has explained the potential of the OEGP approach to overcome the

Copyright © 2006, Idea Group Inc. Copying or distributing in print or electronic forms without written permission of Idea Group Inc. is prohibited.

challenge. The section has also provided the pedagogic background for the OEGP approach, relating it to the educational philosophy of constructivism and the well-established, problem-based learning approach.

The following section of the chapter introduces a number of examples of the OEGP approach in action, illustrating how various aspects of diversity have been tackled by groups of students working on tasks that the authors have set.

Using the OEGP Approach to Accommodate Diversity: Some Examples

The previous section explained the difficulties of using conventional educational techniques for getting students at university to consider the wide range of diversity issues. It also explained why the OEGP approach, with its emphasis on getting students to take shared responsibility for their education, might be an appropriate way of including diversity in the IT curriculum.

This section uses examples of OEGP based coursework undertaken by the authors in their separate universities to show how various aspects of diversity have been addressed in practice. The examples are also used to explain some of the benefits that the OEGP approach offers for educators who adopt it.

The following uses further exemplar scenarios to examine some possible ways in which the OEGP approach could be used to address other diversity issues.

Examples of How the OEGP has Addressed Diversity Issues

Before introducing the actual examples, it should be noted that in none of these cases was "learning about a particular diversity issue," a specific educational objective for the educators concerned. In each case, the diversity issue arose naturally because of the inherent diversity in the student cohort that was being educated. The examples do, however, show that:

- The OEGP approach does accommodate potential problems caused by student diversity;
- Some learning/understanding was achieved by the students concerned, i.e., OEGP may be an effective approach for encouraging student learning for at least some diversity issues;

Copyright © 2006, Idea Group Inc. Copying or distributing in print or electronic forms without written permission of Idea Group Inc. is prohibited.

- In at least some cases, the learning was not limited to the group that was coping with the diversity issue, i.e., there is transferability of learning/understanding between groups; and

- There is some evidence of transferability from one diversity issue to another.

The examples are grouped into three subsections:

1. Cultural, color and ethnic differences (religious differences would almost certainly also have been covered but no data was collected) related to other examples involving students with different educational (knowledge, skill) and motivational backgrounds;

2. Disability (two examples: one involving deaf students and one involving blind students are chosen as representative); and

3. Gender—more specifically, overcoming differences in confidence and leadership qualities between the genders (interestingly, sexual preference/orientation has never been an issue in practice even though there have been gay, lesbian and transsexual students in some of the cohorts).

Examples of Cultural, Color and Ethnic differences

The first group of examples under this heading focuses on "cultural" differences as being simply differences in the background and skill sets of the students involved and show the different sorts of approaches that have been taken by the authors. This is intended to help the reader obtain some feeling for what the OEGP approach is and the sorts of projects it may cover. This is followed by some specific examples of projects where cultural, color or ethnic differences between the individuals could potentially have caused difficulties but where these difficulties did not materialize in practice. Evidence that the students gained insights into the diversity issues involved is reported in the examples.

The first example was designed to enthuse and challenge the students, requiring them to use a wide range of skills and to collaborate amongst themselves and with other students taking a different program of study at the same institution, but to compete against teams from other organizations. The task was to build a team of soccer playing robots to take part in the Robocup world championships. For about one third of the year this was the only task the students were

Copyright © 2006, Idea Group Inc. Copying or distributing in print or electronic forms without written permission of Idea Group Inc. is prohibited.

expected to undertake, and for part of that time they were working with students on a mechanical engineering program who assisted them in building the robots (Daniels & Asplund, 2000). This project was run for several years and, in the later years, the team of robots which the group built that year (there were, of course, different students undertaking the task each year) did take part in the championships, and even win some of its matches. The project achieved its objectives of motivating the students and of getting them to be both industrious and inventive. It also helped them appreciate the need to understand the "culture" in which they were expected to work. In this case the culture was the set of rules and restrictions governing the competition which evolved each year and set new challenges for each cohort undertaking the task. Interestingly, in the context of this chapter, the project has now been replaced by one involving the design and construction of rescue robots since that was perceived to be more gender neutral. Observations that the nature of an assignment can affect the engagement students display towards a subject have also been noted by other educators (Wilson, 2004).

A second example also involves all of the students involved cooperating to achieve a shared goal. In this case the students are studying either Human Factors, Human Computer Interaction or Usability Engineering as one of several modules that they are taking at the same time. The cohort is split into teams and they are expected to produce a single "product" between them. This usually consists in developing a piece of software with different interfaces, and then carrying out a joint evaluation with volunteer subjects. The students have to work in teams to produce their subset of the piece of software, and then they have to cooperate between the teams in order to develop the evaluation material and carry out the survey. (Faulkner & Culwin, 2000). The task, involving both building software and running a survey, makes them address questions of their own skill base—which students are skilled at solving software problems or at arranging schedules or are "good" at approaching potential volunteers. The breadth of tasks means that a wide mix of abilities is needed, and all kinds of student backgrounds are catered for. The OEGP approach thus allows the strengths of the student body to be used to the best advantage by providing very diverse opportunities. It also encourages the students to identify potential weaknesses so that these can be avoided.

In contrast to the first two, in the third example the cohort undertaking the coursework is itself diverse, consisting (in 2004/5) of students drawn from seven degree programs. The students also come from a very wide range of cultural and ethnic backgrounds. The majority of the approximately 200

Copyright © 2006, Idea Group Inc. Copying or distributing in print or electronic forms without written permission of Idea Group Inc. is prohibited.

students (numbers have varied from 150 to 250 over six years) is White European (mostly UK-based, although with representatives from most of the EU and Scandinavian countries) but there are also substantial numbers of students with Asian, African, Afro-Caribbean and Chinese backgrounds. Here, the primary educational objective is to get each team of students to use the knowledge and skills that they have acquired to work with their "clients" to first understand the clients' requirements, and then to design, build and demonstrate a suitable support system. To assist the students in discovering the requirements, the educators take the roles of departmental administrators preparing timetables, who need to obtain rooms in which lectures, tutorials, seminars and laboratories may take place, and university administrators who allocate the rooms for such. Secondary objectives include getting the students to reflect on what they have learnt from the experience (Newman, Dawson, & Parks, 2000) and to draw on the range of skills that are available within the group to accomplish the overall task without unnecessary effort, since it represents only one sixth of the work that they are expected to undertake. A number of sub-tasks are specified, involving deliverables on which the teams get feedback. The students are advised to form teams with as much diversity as possible, but are actually left to choose their own teams. In the first year this task was set and the advice to form "multi-cultural" teams was given, most students ignored the advice and stayed with other students taking the same degree program. However, as time has passed, the success of the "mixed" teams (in terms of marks achieved against effort required) in one year has encouraged greater mixing in subsequent years. For the last two years, the majority of teams have been mixed and, in the current year, even though they have only completed one of the three deliverables, several of the teams that were drawn from a single degree program are already saying (in their evaluation reports) that they now realize they should have included people with different skills in their teams. As already mentioned, there has always been considerable ethnic and cultural diversity in the cohort but, with the exception of some of the students with Asian backgrounds, they have always tended to integrate into mixed teams anyway, without any pressure from the educators. Generally, the performances of the teams that do have a good cultural mix is better than the performance of teams with a homogeneous structure, probably because the prejudices do not go unchallenged. However, no systematic studies have been carried out, so this represents a qualitative rather than a quantitative assessment.

A fourth example is specifically aimed at getting students to consider, and overcome, cultural differences. The students in this case are placed into teams

Copyright © 2006, Idea Group Inc. Copying or distributing in print or electronic forms without written permission of Idea Group Inc. is prohibited.

which span two countries in different continents, introducing potential problems of physical and temporal separation as well as different natural languages (Swedish & US English). Each group is composed of approximately equal numbers of students from both countries, and they are asked to undertake a task which requires collaboration between the two halves of the team (all of the groups are asked to undertake the same task). This approach forces the students to think about and, as the success of the students shows, cope with the difficulties of talking to people who live in the different countries, are in different time zones and who have different cultural expectations and attitudes, as well as a different language. As reported in the student feedback from the module, the Swedish students have found the experiences very rewarding, and employers are pleased to have graduates who have already had the experience of cultural diversity before they start work (Last, Almstrum, Daniels, Erickson, & Klein, 2000).

Examples of Disability

Two examples are given in this subsection, one relates to deaf students, the other to blind and partially-sighted students. These examples are representative. In other cases, students with different physical or psychological challenges (e.g., cerebral palsy, paraplegia, acute anxiety) have been successfully incorporated in teams which have subsequently completed the OEGP task. In every case, both the individual and the team appear to have benefited from the experience by gaining confidence and by becoming more open in their approach. However, it should be noted that in all the cases, the students with the disability were fairly determined individuals, otherwise they would probably not have started their respective university programs.

Deaf Students

In this example, two deaf students were part of a class of about 30 first-year students carrying out a group project. When the students divided into groups, the two deaf students and their communicator were left unassigned. The deaf students had no hearing friends in the student cohort, and the communicator thought their problems necessitated their working separately. The educator insisted that the two deaf students were assigned to a group. Initially, the group thus formed was nervous: the hearing students were not sure what to expect and

Copyright © 2006, Idea Group Inc. Copying or distributing in print or electronic forms without written permission of Idea Group Inc. is prohibited.

the deaf students were worried about working with their hearing counterparts. However, the deaf students proved to have skills that were very useful to the team, and the hearing students soon learned how to communicate effectively with them. The deaf students, in turn, practised speaking aloud and were not permitted to sign unless they also spoke aloud. In other words ,both deaf and hearing students had to learn "manners" for this situation. The deaf students became more confident about speaking in public since this was something they had never had to do previously. The hearing students learned new communication skills (and some signing) which gave them confidence in tackling unfamiliar situations. The deaf students also made new friends and integrated better with their cohort to the extent that for the second OEGP in which they took part, they wanted to be in different teams from each other. They now knew they could make friends with hearing students and vice versa.

Blind and Partially-Sighted Students

The experiences in this case relate to four blind students: one totally blind, two with the ability to detect light but very little other visual ability (both of these two had "seeing eye" dogs) and one partially-sighted individual, who can read magnified print. The four students were in different cohorts, but all of them undertook group project work in their second year at university, where the students were in a situation where they were expected to form their own groups, and the group project work contributed one sixth of the work that the students were expected to undertake in a semester.

The two students with seeing eye dogs, one male and one female, were similar in that they were both direct entrants into the second year of the university course, transferring after successfully completing their first year at a different university. They were both determined and bright individuals, the male eventually proved to be one of the three most academically successful students in a cohort of about 50, and the female had transferred universities because her sighted brother was starting the first year at university and their parents were dead so she felt that she needed to support him. Despite having to make friends before they could find a group, both of these individuals used their considerable personal and social skills to first make friends, then find a group, but they both managed it without requiring any help from the educators. From observation and the personal reports written by the students in the groups as part of the assessment process, both of these students made above average contributions to their respective groups. The female student became group leader, as well as

Copyright © 2006, Idea Group Inc. Copying or distributing in print or electronic forms without written permission of Idea Group Inc. is prohibited.

carrying out more than her share of the task, while the male became "chief analyst/programmer" for the group. Both used their abilities to listen to, and understand, what was being said to very good effect, and their groups had fewer misunderstandings of the requirements than most of the other groups.

The partially-sighted student had worked with a totally blind fellow student in the first year, but that individual had not satisfied the first year assessment criteria. These two students had done everything together in their first year, and had not integrated very much with the rest of the cohort. This meant that the partially-blind student was worried, before the module commenced, about how he would be able to find a group and how he would work within the group. At a meeting with the staff managing the module, it was agreed that he would like to find a group of his own, but if he could not do so the educators would find a way to get him placed with a group. This reassurance was sufficient to give him the confidence to find a group. Once in the group, he contributed well, so much so that by the end of the project, other group members were turning to him when they needed support. The final, and most recent, example involved the totally-blind student who has a helper to escort him between lectures and someone to take notes for him during the lectures. He, naturally, was extremely concerned about how he would manage to join and work with a group, since he had not mixed very much with the other students. However, he was reassured when he was told about the successful outcomes for the other blind students, as reported above, and he did, in practice, find a group very early compared with most of the other students. Furthermore, because of his involvement, the group has decided to consider disability issues as part of their project work and have sought, and gained, permission to do this.

Summary of Experiences with Disabilities

The overall message both from these sets of experience and from experiences with other students with different sorts of physical and mental disabilities (e.g., paraplegic, cerebral palsy, agoraphobia) is that the most important factors in getting a successful outcome are the determination of the student with the disability to contribute to a group and the initial willingness of the other members of the group to accept them. Once these steps are taken, there seem to be fewer difficulties in groups that exhibit significant diversity than in the groups which are apparently homogeneous.

Copyright © 2006, Idea Group Inc. Copying or distributing in print or electronic forms without written permission of Idea Group Inc. is prohibited.

Gender

The OEGP approach naturally puts greater emphasis on collaboration rather than competition, since the task is intentionally larger than can be accomplished by any individual and, by being open-ended, requires all of the group to work together to agree what is to be done and to contribute to doing it. Underwood (2003) suggests that women fare better and feel more comfortable in a cooperative situation, whereas men prefer to compete and both Yieron and Reinhart (1995) and Underwood argue that a collaborative learning environment may well be more successful at drawing female students into the computing community. If this is correct, then the OEGP approach should naturally provide a more comfortable environment for female students. The experiences of the authors certainly bear this out, although it is also necessary to observe that the female students are quite as diverse as their male counterparts and not all female students are shy, retiring or lack confidence in their technical skills. Some of the female students do, indeed, seem to lack confidence and defer to the male students in the groups. However, some of the female students, particularly those in programs where there is a high percentage of males, seem to relish the competitive element and are very likely to take the lead in their group. Nevertheless, one of the important issues in most university computer science programs is the need to encourage more female students to come into the program and to give the female students who do come a greater confidence in their own ability to contribute effectively. The two examples given below focus on this and report experiences where the situation has been adjusted to successfully encourage the female students.

Example 1: Using the Rapporteur Role to Encourage Female Students

For many years, computing has been very much a male preserve, and many of us teaching in the areas of computing and Information Technology have been accustomed to classes which consisted mostly of male students. With the introduction of courses based in Information Technology, this picture has shifted. Classes in Information Technology, and those which cover the "softer" aspects of computing, may often consist of a 50-50 gender split, or even have a predominance of female students. However, women in these classes quite often show a tendency to let their male colleagues take the lead, and are frequently less confident about their abilities, particularly in software development. Members of a cohort who are lacking in confidence or feel shy about

Copyright © 2006, Idea Group Inc. Copying or distributing in print or electronic forms without written permission of Idea Group Inc. is prohibited.

taking part in whole class discussions usually find that the smaller groups required by the OEGP approach provide a much easier place to air their views and to learn to take a more active part. The OEGP naturally requires communication within the group and with the tutor. Where the OEGP involves the whole cohort working together rather than in competition, teams also need to communicate with other teams. One of the authors has found that appointing a student as the rapporteur for the group encourages that individual to act as an administrator for the team they are a part of. They are then also expected to communicate on behalf of their team with other teams. Female students are quite often encouraged by the teams to take on this administrative role, and they will often accept it because it gives them the opportunity to "care" for their team, only to discover a little way down the road that they have more of a communication and leadership role than they envisaged. Gradually, even the shyest are encouraged to take a more active part and this builds their confidence. Making use of, and enhancing, the collaborative nature of the OEGP approach in this way encourages the female students and, quite often, a female student will emerge as one of the spokespersons and leaders for the cohort, and will manage it, making decisions and delegating as necessary. A subtle use of this tactic may encourage female students to take on technical roles as well, which, sadly, they are often reluctant to do. In one case, where a mixed team involving both males and females was deputed to take on the testing and bug reporting, a young women who initially claimed that she would be technically incapable of carrying out the task ended up taking over responsibility for the leadership and organization of the group, after gaining confidence in the rapporteur role. This illustrates the effectiveness of the OEGP approach in helping the students to discover that they possess skills that they did not anticipate that they possessed. This typically happens when the student recognizes that to complete a task the group will need to deploy a skill, or gain knowledge, that no-one in the group appears to possess. The concern for the success of the group overcomes the confidence barrier and leads to the individual gaining the skill or the knowledge in order to ensure that the required task is completed (Faulkner & Culwin, 1999).

Example 2: Using OEGP to Assist in the Recruitment of Female Students

As noted in the previous example, the OEGP approach emphasizes collaboration rather than competition. One of the authors has also found that a suitable

Copyright © 2006, Idea Group Inc. Copying or distributing in print or electronic forms without written permission of Idea Group Inc. is prohibited.

choice of the task for OEGP project work can be used to attract more female students onto a particular module within a degree program. In this case, the OEGP was based on the idea of providing IT solutions for a hospital. The caring, social responsibility aspects of this project proved to be particularly interesting for a section of the female student population, who felt that their skills were particular needful for that type of project. (Daniels, Jansson, Kavathatzopoulos, & Petre, 2000). The success of this choice of task in attracting more female students also encouraged a change in the choice of the OEGP task on another module. As mentioned earlier, in that case the task was changed from the overtly competitive, and primarily male-oriented, world of Robocup (involving the design, construction and deployment of soccer-playing robots) to the design, construction and deployment of rescue robots.

Summary: The OEGP Approach, an Effective Way of Incorporating and Capitalizing on Diversity

The examples that have been given in this subsection, and the many more that could have been given, all show that the OEGP approach accommodates diversity within groups very effectively. The authors also observe that not only do the individual students within groups benefit by working together, but students within other, less diverse groups, may also begin to see the advantages that are offered by having diversity within the group.

The next subsection briefly examines some ways in which the OEGP approach might be used to specifically address particular diversity issues within the curriculum. It also identifies some of the research questions associated with the OEGP approach.

What Next

The previous sections of the chapter have presented a case for the OEGP approach as a very effective way of accommodating issues of diversity that occur naturally amongst students studying in an undergraduate degree program. It has also suggested that there is some evidence that the observed advantages of diversity within a particular group leads at least some of the students in other less-diverse groups to see the advantages of diversity.

Copyright © 2006, Idea Group Inc. Copying or distributing in print or electronic forms without written permission of Idea Group Inc. is prohibited.

This section addresses the question:

"How might the OEGP approach be used to explicitly include some aspects of diversity in the curriculum?"

It uses two examples to show how the approach could be used to address specific issues in diversity. It then identifies a number of research questions whose answers might help improve the uptake of the approach (encouraging staff to try the OEGP approach has been, and remains, a major challenge for the authors).

Designing a Module Based on the OEGP Approach to Help Students Reflect on Particular Aspects of Diversity

As noted earlier in the chapter, the design of a module which will use the OEGP approach to help students gain skills, new knowledge or integrate and reinforce existing knowledge depends on a lot of interrelated factors, many of which will actually be constrained in real situations. This subsection identifies two possible "diversity objectives," and discusses possible module designs that would be likely to achieve the desired educational outcome based on the previous experiences of the authors.

Example 1: Getting Students to Consider People with a Visual Impairment When Designing Generally Accessible Web Sites

Obviously, as described in the title, this would be a partial goal for the module since the task itself could be chosen to meet other educational objectives. Depending on these other educational objectives and the constraints imposed by the existing degree program elements, it might be appropriate to specify a particular subject for the Web site (this could vary from "car sales" to "database design," depending on the students involved) and then add the need to consider people with visual impairments into the constraints. A typical requirement for the groups could be: "demonstrate how the interface would support individuals with, and without, visual impairment" (asking groups to provide a demonstration of what they have done is one effective way of both observing how the group works and of giving a format in which feedback may be given to the group

Copyright © 2006, Idea Group Inc. Copying or distributing in print or electronic forms without written permission of Idea Group Inc. is prohibited.

on what they have done). If it was desirable to encourage the students to give more thought to the issues involved then an additional requirement, a report could be specified (e.g., list the issues that you have considered and describe how each issue has been addressed in your design). If still greater emphasis on the issue was required (and more time was available), then the students could, for example, be asked to design a set of test criteria for the interfaces assess the interfaces provided by other groups and provide a report on their findings.

Example 2: Accommodating Diversity—Designing for Customers in Different Countries

This example could address differences in culture and assumptions as well as differences in natural language. Again, the diversity issues would only be one of several aspects which the module would be addressing (this is a very general comment, diversity is only meaningful in a wider context and, the authors would strongly recommend, it should be addressed in this way). Similar examples have actually been used by two of the authors to help students in Sweden, the US and the UK consider these issues. The Swedish and US students were asked to produce and implement appropriate designs, while the students in the UK carried out evaluations on the designs. In this case, the students doing the designing were producing Web sites and were told to produce sites in English, the challenge being to make the sites accessible to the very wide range of cultures represented in the evaluation cohort in the UK university.

General: Designing for Diversity

More generally, the above two examples will hopefully illustrate the idea that any specific diversity issue could be incorporated in a module which uses the OEGP approach. This can be accomplished quite straightforwardly by adding a deliverable which asks each student group to design for, demonstrate and report on how they had addressed the chosen diversity issue. However, it must be noted that there are limits to the number of issues that may be added to any single OEGP exercise, since it is necessary to ensure that the "reward" (usually marks) for each aspect of the exercise does not become so small that the students can safely omit one or more of the aspects without jeopardizing their overall success.

Copyright © 2006, Idea Group Inc. Copying or distributing in print or electronic forms without written permission of Idea Group Inc. is prohibited.

Deploying the OEGP Approach: Associated Research Questions

The most important research questions, as far as the authors are concerned are probably: "How can teachers be encouraged to try the approach?" and "Why is uptake so limited if the approach is as successful as our observations lead us to believe?" These questions will be discussed in the conclusion. In this subsection, more limited questions will be posed which might be possible to answer via experimental design.

1.   Measuring the skills or knowledge that is obtained and the degree of retention when compared with alternative teaching methods.

It is a fairly common (anecdotal) observation that students learning for an examination seem to have forgotten what they learned by the time the examination is over. In contrast, experience gained from actually carrying out work for oneself and learning from one's own mistakes tends to be retained. The OEGP approach is intended to provide a safe and support-ive environment in which the students may try things out, make mistakes and learn from them. Measuring how much is actually learned and retained and being able to demonstrate this objectively would be very valuable. A longitudinal study of a particular student group to see whether the knowledge and skills are retained over time would be particularly valu-able.

2.   Time spent by staff and students when undertaking an OEGP.

This question addresses two different questions that are frequently asked, and also two concerns that are often expressed by staff who have not experienced a module which uses the OEGP approach. The questions are: "How much time do the students spend on a module based on the OEGP approach?" and "How much time do the educators spend on a module based on the OEGP approach?" The concerns that are frequently expressed are that both staff and students will spend a disproportionate time on the module and, conversely, that the approach allows some students to "get away with doing very little." If a suitable experiment could be designed, the results obtained by studying the two questions would ideally be linked with the outcomes from the previous questions to see whether the learning achieved by the students was at least commensurate

Copyright © 2006, Idea Group Inc. Copying or distributing in print or electronic forms without written permission of Idea Group Inc. is prohibited.

with the effort that was put in or, as the authors believe, proportionately greater.

3.   Obstacles, real and perceived, in addressing diversity issues using the OEGP approach.

4.   Designing experiments to assess these questions in a way to avoid disadvantaging some students.

The traditional experimental designs require comparable sets of experimental subjects to be "processed" using different techniques. The results would then be compared. However, when the subjects are students studying for a degree and the experimental procedures are different teaching methods intended to help them with that study, the concept of "double blind" testing, such as is used to eliminate bias in drug tests, seems completely impossible to undertake. Even if the students could be split into two (or more) comparable groups and each group could be subjected to different teaching methods, it would not be easy to prevent knowledge and skill transfer between the groups outside the structured teaching environment. Furthermore, if one of the groups performed significantly better than the others then the students in the groups that performed worse would have a prime facie case that they were discriminated against and entitled to compensation.

Conclusion

Starting from the premise that education should have a role to play in the development of well-adjusted citizens and workforces of the increasingly diverse societies of the future, it would be reasonable to ask how diversity may be incorporated into the educational curriculum. This chapter has suggested that the OEGP approach would be an effective way of including a consideration of some diversity issues in the university curriculum. However, given the claimed success of the OEGP approach for dealing with a variety of educational and social questions, it might seem strange that the use of the OEGP is not more widespread than it apparently is. Several possible concerns are discussed below, but it is also possible to consider that a fear of diversity is one reason for the slowness in the uptake of the OEGP approach. University teaching, particularly in science, has traditionally been based round the lecturing paradigm, and most of the methods of assessing the performance of lecturers are

Copyright © 2006, Idea Group Inc. Copying or distributing in print or electronic forms without written permission of Idea Group Inc. is prohibited.

geared to the lecturing approach. Using the OEGP approach inevitably means that some of the assessment elements which are used to decide whether a lecturer is competent (e.g., was the lecturer well prepared, did they have a plan for the lecture, did the lecture have an appropriate structure, etc.) will not be fulfilled and, therefore, it is inherently risky and may threaten career progression. This worry may only be addressed by overcoming the prejudices and gaining acceptance that using the OEGP approach as a supplement to the more conventional lecturing approach does bring benefits in learning and retention.

Other concerns are rather easier to address since they are not institutionalized in the assessment procedures which are prescribed for the educators.

To begin with, one of the biggest reasons for resistance to the use of the OEGP comes from both staff and students, and that is that the OEGP cannot be assessed fairly. Many authors have commented on the seemingly difficult task of deciding who gets what and coping with "free wheelers.". All three authors have addressed these problems in different ways, and although anyone using the OEGP would not deny that there appears to be a problem, it is not insurmountable. One technique that may be used is for the teams to have regular monitoring meetings with the tutor running the OEGP. This allows the tutor to ensure that all students are working consistently and doing their fair share. Logbooks, or minutes, may be kept by the teams in order to ensure a record of each student's contribution. Students may be asked to "pay" their fellow team members, thus allowing them to comment on the effectiveness of their teammates and themselves. These "payments" may then be used to decide how marks might be distributed. The OEGP might of itself contribute very little to the final assessment mark. For example, students might be required to provide a final report on what they did, or the teamwork could be the process by which further work is done. One author uses the OEGP to build software which is then used in a survey. The data available from the survey is then used by the students to write a "conference paper," which forms the majority of the assessment marks. In this way, the OEGP is the process by which the work is done, but it isn't the entirety of the exercise and forms very little of the final marks. It has to be said that in the experience of the three authors, students are very honest about their contributions to the team effort. They are unwilling to let down their fellow teammates in the first place, and, if their effort has been less than 100%, they usually confess to that and agree to having their team mark component reduced. Most teams are quite realistic about what they have accomplished. Again, this very process of addressing the diverse nature of each student's contribution can help students to evaluate and assess their own contribution, and is part of the skill base for cooperative behavior.

Copyright © 2006, Idea Group Inc. Copying or distributing in print or electronic forms without written permission of Idea Group Inc. is prohibited.

There is also resistance to the OEGP because staff are unsure as to how they will manage disputes should they arise. However, if disputes are seen as part of the process of learning cooperation and compromise, then they cease to be negative and become a positive part of the learning process. When disputes occur, students need to be encouraged to find out why they have occurred and to talk through possible solutions. When people work together, there will always be disputes but these do not have to be negative and learning how to deal with them is necessary. It is better to learn in the safe environment of the OEGP than in the workplace. Staff may wish to help this process, but they should not be a substitute for the compromising that will need to occur. Students may sometimes ask for interventions from staff, and these requests will need to be dealt with firmly and kindly, but finally learning to deal with diversity is all about finding solutions that everyone can accept and students have to address that.

OEGP topics may also be problematic. It is easier by far to have a few assignment topics with clear-cut answers which can be used in rotation. Finding a practical and useful topic for an OEGP is not always easy. However, on the positive side the OEGP can be used to introduce exciting new topics which would otherwise not find their way into the educational diet and are perhaps too small for an entire module. Again, this can in its turn be a way of introducing diversity into the curriculum.

The OEGP requires the tutor to cease being an all-knowing guru who answers all questions and shows the way. The tutor engaged with an OEGP acts as a guide and a mentor, offering advice only when he or she needs to. The OEGP is a cooperative environment, not just for the students, but also for the tutor. This is particularly the case when the topic being covered by the OEGP is a research one. Some staff may find this shift from being the font of all wisdom to an adviser or signpost difficult to adjust to. Perhaps the biggest hurdle, though, is one of custom. It is not easy being a teacher. Lecturing is very like starring in a play where there is no real script and the audience is allowed to join in as they wish. For some lecturers, the OEGP seems to take away even more of the script. Thus, shifting to an OEGP approach may be seen by some as letting go of control. This is not always an easy decision to make, but the rewards for both staff and students should not be underestimated. Perhaps the best approach for anyone considering an OEGP is to try one occupying only a few weeks, or to try it first in a team-teaching environment, where there are other lecturers to offer support.

As societies confront the need to ensure the participation of all sections of their communities, so the challenge of coping with diversity will come more to the

Copyright © 2006, Idea Group Inc. Copying or distributing in print or electronic forms without written permission of Idea Group Inc. is prohibited.

forefront. Societies can legislate to ensure that all of its people have the chance to take part in all walks of life and to enjoy the fruits of society equally. However, the real challenge comes when people live with the genuine consequences of the attitudes which such legislation seeks to foster. All people, whatever their racial background, color, creed, sexuality, physical and cognitive abilities, deserve to take their place in society on an equal footing. The challenge for society is to ensure that its people are not weighed down by past prejudices. To a great extent, education can help to foster a spirit of cooperation and positive acceptance of the differences that people exhibit. It is not simply that society needs to offer people with disabilities, for example, the chance to take part in the community, but that society needs to recognize that the very differences betweens its people are the source of much strength. Homogeneity produces fewer novel and exciting solutions than heterogeneity does. When students work alone, they witness only their own backgrounds, assumptions, skills and propensities. By asking them to work with others, educators can show the citizens of the future how differences are the strength of society. The OEGP, by encouraging and fostering a spirit of mutual respect and cooperation, can help shape the workforce and citizens of the future so that the legislation which is now necessary to protect minorities will become unnecessary. The modern workforce needs to be one without harmful prejudices. By subjecting students to the problems and joys of working with diverse people now, we ensure that they are equipped to deal with the increasingly diverse nature of the society they live in and will have to work in. The OEGP can do this in a safe environment so that attitudes and practices may be tried out and evaluated.

References

Brooks, M., & Brooks, J. (1999). The courage to be constructivist. *Educational Leadership, 57*(3), 18-24.

Cantwell, W. (2004). A study of learning environments associated with computer courses: Can we teach them better? *Journal of Computing Sciences in Colleges Archive, 20*(2), 267-273.

Christie, A. (2002). Perceptions and uses of technology among adolescent boys and girls. In D. Warson & J. Andersen (Eds.), *Networking the*

Copyright © 2006, Idea Group Inc. Copying or distributing in print or electronic forms without written permission of Idea Group Inc. is prohibited.

learner, computers in education (pp. 257-265). Dordrecht: Kluwer Academic Publishers.

Copley J. (1992). The integration of teacher education and technology: A constructivist model. In D. Carey, R. Carey, D. Willis, & J. Willi (Eds.), *Technology and teacher education* (p. 681). Charlottesville, VA: AACE.

Daniels, M., & Asplund, L. (2000). Multi-level project work: A study in collaboration. In the *Proceedings of the 30th ASEE/IEEE Frontiers in Education Conference*, Kansas City, USA (pp. K4C-11 - K4C-13).

Daniels, M., Berglund, A., Pears, A., & Fincher, S. (2004). Five myths of assessment. In the *Proceedings of the 6th Australasian Computing Education Conference*, Dunedin, NZ (pp. 57-61).

Daniels, M., Faulkner, X., & Newman, I. (2002). Open ended group projects, motivating students and preparing them for the "real world." In *IEEE Proceedings of 15th Conference on Software Engineering Education and Training* (pp. 128-139). New York: IEEE.

Daniels, M., Jansson, A., Kavathatzopoulos, I., & Petre, M. (2000). Using a real-life setting to combine social and technical skills. *IEEE Frontiers in Education Conference* (pp 6-9). New York: IEEE.

Faulkner, X., & Culwin, F. (1999). From tuttles to brewsers: Integrating HCI and software engineering using the whole class project. In *Proceedings of Project '99,* University of Exeter.

Faulkner, X., & Culwin, F. (2000). Enter the usability engineer. In the *Proceedings of ITiCSE 2000*, Helsinki, Finland (pp. 61-64).

Gurin, P., Nagda, B., & Lopez, G. (2004). The benefits of diversity in education for democratic citizenship. *Journal of Social Issues, 60*(1), 17-34.

Jenkins, T. (2001). The motivation of students of programming. *Proceedings of ACM ITiCSE* (pp 53-56). Canterbury, UK: ACM Press.

Kolb, D. (1984). *Experiential learning: Experience as the source of learning and development.* New York: Prentice Hall.

Kolmos, A., & Algreen-Ussing, H. (2001). Implementing a problem-based and project organized curriculum. *Das Hochschulwesen, 1*, 15-20.

Last, M., Almstrum, V., Erickson, C., Klein, B., & Daniels, M. (2000). *Proceedings of the 5th annual SIGCSE/SIGCUE ITiCSE Conference*

Copyright © 2006, Idea Group Inc. Copying or distributing in print or electronic forms without written permission of Idea Group Inc. is prohibited.

on Innovation and Technology in Computer Science Education (pp. 128-131). Helsinki, Finland: ACM Press.

Newman, I., Dawson, R., & Parks, L. (2000). Reflecting on the process, some experiences of teaching students to think about how they produce software in a real environment. In *INSPIRE V Quality & Software Development Teaching and Training Issue* (pp. 25-36). UK: British Computer Society.

Underwood, J. (2003). Student attitudes towards socially acceptable and unacceptable group working practices. *British Journal of Psychology, 94*(3), 319-337.

Yerion, K., & Rinehart, J. (1995). Guidelines for collaborative learning in computer science, *ACM SIGCSE Bulletin archive, 27*(4), 29-34.

Copyright © 2006, Idea Group Inc. Copying or distributing in print or electronic forms without written permission of Idea Group Inc. is prohibited.

Chapter X

Attack of the Rainbow Bots:
Generating Diversity through Multi-Agent Systems

Samuel G. Collins, Towson University, USA

Goran P. Trajkovski, Towson University, USA

Abstract

Many in IT education—following on more than twenty years of multicultural critique and theory—have integrated "diversity" into their curricula. But while this is certainly laudable, there is an irony to the course "multiculturalism" has taken in the sciences in general. By submitting to a canon originating in the humanities and social sciences—no matter how progressive or well-intentioned—much of the transgressive and revolutionary character of multicultural pedagogies is lost in translation, and the insights of radical theorists become, simply, one more module to graft onto existing curricula or, at the very least, another source of authority joining or supplanting existing canons. In this essay, we feel that

Copyright © 2006, Idea Group Inc. Copying or distributing in print or electronic forms without written permission of Idea Group Inc. is prohibited.

introducing diversity into IT means generating this body of creative critique from within IT itself, in the same way multiculturalism originated in the critical, transgressive spaces between literature, cultural studies, anthropology and pedagogy. The following traces our efforts to develop isomorphic critiques from recent insights into multi-agent systems using a JAVA-based, software agent we've developed called "Izbushka."

Multiculturalism in Science

In this second century of U.S. multiculturalism, it is an impossible—and perhaps pointless—task to delineate the rapidly brachiating strains of multiculturalism extant today, a list that would have to include multiculturalisms practiced in educational settings, government and corporations. Nevertheless, Powell (2003) suggests a useful typology:

More specifically, "multiculturalism" will be defined here in at least three distinct, yet interrelated, ways: as a historical phenomena that originates with the social activism of the 1960s and 1970s, as a critique where a wide array of scholars and activists continue to demand their own cultural identity in their own terms, and as a theoretical movement that self-consciously sets out to theorize a multiplicity of cultural perspectives in what is often called a "relational" or "dialogic" context. (p. 152)

Although Powell introduces this typology by way of historicizing multiculturalism, it is also useful as a description of extant multiculturalisms.

First, we might note the demographic fact that the sciences have become more diverse over the past three decades as the percent of native-born, white-male PhDs in the sciences and engineering has declined. By 2000, a National Science Board study showed, the number of foreign-born PhDs in the sciences increased to 38%, almost doubling the percent in 1990 (NSB, 2003). Moreover, the modest increase in the number of native-born PhDs is "attributable to the rise in the number of women and minorities earning PhDs" (NSF, 2003, p. 21).

Secondly, as part of the sweeping critique of the civil rights movement, there have been various efforts to reform the science "canon" to include women, scientists of color and non-Western scientists. As Donna Riley (2003) writes,

Copyright © 2006, Idea Group Inc. Copying or distributing in print or electronic forms without written permission of Idea Group Inc. is prohibited.

An obvious problem in teaching thermodynamics rests in the fact that the traditional body of knowledge is wholly Western centered, with predominantly white, male, upper-class heroes. It is possible with a little digging in the history of science literature to turn up countercurrents in this stream. (p. 151)

Thus, Riley uses "Maria the Jewess" to demonstrate early insights into thermodynamics, and others have referenced the contributions of peoples from Africa, Asia and the Middle East (Hess, 1995). This movement towards inclusion—however slow and uneven—might be said to be the baseline context for a more globalized, more diverse scientific community.

But it is Powell's third type—the theoretical movement—that has the most far-reaching implications for the sciences in general, and science education in particular. One side of that theoretical development, associated with Science and Technology Studies, has proven especially galvanizing for the science community. In those critiques, "value-free" science is unmasked as the effect of ideological discourse associated with Western, white and male hegemony. Laying down the gauntlet, Andrew Ross (1996) writes:

If stable sciences really are objective fields of knowledge and inquiry, why have so many (seismography, oceanography, and microelectronics, to name a few) evolved directly from military R&D as part of this spin-off system that is habitually cited to justify the benefits to society of the vast military budget? (p. 5)

From the "strong programme" of the Edinburgh school to Latour's accounts of processes of inscription, Science Studies has represented scientific practice as agonistic, interested and imbricated in sociohistorical contexts (Latour & Woolgar, 1970; Latour, 1996).

Against, for example, the objective claims of primatology, Donna Haraway's *Primate Visions* illustrates the ways patriarchy has not only impacted the formation of primatology as a discipline, but has also (over)determined the sorts of questions being asked (Haraway, 1989). Others have looked to the tools of science as "reified theory,"… "with unquestioned assumptions" about gender and knowledge "hard-programmed into them" (Traweek, 1988, p. 49). For example, by suggesting that Artificial Life scientists build their simulations of "life-as-it-could-be" with specific (but untested) assumptions about "life-as-

Copyright © 2006, Idea Group Inc. Copying or distributing in print or electronic forms without written permission of Idea Group Inc. is prohibited.

we-know-it," Stefan Helmreich (1998) questions Darwinistic competition, stratification and scarcity as the "natural" constituents of life and, through evocations of alternative understandings of evolution, makes room for alternative genders and sexualities in "life-as-it-could-be."

Particularly galling to some scientists (e.g., Andrew Sokal) have been the non-science origins of many of these critical works; indeed, science studies has been demonstrably ecumenical, incorporating work from literature, anthropology, history and cultural studies. Part of the problem is the assumption that scientific inquiry is a "text" to be considered, *inter pares*, on the same terms as novels, advertising and movies—certainly a far cry from the separate status Robert Merton (1973) carved out for science in the mid-twentieth century.

However, multiculturalism's theoretical critique has not just run one way—from literature and cultural studies to science. Or, rather, much of the multicultural critique of the sciences only seems to come from "outside" if we accept the ideological division of the sciences from the humanities. But between the cognitive sciences, cybernetics, chaos theory, poststructuralism, biogenetics, etc., that line is (increasingly) blurred. For example, in the wake of PCR (polymerase chain reaction) and genetic engineering, academicians from the "other side" of the quadrangle have been inspired to deconstruct "nature" in light of what Hegel termed "second nature," which here refers to the technology and information-infused scapes of the late-twentieth and early twenty-first centuries. This involves the (occasionally forced) appropriation of scientific terminologies and theories for generative, root metaphors (Ritchie, 2003). To be sure, these appropriations have been selective, for example, Lynn Margulis' work on endosymbiosis or Helmreich's appropriations of nonfiliative descent among extremophile microrganisms (Helmreich, 2003; Parisi, 2004), artificial life, emergence, complexity and chaos.

Deluze and Guattari have cribbed various examples from biology as a starting point for their work in *A Thousand Plateaus* (1987), basing their ideas of rhizomatic assemblage and machinic phylum on phenomena like the symbiosis of the Australian wasp and the orchid. Non-genealogical descent has proven suggestive to many disciplines, among them a feminism concerned with disrupting sexuality as a primarily reproductive economy and anthropology, which looks to these recent insights from bioengineering in order to critique models of kinship, which, just a generation before, had been utilized by anthropologists to critique biology, especially work that "naturalized" the nuclear family as the "unit" of kinship and social organization (Strathern, 1992).

Copyright © 2006, Idea Group Inc. Copying or distributing in print or electronic forms without written permission of Idea Group Inc. is prohibited.

Systems theory and information sciences have been no less suggestive, following on the work of Donald MacKay as an alternative to Shannon and Weaver's quantitative operationalization of information as a ratio of signal to noise (Terranova, 2004). MacKay's definition of information, on the contrary, emphasizes both content and frame. As Hayles (1999, p. 56) summarizes:

Arguing for a strong correlation between the nature of a representation and its effect, MacKay's model recognized the mutual constitution of form and content, message and receiver. His model was fundamentally different from the Shannon-Weaver theory because it triangulated between reflexivity, information, and meaning. In the context of the Macy Conferences, his conclusion qualified as radical: subjectivity, far from being a morass to be avoided, is precisely what enables information and meaning to be connected.

Combined with models of "distributed cognition" that reject the artificial separation of mind, body and environment, this has led some to utilize "autopoiesis," a development of cybernetics and systems theory emphasizing the "structural coupling" of systems to their environment such that the organism can be said to make itself and its environment (Maturana & Varela, 1980). In the computer sciences, this has meant more dynamic approaches to simulation, multi-agent systems, artificial intelligence and artificial life, among other things. As Stefan Helmreich (1998) writes:

As with metaphors drawn from genetics, the idea of a stochastic, dynamic system has also proven suggestive to non-scientists, especially in the critique of static, organizational models and in the characterization of social systems as dynamic and emergent.

All of these have impacted multicultural thought by naturalizing diversity, here construed in a Bergsonian fashion that challenges teleologies, closed systems and linear equations, and by undermining the primacy of the Lockean subject by supplanting a bounded, monadological self with more shifting, "dividual" theories locating the self at the conjuncture of multiple contexts and multiple discourses (LiPuma, 2001). All of these suggest a heterogeneous, changing world where "difference" is always undermining "identity," a powerful critique of essentialist definitions of race, gender and nationality.

Copyright © 2006, Idea Group Inc. Copying or distributing in print or electronic forms without written permission of Idea Group Inc. is prohibited.

These insights are also transformative of science, replacing a "consensus" model of scientific inquiry with something more agonistic and temporary, i.e., a notion of scientific inquiry ironically closer to the way actual practitioners see their field (cf. Traweek, 1988). In this milieu, "diversity" brings with it the possibility of new ideas and creativity. As Riley writes:

Diversity has come to be valued to an extent in the workforce for its contribution to creativity. The more perspectives held in a project group, the greater number of alternatives generated and the more likely that best, most innovative solution will emerge. (Riley, 2003)

In the wake of tragedies like the Challenger and Columbia shuttle disasters, where the hierarchical organization of NASA has been said to have contributed to the accidents by stifling dissent through rigid hierarchies delimiting communications between different departments, this kind of "diversity" is certainly welcome. This includes cultural diversity as well. As Sandra Harding (1994, p. 323) writes:

Just as modernization pressures are reducing the diversity of plant, animal, and even human genetic pools, so, too, they are reducing the diversity of human cultures and the valuable human ideas developed in them. These scientific legacies are interesting and valuable to preserve for their own sake–but they can also make even greater contributions to modern science.

"Science" conceived as an activity unfolding across heterogeneous cultures is valuable for at least two reasons: 1) Science undertaken in non-Western milieus (e.g., health care and engineering projects through development agencies) has to be planned in cultural contexts, and 2) Cultural difference generates different perspectives on problems.

This, for example, has been one of the arguments for the continuation of the H-1B visa program in the US, suggesting that, among other things, cultural difference has been one of the engines of innovation in Silicon Valley (English-Lueck, 2002).

Ironically, a more agonistic, heterogeneous science is closer to the ways practitioners actually characterize their work, as opposed to the way science is presented in textbooks and popular accounts. Sharon Traweek writes that

Copyright © 2006, Idea Group Inc. Copying or distributing in print or electronic forms without written permission of Idea Group Inc. is prohibited.

one of her informants characterized Mertonian characterizations of science as "'an adolescent fantasy which keeps the students working' through their graduate school years and into the postdoctoral period, when they begin to get some rewards" (Traweek, 1988, p. 80). These ideal characterizations of the slow advance of science through the selfless research of "great men" is belied by the adversarial, agonistic and uncertain world of science practiced today, particularly a science more and more competitive for funding, patents and profits.

Nevertheless, science education generally projects knowledge as consensual, noncontroversial and paradigmatic. It is, for the undergraduate, not something to be questioned, but to be memorized. The same might be said for IT as for engineering: "from professor's notes to student's notes and through the minds of neither."(Riley, 2003,139). Not only does this obscure the creative processes that make IT possible, but these accounts reinforce knowledge as something that students stand on the receiving end of only, i.e., the "container" type of education, where knowledge is construed as a "content" to be transmitted to empty vessels of students. As Reid (2000) writes of higher education in general,

Educational institutions tend to define students by their shortcomings: students can't write; they have no sense of history; they have bad work habits; they're undisciplined.

In IT, we might extend the list to include not only programming languages, matrices, logic and computer systems architecture, but also the "feel" for problems, in the sense of questions of social organization and culture, addressed in courses like "Software Project Management."

Not surprisingly, one of the foci for multicultural critique has been pedagogy itself. From Henry Giroux's "insurgent multiculturalism" and Bell Hooks's "transgressive" pedagogy to Grossberg's "radical" pedagogy, multicultural theorists have not only continued the critique of academic canons begun in the 1960s, but have extended it to the institutions, discourses and practices that (over)determine the reproduction of existing inequalities in higher education. What these all have in common, however, is, on some level, a capitulation. That is, multicultural critique demands that we upset existing structures of the classroom—the interpellation of the subject positions professor and student — with something that reflexively questions this agency by way of transforming

Copyright © 2006, Idea Group Inc. Copying or distributing in print or electronic forms without written permission of Idea Group Inc. is prohibited.

learning itself and, ultimately, the world around the classroom (Reid, 2000).

By facilitating the articulation of marginal voices, by allowing students to "take control" of classroom activities, we also nudge students towards a ideological critique of society's status quo at the site of that status quo's formation, i.e., what Brian Massumi terms "tactical sabotage" — not the replacement of one hegemon with another, but an unsettling critique that leads students to question hegemonic institutions and practices altogether.

At the same time, these approaches open up the possibility of diverse and creative outcomes. This is one of its chief attractions for IT education. Indeed, the IT classroom offers in many ways the ideal space for transgressive pedagogies, not only because of the structure of classroom learning, but because recent theories in artificial intelligence and multi-agent systems are in many ways inimical to the "transmission" model of education, where knowledge is content transmitted between a sender to a receiver.

For example, since the 1950s, AI research has undergone an isomorphic period of critique and questioning, resulting in the rejection of the "brain as computer" model that dominated the field from the 1950s until the 1970s (Clark, 2001; Johnston, 2002; Woolridge, 2002). There are two parts to this critique. First, the critique of a monological model of intelligence premised on a strict division of mind and body and a "representational model" of being-in-the-world, where "intelligence" is a function of a symbolic representation of the world (Shaviro, 2003). The second, taking cues from ethology, and especially herd behaviors such as flocking, rejects hierarchical models of intelligence as the best way to model intelligence in non-human agents. As Johnston (2002, 493) summarizes,

In contrast, the new AI gives primary importance to the "bottom-up" processes by which intelligence emerges and evolves in biological life, particularly in interactions with the environment that enhance the agent's present situation and increase[s] its chances for survival, or in which new kinds of organization and cooperation among multiple agents emerge.

Both of these critiques are articulated by Rodney Brooks in his work with Anita Flynn and others in the 1980s and 1990s. In Brooks and Flynn's then-controversial 1989 article, "Fast, Cheap and Out of Control," the "symbolic" approach, with its centralized control and its internal representations, is

Copyright © 2006, Idea Group Inc. Copying or distributing in print or electronic forms without written permission of Idea Group Inc. is prohibited.

completely rejected for a "subsumption architecture." As they write of Genghis, the paradigmatic example of this reactive architecture (1989, p. 481):

Nowhere in the control system is there any notion of a central controller calling these behaviors as subroutines. These processes exist independently, run at all times and fire whenever the sensory preconditions are true.

Brooks later describes this as the rejection of a "horizontal decomposition" for a "vertical decomposition" modeled on animal behavior and composed of parallel tracks "stacked vertically" (Murphy, 2000, p. 106). Each "track" need not possess the same representations of the environment, belying the idea that there can be more or less "correct" representations of the environment. Instead, as Brooks and Flynn explain (1989, p. 479):

It is entirely plausible for different parts of the system to "believe" wildly inconsistent things about the world. Of course, belief is all in the mind of an outside beholder as there are no explicit symbolic representations of any believed facts within the subsumption architecture.

In a later, retrospective article, Brooks (1997) amplifies this point:

But as, the specific goals of the robot are never explicitly represented, nor are there any plans—the goals are implicit in the coupling of actions to perceptual conditions, and apparent execution of plans unroll in real time as one behavior alters the robot's configuration in the world in such a way that new perceptual conditions trigger the next sequence of actions.

Putting aside the different objections to subsumption architecture, e.g., that there are schemas in the "reactive paradigm" (e.g., the wiring itself) and that most scientists have since rejected more catholic versions of the reactive paradigm for hybrid approaches combining subsumption architectures with evolutionary programming and other forms of computation, this approach suggests critical and subversive approaches to the IT classroom.

To begin with, Brooks's work suggests the power of diversity: Optimal outcomes result from systems where agents do not hold the same beliefs and desires. By removing the "middle-man" in internal representations and planning

Copyright © 2006, Idea Group Inc. Copying or distributing in print or electronic forms without written permission of Idea Group Inc. is prohibited.

algorithms, subsumption speeds reaction and improves adaptability. This is a powerfully subversive idea in a classroom structured according to a more-or-less unilinear approach, where skills and theories must be acquired in an ordered sequence before students can accede to the next level of instruction. Indeed, one of the advantages of Brooks's model is the way it models the ability of living agents to act on incomplete or even contradictory knowledge. Not only is this an example of Varela's "enaction," as parts of systems and agents structurally couple to their environments but it also naturalizes radical difference, as "agents" making up a system need not "share" representations and scheme to be effective; in fact, Brooks makes the opposite argument. In order to effectively act in an unknown, dynamic environment, it's better if agents do not believe the same thing. This is the chief advantage, in fact, in using "microrovers" or "gnat robots" for extraplanetary exploration. Brooks and Flynn (1989, p. 484) tell us:

One should not think of gnat robots as machines which are told what to do, but rather as autonomous creatures that when turned on, do what is in their programmed nature to do.

Indeed, one of the most intriguing legacies of Brooks's approach amounts to nothing less than a radical deconstruction of what might constitute an "agent" in the first place (Johnston, 2002, p. 485).

Does it denote a class of subjects, objects, or functions? From its use in phrases like "Modeling cognitive agents," "designing autonomous agents," or simply "embodied agents," we can infer that an agent can be a person, animal, insect, robotic machine, or even a body of code (i.e., a software program).

After earlier insights into cybernetic theory from Gregory Bateson and others, we might interpret this as a perspectival model of agency, where identity and intentionality are problems of the observer and are ultimately constructed through that local, contingent relation (Bateson, 1984; Hayles, 1999). Moreover, the turn to multi-agent systems subverts enlightenment models of the Lockean individual. As Woolridge (2002) cautions, there is no such thing as a single-agent, multi-agent system; the "divdiual" relationships linking autonomous agents are ontologically prior to the "individual."

Secondly, this optimization of difference is a stochastic process: difference begets difference in a dynamic systems environment. This open-ended, emergent alterity has been one of the chief objections to subsumption robots. Woolridge (2002, p. 71) explains that:

Copyright © 2006, Idea Group Inc. Copying or distributing in print or electronic forms without written permission of Idea Group Inc. is prohibited.

One major selling point of purely reactive systems is that overall behaviour emerges from the interaction of the component behaviours when the agent is placed in its environment. But the very term 'emerges' suggests that the relationship between individual behaviours, environment, and overall behaviour is not understandable. This necessarily makes it very hard to "engineer" agents to fulfill specific tasks.

Indeed, the turn back to computations in multi-agent systems is at least partly attributable to the pragmatic capitulation to predictable results and behaviors, a capitulation to the instrumental needs of business and the defense industry.

In the multicultural classroom, this idea of a multi-agent system leads to a rejection of many of the underlying assumptions of IT education, including:

1.   Western models of the individual as a stable configuration of faculties (reason, memory);
2.   A meritocratic model of education where students are judged individually according to their achievement of the desirable end-state;
3.   Learning as a linear process with a discrete beginning and ending; and
4.   A predetermined end-state of the measure of success in the classroom.

In the following, what we have tried to do is design a classroom activity where students might articulate all of these critiques against the backdrop of multi-agent systems design and, by learning about the "real" state of the world, reflexively critique institutions of education and their own interpellations within that system (Reid, 2000)

The Tool

As a result of our work in multicultural theory, we became interested in developing a "0-context" tool where we might observe emergent interactions between human- and non-human agents in such a way that results are not simply artifacts of pre-existing metaphors—physical, social and cultural. By "emergence," we refer not to some mystical process wherein research results are "inexplicable" (a charge sometimes leveled at the sciences of complexity) but

Copyright © 2006, Idea Group Inc. Copying or distributing in print or electronic forms without written permission of Idea Group Inc. is prohibited.

to the possibility that we may find new, generative metaphors for understanding online, multi-agent systems in the course of our analysis, what has been called an "unprogrammed functionality" (Clark, 2001, p. 114). Likewise, while we recognize that no context can ever be at "0" (there are always contexts, schema, syntax and so on), we would suggest that there are nevertheless ways to introduce what Walter Benjamin called the "uncanny."

Accordingly, we developed an online, environment-agent we've called "Izbushka" (after Baba Yaga's semi-sentient hut) that couples structurally with human agents, the goals of which emerge in the course of human- and non-human interaction. A blank screen first confronts human agents, interacting with Izbushka. "Clicking" onto the screen illuminates a square in a grid displaying shapes and patterns in different colors with accompanying sounds, and subsequent clicks illuminate adjacent squares but may also change the patterns and colors of already illuminated squares. The "goal" of human agents will be to discern the goal of the simulation. Is it to illuminate the entire screen in similar patterns, shapes, colors or sounds? Or to build sequences of different patterns, shapes, colors or sounds? Or to "black out" the entire screen by following sequences of clicks on adjacent squares in a pattern? Is "success" signaled by certain sounds, failure signaled by others? What human agents will not know is that Izbushka's goals (its "drives") depend upon the choices of human agents, i.e., the "goal" of the simulation depends upon the interaction of human and non-human agent and, additionally, may change in the space of the simulation.

While interacting with Izbushka, participants generate data in several, different ways. First, they leave a cache of keystrokes and environments, the record of their "structural coupling" with Izbushka. Second, human agents may communicate with each other through a "chat" window at the bottom of the screen; transcripts from chat sessions are synchronously logged along with interactions. Third, they may talk to each other in person.

All of these are "representations," i.e., ways of conceptualizing Izbushka and online interaction in general. However, after Bickhard (1993, 1995), we reject a "substance"-based approach to representation for a "process" approach based on the agent's dynamic interactions with an environment. In this enactivist approach, "concepts" are seen as processes that direct the sensory-motor flux in the coupled agent-environment dynamic system rather than as varied "images." That is, data analysis results in a range of perspectives on representation nested inside each other like a series of boxes. The first "box" looks at dynamics of learning through agent interactions, the second at "learning" as an imitative and dialogic process between members of teams

Copyright © 2006, Idea Group Inc. Copying or distributing in print or electronic forms without written permission of Idea Group Inc. is prohibited.

interacting and communicating with each other. Finally, the third "box" takes on "meta-perspectives" on the system defined as agents + environment + emergent culture, in other words, new models of online interaction in cyberspace.

One of the goals of this project is to prompt the participants in the experiments to shift perspectives (the *problem of the observer* in cybernetics) in order to consider multi-agent systems as, respectively,

1.   A component of HCI;
2.   As generative of new models for human-human and human-machine interactions in contemporary organization; and
3.   As part of an emergent cyberculture.

In other words, we ask participants to consider multi-agent systems as a simulation of human social and cultural interaction and as a laboratory for the generation of new organizational structures. Do simulated, multi-agent systems emulate human multi-agent systems with respect to language, learning and social interaction?

If we consider culture as inclusive of material artifacts, practices, social structures and communications, then we must consider online environments as part of the process of culture change (Hakken, 2003). It is our belief that multi-agent systems composed of human- and non-human agents are the bellwether of future ethnogenesis (the creation of new cultures). And yet, we cannot hold these new cultures apart from cultural heterogeneity. Through this kind of activity, we hope to show undermined "monocultural" assumptions in the classroom and in society-at-large.

Technical Background: Ishbushka/E-Popisicle Setup

Ishbushka is a flexible online environment, realized with the purpose of supporting our theoretical work in the domain of the Interactivist-Expectative Theory on Agency and Learning (IETAL) (Stojanov et al., 1997a), and its multi-agent version MASIVE (Multi-agent Simulated Interactive Virtual Environments) (Trajkovski, 2001, 2003a, 2003b). It has come out of the class-

Copyright © 2006, Idea Group Inc. Copying or distributing in print or electronic forms without written permission of Idea Group Inc. is prohibited.

room, and all steps of its development have witnessed a significant involvement of undergraduate and graduate students. We explore use of the inborn schemas in humans (Piaget, 1945), their use of contextual information (Stojanov et al., 1997b), as well as the phenomenon of imitation (Rizolatti et al., 1996) and information interchange (Trajkovski, 2003a; Trajkovski, 2003b). The Ishbushka/ e-POPSICLE (POPSICLE: Patterns in Orientation: Patter-aided Simulation Interactive Context Learning Experiment) is a flexible online experimentation workbench to study of the use of contextual information in human subjects.

What motivated the implementation of this project? In the past eight years we worked on the theoretical aspects of IETAL and MASIVE. We have several simulation studies. Heavily influenced by Piaget, the theory IETAL expresses our beliefs of how humans learn, and MASIVE sheds light on the learning in societal setting. By gathering data from humans in, at first, simple virtual environments, we were able to calibrate our simulation models, and study, in a simulation environment phenomena in human learning, especially in contextual learning in an environment where the phenomenon of perceptual aliasing is present (as well as social phenomena, and especially the emergence of those phenomena). By gathering data from a control group and groups from different cultural milieus, we are planning to conduct a few cross-cultural studies.

The original POPSICLE experiment (Trajkovski et al., 2003), that Ishbushka is based on, used a set of small mazes (5x5) with obstacles, whose squares (tiles) are of several different colors. The goal—place where the agent satisfies its drives (food, water)—is placed in a single place in this environment. In all of the environments, stepping on tiles of a particular color leads to the goal tile. In different stages of the experiment, a different amount of information is presented to the subject (instructions, context). The subject does not get to see the whole environment. In different stages of the experiment, he or she sees either the color of the square (tile) of the maze they are on (context 0), or of the present tile and the immediate neighboring tiles (context 1) (Stojanov et al., 1997b). As the experiment goes on, the subject(s) are provided with more information on the environment itself.

The present platform enables the POSICLE to be deployed online, which would account for better comfort of the test subjects, and no interference between them. We are currently working on packaging e-POPSICLE to give the appearance of a game, as we have studied the phenomenon of stress during the original experiment, have concluded that we need to implement an instrument to boost the motivation of the subjects (Trajkovski et al., 2005).

Copyright © 2006, Idea Group Inc. Copying or distributing in print or electronic forms without written permission of Idea Group Inc. is prohibited.

For an agent to perform efficiently, good special representations are a must. The agent should gain this knowledge during its interaction with the environment. This model accounts for—amongst other real world phenomena—the phenomena called perceptual aliasing, when, due to sensory resolution limitations, two locally distinct places in the environment are perceived the same by the agent (Stojanov & Trajkovski, 1998).

If we speak in terms of graphs, we may depict this situation with a graph whose nodes are labeled and these labels may be same for different nodes. The only way a node can be recognized as different then is to examine its context. Context of a node is a tree-like data structure defined recursively as all followers of the node together with their contexts (Stojanov et al., 1997b).

Let $V=\{v_1, v_2, ..., v_n\}$ be the vertices and $A=\{s_1, s_2, ..., s_m\}$ the action repertoire of the agent Petitage. Let $G_s = (V, r_s)$, $s \in A$, where $r_s \subseteq V \times V$, be an oriented regular graph with matrix of incidence of the relation r_s for every $s \in A$ that contains exactly one element 1 in each column,. is the graph of general connectivity of the family of graphs $\{G_s : s \in A\}$. If the G' is connected, then the triplet $G=(V, A, r)$ – where $r \in (V \times V) \times A$, defined as follows: $((v_1, v_2),s) \in r$ if and only if $(v_1, v_2) \in r_s$ $v_1, v_2 \in V$, $s \in A$ – is an oriented graph with marked edges. Let $L=\{l_1, l_2, ..., l_k\}$ be a set of labels and $f: V \to L$ a surjective mapping (labeling of the vertex set of G, i.e., the perceptual repertoire of the agent). The quintuple $G''=(V, A, L, r, f)$ is called *Designer Visible Environment* (DVE). The product $L_D=V \times L$ is called designer visible *label set*. The designer knows how the agent perceives a vertex, and takes in consideration the perception repertoire and resolution of the agent. The relation r induces the relation r''' $\in (L \times L) \times A$, defined by the means the following expression: $((f(v_1), f(v_2)),s) \in$ r''' if and only if $((v_1, v_2),s) \in r$. The graph G''' = (L, r''', A) represents the *Agent Visible Environment* (AVE).

The agent perceives the environment in a certain way; the perceptual aliasing is a phenomenon accounted for. Based on the agent's visible environment, via the interactions with the environment, the agent builds its intrinsic representation of the environment. The intrinsic representation is later used in the agent's quest to satisfy its drives.

In other words, the designer, us, can see the whole environment, which is not—as it has been many times the case in classical AI—spoon-fed to the agent. The IETAL agent interacts with the environment, and that is how it learns it, or portions of the Umwelt it is in. When Petitagé—pronounced the same as Piaget (petit-age: of young age)—(Stojanov, 1997a)—the IETAL agent "enters" an

Copyright © 2006, Idea Group Inc. Copying or distributing in print or electronic forms without written permission of Idea Group Inc. is prohibited.

environment it is not familiar with, it tries to execute its internal inborn programming—inborn schema (Piaget, 1945).

Based on the topology of the environment (positions of obstacles) the agent can execute (or not) actions from the inborn schema. The successful actions executed from the schema and the percepts associated with the actions in the subschema build the intrinsic representation of the environment of the agent. Bumping into an obstacle, a wall, increases the pain units. Apparently, the drive to keep the pain to a minimum is one of the agent's drives.

Given the algebraic representation above, the learning procedure goes as shown in Figure 1. If there is an existing entry in the contingency table that

Figure 1. Learning in an IETAL agent

```
Generate_Intrinsic_Representation (G: Interaction_Graph, ξ: Schema;
        GIR: Assotiative_Memory, Δ: SetOfDrives)
BEGIN_PROCEDURE
        Initialize (R_Δ=∅);
        Initialize_Position (G; Position);
        Try (Position, ξ; (B₁, S₁));
        Add ( [(λ, λ), (B₁,S₁)]; R_Δ); // λ is empty schema
        WHILE (Active_Drive_Not_Satisfied) DO
        BEGIN_WHILE
                Try (Position, ξ; (B₂, S₂));
                Add ([(B₁, S₁), (B₂, S₂)]; R_Δ);
                (B₁, S₁):=(B₂, S₂);
        END_WHILE
        Propagate_Context ( (B₁, S₁), drive; GIR).
END_PROCEDURE


Try (Position: Location_In_Interaction_Graph, ξ: Schema;
        (B, S): Percepts_Actions_Pair)
BEGIN_PROCEDURE
        S:=λ;
                TryIn (Position, ξ; (Add (S, Currfent_Percept), B) );
        REPEAT
                TryIn (Position, B; (Add (S, Current_Percept), B)[)]
        UNTIL NOT enabled (B)
END_PROCEDURE


Propagate_Context (δ: drive; GIR: Assotiative_Memory)
BEGIN_PROCEDURE
        N:=0;
        WHILE (B₁, S₁) ∈ Projection_δ (GIR) DO
        BEGIN_WHILE
                Projection_δ (GIR) := exp(-N);
                INC (N)
        END_WHILE
END_PROCEDURE
```

Copyright © 2006, Idea Group Inc. Copying or distributing in print or electronic forms without written permission of Idea Group Inc. is prohibited.

Figure 2. Emulating abstract agents on humans: S-Stimulus, A-action repertoire

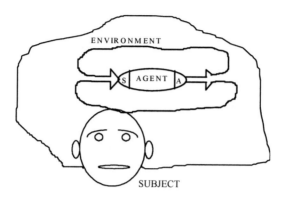

expresses previous experience of the agent when it has executed the same subschema and registered the same array of percepts, it expects the next execution of the schema to be the same. If that does not happen, it accumulates surprise units.

The drives play a central role in the learning procedure and the agent's view of the environment. Based on the set of active drives, the agent strives to satisfy those goals. When hungry, only hunger-related entries in the associative memories matter to Petitage (that might be completely irrelevant to the satisfaction of the, say, thirst drive). For a discussion on the drives, contingency tables, and the emotional contexts, see, for example (Trajkovski, 2003). We have studies and modeled the agent's model drives algebraically with L, R and S fuzzy algebraic structures, based on the Maslow hierarchy of drives (Maslow, 1970).

In conclusion of the model, an agent is defined when its sensory/perceptual abilities/resolutions S are known (the labeling f above), as well as its action repertoire A, its set of drives Δ and its inborn schema ξ. Knowing this we can now explain how we can emulate abstract agents in bio, i.e., human, agents with linguistic abilities.

In the sense of IETAL, humans are the only linguistically competent agents (Stojanov et al., 1997). Humans are able to filter out all other stimuli and it is in this sense that we say that we are emulating an abstract bio-agent (Figure 2).

We define the S and A agents by telling the subject what inputs he or she should pay attention to and what possible motor actions he or she is allowed. In different stages of the experiment, different information is given to the object(s)

Copyright © 2006, Idea Group Inc. Copying or distributing in print or electronic forms without written permission of Idea Group Inc. is prohibited.

of the experiments to define S: "On the screen you will be seeing patterns like this" (demonstration of the patterns). To define A the subject is told: "You are allowed to press or not to press these buttons" (experimenter shows the buttons to the subject). Schemas are defined similarly. An example may be the following "Follow the tiles colored yellow." An example of external goal creation is the following: To define the "react as fast as you can" goal, the subject is told: "find the food."

This concludes the definition of the abstract agent. Having defined all the initial elements, the experimenter can now observe various aspects of the agent's sojourn in that particular environment. Of particular interest are the structures that emerge during the agent-environment interaction. These are the networks of concept/behaviors.

The focus of the experiment is to study the inborn navigational patterns and the development and the use of one's associative memory throughout the experiment.

There are three distinct ways of conducting experiments for POPSICLE distinguishable by who/what is traversing the environment as the test subject. Test subjects may be human subjects, robotic agents or simulated agents. These fundamental differences drive the experiments in terms of what factors are going to be measured and how this data will be collected.

Previously there have been experiments conducted using all three of the aforementioned methods. In the spring of 2004, Towson University's robotics lab began working on a POPSICLE study using robotic agents. In the summer of that year, a small group of Towson Students began working with POPSICLE using computer-simulated agents. That group of students was organized into two subgroups, each working independently on their own simulation.

A few years ago, there was a project undertaken to study POPSICLE using human subjects. This software package and the experiments conducted using them, although successful, left room for improvements to be made. The experiment needed the ability to be administered to a larger group of test subjects. The original test group was less than 100 subjects. Also there were improvements to be made in the collection of the data and the validation of subjects as being motivated to take part in the experiment and attempt to learn the patterns involved rather than by responding randomly.

The e-POPSICLE project is a new implementation of this POPSICLE software for human subjects. It does not use any of the code or design from the previous iteration, but it will feature improvements in terms of administration, data-gathering and overall scale. It is available for public use.

Copyright © 2006, Idea Group Inc. Copying or distributing in print or electronic forms without written permission of Idea Group Inc. is prohibited.

Figure 3. Flow diagram for e-POPSICLE

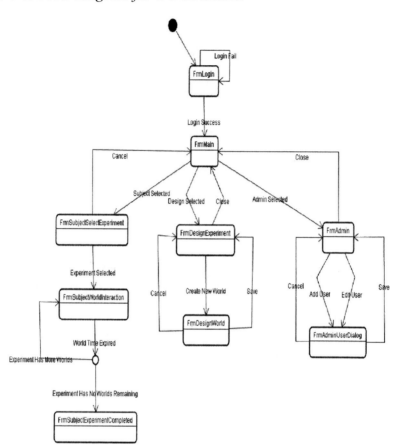

The e-POPSICLE modules are publicly available within a CVS system, that serves as a repository for the bigger system that we are building. In addition to the human subject test bed, we are incorporating also a flexible simulation tool that will enable us to calibrate the simulation based on the human subject data, and observe realistic simulations in the study of emergent social phenomena.

The flow diagram for this application is given in Figure 3, and its general class structure in Figure 4.

This section comments on the programming language and database management systems choices this project has been coded in.

Programming Language: The software is developed using a common high-level programming language. This will support future work and improvements

Copyright © 2006, Idea Group Inc. Copying or distributing in print or electronic forms without written permission of Idea Group Inc. is prohibited.

Figure 4. Overview of the class diagrams in the e-POPSICLE Web application

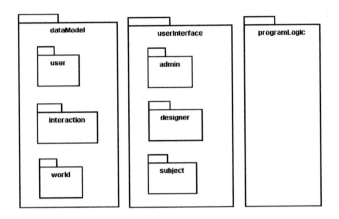

to the software by using technology that others are familiar with. Initially C# and Java were considered as options for the project. After some initial testing it was decided that the project would be coded in Java. This was due to several factors, among which are cross-platform compatibility and program extensibility. Java runs on any system that has a Java virtual machine installed, and Java code may also be integrated into web applications using applets or servlets which further increase the options for program deployment.

The software is functionally dependent upon data in order to operate and to process the experimental results. Although XML was initially considered as an alternative, it was decided that a database was necessary. Two different database packages were considered: My-SQL, and Oracle. Both of them offer similar functionality and services, but My-SQL was chosen because of its popularity with the open-source community. It is easy to set up a My-SQL server at home. This being said, the software must be designed in such a way that the database connectivity layer can easily be abstracted from the program and replaced if needed.

A user is defined by a login and the roles assigned to it. There are three identified roles: Administrator, Designer and Subject. It is possible for a user to have multiple roles.

Administrators represent the highest level of user. These users manage user accounts. They have the ability to create, modify and delete users. This includes

Copyright © 2006, Idea Group Inc. Copying or distributing in print or electronic forms without written permission of Idea Group Inc. is prohibited.

Figure 5. User class structure

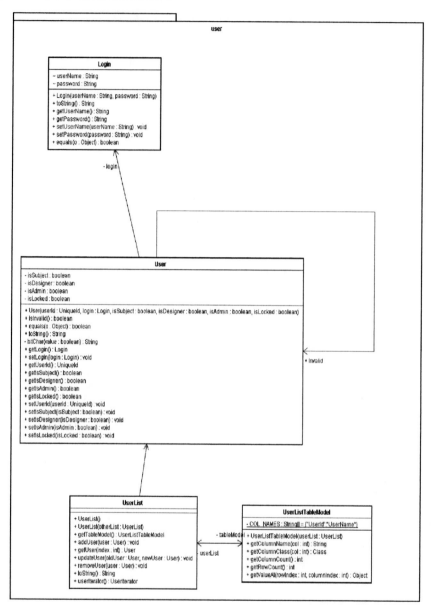

changing passwords and assigning roles. Designers are the next highest level of user.

Designers create the experiments for subjects to interact with. Experiments may only be created, since deleting or modifying one would invalidate the test data associated with it. Subjects are the lowest level of privileged user. They

Copyright © 2006, Idea Group Inc. Copying or distributing in print or electronic forms without written permission of Idea Group Inc. is prohibited.

Figure 6. The world class

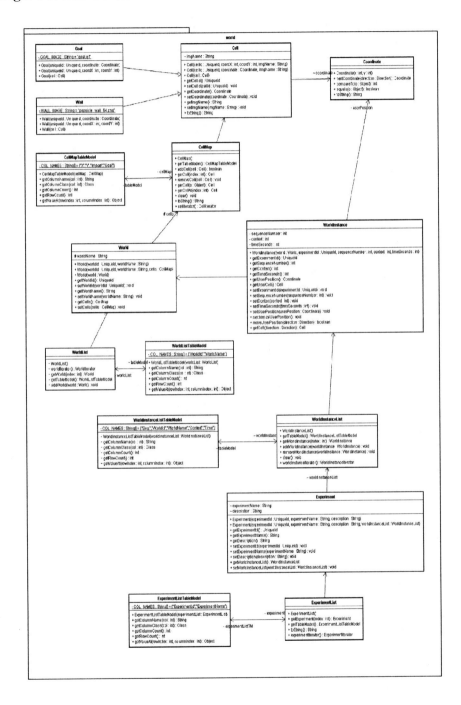

Copyright © 2006, Idea Group Inc. Copying or distributing in print or electronic forms without written permission of Idea Group Inc. is prohibited.

Figure 7. The data model

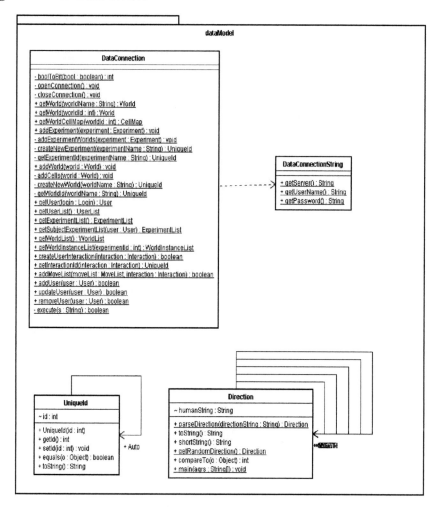

interact with the experiments in order to generate test data. A world is a two-dimensional representation of an environment. It may be visually represented as a matrix, where each element, here on referred to as a cell, contains an image.

The class diagrams for World, Data Model, Program Logic and the User Interface, depicted in Figure 4, are given in Figures 5-9, respectively.

There are two specializations of a cell: wall and goal. A wall is a cell that cannot be entered but contains a pre-defined wall image. A goal represents the place in the world where the subject is attempting to navigate to and contains a pre-defined goal image. A world may have multiple goals. It may also have multiple walls. For efficiency, it is not necessary to store the world as a true matrix and

Copyright © 2006, Idea Group Inc. Copying or distributing in print or electronic forms without written permission of Idea Group Inc. is prohibited.

Figure 8. Program logic of the application

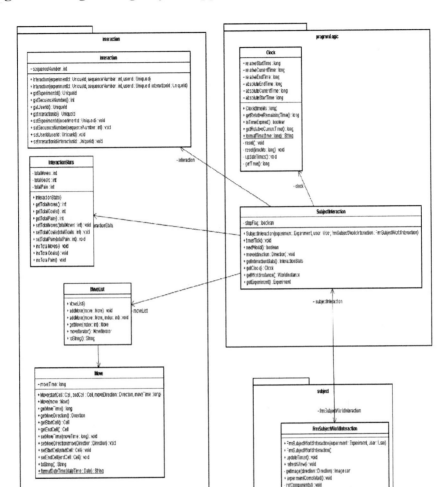

include the walls. Since the walls are essentially null cells, they do not need to be stored at all. This results in a savings on physical memory for the database.

An experiment is a sequence of worlds, each with an associated time limit and context. Valid contexts are 0 and 1. These represent the distance that a subject can see relevant to the current cell. Specifically, a context of 0 means that the subject can only see the cell that he is in currently. A context of 1 means that the subject can see the cell he is in and the immediately adjacent cells. For each

Copyright © 2006, Idea Group Inc. Copying or distributing in print or electronic forms without written permission of Idea Group Inc. is prohibited.

Figure 9. User interface class definition

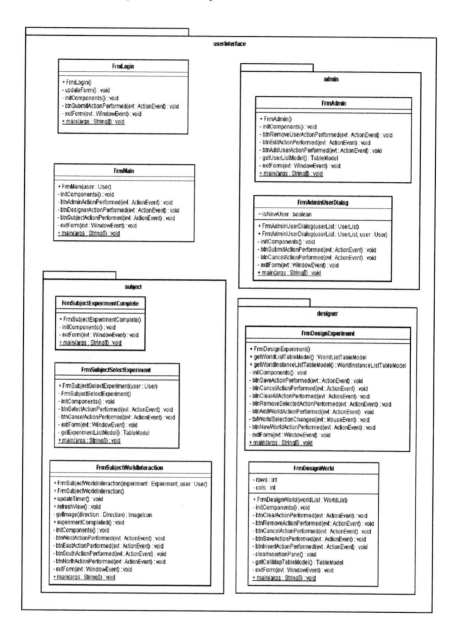

world in the experiment, the subject will try to navigate to a goal as many times as possible before the time limit expires. The user is repositioned to a random cell initially and each time he successfully finds the goal.

As the subject interacts with the experiments, the program creates a table entry for each move the subject makes.

Copyright © 2006, Idea Group Inc. Copying or distributing in print or electronic forms without written permission of Idea Group Inc. is prohibited.

Figure 10. Administrator's (designer's) view when designing experiment scenarios

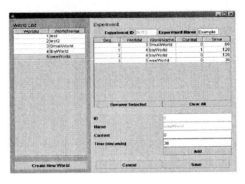

Figure 11. Interface for creating the world

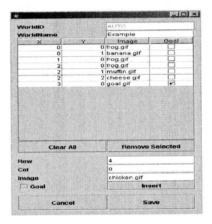

Figure 12. User interface when conducting a segment of the experiment with context 0

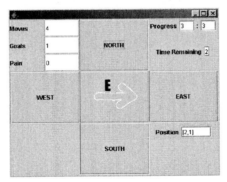

Copyright © 2006, Idea Group Inc. Copying or distributing in print or electronic forms without written permission of Idea Group Inc. is prohibited.

Figure 13. Worldview in context 1

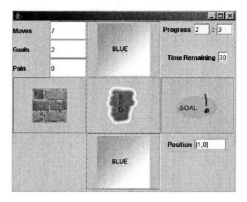

Figure 14. Steps to food of a simulated agent (Stojanov et al., 1997a) (Plotted are the steps to food versus the number of activation of the food drive.)

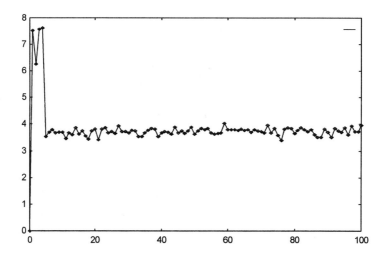

Copyright © 2006, Idea Group Inc. Copying or distributing in print or electronic forms without written permission of Idea Group Inc. is prohibited.

Figure 15. A typical trend in inter-action time of a human agent in a POPSICLE experiment scenario (Trajkovski, 2003) (Milliseconds to next action are shown versus the number of actions on the x-axis.)

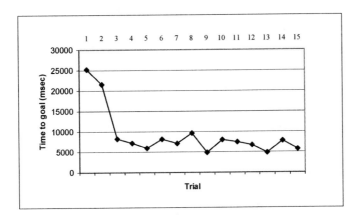

Figure 16. The human agents are linguistically competent (Four times during the initial POPSICLE experiment, they work together as a pair, and get to exchange the acquired concepts linguistically.)

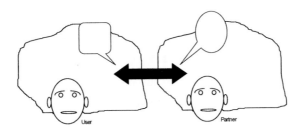

Figure 17. One of the environments—the color-coding used is as follows: 1-red, 2-yellow, 3-green, 4-blue 9-black (obstacle)

Start	1	1	1	1	
	3	3	9	2	1
	2	3	3	9	1
	4	2	2	4	1
	4	4	9	4	Goal

Copyright © 2006, Idea Group Inc. Copying or distributing in print or electronic forms without written permission of Idea Group Inc. is prohibited.

Figure 18. An instance of context 0—a blue tile

4

Figure 19. Instance of the environment of context 1. The center tile is the current position. The surrounding tiles represent possible directions of navigation. The upper square is black and represents an obstacle.

	9	
1	1	Goal
	4	

This entry contains the time (accurate to the millisecond), subject's location, direction of the attempted move, and whether the move was successful. A move would be unsuccessful in the case where a subject attempts to move into a wall. The number of unsuccessful moves may be an indicator of whether a subject is motivated and attempting to find the goal by learning paths, or the user is simply clicking randomly and hoping to land on the goal eventually. Initial data analysis studies the mean time between click for a variety of experiments. In studying this it is necessary to validate this mean time against the percentage of failed moves in order to confirm that the subject is actually trying.

With IETAL and MASIVE we have built cognitive models for human individuals and societies. For successful simulation and study of phenomena with these models, data from human subjects is needed to calibrate the implementation of the model for simulation purposes. This paper presents an online system implemented for the purpose of studying use of context in orientation by humans inhabiting simple virtual environments. All the classes developed for this application are a subset of a larger system, available in a CVS environment that also contains a simulation module for studying IETAL and MASIVE phenomena. The objective of this paper is to popularize the e-POPSICLE environment, and share it with the academic society interested in collaboration.

We are finishing up the simulation counterpart of e-POPSICLE, based on our interactivist uni- and multi-agent theories. This whole system will provide for a comprehensive framework and experimental workbench to study learning in

Copyright © 2006, Idea Group Inc. Copying or distributing in print or electronic forms without written permission of Idea Group Inc. is prohibited.

Figure 20. The POPSICLE scenario – the environment numbers (second column) correspond to the various DVEs used in the experiment

Part	Env	Context	Seat 1	Seat 2	Dura-tion	Observa-tions
1	1	0	User	Partner	3min	Figure 22
2	Figure 17		Both		3min	
3	2	1	User	Partner	3min	Figure 24
4	Figure 23		Both		3min	
5	3	0	User	Partner	3min	Figure 26
6	Figure 25		Both		3min	
7	4	1	User	Partner	3min	Figure 28
8	Figure 27		Both		3min	

Figure 21. Information given to subjects in the different stages of the experiment and for the four different environments

Env.	Information
1	None
2	"There is a pattern to be followed."
3	"One color leads to the goal."
4	"Follow green to the goal."

humans, communication and influence of information in multi-agent environments, emergence of language, formation of concepts and other individual and social phenomena, from the perspective of our theories on agency, learning, and interaction in uni- and multi-agent environments. At the same time, we are conducting experiments in the domain of Developmental/Cognitive Robotics, where we use "observe-the-phenomena" in realistic environments, using robotics agents.

At the present time, we are investigating a shift in the model where, instead of the algebraic model, we will be using a dynamic model "of the mind". The initial observations have been promising in the sense that we can establish parallels between the two models. This means a shift from a discrete to a continuous model. For example, a row in the contingency table of the intrinsic representation in the discrete model would correspond to an attractor in the "continuous" intrinsic representation.

Copyright © 2006, Idea Group Inc. Copying or distributing in print or electronic forms without written permission of Idea Group Inc. is prohibited.

Background: Multi-Agent Isbushka

The concept of learning by imitation is certainly not a new one. Thorndike (1898) defines it as "[imitation is] learning to do an act from seeing it done," whereas Piaget (1945) mentioned it as a major part when offering his theory for development of the ability to imitate, going through six stages. After Piaget, the interest in (movement) imitation diminished, partially because of the prejudice that "mimicking" or "imitating" is not an expression of higher intelligence (Piaget, 1945). Imitation is, though, far from being a trivial task. It is rather a highly creative mapping between the actions and their consequences of the other and oneself (visual input-motor commands-consequences evaluation) marked by the discovery of the so called "mirror neurons"—neurons that fire while one is performing some motor actions or look at somebody else doing the same action (Rizolatti et al., 1996). The imitation is the base of the MASIVE extension of IETAL.

The JAVA tool we've developed, Izbushka, is a dynamic environment. Using separate keys, the agents move up, down, left and right in the DVE. However, the environment that the agent sees at any given time is a subset of the DVE (Figure 17).

The tester presents to the subjects of the experiments instances of the environment on two different context levels. Context 0 (example in Figure 18) presents the subject with a single colored tile. There are no clues given to whether it is possible to move up, down, left, or right. The subject must use trial and error to navigate.

In context 1 (example in Figure 19) the subject is given the current tile he or she is on and the adjoining tiles. All the tiles show their respective colors. This includes the colors for obstacles, which are black, and the goal, which is gray. The borders are also represented by black squares, although they are not identified as borders specifically. Once the goal is found, the subject is at the same initial position, and within 3 minutes tries to find the goal as many times as possible.

Testing was administered via computer terminals in a computer lab. The batches were between 10 and 24 subjects in size. Each batch was assigned a class number and paired off. In each pair one subject was designated the "user," and the other the "partner." Each subject was given a set of instructions that told them that they would be placed in an environment with obstacles and a goal.

Copyright © 2006, Idea Group Inc. Copying or distributing in print or electronic forms without written permission of Idea Group Inc. is prohibited.

They were given the procedures for navigation and told to find the goal as many times as possible in three minutes. When the test began they were presented with context 0. No other information was given about meanings of the color tiles. They were not told whether the environment changed or whether the starting point changed.

After the three-minute time period, each "partner" would join the "user" (Figure 20). At this point they were to perform the same task only as a team. Here, once they realized it was the same environment, they were expected to exchange information and performance would be enhanced. When the time limit had expired, the team was presented with a questionnaire that asked whether they had used any search pattern. If they had, they were to explain what it was. Next, they were asked if the had noticed any patterns within the environment. Again, if they had, they were to explain.

Upon finishing the questionnaire, the team would split up. Now each person would be told it was a new environment. They were also told they would receive more information. This information came in the form of context 1. They were again given three minutes to find the goal of this new environment as many times as they could. Once the time limit had expired they got back into their teams to do this environment at context 1.

Figure 21 overviews the information given to subjects in for each of the environments.

There were four sets like this (Figure 20). Each set included a new environment, a single person trial and a team trial. In set one no information was given about the environment or the colors. In set two the subjects were told there was a pattern that could be found in the environment. In set three the pattern was explained. One of the colors led to the goal. Finally, in step four the subjects were told which color led to the goal.

Figure 22. Subjects' observation on the first environment used in the POPSICLE experiment

1.	Four right, four down.
2.	Left, with up or down accordingly.
3.	A left, and 3 or 4 up/down pattern.
4.	I got jammed in the upper right corner and then went down four spaces to the goal.
5.	Red signals meant we were going to get stopped, green meant we were going in the right direction.
6.	Move right until blocked, then move down until reaching goal.

Copyright © 2006, Idea Group Inc. Copying or distributing in print or electronic forms without written permission of Idea Group Inc. is prohibited.

Figure 23. Environment 2 (parts 3 and 4 of POPSICLE)

3	3	9	4	2
3	2	2	2	2
3	2	9	4	4
9	2	4	4	1
0	2	9	1	1

Figure 24. Subjects' observations on the environment in Figure 23

6	Go to the left and towards the bottom of the screen. The pattern seemed to be left and down toward the bottom of the screen.
7	Down, right, down, down, down, left.
8	Follow the yellow squares.
9	Down, right, 3 times down, left, goal
10	Right one, down five and left one.

Figure 25. Environment 3 (parts 5 and 6 of the experiment)

4	0	4	1	1
4	9	4	9	1
4	4	4	9	1
9	2	3	2	2
1	3	2	3	3

The parameters that were measured were the interaction times, the parameters in the success of finding food, as well as the amount of pain (hitting an obstacle) encountered in the quest for food. From the data collected, we are able to extract data on the sequences used while in the environment, to attempt a study in the inborn schemas area (Piaget, 1945).

Subjects' Observations

The first environment is given in Figure 17. The parts 1 (individual) and 2 (collaborative work of the subjects) of the experiment use this environment. Some of the subjects' observations, in his or her own words, are given in Figure 22. Figures 23, 25 and 27 represent the second, third and fourth environments, which were used for parts 3, 4, 5, 6, 7 and 8 of the POPSICLE experiment respectively. The respective subject observations are given in Figures 24, 26 and 28.

Copyright © 2006, Idea Group Inc. Copying or distributing in print or electronic forms without written permission of Idea Group Inc. is prohibited.

Figure 26. Subjects' comments on the environment in Figure 25

6	Down, down, right, right, up, up.
7	Count the movements.
8	The square stayed blue, with movements of two-down, right, then up.
	However, we think the color of the square is a secondary need to find the goal.
9	Stay with the blue squares
10	There wasn't a specific strategy.

Figure 27. Environment 4, used in the last two parts of the experiment.

2	2	9	4	2
4	1	3	3	3
1	4	3	9	0
2	9	3	1	9
3	3	3	4	2

Figure 28. Subjects' comments on the environment in Figure 27

6	Right and down.
7	Right, down, right, right, right, down
8	The gray square may be the goal.

Results and Interpretations

In Figure 29, a typical learning curve is given for part 1 of the experiment. After a while, the time needed to reach the goal stabilizes. The slope is emphasized more in the early stages of the experiment (especially parts 1 and 2).

Identifying the unsuccessful subjects was an important goal of the experiment. While further examination of the data is needed to investigate the reasoning of this small group of participants, out of the 75 subjects that participated in the experiment, our observations during its implementation were that the subjects were not concentrating well on the task and/or had trouble interfacing with the computers. Although we wanted to statistically analyze the data collected from successful sessions, Figures 29 and 30 show that these sessions do not influence significantly the behavior of the observed aggregated data.

Figure 33 presents a typical form of the time when action is fired by the subject, relative to the time when the subjects left the starting tile. Figure 34 shows a

Copyright © 2006, Idea Group Inc. Copying or distributing in print or electronic forms without written permission of Idea Group Inc. is prohibited.

Figure 29. Typical learning curve for POPSICLE part 1

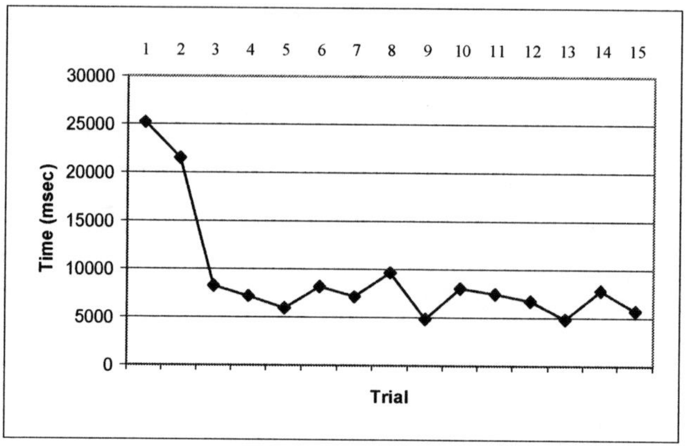

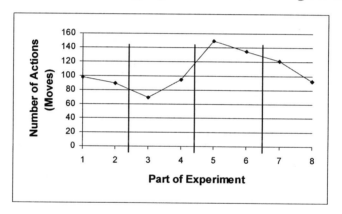

Figure 30. Average number of keystrokes of unsuccessful subjects. The vertical lines denote the change of environments during the experiment.

typical graph of the time between actions of a subject. It reflects the time the subject needed to decide what action to take. In most cases this time shows a decreasing trend.

The subjects were getting tired, especially after the third environment. The loss of concentration and the time and space constraints that were imposed on the experiment attribute to the unexpected jump in the time to goal when the subjects used the fourth environment.

There could also be a different explanation for this. Some reactions to the experiment in the questionnaires indicate alternative comprehension of the

Copyright © 2006, Idea Group Inc. Copying or distributing in print or electronic forms without written permission of Idea Group Inc. is prohibited.

Figure 31. Average time (in milliseconds) to goal (The upper curve is based on cumulative data, the lower one, on data without the unsuccessful subjects.)

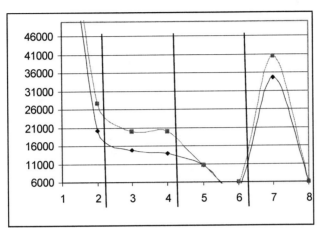

environment, meaning that not all subjects understood it as a maze-type of environment, but developed their own intrinsic representation of the environment. With the more information they were given as the experiment was progressing, they were forced to revise their expectancy tables, in the sense of IETAL.

The number of participants in the POPSICLE experiment was 75. As expected, this experiment showed that in most cases, initially, reaction times are relatively long, decreasing as the experiment continues. The pain (hitting the obstacle) in most cases decreases. After the pairing, the pair does better in the environment than when the user and the partner worked individually within the same environment.

The subjects were asked to answer a short list of questions after each component of the POPSICLE. Some of the responses, especially those on the first component where the only instruction to the subject was "to find the goal" were extremely interesting, which are motivating towards a closer investigation in the domain of inborn patterns: "I went as far right as I could, and then down as many times as possible, and then hit the goal." Others were expressing their observations in terms of contextual data: "It seems that the pattern is working in a sequence of three before you have to switch directions," or: "I noticed that I always see a red square about three moves away from the goal."

Copyright © 2006, Idea Group Inc. Copying or distributing in print or electronic forms without written permission of Idea Group Inc. is prohibited.

Figure 32. Average pain (hitting an obstacle) to goal. The upper curve is the cumulative data on all subjects, the lower on only the successful subjects.

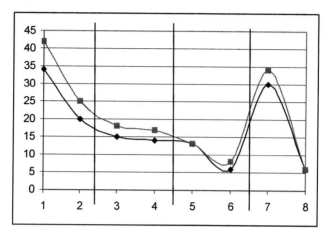

Figure 33. Time to action. The graph shows a typical form of the time of keystrokes in every segment of the steps, counting as 0 the time when the subject is

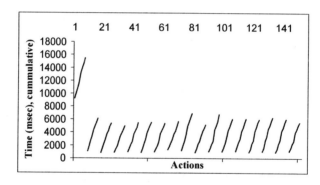

Some had trouble expressing the observations linguistically "Yes, there is definitely a pattern—I can do it, but cannot really write it down." All of the above statements add additional motivation to the POPSICLE team for further investigation of the presently available data, and modification of the experiment in order to more closely investigate different aspects of the phenomena at hand.

Copyright © 2006, Idea Group Inc. Copying or distributing in print or electronic forms without written permission of Idea Group Inc. is prohibited.

Figure 34. Time between actions (decision time). This example is from a subject in experimental phase 5.

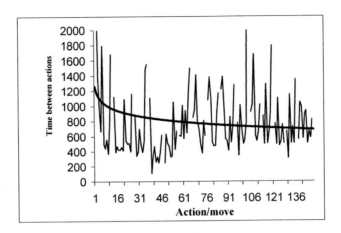

The lessons learned from POPSICLE will further help us calibrate our simulations of the agents in the IETAL, and MASIVE theories. The subjects' reactions are indications of a limited (for such a small environment), but valuable, variety of inborn schemas, in the sense of Piaget (1945). That will help us calibrate better our existing model and the fuzzy algebraic model based on our original work on fuzzy lattices and relations (Tepavcevic & Trajkovski, 2001), and previous work on brain waves (Trajkovski, 2003b).

An immediate goal is the analysis of the interrelation between the data obtained between pairs of subjects that worked together. For the (individual) parts 1, 3, 5, and 7, we are developing Internet environments, where volunteers would further provide us with data on the patterns in orientation.

Now that we have learned our initial lessons, the multi-subject parts of the experiments will be supplemented by information from a more comprehensive questionnaire with a smaller population.

In conclusion, POSICLE provides valuable kick-off information for our simulation environments, and lays the groundwork and direction for further explorations.

Copyright © 2006, Idea Group Inc. Copying or distributing in print or electronic forms without written permission of Idea Group Inc. is prohibited.

Technical Lessons from Isbushka

Teaching and Learning

The POPSICLE/Izbushka environments are all the result of significant involvement of students in the process. There were three basic modalities in which they were involved directly in the implementation process.

The experiment was conceptually developed within a small autopoietic classroom of an upper undergraduate elective Artificial Intelligence course. Due to the small size of the class, and based on talks about the instructor's personal research interest in cognitive science and theories of agency and learning, the students and the instructor came up with the concept of POPSICLE. The experiment was pre-tested, and preliminary decisions were made on the flow of the experiment. As a mini-project within the human-computer interaction module of the course, they developed a simple JAVA-based interface for the POPSICLE environment.

Another of the processes happened in the graduate classroom in Summer 2004, as a part of a course in Object Oriented methodology. Following our decision to have a hands-on, rather than all-theory summer, intensive course, we needed a project that would not only enable the students to experience the development of a medium-size environment, but also enhance their programming skills, and give them first-hand experience with a lot of software engineering decision making dilemmas on the go.

One-semester courses are quite restricting—timewise that is—when the goal is implementation of a project the size of POPSICLE. Not only did the participants need time for evaluating technical options, they also had a number of other courses to take care of; therefore, a balanced approach was more than necessary. A selected group of students, after completing the courses, decided to participate in some of the project modules within the frames of their graduate project work. Some of the undergraduate students decided to do so within the independent study options that they may opt to take.

In conclusion, the POPSICLE project has proven itself as a very useful and fruitful project for classroom infusion in the teaching of a wide range of topics, especially programming (JAVA, and a variety of JAVA-based libraries), design and implementation of interfaces, software engineering approaches, object-oriented programming, etc.

Copyright © 2006, Idea Group Inc. Copying or distributing in print or electronic forms without written permission of Idea Group Inc. is prohibited.

With the raw data collected from the experiments, students apply their knowledge of statistics and data mining techniques.

Building Agents and Societies

Intelligent agents, agency and multi-agent systems are the applied areas where POPSICLE may be used as a case study, to learn important lessons on what agents are, the imminent parameters of learning, learning algorithms and how they work, how agents communicate between themselves, what type and amount of information agents (may) exchange and how information exchange influences the learning in a multi-agent setting.

It is exactly because of this goal of the overall project that we have decided to include the simulation, uni- and multi-agent part, in the CVS environment. Not only because this part of the project emphasizes programming, interfaces and engineering of software, but also since it provides for an environment in which students with other than a software engineering focus can experiment with intelligent agents and societies and modify parameters of learning, without having to have too sound a technical knowledge.

Multicultural Lessons from Isbushka

Diversity of Agents

The experiments within the initial POPSICLE show that people learn in different ways. They conceptual the environment in different fashions; their observations are all different. Some manage to make out a satisfactory conceptualization of the environment within the frames of the 3-minute parts/sessions of the experiment, some did not. From the post-experiment interviews, many of them got stressed in one way or another (therefore the part 7 and 8 curves seem not to be in concert with the phenomena observed in parts 1-6).

Izbushka takes these initial insights even further. More than just an appreciation for difference (people perceive differently), Izbushka ontologically grounds diversity; without the brachiation of drives, perceptions and interpretive

Copyright © 2006, Idea Group Inc. Copying or distributing in print or electronic forms without written permission of Idea Group Inc. is prohibited.

frames, there is no Izbushka—it only works in the course of difference. This is similar to Henri Atlan's reinterpretations of the information circuit around the importance of noise, an insight Michel Serres takes up in *The Parasite*. In these works, it is noise that enables information, rather than, as with Shannon, the minimization of noise in a ratio of signal-to-noise. As Mark Taylor (2001, 136) paraphrases:

Insofar as an organism is understood as a communications system, noise plays a critical role in both its functioning and disfunctioning. [. . .] Noise, according to Atlan, is an "aleatory aggression" on the part of the environment, which, on the one hand, increases the disorder of the system, and, on the other hand, provides the occasion for the emergence of a more complex order.

In a multi-agent system like Izbushka, "noise," the missed keystrokes, the babble of confusion, the multiplication of interpretive frames, is the only way the simulation can take shape. The "noise" generates interpretations on the part of human- and non-human agents that, in turn, are constitutive of the environment. That is, we have to think of this multi-agent system autopoietically, as the self-organization of a system composed of human and non-human agents where "order" and "meaning" can only emerge in the course of disorder and nonsense.

This may even be a direct relationship. The more disorder, the more opportunities for order; the more nonsense, the multiplication of new opportunities for sense-making. Notice that complete entropy is as undesirable here as complete order; the activity only works in the space of the dialectic. Although physically we exhibit few significant differences, humans nevertheless differ psychologically, socially and culturally; these differences are vital to the functioning of the system. Without this important source of "noise," to go back to Atlan, there can be no meaning, or, to place this in relation to IT education, without diverse peoples following diverse questions, there can be no knowledge.

Other questions also arise. Should we all speak one language, hold the same beliefs? If we do, is that a limiting frame?

Critique Bias

Investigations into the behavior of the human subjects during the POPSICLE experiment lead us to believe that it is necessary to keep their motivation high

Copyright © 2006, Idea Group Inc. Copying or distributing in print or electronic forms without written permission of Idea Group Inc. is prohibited.

(Trajkovski et al., 2005). We have experimented with the implementation of a video game-like environment that will be motivating the subjects to score as many points as possible, actually awarding them for finding shorter paths to the goal from the start. Will the goal now be to "win" the simulation? Will this defocus the subject, and produce unusable data for the study?

If it's not winning, then what is the goal? The co-construction of a pattern and the production of divergent perspectives. Is the goal of social action always to "win"? Students reflect on the biases they bring to the simulation, and where those biases came from.

Isomorphisms to Invention, Contemporary Organizations and Diversity

Infusion of student research in the educational process, undergraduate or graduate, is very risky. Apart from having to frequently intervene (and as social workers at times), we have to be very sensitive in approaching these students. These partnerships are in general very time consuming. Students might not—and usually do not—have a clear picture of what research entails. Course length and other structured ways of organized education usually work out so that researchers cannot work with the same team for longer than one semester. But the process is isomorphic to invention, nevertheless. This kind of activity is a better description of discovery, with all its unstructured, chaotic, serendipitous elements. Is there a single goal in an organization (corporation, government, scientific laboratory) or is there a variety of goals? Which model is better?

Goals Emergent in the Context of Emergency

One classic example of emergence in robotics involves Hallam's and Malcom's (1994) wall-following robot.

This robot follows walls encountered to the right by means of an inbuilt bias to move to the right, and a right-side sensor, contact activated, that causes it to veer slightly to the left. When these two biases are well calibrated, the robot will follow the wall by a kind of "veer and bounce" routine. (Clark 2001,112)

While Clark wonders if this counts as genuinely emergent behavior, it shares some characteristics of other behaviors termed emergent, including flocking, in that both might be described as a shift in frames, i.e., the shift in the position of the observer. From the perspective of the wall-following robot, for example,

Copyright © 2006, Idea Group Inc. Copying or distributing in print or electronic forms without written permission of Idea Group Inc. is prohibited.

there is no "emergent" behavior, since there is no symbolic representation of "wall." Instead, the robot is merely acting on its program, and the "emergent" dimensions only exist in the minds of humans who find this wall-following pattern unexpected and interesting. Adaptive advantage aside, is "flocking" really different? In order to be "emergent," flocking needs an observer to place it in a different frame, i.e., a scopic panorama of the whole flock against a landscape rather than the perspective of a single, animal agent.

But this is not to debunk in any way theories of emergence nor suggest that attempts to mathematically model emergence aren't useful, although it does gesture to a certain polysemy in how scientists have operationalized that idea. Instead, we would suggest that there is a power to these kinds of perspectival shifts. By moving through different conceptual frames and multiplying perspectives, new possibilities may emerge, new "unprogrammed functionalities" that may prove adaptive and ultimately transformative, but are in no way "chaotic." This is close to Henri Bergson's idea of "creative evolution," where "each form flows out of previous forms, while adding something new, and is explained by them as much as it explains them" (quoted in Ansell-Pearson, 2002, p. 71).

In many ways, this is a synecdoche for the diversity in IT. Multiplying perspectives and upsetting the standard, stereotypical frames generate new ideas and contribute to the pace of innovation. As we have argued, there's no need to look far afield and import alternative "canons" of theory into IT; the potential has been here all along, evidenced here in an interesting, but by no means unusual, classroom activity.

Acknowledgments

The work on this paper has been funded in part by the National Academies of Sciences under the Twinning Program supported by contract no. INT-0002341 from the National Science Foundation. The contents of this publication do not necessarily reflect the views or policies of the National Academies of Sciences or the National Science Foundation, nor does mention of trade names, commercial products or organizations imply endorsement by the National Academies of Sciences or the National Science Foundation.

Copyright © 2006, Idea Group Inc. Copying or distributing in print or electronic forms without written permission of Idea Group Inc. is prohibited.

References

Ansell-Pearson, K. (2002). *Philosophy and the adventure of the virtual.* New York: Routledge.

Bateson, M. (1984). *With a daughter's eye.* New York: William Morrow and Co.

Brooks, R. (1997). From earwigs to humans. *Robotics and Autonomous Systems, 20,* 291-304.

Brooks, R., & Flynn, A. (1989). Fast, Cheap and Out of Control. *Journal of the British Interplanetary Society, 42,* 478-485.

Clark, A. (2001). *Mindware.* New York: Oxford University Press.

Deleuze, G., & Guattari, F. (1987). *A thousand plateaus.* Minneapolis: University of Minnesota Press.

English-Lueck, J. (2002). *Cultures@SiliconValley.* Stanford: Stanford University Press.

Ferber, J. (1999). *Multi-agent systems.* New York: Addison-Wesley.

Haraway, D. (1989). *Primate visions.* New York: Routledge.

Harding, S. (1994). Is science multicultural? *Configurations, 2.2,* 301-330.

Hayles, N. (1999). *How we became posthuman.* Chicago: University of Chicago Press.

Helmreich, S. (1998). *Silicon second nature.* Berkeley: University of California Press.

Helmreich, S. (2003). Trees and seas of information. *American Ethnologist, 30*(3), 341-359.

Hess, D. (1995). *Science and technology in a multicultural world.* New York: Columbia Universty Press.

Johnston, J. (2002). A future for autonomous agents. *Configurations, 10,* 473-516.

Latour, B. (1996). *Aramis, or the love of technology.* Cambridge: Harvard University Press.

Latour, B., & Woogar, S. (1979). *Laboratory life.* Beverly Hills, CA: Sage Publications.

LiPuma, E. (2001). *Encompassing others.* Ann Arbor: University of Michigan Press.

Copyright © 2006, Idea Group Inc. Copying or distributing in print or electronic forms without written permission of Idea Group Inc. is prohibited.

Maslow, A. (1970). *Motivation and personality* (2nd ed.). New York: Harper & Row.

Maturana, H., & Varela, F. (1980). *Autopoiesis and cognition.* Dordrecht: Reidel.

Merton, R. (1973). *The sociology of science.* Chicago: University of Chicago Press.

Murphy, R. (2000). *Introduction to AI robotics.* Cambridge: MIT Press.

National Science Board. (2003). *The science and engineering workforce.* Washington, DC: U.S. Government Printing Office.

Parisi, L. (2004). Information trading and symbiotic micropolitics, *Social Text, 80*(22), 3.

Piaget, J. (1945). *Play, dreams, and imitation in childhood.* Norton: New York.

Powell, T. (2003). All colors flow into rainbows and nooses. *Cultural Critique, 55,* 152-181.

Reid, A. (2000). Free action or resistance. *Theory and Event, 4*(3).

Riley, D. (2003). Employing liberative pedagogies in engineering education. *Journal of Women and Minorities in Science and Engineering, 9,* 137-158.

Ritchie, D. (2003). Argument is war. *Metaphor and symbol, 18*(2), 125-146.

Rizolatti, G., Fadiga, L., Gallese, V. & Fogassi, L.(1996). Premotor cortex and the recognition of motor actions. *Cognitive Brain Research, 3*(2),131-141.

Ross, A. (1996) Introduction. *Social Text, 46/47*(1-2), 1-13.

Shaviro, S. (2003). *Connected.* Minneapolis: University of Minnesota Press.

Stojanov, G., Bozinovski, S., & Trajkovski, G. (1997) Interactionist-expectative view on agency and learning. *IMACS Journal for Mathematics and Computers in Simulation, 44,* 219-310.

Stojanov, G., Bozinovski, S., & Trajkovski, G. (1997). Representation vs. context: A false dichotomy: Introducing intrinsic representations. In *Proc. 3rd European Conference on Cognitive Sciences (ECCS) – Workshop on Contex* (pp. 227-230). Manchester, UK.

Stojanov, G., & Trajkovski, G. (1998). Spatial representations for mobile robots: Detection of learnable and unlearnable environments. In *Proceed-*

Copyright © 2006, Idea Group Inc. Copying or distributing in print or electronic forms without written permission of Idea Group Inc. is prohibited.

ings of the First Congress of Mathematicians and Computer Scientists of Macedonia (pp. 151-156). Ohrid, Macedonia.

Strathern, M. (1992). *Reproducing the future.* New York: Routledge.

Taylor, M. (2001). *The moment of complexity.* Chicago: University of Chicago Press.

Tepavcevic, A., & Trajkovski, G. (2001). L-fuzzy lattices: An introduction. *Fuzzy Sets and Systems, 23,* 209-216.

Thorndike, E. (1898). Animal intelligence: an experimental study of the associative process in animals. *Psychological Review Monograph, 2,* 551-553.

Trajkovski, G. (2001). An imitation-based approach to modeling homogenous agents societies. Progress. In P. Brazdil & P. Jorge (Eds.), *AI knowledge extraction, multi-agent systems, logic programming, and constraint solving* (pp. 246-252). New York: Springer.

Trajkovski, G. (2003). Fuzzy sets in investigation of human cognitive processes. In A. Abraham & A. Lakhmi (Eds.) *Recent advances in intelligent paradigms* (Chapter 18). New York: Springer.

Trajkovski, G. (2003). MASIVE: A case study in multiagent systems. In H. Yin, N. Allison, R. Freeman, J. Keane, & S. Hubbard (Eds.), *Intelligent data engineering and automated leaning* (pp. 249-254). New York: Springer.

Trajkovski, G. (2003). *Representation of environments in multiagent systems.* Unpublished doctoral dissertation, SS Cyril and Methodius University, Skopje, Macedonia (in Macedonian).

Trajkovski, G., & Stojanov, G. (1998) Algebraic formalization of environment representation. *Agents Everywhere,* HU, 59-65 (pp. 29-65). Budapest: Springer

Trajkovski, G., Stojanov, G., & Vincenti, G. (2005). Extending MASIVE: The impact of stress on imitation-based learning. In *Proceedings of the 6th ACIS SNPD Conference* (pp. 330-365). Towson, MD: Towson.

Traweek, S. (1988). *Beamtimes and lifetimes.* Cambridge: Harvard University Press.

Woolridge, M. (2002). *An introduction to multiagent systems.* New York: John Wiley & Sons.

Copyright © 2006, Idea Group Inc. Copying or distributing in print or electronic forms without written permission of Idea Group Inc. is prohibited.

Chapter XI

Adaptive Technology in a Computing Curriculum

Blaise W. Liffick, Millersville University, USA

Abstract

This chapter describes how adaptive technology (AT) for the disabled can enhance a computing curriculum. It argues that computer professionals will naturally have an increasing role in the support of AT, as a result of economic, legal and social pressures, and that as a consequence AT topics should be covered within a standard computing curriculum. Ideas for integrating AT topics into computing courses are presented, along with an outline of an advanced course on AT from a computer science perspective. A model AT laboratory for supporting these efforts is described. The author hopes that this chapter will encourage computing educators to use AT topics as examples within their courses, ultimately leading to a computing workforce that is ready, willing and able to provide fundamental AT services to those with disabilities.

Copyright © 2006, Idea Group Inc. Copying or distributing in print or electronic forms without written permission of Idea Group Inc. is prohibited.

Introduction

The term *diversity* is most often used in relationship to either gender or ethnicity, along with all of the thorny issues of discrimination, imbalanced economics and social conflicts. Computer systems, however, typically work the same regardless of a user's gender or ethnicity. While design bias in a particular system might be shown at times to favor or discourage a particular group, by and large computerized systems are accessible to any user regardless of gender or ethnicity—problems of accessibility tend to be social or economic, not technical.

The same cannot be said, however, for those with disabilities. Basic accessibility, e.g., being able to start a program, issue commands, access media, etc., is a problem with computer systems used by those with disabilities, resulting in a large percentage of the population encountering significant difficulties in using modern technology. This chapter introduces this problem along with curricula aimed at educating future computing professionals on how to develop universally accessible systems. It shows how incorporating systems for the disabled into standard computing degree programs not only serves the need for better accessibility, but also provides interesting applications for computing students that enhance the overall learning experience.

Background

Adaptive technology (AT—also known as *assistive technology*) is computer hardware and/or software used to increase, maintain or improve the functional capabilities of individuals with disabilities. Although AT actually has a much broader definition, including, for instance, mechanical devices such as standard wheelchairs or walkers, foam supports for arranging posture, etc. (Cook & Hussey, 2002), the focus of this chapter is clearly on computerized devices and software.

It doesn't take a very long look at disabilities statistics (Cunningham & Coombs, 1997) to give one pause. Nearly 20% of Americans are disabled, with half that number being classified as "severe." There are some 700,000 newly disabled Americans each year. One of each 100 babies born in this country has a disability. By the year 2030, 26% of Americans will be over age 65, virtually all of whom will be coping with age-related disabilities or

Copyright © 2006, Idea Group Inc. Copying or distributing in print or electronic forms without written permission of Idea Group Inc. is prohibited.

limitations. Some 10% of all college students have a disability. Nearly three quarters of the disabled are unemployed.

Adaptive technology is increasingly available to either help compensate for a disability or to provide accessibility to information and services; in general, improving the quality of life of the disabled. Computer professionals, especially those involved in human-computer interaction (HCI), have an expertise in developing and evaluating devices from a usability perspective. However, currently this expertise is too seldom directed at the AT field. As a consequence, many AT devices are poorly designed from a usability perspective, resulting in extensive training needs, poor utilization by clients and frequent abandonment of the AT by users. The poor matching of devices to persons with disabilities exacerbates this, leading to nearly one third of AT being abandoned within three months (Scherer, 2000). Finally, the complexity of many AT devices is often an impediment to potential users, requiring extensive computing experience to take full advantage of features.

Those who are most often called upon to provide service for AT, such as occupational therapists or speech-language pathologists, are also typically not well prepared for the complexities of computerized devices. This lack of skill is due to a number of factors. To begin with, the degree programs for persons entering this field are by necessity general in their approach to the disabled population and focus on the fundamentals of human anatomy, biomechanics, neurology, cognitive psychology, pathologies and the health care system— often without a single course on adaptive technology. Even more specialized professional degree programs, such as speech-language pathology or special education, have little room in their curricula for more than a cursory introduction to AT. Finally, the complexities of some systems require extensive computer knowledge to install, configure and maintain, especially when things go wrong.

The intricacies of high-tech AT devices require a level of computer sophistication that is much higher than that typically possessed by those who provide primary services to the disabled. While many of the devices (e.g., a trackball) are simple to install and configure, the real difficulties involve issues such as interoperability (or *in*operability, as the case may be), and dealing with a complex system when something goes wrong. A recent email posted to an AT listserv (personal communication, September 27, 2004) from a desperate service provider illustrates: "I am looking for some help when backing up a [particular type of augmentative communication device] ... to Windows XP. I tried yesterday with no success...does anyone know any tricks/tips that may help me out?" Unfortunately, this type of request for technical support is not

Copyright © 2006, Idea Group Inc. Copying or distributing in print or electronic forms without written permission of Idea Group Inc. is prohibited.

the least bit uncommon. Another post to the AT listserv (personal communication, December 5, 2004) illustrates the frustrations that develop when no one is ready to take responsibility for problems that develop: "Too few people on site have the chance to educate themselves about how the specific technology works.... And the [school] district's computer network troubleshooter knows computers, but not assistive tech, so he sometimes can't help out much either!" Clearly there is a need for professionals who can bridge this gap.

The Role of Computer Professionals in AT

Computer professionals are needed by AT developers to research and develop new AT devices and techniques. Beyond that, computing professionals are also needed for providing numerous levels of support to those who use AT, including evaluations of products, installations, upgrades, backups and configurations.

To begin with, as employers strive to comply with the requirements of laws such as the Americans with Disabilities Act (ADA) to provide reasonable accommodations to employees who are disabled, computer personnel will be required to provide the technical support for AT devices and software. This occurs both as companies hire more disabled employees, and as they are required to provide support for current employees who become disabled.

In addition to the legal requirements of the ADA, Section 508 of the Rehabilitation Act and similar laws, there are good economic reasons for companies to provide complete accessibility to company information, services and products. No company wants to create barriers to anyone who wants to be a customer. Companies need to ensure that their Web sites as well as printed documents, forms, etc., are in formats as accessible as possible. Developing accessible Web sites requires special knowledge about accessible Web design, as well as knowledge of AT systems such as screen-reading software. Conversion of printed documents into accessible formats requires knowledge of special software and hardware. These responsibilities to ensure universal accessibility are most likely to fall upon computing personnel to handle.

AT in a Computing Curriculum

One of the topics of a typical human-computer interaction (HCI) course is the diversity of users. This is usually discussed in a variety of ways, including

Copyright © 2006, Idea Group Inc. Copying or distributing in print or electronic forms without written permission of Idea Group Inc. is prohibited.

physical and cognitive skills, personality types, cultural and international differences, novices versus experts, age differences, etc. The concept of universal usability, that takes the "diversity of human abilities, backgrounds, motivations, personalities, cultures, and work styles" (Shneiderman & Plaisant, 2005, p. 24) into account, is of growing interest within the HCI community.

One of the areas that is least discussed in HCI courses, however, is differences due to disabilities. In a recent survey of 16 of the most widely used HCI textbooks, only two of those books contained sufficient mention of disabilities issues to warrant a reference in the book's index (Liffick, 2003). The total page coverage of the topic in all of these books combined was just six pages. Outside of HCI, there is virtually no mention of disabilities within computing curricula. However, given the size of the disabled population, and the importance of computer technology in the ultimate support of that population, it is vital to incorporate disabilities issues into a computing curriculum. Furthermore, AT provides a rich source of practical examples for software and hardware development within a computing curriculum, giving students more concrete examples of how their work impacts the real world. In addition, including AT in the curriculum opens up opportunities for service learning projects for students, allowing them to work on real-world problems while providing invaluable services to disabilities service agencies.

Finally, one significant pedagogical issue is the egocentric nature of most students. One of the necessary skills that is difficult to teach is the ability to design systems from the perspective of others, i.e., user-centered design. Students tend to look inward for user models, in part because the assignments they are given require nothing more—they use simple, standard I/O techniques so that the user interface requires little thought to develop. As a consequence, students tend to design with the tacit assumption that *they* are the typical user. This may easily be seen in how students test their programs for bugs, using only obvious data instead of comprehensive test cases. One of the significant benefits of using AT examples and assignments is that students are forced out of themselves when thinking about how a system is going to be used. The result is professionals who can think beyond themselves for solutions, who naturally take users into account in their designs and who easily adopt universal design strategies (Center, n.d.).

Copyright © 2006, Idea Group Inc. Copying or distributing in print or electronic forms without written permission of Idea Group Inc. is prohibited.

Curriculum Ideas

AT may be used as applied examples in many of the classic areas of computer or information science, including architecture, operating systems, artificial intelligence, software engineering, human-computer interaction, networking and Web development. Incorporating AT examples into these courses fits very well into curriculum models such as those promoted by the ACM for computer science, information science and software engineering (ACM, 2005). It also fits well within the accreditation guidelines of ABET (ABET, n.d.).

The ACM Computing Curricula 2001 model curriculum (Computing, 2001) is organized as a series of knowledge units related to the fourteen areas listed in Table 1. All but one of these areas (CN) contain elements of core topics, with most also containing advanced topic elements. The following sections illustrate how AT fits within many of these topic areas. In addition, of course, programming with an application to AT fits within the more general topics related to the design and implementation of software, such as in the Programming Fundamentals and Software Engineering topics.

An additional common thread related to AT that runs throughout a computing curriculum is accessibility and its relationship to universal design principles (Center, n.d.). Just as we have concepts about what makes software "good" or "bad" from a design or implementation perspective (e.g., programs should be well documented, include appropriate indentation, use appropriate algorithms, etc.), we can also apply criteria to judge how usable and accessible a

Table 1. ACM computing curricula 2001 areas of knowledge

Discrete Structures (DS)
Programming Fundamentals (PF)
Algorithms and Complexity (AL)
Architecture and Organization (AR)
Operating Systems (OS)
Net-centric Computing (NC)
Programming Languages (PL)
Human-Computer Interaction (HU)
Graphics and Visual Computing (GV)
Intelligent Systems (IS)
Information Management (IM)
Social and Professional Issues (SP)
Software Engineering (SE)
Computational Science and Numerical Methods (CN)

Copyright © 2006, Idea Group Inc. Copying or distributing in print or electronic forms without written permission of Idea Group Inc. is prohibited.

given program is in terms of its interface, how well a program's interface meets the needs of its intended users or how universal an interface design is. These concepts cut across the entire curriculum of computing, since they may apply to every program a student develops in the same ways that good design and implementation criteria are applied.

Architecture and Organization (AR)

Within the core section of this category are topics related to input/output (I/O fundamentals, such as handshaking, buffering, etc.), along with a discussion of various bus structures. Since many of the AT devices involve connection to general computer systems via, for instance, a USB connection, the interfacing of such devices provides an excellent example of hardware issues. In addition, AAC devices are typically interfaced to general computers either to provide a backup mechanism (requiring students to learn about data transference mechanisms) or as specialized input devices. On a more general level, the use of I/O devices such as touchscreens would add interest to discussions about innovative hardware.

Operating Systems (OS)

As in the case of the architecture area, operating systems provide a rich topic area for introducing AT into a computing curriculum. Interrupt-driven devices, device management and drivers, embedded systems and hand-held devices are all areas of concern for AT development. In addition, a comparative study of the accessibility issues between Windows®-based and Unix-based systems would highlight not only disabilities issues but also general issues related to the OS user interface.

Net-Centric Computing (NC)

The inaccessibility (at least initially) of much of the technology developed for the World Wide Web pervades this area. Discussing emerging net technologies and assessing "their current capabilities, limitations, and near-term potentials" is one of the learning objectives for an introduction to this core topic area (Computing, 2001, p. 108). This should be done in the context of how these

Copyright © 2006, Idea Group Inc. Copying or distributing in print or electronic forms without written permission of Idea Group Inc. is prohibited.

innovations affect the ability of AT users to access information via the Web. A detailed investigation of mobile and wireless computing would also be beneficial. For instance, there are some indications that Bluetooth® technology might be useful in connecting AT to computers, providing a better connection method for those who have difficulty connecting cables.

Human-Computer Interaction (HU)

This area is, of course, a natural fit for discussions about disabilities and AT. One of the major topics of HCI is accommodating human diversity, which would include issues of cognitive and physical differences in addition to the usual international differences. User-centered design is fundamental to this area, and could be used to introduce students to particular user populations, particularly those with specific disabilities. Usability testing of AT devices, or systems not meant specifically for use by those with a disability, may be used to introduce evaluation techniques. A section on graphical user-interface design includes "choosing interaction styles and interaction techniques," which could be used to introduce interaction methods and devices to meet the needs of particular disabled users, such as scanning (Computing, 2001, p. 120). Speech recognition is another area that lends itself easily to discussing accessibility issues. Finally, AT devices provide a much wider set of input and output options than most users encounter. Their specific characteristics and use would provide valuable examples both for selecting interaction methods for a specific application and for quantitative analysis of potential user performance.

Graphic and Visual Computing (GV)

Core learning objectives include an understanding of various input devices and emerging technology for creating and displaying graphics. For example, touchscreen technology is now widely used in augmentative/alternative communication (AAC) devices. A discussion of the tradeoffs between using dynamically- and statically-displayed interfaces for such devices would provide an excellent example of the issues surrounding device capabilities and selection criteria.

Copyright © 2006, Idea Group Inc. Copying or distributing in print or electronic forms without written permission of Idea Group Inc. is prohibited.

Intelligent Systems (IS)

Many techniques that have found their way into AT systems originated within the field of artificial intelligence (AI), such as speech generation and recognition. The development of intelligent agents to provide personal assistants for those with disabilities provides a concrete example of the need for such methods. Personal robotics to aid those with disabilities is another useful example that fits well within this area. Semantic word prediction methods are also important methods that use AI techniques.

Information Management (IM)

"This area includes the capture, digitization, representation, organization, transformation, and presentation of information...." (Computing, 2001, p. 139). Part of this includes topics related to hypertext and hypermedia. Accessibility to hypermedia has frequently been troublesome for those with disabilities, particularly the visually impaired. Methods to ensure universal access are an important part of this topic.

Social and Professional Issues (SP)

This area provides an obvious ground for discussing disabilities issues on a more general level than in the other sections. Concerns about the social context of computing should introduce accessibility as a problem of disenfranchisement of the disabled. Accessibility tools, such as voice generation systems, often require licensing agreements, introducing concerns about intellectual property rights. The social impact of using a synthesized voice could also be discussed. Economic issues related to the high unemployment rate among the disabled should also be addressed as an accessibility issue.

An Adaptive Computing Course

Figure 1 gives an outline for a complete course in adaptive technologies that would fit well in any computing curriculum as an advanced elective. The main prerequisite is advanced programming skills. A human-computer interaction

Copyright © 2006, Idea Group Inc. Copying or distributing in print or electronic forms without written permission of Idea Group Inc. is prohibited.

Figure 1. An adaptive technologies course description

Title: Adaptive Technologies

Description:
Topics in this course include the universal design principle; user-centered design; interfacing specialized hardware devices; interaction methods such as Morse code, voice recognition and generation, scanning techniques, word expansion and word prediction; modes of communication, such as single or multi-switch, audio and voice and alternative languages; web accessibility; and usability testing as a means of user/device evaluation and product acceptance.

Objectives:
The successful student will:
- Be able to identify the major types of disabilities
- Be able to match disability types to specific adaptive technology
- Demonstrate skill at interfacing and installing a variety of adaptive devices
- Demonstrate skill at making Web sites accessible
- Demonstrate understanding of built-in accessibility controls for the Windows® environment
- Demonstrate understanding of augmentative-alternative communication devices
- Demonstrate ability to perform usability testing as an assessment tool
- Demonstrate understanding of various interaction methods

Course Topics

I.   The Disabled User
    A.   Visual Function
    B.   Auditory Function
    C.   Somatosensory Function
    D.   Cognitive Function
    E.   Motor Control
II.   Disabilities Legislation
III.   Universal & User-Centered Design
IV.   Basic Human-Computer Interaction Practices
    A.   I/O devices
    B.   I/O methods
    C.   Models of interaction
    D.   Human Factors
    E.   Usability studies
V.   Control Interfaces
    A.   General characteristics
    B.   Selecting control interfaces for the user
    C.   Direct selection
    D.   Indirect selection
    E.   Integrated control systems
VI.   Augmentative/Alternative Communication
    A.   Communication systems
    B.   Multimodal communication
    C.   Conversational needs
    D.   Graphical output needs
    E.   Control interface
    F.   Selection method
    G.   Selection set
    H.   Selection technique
    I.   Accelerating/extending vocabulary
    J.   Vocabulary storage
    E. K.   Text editing

    L.   Output control
    M.   Speech output
    N.   General computer and Internet access
VII.   Visual Impairment Aids
    A.   Screen magnification
    B.   Text to Braille
    C.   Text to speech
    D.   Electronic travel aids
VIII.   Speech Synthesis
IX.   Speech Recognition
X.   Web Accessibility
XI.   Wireless AT Devices
XII.   AT for the Elderly
XIII.   User evaluation and assessment
    A.   AT abandonment issues
    B.   Language Analysis Monitoring
    C.   Evidence-based practice
    D.   Usability study as evaluation tool

(HCI) course could also be a natural prerequisite, in which case the general overview of HCI could be eliminated from this course.

In looking at the list of topics, one might expect this course to be more at home in a field such as occupational therapy or speech-language pathology. However, the emphasis of this course is on how these systems are constructed, not just on how to operate them. For instance, one technique with a significant basis

Copyright © 2006, Idea Group Inc. Copying or distributing in print or electronic forms without written permission of Idea Group Inc. is prohibited.

Figure 2. An example of word prediction using the WiViK® on-screen keyboard system

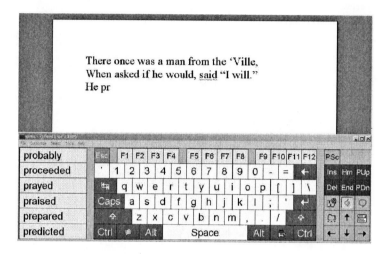

in computer science (specifically artificial intelligence) is word prediction. Figure 2 shows the WiViK® on-screen keyboard system with word prediction being used to enter text into a general word processing program. In the earliest prediction systems, a simple lexical matching was performed, which looked only at all the words that begin, for instance, with "pr." Today, words are predicted semantically (as in the figure), taking the context of the potential next word into account in addition to the lexical elements. This semantic analysis is derived from natural language processing. Speech synthesis and speech recognition also developed out of the artificial intelligence field, and are also presented in the course from that perspective.

A Model AT Laboratory

Can a typical computing program support the lab requirements of incorporating AT topics into the curriculum, or for an entire course on adaptive technologies? There are clearly some start-up costs in doing so, and some of the potential equipment and software is quite expensive. The most sophisticated screen-reading systems, for instance, cost between $1,000 and $1,500. Augmentative/alternative communication (AAC) devices range between about $3,500 and $8,000. Head-tracking systems range up to nearly $1,800.

Copyright © 2006, Idea Group Inc. Copying or distributing in print or electronic forms without written permission of Idea Group Inc. is prohibited.

Table 2. Some of the special AT hardware and software available in the model lab

WiVox® Text-to-Speech System
CAST E-Reader Text-to-Speech System
Kurzweil 1000 Text-to-Speech System
JAWS® Screen Reading System
ZoomText Screen Enlargement System
IntelliKeys® Keyboard
Discover: Board Keyboard
Discover: Switch System
IBM ViaVoice Speech Recognition
Dragon NaturallySpeaking Speech Recognition
WiVik® On-Screen Keyboard with Word Prediction
KeyREP Word Prediction System
Penny & Giles Roller Plus Trackball
Penny & Giles Roller Plus Joystick
Tracker 2000 Head Tracking System
Words+ EZKeys Communication System
Words+ IST Switch Interface
Prentke-Romich Pathfinder AAC Device

Table 2 shows a listing of AT systems that were purchased for the model Adaptive Computing Lab (ACL) supported by a National Science Foundation (NSF) grant (Liffick, 2002). There are several purposes for these specific systems. First, they provide examples of some of the typical AT that is currently available—it is important to familiarize students with the current state of the art. It is also useful for students to gain experience in installing and operating these systems, particularly since some systems may conflict with each other. Second, when several systems of the same type (e.g., screen readers) are available, students may perform comparative studies of techniques and features, an important skill when faced with evaluating products for possible use with a given individual. Third, they provide models on which to base student projects, or devices students can use within those projects. Finally, such systems provide platforms on which students may conduct usability studies.

This model lab emphasizes three particular areas of AT: screen readers, alternative access devices and AAC devices. These correspond to AT in the areas of visual impairment (with some crossover into cognitive impairment), physical impairment, and augmentative/alternative communication, representing three of the largest categories of disabilities that could benefit from computerized AT.

Copyright © 2006, Idea Group Inc. Copying or distributing in print or electronic forms without written permission of Idea Group Inc. is prohibited.

Devices for the Visually Impaired

The text- and screen-reading software used in the lab provides a wide range of capabilities, from simple text reading to sophisticated systems intended for use by the blind, and from the Narrator system built into Microsoft Windows® to professional level systems. Some of these systems (e.g., CAST E-Reader) are also useful for those with cognitive or learning disabilities, highlighting words as the system reads them or assisting in writing tasks with verbal support. The Kurzweil system also provides for scanning in text using optical character recognition, converting printed text to electronic form. The JAWS® system from Freedom Scientific is one of the most popular systems used by those who are blind.

Devices for the Physically Impaired

For the physically impaired, the objective is to provide as wide a range of input options as possible. Alternative keyboards such as IntelliKeys® and Discover: Board is one approach (see Figure 3). The IntelliKeys® system is particularly versatile, providing numerous replaceable overlays and the creation of customized keyboards. Other options for alternatives to standard keyboards might include miniature keyboards or chording keyboards (similar to a court stenographer's keyboard).

Alternative pointing devices, such as a trackball or joystick, are also important. While in some instances standard versions of such devices are usable, in others

Figure 3. A workshop participant using an IntelliKeys® keyboard

Copyright © 2006, Idea Group Inc. Copying or distributing in print or electronic forms without written permission of Idea Group Inc. is prohibited.

Figure 4. A specially designed trackball and joystick by Penny & Giles

a sturdier or specialized version is required. Figure 4 shows a trackball and joystick designed specifically for more "heavy duty" use. They incorporate components that can handle physical abuse and are moisture resistant. They also contain keyguards that allow someone with limited use of their arms or hands to have designated gripping points for all buttons. In addition, the devices include special buttons, such as a locking selection to facilitate dragging operations, and an X/Y direction-locking button to limit cursor motion to a single direction.

A head-tracking device provides pointing for those with limited control of their hands. The type provided in this model lab (Tracker 2000 from Words+) uses an infrared beam that detects a reflective dot the user positions on their forehead or glasses. This device illustrates issues related to range of motion, fault tolerance and user fatigue in addition to being an interesting example of infrared range finding and position translation.

On the extreme end, control of a computer with just single switches combined with special scanning software completes the spectrum of access methods. These devices provide an opportunity to demonstrate various switch types, such as a microswitch, eyebrow switch, infrared switch or sound-activated switch. These devices are used with individuals who have the most limited ranges of motion. They are used to illustrate scanning as an interaction method. Speech recognition systems are another way of providing access to computer systems for those with limited mobility.

Copyright © 2006, Idea Group Inc. Copying or distributing in print or electronic forms without written permission of Idea Group Inc. is prohibited.

AAC Devices

It is unlikely that a computing lab can afford more than a couple of AAC devices at most because of their high cost. Such devices range from PDA-sized systems costing $3,000-$4,000 to systems based on laptops costing more than $8,000. Nearly all AAC devices offer dynamic displays with touch-screen technology as the main interaction method. The notable exception is the Pathfinder from Prentke-Romich Corporation, which offers both a small dynamic interaction window and a static keyboard area with up to 128 keys (see Figure 5). One of the interesting issues that invites scientific study is the relative communication speeds of such devices. Other aspects of these devices that can be studied include cognitive load issues for the user.

One of the enduring problems of the AAC field is how to select a particular device for a given individual. Much interesting work may be done by students investigating ways to reliably match devices to users.

Finally, AAC users would typically like to be able to use their AAC device as their interface method to a standard computer for all the usual functions for which anyone uses a computer: email, word processing, spreadsheets, Web access, etc. Some AAC devices are much better suited to this use than others. One of the frequent complaints of AAC users is the difficulty of setting up their devices in this way. In addition, connecting AAC devices to PCs is also done to provide a backup method for the device and for providing a monitoring method for evidence-based practice evaluations (Hill & Romich, 2002). Such

Figure 5. The Prentke-Romich Pathfinder AAC device, with 128-key iconic keyboard and dynamic touchscreen display

Copyright © 2006, Idea Group Inc. Copying or distributing in print or electronic forms without written permission of Idea Group Inc. is prohibited.

uses provide numerous opportunities for computing students to test their expertise in hardware and software configuration and interfacing.

Software Product Trial Versions

Many software products have a free trial version available for download, including emulations of some of the AAC devices. While these are somewhat useful for a lab of this sort, they are usually either reduced systems (with features such as *save* disabled) or have a limited timeframe of usability (e.g., 30 or 90 days). Most vendors require registering to obtain the trial download, and the systems frequently are configured to prevent reinstallation once the trial period has expired (even with a fresh download). Some developers are open to negotiating less restrictive configurations of the trial versions of their products for educational laboratory use, however.

Operating System Issues

One issue that should be addressed in an AT lab is the Windows®-centric nature of most AT systems, which has occurred for obvious reasons. However, there are strong reasons to include both Apple Macintosh and Unix-based systems within the lab. Doing so certainly opens up interesting project opportunities for students, such as developing drivers for AT hardware for these other operating systems.

Additional Resources

While there are no textbooks specifically written on adaptive computing from a computer science perspective, there are numerous texts on AT that go beyond the superficial level of AT devices and software. Cook and Hussey (2002), in particular, provides many technical details of control interfaces, selection techniques and AAC devices, in addition to an excellent overview of the human factors involved in disabilities. Scherer (2000) provides extensive context for understanding the psychology of AT and users with disabilities, along with an introduction to her "Matching Person and Technology" model for AT-related assessments. Galvin and Scherer (1996) is a collection of articles covering the evaluation, selection and maintenance of AT, in addition to

Copyright © 2006, Idea Group Inc. Copying or distributing in print or electronic forms without written permission of Idea Group Inc. is prohibited.

governmental policy, legislation and funding of AT. Beukelman and Mirenda (1998) is a bit dated technologically, but still offers a definitive discussion of augmentative/alternative communication issues and techniques.

More technical discussions of AT may be found in the proceedings of several conferences, particularly ASSETS, sponsored by the Association for Computing Machinery's (ACM) Special Interest Group on Accessible Computing (SIGACCESS, n.d.). Another ACM group that supports work in this area is the Special Interest Group on Computer-Human Interaction (SIGCHI, n.d.), which also hosts an annual conference. The HCI International conference (HCI, 2005) offers tracks on ergonomics, universal accessibility, usability and cognitive science. There are also two AT conferences in particular that are excellent places to learn about AT products: Closing the Gap (Closing, 2005) and the California State University at Northridge Center on Disabilities annual conference (CSUN, 2003).

There are, of course, numerous online resources related to AT and disabilities, including Web sites, online newsletters, listservs, distance learning opportunities, etc. Many of these resources have been posted to the Millersville University Department of Computer Science Adaptive Computing Lab's Web site (http://cs.millersville.edu/labs/acl.html). It includes links on research and education, accessibility, advocacy and support, companies and vendors of AT products and additional information about the lab.

Potential Impact of Including
AT in a Computing Curriculum

Incorporating AT topics within a computing curriculum is a straightforward way to help meet the ACM and ABET curriculum guidelines for including social, ethical and legal issues within a computer or information science degree program. For instance, although the technology of AAC devices may provide a voice for those who have none, there are problems related to the artificiality of the voices projected: Recipients may have difficulty understanding the voice because of oddities of pronunciation and the lack of natural prosody; the speed of generation is very slow compared to natural speech, which causes conversational difficulties; and there are some perceptions of a lack of intelligence on the part of AAC users. Legal issues could include the application of disabilities

Copyright © 2006, Idea Group Inc. Copying or distributing in print or electronic forms without written permission of Idea Group Inc. is prohibited.

laws such as the Americans with Disabilities Act or Section 508 of the Rehabilitation Act, or the need for licensing agreements for use of voice synthesizers in AAC products. The ethics of creating systems that are inaccessible to the disabled could also be explored.

Including AT topics will also make students more competitive in the job market. American companies are required by law to make reasonable accommodations for disabled workers and to provide accessibility to information and services for disabled consumers. In addition, this educational experience opens up employment opportunities within the AT field itself, on both the development and after-sale support sides. There are several thousand AT products now available which need computer professionals to provide support. In a field that has seen a massive retrenchment in recent years along with foreign outsourcing, the AT field is one that will continue to require significant amounts of hands-on, face-to-face support.

Finally, as AT topics are brought into the mainstream of computing degrees, it is likely that the number of disabled entering the computer field will increase. It will open up career opportunities for the disabled, especially when coupled with businesses willing to allow such employees to telecommute. Once the issue of access is resolved, the person on the other end of the network could be indistinguishable from anyone else in the office.

Conclusion

This chapter has presented adaptive technology for the disabled as an issue of diversity within the computing field on several levels. First, providing more career opportunities with computing for those with disabilities seems a natural fit in many ways: Many of the disabled are technologically savvy out of necessity; sophisticated computing systems may be used to minimize limitations of disabilities, and telecommuting opportunities have obvious advantages for both employer and disabled employee. The result should be that many of those with disabilities would find a natural home within the computing field.

Second, it is important for the computer field to take a stance against creating additional barriers for those with disabilities. As new interaction technology is developed, we must make certain that accessibility is maintained. Just as it is now considered unethical to design buildings that block access for those in

Copyright © 2006, Idea Group Inc. Copying or distributing in print or electronic forms without written permission of Idea Group Inc. is prohibited.

wheelchairs, so, too, should it be considered unethical to create technologies that would be inaccessible to the disabled.

Finally, computer professionals should be trained from the onset in the skills of universal design. This requires that they be educated to design systems with the needs of all users taken into account. User-centered and universal design principles should be introduced into the mainstream of computing degree programs. By using examples and assignments that have an adaptive technology component, we help our students develop the skills needed to develop truly inclusive systems, accommodating the widest range of diversity possible.

Acknowledgments

The author wishes to thank the National Science Foundation for its support of this work with the CCLI-EMD grant "Integrating Assistive Technology into an Undergraduate Computer Science Curriculum from an HCI Approach" (DUE-0230969).

References

ABET accreditation evaluation guidelines. (n.d.). Retrieved January 5, 2005, from http://www.abet.org/criteria.html

ACM curricula recommendations. (2005). Retrieved January 5, 2005, from http://acm.org/education/curricula.html

Beukelman, D. R., & Mirenda, P. (1998). *Augmentative and alternative communication* (2nd ed.). Baltimore: Paul H. Brookes Publishing Co.

Center for universal design. (n.d.). Retrieved January 5, 2005 from http://www.design.ncsu.edu/cud/

Closing the Gap. (2005). Retrieved January 7, 2005 from http://www.closingthegap.com/index.lasso

Computing curricula 2001: Computer science. (2001). Retrieved January 5, 2005 from http://www.computer.org/education/cc2001/final/cc2001.pdf

Cook, A., & Hussey, S. (2002). *Assistive technologies principles and practice* (2nd ed.). St. Louis, MO: Mosby, Inc.

Copyright © 2006, Idea Group Inc. Copying or distributing in print or electronic forms without written permission of Idea Group Inc. is prohibited.

CSUN Center on Disabilities. (2003). Retrieved January 7, 2005, from http://www.csun.edu/cod/

Cunningham, C., & Coombs. N. (1997). *Information access and adaptive technology*. Phoenix, AZ: Oryx Press.

Galvin, J. C., & Scherer, M. J. (1996). *Evaluating, selecting, and using appropriate assistive technology*. Gaithersburg, MD: Aspen Publishers.

HCI International. (2005). Retrieved January 6, 2005 from http://www.hci-international.org/

Hill, K., & Romich, B. (2002). A Language activity monitor to support AAC evidence-based clinical practice. *Assistive Technology, 13*(1).

Liffick, B. (2002). *Integrating assistive technology into an undergraduate computer science curriculum from an HCI approach*. Retrieved January 5, 2005, from http://www.nsf.gov/awardsearch/showAward.do?AwardNumber=0230969

Liffick, B. (2003). Assistive technology in computer science. *Proceedings of the International Symposium on Information and Communication Technologies ISICT03* (pp. 46-51). Trinity College, Dublin, Ireland.

Scherer, M. (2000). *Living in the state of stuck: How assistive technology impacts the lives of people with disabilities* (3rd ed.). Cambridge, MA: Brookline Books.

Shneiderman, B., & Plaisant, C. (2005). *Designing the user interface* (4th ed.). Boston: Addison Wesley.

SIGACCESS. (n.d.). Retrieved January 6, 2005 from http://www.acm.org/sigaccess/

SIGCHI. (n.d.). Retrieved January 6, 2005 from http://www.acm.org/sigchi/

Copyright © 2006, Idea Group Inc. Copying or distributing in print or electronic forms without written permission of Idea Group Inc. is prohibited.

Chapter XII

Tessellations:
A Tool for Diversity Infusions in the Curriculum

Reza Sarhangi, Towson University, USA

Gabriele Meiselwitz, Towson University, USA

Goran P. Trajkovski, Towson University, USA

Abstract

Introducing diversity topics in the natural, mathematical and computer sciences is a hard task, since these disciplines are traditionally labeled as "diversity-unfriendly," due to their primary foci of study. In this chapter we illustrate how tessellations may be used as a tool for infusion of multicultural topics, as well as a framework, designed after the Towson University course "Computers and Creativity," where these concepts have been successfully implemented.

Copyright © 2006, Idea Group Inc. Copying or distributing in print or electronic forms without written permission of Idea Group Inc. is prohibited.

Introduction

Diversity is an omnipresent buzzword in academic circles in the continuing efforts to diversify the curricula. The term "diversity" is hard to define, but everyone seems to understand it as plethora of varieties. We can define it as narrowly or as widely as needed in a given discourse, but the bottom line is that diversity is "being aware of what is there." Due to the nature of the subject, it seems easy to have whole courses or significant modules on women's issues, gender, national origins, disability, etc., in the social sciences and the humanities. However, the natural, mathematical and computer sciences are believed to be more hostile to these topics. The infusion of diversity in such courses cannot be done as explicitly as in some other disciplines, but many of us do it every day in our classrooms.

In order to illustrate the micro infusion of diversity topics in teaching "diversity-unfriendly" disciplines, here are some tidbits that can be used not only to achieve the educational goal of a lecture, but also go the extra mile. They refer to the computer sciences specifically. Instead of showing the students how to build tables in Excel on a generic example using data on the imaginary "ACME Tomato Company" (Parson et al., 2001), use data on the Gross National Products of various countries, for example. When discussing the Fibonacci numbers, and the recurrence relations, tell the story of Fibonacci, whose real name is Leonardo and came from Pisa (the town of the Leaning Tower of Pisa), and make a side-point on the role of this Italian genius from some 800 years ago in the introduction of the Arabic numerals and the positional numbers system in Europe. In Human Computer Interaction-related topics, spend some time discussing Equal Opportunity Computing, i.e., computing for people with disabilities. When discussing computer security, privacy and ethical issues, spice it up with the geographical distributions of the domiciles of the viruses, while stressing that the different laws that different countries have with respect to Internet privacy. Often what is legal in one country is not necessarily legal in others.

Rather than theorizing on how to integrate diversity topics in the curriculum, this chapter showcases the use of the tessellation theory as a tool for infusion of multicultural topics, and presents the Towson University course, "Computer and Creativity" (Meiselwitz, 2005), where tessellations suitably fit the educational goals.

This chapter is organized as follows: In the next section we discuss the tessellations and tilling from a mathematical perspective, and its foundations in

Copyright © 2006, Idea Group Inc. Copying or distributing in print or electronic forms without written permission of Idea Group Inc. is prohibited.

art. Afterward, we overview the course in "Computers and Creativity" and discuss the introduction of diverse topics within it. The subsequent section discusses technical and other considerations, and observations of the use of tessellations in the course. The last section concludes the work presented in the chapter.

Tessellations in Mathematics and Art

This section will present ways in which computers are employed to introduce the idea of tessellation to students. Here we overview briefly the basics of tilings, and their foundations in mathematics and art. Studying designs whose construction is based on repeating patterns provides a rich source for introducing the concept of infinite groups to undergraduate students in mathematics, and to others where these concepts are not introduced as formally.

Despite the large numbers of artwork with repeated patterns in one and two-dimensional spaces over time and cultures, the study of their mathematical properties began much later, with the work of Johannes Kepler (White & Brewda, 2003). The designers and geometers of the past created friezes and tessellations of all possible classes, but they never discovered that their creations could be classified based on their symmetries.

Mathematically, based on the four rigid transformations in a plane (isometries), all one-dimensional, one-color patterns (friezes, bands, borders) may be categorized into seven classes. Likewise, two-dimensional patterns (wallpaper

Figure 1. The seven one-dimensional repeating patterns, Frieze groups, extracted from artworks of different cultures and periods in time.

Copyright © 2006, Idea Group Inc. Copying or distributing in print or electronic forms without written permission of Idea Group Inc. is prohibited.

Figure 2. (a) A P4m wallpaper pattern, and (b) a P31m wallpaper pattern

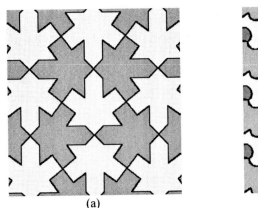 

(a)   (b)

patterns, crystallographic groups) of one color are divided into seventeen classes. During the 1920s, the classifications of one- and two-dimensional patterns became known (Niggli, 1924; Polya, 1924). The seventeen two-dimensional patterns were published in 1891 (Fedorov, 1891), but did not become widely known until later.

Disciplines other than mathematics benefit by the studies and applications of repeating patterns. Figure 1 presents the seven frieze groups extracted from artwork of different cultures and periods in time.

In 1924, Polya first illustrated the 17 wallpaper patterns (Polya, 1924). Escher studied the rules that governed these patterns and made several sketches of them in his copybook. In addition to Alhambra designs, these illustrations were a source of inspiration for Escher.

Today we have many software packages to use when studying tessellations. *Tessellation Exploration* is a software utility designed to create tilings using basic geometric figures such as triangles and quadrilaterals. The software is able to tessellate with 33 different types of tiles; it has been developed based on the Heech classification of the 28 types of asymmetric tiles that can fill the plane in an isohedral manner without using reflections (Schattschneider & Dolbilin, 1998). The other five utilities in this software are tiles that utilize reflections. In addition to creating wallpaper patterns, this utility provides an environment that helps students analyze isometries used in a tiling.

Figure 2 represents two renditions of Polya's illustrations which are performed in Tessellation Exploration. Figure 2 (a) is identified as D°4 by Polya (1924).

Copyright © 2006, Idea Group Inc. Copying or distributing in print or electronic forms without written permission of Idea Group Inc. is prohibited.

The basic shape to construct this pattern in Tessellation Exploration is a triangle. The isometries employed are a reflection and a quarter rotation. The mathematical notation for this pattern is P4m. It belongs to the square lattice of wallpaper patterns and its highest order of rotation is 4. It can be generated by 1/8 of its square unit. Figure 2 (b) is the rendition of D°3 Polya's illustration, which has been created based on a triangle, two isometries of a reflection and a rotation of 120°. The mathematical notation for this pattern is P31m. It is in the hexagonal lattice with the highest order of rotation 3. It can be generated by 1/6 of a hexagon unit.

Tessellation Explorations creates Escher-like tilings with ease and thus is an excellent environment for illustrating how mathematics can help in the production of art. On the main menu of this software, click on "Create a New Tessellation." Then, the "Choose a Base Shape" screen appears along with a triangle, quadrilateral, pentagon and hexagon. Select one of them, the quadrilateral for example, and click "Quadrilateral" and then "Next" to continue. Then the "Choose the Moves" screen appears. Now we select the transformations that we would like to use in our tessellation. The transformations that we choose determine the following:

1.   How the sides of the polygon are transformed to create the base tile.
2.   How the base tile will be transformed to create the tessellation.

On "Choose the Move," you have the choice of selecting a single transformation or a certain combination of transformations. We choose, for instance, the "Slides" tab and click "Create My Own." A tile appears on the "Tessellation Creator," ready for us to shape and add our artwork.

To shape the tile you need to use the following tools: ⬆, 🖐, and ✏. The first tool, ⬆, is the "Resize the Tile" tool. Click ⬆ and drag a corner handle that appears around the tile. As the tile is resized, the tessellation on the left side of the screen changes. The next tool, 🖐, is the "Shape the Tile" tool. There are two ways to shape the tile using 🖐: You can move a vertex point and you can add points to the tile's outline. The last tool, ✏, is the "Delete Points" tool. To delete points that you have added, click on ✏ and then click on an unwanted point. The point is removed and the side returns to its previous form.

Copyright © 2006, Idea Group Inc. Copying or distributing in print or electronic forms without written permission of Idea Group Inc. is prohibited.

Figure 3. Pegasus: Escher-inspired tiling

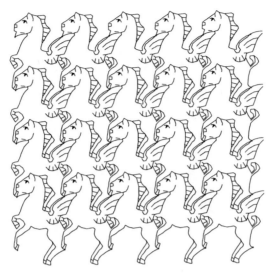

The *Geometer's Sketchpad* (www.keypress.com) is another package that may be used in exploring tessellations. It is a visual geometry software program, based on the rules of constructions using compass and straightedge. Using the buttons to the left of the screen (, , , ,) this utility draws objects such as points, line segments, rays, lines and circles. In this chapter, we introduce this utility and use it in order to construct geometric objects.

Figure 3 is a tessellation that is created using the Geometer's Sketchpad. Careful examination of this figure reveals that one base tile is being replicated via duplication by translations horizontally and vertically, with a perfect fit to the adjacent tiles, and second, the magnitudes of the horizontal and vertical translations are the same. This suggests that a square is somehow involved in designing our base tile. We also observe that the left part of the tile's outline is identical with its right. Moreover, the top part of the tile's outline is the same as its bottom.

Figure 4.a shows a square with four sides of *a, b, c* and *d*, and it also shows that side *a* has been modified. Figure 4.b shows a translation that takes this modification to the opposite side, *c*. Figure 4.c presents a modification on side *b*. The final image shows how a translation takes this modification to side *d* and completes the creation of our base tile.

Copyright © 2006, Idea Group Inc. Copying or distributing in print or electronic forms without written permission of Idea Group Inc. is prohibited.

Figure 4. Creating the base tile of Figure 3 in the Geometer's Sketchpad

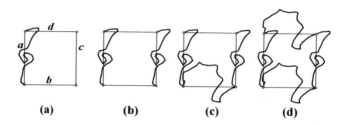

(a)   (b)   (c)   (d)

David Hilbert wrote, "In mathematics, as in any scientific research, we find two tendencies present. On the one hand, the tendency toward abstraction seeks to crystallize the logical relations inherent in the maze of material that is being studied, and to correlate the material in a systematic and orderly manner. On the other hand, the tendency toward intuitive understanding fosters a more immediate grasp of the objects one studies, a live rapport with them, so to speak, which stresses the concrete meaning of their relations. As to geometry, in particular, the abstract tendency has here led to the magnificent systematic theories of Algebraic Geometry, of Riemannian Geometry, and of a sense of algebra. Notwithstanding this, it is still as true today as it ever was that intuitive understanding plays a major role in geometry. And such concrete intuition is of great value not only for the researcher, but also for anyone who wishes to study and appreciate the results of research in geometry" (Hilbert, 1996). What we may be able to add to the above statement is: the use of technology and computers has extensively enhanced our abilities to intuitively comprehend various concepts in mathematics and science, and the ways that cultures represent them in their arts.

Computers and Creativity: Course Framework

In this section we discuss a framework for a course in computers and creativity that serves as an environment for the use of tessellations in our efforts to enhance diversity.

Computers and creativity are often considered a difficult combination, and many computer science departments stay away from offering creative computer courses in their curriculum. Computer art is often taught in art departments for upper-level students. However, much of the material taught in those

Copyright © 2006, Idea Group Inc. Copying or distributing in print or electronic forms without written permission of Idea Group Inc. is prohibited.

upper-level courses concentrates on sophisticated software that takes time and skill to master. At Towson University, we decided to develop a course model for computer novices and introduce the beginning computer user to creativity and computer science. The course, "Computers and Creativity," introduces students to computer science using a different approach—by introducing the computer to experience creativity.

Computer sciences often concentrate on teaching sciences and mathematics first, and then introducing students to computer applications. The majority of computer science curricula contain few course offerings of computing in arts and humanities. Computer science students are dominantly practical, and their orientation is often towards job-oriented skills (Hertlein, 1977). Although skills in graphic arts are highly valued in industry, many computer science students are intimidated by computers in arts (Eber & Wolfe, 2000). They often possess the technical ability to master the software, but have little or no experience in applying creative thinking in their products.

Technology has become present in all aspects of living, and as a result, people's work and leisure are merging. Engineers and artists become collaborators. Engineers are noticing how people really work, and incorporate many of their observed uses into new tools, while artists are infusing themselves into the computer communications industry (DeKoven et al., 1994). In an attempt to incorporate these changes into our computer science curriculum, we created a course to serve as a connector between the two disciplines of computer science and fine arts. Our goal at Towson University was to create a computer course for beginners, centering on experiencing creativity using computers, with emphasis on experience, and to enable students in this course to have the possibility to experience the computer as a creative instrument.

We built an entry-level computer science course, titled: "Computers and Creativity." It is classified as a general education course in the category: "Creativity and Creative Development." The course is a 15-week, three-credit course and consists of a lecture and a laboratory component. The course's main objective is to provide the environment and tools so that the computer may be used to express and enhance creativity. Students experience traditional creative forms such as tessellations, drawing, painting, photography and writing as well as creative forms unique to computer technology, such as computer graphics, multimedia, dynamic presentations, computer-based animation, World-Wide-Web publishing, digital photography and movies, virtual reality and the use of computers for music publishing and performance. Computer

Copyright © 2006, Idea Group Inc. Copying or distributing in print or electronic forms without written permission of Idea Group Inc. is prohibited.

concepts which are relevant to the use of the computer as a creative tool are studied.

The course consists of four units, each unit lasting three-four weeks. The first unit is an introduction unit and introduces the student to basic ideas of creativity, mathematics and art. It also introduces basic computer concepts. Unit 2 covers computer-based drawing, painting and animation. Several tools are used to illustrate concepts and express creative ideas. Students are encouraged to implement any idea that they have, and there are very few restrictions on suitable projects. The third unit introduces the Web design and development process using application development tools and considering basic design rules. The final unit, unit four, works with sound manipulation and also contains the final project. This project is a showcase for the student; they may create any project they are interested in as long as they use the tools that they have used during the semester.

The course introduces the student to many creative areas in computing, not just one particular product or a few application areas. Students learn a variety of tools, and spend approximately half of their total class time in labs. Assignments are only minimally structured in order to allow students to bring in their individual idea of creativity. Considering that creativity is highly individual, this course is strongly based on a constructivist learning approach. Constructivist learning environments focus on what a person knows; the interpretation and construction of individual knowledge representation, and the promotion of higher-order thinking. Social context is increasingly important in the meaning-making process and is incorporated as much as possible. Learning in a constructivist environment is seen as an active process, where individuals take responsibility for their learning processes and experience. This theory promotes a holistic view of learning and supports the idea that there is no exactly "right" or "wrong" way of learning, and seems to be a natural fit to teach computers and creativity (Jonassen & Land, 2000).

To illustrate, when working with computer-based drawing, students are given the objective that they must show mastery of using several tools (freeform shapes, geometrical shapes, text tool, etc.) and they may choose the topic of their drawing. Many objects that are produced over the length of the course are also being re-used, showing connections between various tools and techniques. In an early assignment, students take digital photographs of each other and themselves and learn to edit these photographs with photo editing software. This digital photograph is then used in several other assignments, in computer based animation for example, to produce special effects.

Copyright © 2006, Idea Group Inc. Copying or distributing in print or electronic forms without written permission of Idea Group Inc. is prohibited.

Constructivism is a paradigm honoring the situated nature of knowledge and enables students to experience an individual knowledge-building process in an authentic, collaborative environment. Knowledge grows when multiple perspectives are shared in collaboration with other learners (Brown et al., 2001). Learning is seen as a process of working toward a more complete and coherent understanding; students are actively engaged in the knowledge-construction process and take ownership for their own learning process.

To foster a constructivist learning process, this course encourages collaboration. Students may work in teams, but they are not required to do so. To encourage collaboration and display of the artwork that students have produced, the course uses an online learning environment, Blackboard. All assignments in this course contain personal elements (like a personal digital photograph) or are in file formats that are copy protected. This allows us to share all of the artwork in a discussion board online. This encourages communication and collaboration as students are asking other students about certain techniques or making general comments about their posted artwork.

Integrating Projects

This section discusses the use of the tessellations in the "Computer and Creativity" course at Towson University.

The Tessellation Exploration and the Geometer's Sketchpad software packages are extremely helpful in the early stages of the "Computer and Creativity" course, and fit perfectly into the instruction goals. Being tools with friendly interfaces, they make the general student population comfortable using them. Many of the students in an introductory course are still uneasy about using computers, so these software packages help them overcome the technological anxiety, and focus on the application, rather than the hardware issues.

Each unit contains a small unit project that is shared with the class, including a description of the history of the motivating object. Students vote on the most successful assignment, after having read all the data on their classmates' projects.

In an in-class discussion and presentation of the unit projects, the students have proven eager to learn about the history of many of the motivating pieces, and they do not hide their astonishment at the multitude of creative discoveries.

Copyright © 2006, Idea Group Inc. Copying or distributing in print or electronic forms without written permission of Idea Group Inc. is prohibited.

In addition to the smaller unit projects, students also produce a more extensive term project. The integration of projects gives our students a chance to see the material in a practical context, and it also allows them to implement the material in a context that is meaningful for the individual student.

While having their creativity and experimental spirits challenged, the students learn about different cultures, people, habits and ways of life. Many of the objects tell exquisite stories. The atmosphere in the class is nurturing and motivated, while students are competing to come up with their best ideas and designs, and ultimately "educating" in the multicultural sense.

The Recipe for the Course

In this section we discuss the modules that we implement in the "Computer and Creativity" course in order to help other educators interested in using them.

We have divided the course into modules. Modules allow the instructor to cover a multitude of topics and make the course more flexible. They can be rearranged or adapted as needed. Using the modular approach makes it easy to adjust this course to be taught in semesters of varying length. The course is divided into four units, each covering approximately three to four weeks. A small student project is part of each unit and will tie together all items that have been covered during each unit. These small projects give the students a chance to show what they have learned and allow the instructor to assess their learning. Students are encouraged to work in teams, but they are not required to do so.

The structure of all units is very similar. The first week introduces the topic by covering general concepts and skills, background (in any sense of the word) and historical perspectives. The second week expands on general concepts and functionality. Advanced concepts are introduced during week three. Completing the unit in week four, students get a chance to put all the learned material together in context and demonstrate what they have learned by producing a small project. Depending on the topics covered and the time available for each unit, the unit project may concentrate on material from previous weeks only, or could introduce further elements relevant to the unit.

Unit 1: Tessellations

In this unit the student is introduced to general concepts of mathematics and arts and will acquire necessary background information, including historical per-

Copyright © 2006, Idea Group Inc. Copying or distributing in print or electronic forms without written permission of Idea Group Inc. is prohibited.

spectives. Geometry concepts, terms and constructions are studied using tessellations. The software used for this unit are the Geometer's Sketchpad and Tessellation Exploration. The subunits are as follows:

1. Introduction to mathematics and arts
2. Basic exercise using Tessellation Exploration
3. Advanced exercise using the Geometer's Sketchpad
4. Small student project

Exercises in this unit may be supported by studying architectural and archeological items. In one of the assignments, students will visit the local museum and study artwork for their tessellation assignment. The small student project for this module requires the students to integrate the computer skills that they have learned, as well as demonstrate an appreciation for cultural influences and diversity. By visiting a local art museum, students can clearly see connections between art and mathematics.

Unit 2: Computer-Based Animation

Unit 2 introduces the student to the basics of computer- based animation. Software packages used in this unit are *Photo Editing Software* and *Macromedia Flash*.

5. Introduction to drawing and painting
6. Basic animation
7. Advanced animation
8. Small student project

All assignments in this unit encourage students to bring in their personal ideas and interests. In drawing and painting, students share an illustration of a personal or professional interest; for example, organizations they belong to or they want to support. Advanced animation works with digital photographs students have taken earlier in the course. Many students choose to use elements of their own background and culture and share the results with the class.

Copyright © 2006, Idea Group Inc. Copying or distributing in print or electronic forms without written permission of Idea Group Inc. is prohibited.

Unit 3: Web Design and Development

9.   Introduction to HTML and simple design rules
10. Basic Web design
11. Advanced Web design
12. Small student project

This unit covers basic principles of design and development. Students learn about Web design and produce their own Web sites. This is a very practical unit and many students come to this unit with a number of ideas that they want to implement on their Web sites. Multiculturalism is included in several projects for this module. Students use the Internet to find recipes, perhaps from their own culture, and share them. They also research a foreign country, again perhaps with personal connections, and use this information to create a Webpage travel brochure. Many students choose to report about their own family, town or country. Software used in this unit is *Microsoft FrontPage*.

Unit 4: Term Project

The term project connects all other units and brings together all elements of the single units. This project is very extensive and requires work above and beyond all the assignments completed during the semester. This unit starts with a planning phase, during which students work on the design for their final project. Students have to choose a project that demonstrates their mastery of concepts and skills from earlier units. A student may choose any or all of the three areas that were covered in units 1, 2 and 3. They may produce an extensive tessellation project, an extensive computer-based animation project, an extensive Web page project or a combination of all three. There are no restrictions on the topics.

These projects are presented to the class by the individual students or student teams at the end of the course. In addition to receiving a grade for these projects, students vote for the best project. This produces a lively discussion and also a positive competitive spirit. Students are very eager to share details about their personal lives, cultures and backgrounds. In a broader sense, this term project brings together not only the content of all the units that were taught in this course, but also different cultures, backgrounds, goals and personal interests of students.

Copyright © 2006, Idea Group Inc. Copying or distributing in print or electronic forms without written permission of Idea Group Inc. is prohibited.

Figure 5. Sample course syllabus for the computers and creativity course

SAMPLE COURSE SYLLABUS: COMPUTERS AND CREATIVITY

Course Description: Creative activities involving geometric concepts and skills, symbolic manipulation, computer animation, Web publishing, artwork and multimedia. Additional lab time required.
Prerequisite: None
Credit Hours: 3

Course Objectives: This course is a bridge between sciences and arts. The course provides the environment and tools so that the computer may be used to express and enhance creativity. Traditional creative forms such as drawing, photography and writing will be explored as well as creative forms unique to sciences, such as tessellations, computer graphics, computer-based animation, World-Wide-Web publishing and multimedia. Mathematical and computer concepts that are relevant to the use of the computer as creative tools will be studied.
Attendance Policy: Students are expected to attend each class meeting and laboratory meeting as required. Students are required to notify the instructor via e-mail if they are unable to attend a class meeting. Written documentation of the reason for the absence may be requested by the instructor and must be submitted for the absence to be excused.
Assignments and Grading: The course grade will be based on 4 quizzes (50 points each, 200 points total), 12 assignments (180 points total) and a final project (120 points). The grade ranges are as follows: A (450-500 points), B (400-449), C (350-399), D (300-349), and F (below 300).
All work MUST be turned in by the assigned deadlines or a grade of zero will be assigned. No late assignments will be accepted. Assignments will be turned in online using the Blackboard system.
Policy on Academic Integrity: Academic honesty according to the Academic Integrity Policy of (*)[?] University is expected in this class for all work submitted for a grade. This policy will be strictly followed. Students are responsible for reading, understanding and following this policy.

Course Outline:
Unit 1 – Tessellations:
Introduction to mathematics and arts (10 points)
Basic exercise tessellation exploration (10)
Advanced exercise tessellation exploration (20)
Small student project (20)
Unit 2 – Computer-based animation
Introduction to drawing and painting (10)
Basic animation (10)
Advanced animation (20)
Small student project (20)
Unit 3 - Web design and development
Introduction to HTML and simple design rules (10)
Basic Web design (10)
Advanced Web design (20)
Small student project (20)
Unit 4 – Term Project
Term project design (40)
Term project development (60)
Term project presentation (20)

Logistics

A course of this type requires quite a bit of planning. Many of the assignments cannot be turned in on paper and require an online medium. To support this course, either the World Wide Web or a course management system is required. In our case, we are using Blackboard, an online learning environment. All student assignments are submitted electronically, and grades are posted to the online grade book.

Copyright © 2006, Idea Group Inc. Copying or distributing in print or electronic forms without written permission of Idea Group Inc. is prohibited.

We heavily use the discussion board feature of Blackboard in this course. Assignments are posted to the discussion board, which serves as a showcase for all our creative work. Students have a chance to check out their classmates' work, and this online student-to-student communication enriches the students' learning process and creates a sense of community. It encourages student dialogue online, as students compliment each other's work or ask for explanations of interesting techniques.

Communication is essential for this course. Using an online medium, we have noticed that many students expect immediate feedback if they have a question. A short response time between instructor and student definitely encourages student motivation and participation. We often find ourselves communicating with students outside of regular business hours, for example, during evening hours or weekends, and this may be very time-consuming for the instructor.

But not only does the instructor spend more time, the online setup also presents additional material to master for the student. This may be a little challenging, especially since this class is a lower-level class and the overwhelming majority of the students is freshmen and sophomores. However, we find that students are coming to college with better computer knowledge due to better preparation in high school and that they catch on very quickly. At our institution we also offer a computer literacy seminar, that covers basic computer concepts like e-mail, the Internet and course management systems which many incoming freshmen take.

This course also requires many different software packages, some of them quite elaborate and/or pricey. This can be a hardship for departments if laboratories are limited or if funds are inadequate to purchase, maintain and upgrade software.

Possible Modifications

One of the advantages of this course model is its scalability and ease of modification. If necessary, the number of units may be extended or reduced. Additional topics could be introduced, sound, for example. If needed, topics can be eliminated, for example, for shorter semester durations or if a particular software is not available.

In addition to modification of the number of units, the number of topics covered per unit may also be altered. Expansion of topics may further deepen the student's understanding, and allows instructors to emphasize particular sub-

Copyright © 2006, Idea Group Inc. Copying or distributing in print or electronic forms without written permission of Idea Group Inc. is prohibited.

jects of their choice. If required, the small unit projects could be eliminated, thus reducing the number of topics covered per unit. However, we do not recommend this since students enjoy these projects and also get a chance to apply and show the mastery of the material they have learned. Working on the small projects also prepares the students for the large final project.

Student Comments

We have informally collected some student comments and would like to share some of those with you. This is a very popular course and students especially like that the course is multifaceted and that they may bring in their personal backgrounds and interests. Students comment very positively on the multicultural element in this course, and they enjoy experiencing material in a more holistic approach

Following are some student comments:

- "I really liked student's homepages, especially when they reported about other countries."
- "This is the only course where you can have fun."
- "In this course I learned something that I can actually use (and) in other courses."
- "I never thought that I would be able to do this."
- "It's fun to see everything coming together."

Conclusion

In this chapter we illustrated a course where multicultural infusion has been done via tessellations. Students have produced an amazing showcase of work, and many students have developed the ability to use the computer to express their creativity. Many products are far from being perfect pieces of art and most definitely would not win a prize at an exhibition. However, the goal of this course is not to produce high-level artistic work. The goal is to merge the ideas of art and computing sciences and to provide the environment for the student to experience this fusion. We find that the encouragement to experience art in

Copyright © 2006, Idea Group Inc. Copying or distributing in print or electronic forms without written permission of Idea Group Inc. is prohibited.

an individual context is highly motivating for our students, and many students are relieved to find out that they have the freedom to produce artwork that is allowed to be imperfect. It frees the student from art anxiety, and we achieve astonishing results once a student frees him- or herself from this stage fright and performance anxiety.

References

Brown, J., Collins, A., & Duguid, P. (2001). Situated Cognition and the Culture of Learning. In D. Ely & T. Plomp (Eds.), *Classic Writings on Instructional Technology*. Englewood, CO: Libraries Unlimited.

DeKoven, J., Binkley, T., Entis, G., Maxwell, D., & Smith, A. (1994). Computer technology and the artistic process: How the computer industry changes the form and function of art. *Proceedings of the 21st annual conference on computer graphics and interactive techniques* (pp. 494-495). New York: ACM Press.

Eber, D., & Wolfe, R. (2000). *Teaching computer graphic visual literacy to art and computer science students* (pp. 24-26). New York: ACM Press.

Fedorov, E.S. (1891). Simmetriya pravil'nyh sistem figur [Symmetry of Regular Systems of Figures]. *Zap. Mineral. Obch, 28*(2), 1-146.

Geometer's Sketchpad: Dynamic Geometry® Software for Exploring Mathematics. Key Curriculum Press. Retrieved February 26, 2003, from http://www.keypress.com/catalog/products/software/Prod_GSP.html

Hertlein, G. (1977). Computer art for computer people. *Proceedings of the 4th annual conference on computer graphics and interactive technique* (pp. 249-254). New York: ACM Press.

Hilbert, D. (1996). *The Emergence of Logical Empiricism*. New York: Garland Publishing.

Jonassen, D., & Land, S. (2000). *Theoretical foundations of learning environments*. Mahwah, NJ: Lawrence Erlbaum Associates, Inc.

Meiselwitz, G. (2005). *Homepage – Teaching*. Retrieved February 23, 2005, from http://pages.towson.edu/meisel

Copyright © 2006, Idea Group Inc. Copying or distributing in print or electronic forms without written permission of Idea Group Inc. is prohibited.

Niggli, P. (1924). Die Flächensymmetrien homogener Diskontinuen. *Z. Kristall, 60,* 283-298.

Parsons, J., & Oja, D. (2001). *New Perspectives on MS Office 2000 – Brief.* Boston: MS Course Technology.

Polya G. (1924). Über die Analogie der Kristalsymmetrie in der Ebene [trans]. *Z. Kristall, 60,* 278-282.

Schattschneider, D., & Dolbilin, N. (1998). *Catalog of Isohedral Tilings by Symmetric Polygonal Tiles.* Retrieved February 1, 2003, from http://www.mathforum.org/dynamic/one-corona/

White, C., & Brewda, S. (2003). *Translations of Works by Johannes Kepler.*Retrieved February 1, 2003, from http://www.schillerinstitute.org/transl/trans_kepler.html

Copyright © 2006, Idea Group Inc. Copying or distributing in print or electronic forms without written permission of Idea Group Inc. is prohibited.

Chapter XIII

Training Faculty for Diversity Infusion in the IT Curriculum

Goran P. Trajkovski, Towson University, USA

Abstract

In this chapter we offer a flexible training environment and strategies for diversity infusion in the Information Technology curriculum. The chapter overviews "My First Diversity Workbook," and the ways in which it may be used in diversity training for faculty. The major part of such workshops consists of four parts. In the first part, the trainer talks about his or her positive experiences of diversity infusion in the curriculum, and serves as a motivational component of the training. The second and third components explain how to get inspired for micro and macro infusion of topics in the curriculum from the outside and the inside. By using external examples and facts, or internal experiences and introspections, the instructors may successfully diversify a unit lesson or the whole curriculum. In the fourth component, the trainer talks about continuing to share classroom experiences after the workshop is done—usually online, within the

Copyright © 2006, Idea Group Inc. Copying or distributing in print or electronic forms without written permission of Idea Group Inc. is prohibited.

framework of an e-group. We describe fitting these four components into two different contexts, and outline in detail the schedule and experiences of participants from those two workshops, custom-tailored to the needs of the institution that the training was designed for. These workshop patterns are fully replicable. The chapter not only describes the author's strategies in covering the topics, but also provides a selection of sources that the trainer and the participants may use when replicating or modifying these trainings.

Introduction and Rationale

With the number of studies of scientific laboratories and scientific research in other countries, social scientists have amassed data on a variety of different institutional, organizational and cultural formations that might be said, despite their differences, to produce good science (Traweek, 1988; Coleman, 1999). Scholars like Itty Abraham (2000) look to the different ways research was conducted in the formation of India's Giant Metrewave Radio Telescope (GMRT), analyzing the different ways this became "a totally Indian project" (Abraham, 2000). Moreover, laboratory studies within Europe and the United States suggest that research organizations display considerably heterogeneity, confirming the idea that different institutions have different "cultures," i.e., different ways of interacting, hierarchies and ways of communicating (Knorr-Cetina, 1981; Latour, 1979). Identifying diversity internationally and intra-nationally, however, leaves unanswered the question of diversity as a resource, and the effects of "diversity" (however defined) upon the day-to-day organizational behavior.

It is our belief that "diversity" should go beyond just the inclusion of different, underrepresented populations; integrating diversity into the classroom should also mean transforming some of the basic institutions of research and pedagogy at the undergraduate level. To truly incorporate diversity, as David Hess (1995, pp. 252-253) notes, the "culture" of science education itself should be open to transformation from within. Indeed, as Downey and Lucena(1997) suggest, targeting underrepresented populations for inclusion in engineering may not yield positive results unless the "culture" of engineering education itself changes—i.e., the way engineers are socialized.

Copyright © 2006, Idea Group Inc. Copying or distributing in print or electronic forms without written permission of Idea Group Inc. is prohibited.

This brings us to the true promise of diversity: the experimentation with different ways of teaching and learning which may result in new forms–a bonafide creative, recombinatory process. Just as management theory in IT has experimented with Taiwanese guanxi networks and various strains of Japanese-inspired "quality circles," science education has much to gain through experimentation in the transformation of pedagogies with the inclusion of cross-cultural diversity. In fact, this kind of experimentation may be vital to the continued development of the sciences themselves.

Later in her career, and partly as a result of her involvement, along with Gregory Bateson, in first-generation cybernetics and the Macy Conferences on Cybernetics in the late 1940s and 1950s, Margaret Mead became interested in small-group dynamics, e.g., the way one might model decision making and other social processes by way of negative and positive feedback loops in a way isomorphic to Norbert Wiener's discussions of living- and non-living systems (although Wiener himself was not very hopeful that cybernetics could be used to model social- and cultural behavior). She began to consider the small group itself as an agent of microevolution, or what she called an "evolutionary cluster." In her last, sustained, scholarly work, *Continuities in Cultural Evolution* (1964), Mead defined the evolutionary cluster as "an intercommunicating group of human beings who stand at some crucial point in the process of culture change". Her insight is that what is oftentimes ex post facto glossed as "genius" is, in fact, the product of a network of individuals acting together under certain conditions. While engineering "genius" is an impossibility, Mead nevertheless believed that it might be possible to create "the conditions within which clusters including highly gifted people are likely to form and contribute to human culture" (p. 67).

For Mead, this was a project to be carried out on a global scale. If we look to "clusters" of individuals rather than the lone (and ethnocentric) "genius," then we might expect them in every cultural and social context. Everyone on the planet, she reasoned, might have some vital contribution to make to the advancement of the sciences (p. 262). And, indeed, this participatory research was, for her, vital to the continued spread of democratic ideals.

While many of Mead's ideas were limited by that first generation of cybernetic modeling (with its functionalist cycles of feedback) and the tendency to apply spurious teleologies to the development of human culture, the notion that diversity is worth pursuing for its own sake as a source of creativity is an idea that we have found attractive. Taking inspiration from Mead's "evolutionary clusters" and using more contemporary, cybernetic modeling through robotics,

Copyright © 2006, Idea Group Inc. Copying or distributing in print or electronic forms without written permission of Idea Group Inc. is prohibited.

we propose to bring together diverse, creative students to work in small groups on creative, research projects.

More than simply welcoming diversity into science education, we want to include students in the formation of research itself. More than that, we want them to realize the extent to which science and technology are part of everyday life irrespective of culture, identity and academic discipline. In doing so, we hope to spur both increased participation in the sciences as well as genuine, unforeseen creativity and novel insight.

Typically, people in the US understand technology as something that develops according to its own logic and that affects social and cultural life from the outside: in other words, technological determinism. Anthropological studies of science and technology have generally tended to reproduce that, either through the study of environmental determinism or through the examination of the impacts of technology transfer on developing populations. The problem with such studies is that they invariably underestimate the roles of science and technology. While technology and science certainly impact social and cultural life, they do so in the context of that social and cultural life. Indeed, in some instances, technologies take on their own agency. For example, the automobile might be better appreciated as an agent in itself, particularly with regard to the development of roads, highways and interstates. Our interactions with the automobile in the twentieth century as an agent lead to an assemblage of developments, including changes in residence, family, work, education and so on. In his study of the development of CAD/CAM in the 1980s, Downey (1995) makes the argument that, under these conditions, we should see these computer-assisted design programs as agents interacting with other human and non-human agents because "in positioning the new technology agents also reposition themselves" (p. 366). That is, scientific knowledge does not just "impact" society; it enters the social fabric and restructures society and culture, in turn affecting the development of new knowledge and technologies. This model of science and technology configures them as intrinsic rather than as extrinsic to society.

These sorts of questions, whereby the border between "human" and "non-human" is blurred in the production of scientific knowledge, are common to anthropologies of artificial intelligence (AI) and artificial life. Are the intelligent systems we build similar to our own cognition? Isomorphic? The initial "Turing test" claims that AI would be on some level indistinguishable from human intelligence have since been refined. Few people would claim that machines will develop human intelligence; nevertheless, AI remains singularly important in the

Copyright © 2006, Idea Group Inc. Copying or distributing in print or electronic forms without written permission of Idea Group Inc. is prohibited.

modeling of human intelligence and interaction. The other side of the Turing question, however, remains unanswered. What happens when our own forms of cognition, communication and interaction become more machine-like? As Stefan Helmreich (1998) points out in his ethnography of artificial life research at the Santa Fe Institute, researchers routinely "imagine the life process as a program" (p. 123). The world itself (metaphorically) resembles a computer; the computer, in other words, transforms the world in its own image even as engineers and programmers seek to model the world on the computer. It is these agential transformations that anthropologists find most interesting, that is, the ways in which people and their machines have mutually re-ordered their social and cultural worlds.

Whether or not one can equate AI with human intelligence or artificial life with biological life is, in this sense, beside the point. Both of these are *sine qua non* sites for thinking about human lives and cognitive functions in the context of a world structured by IT, about the flows between them and about boundaries that might be erected or traduced. This seems similar to Bateson's 1972 parable:

Consider a man felling a tree with an axe. Each stroke of the axe is modified or corrected, according to the shape of the cut face of the tree left by the previous stroke. This self-corrective (i.e., mental) process is brought about by a total system, trees-eyes-brain-muscles-axe-stroke-tree; and it is this total system that has the characteristics of immanent mind. (Bateson, 1972, p. 318)

One of the interesting areas where the question of the interactions and similarities of human- and non-human agencies is thrown into relief is autopoiesis, a development of cybernetics and systems theory originating with the work of Humberto Maturana and Francisco Varela in the 1970s and culminating with their 1980 book, *Autopoiesis and Cognition: The Reduction of the Living*. According to Varela (1979, p. 13):

An autopoietic system is organized (defined as a unity) as a network of processes of production (transformation and destruction) of components that produces the components that: (1) through their interactions and transformation continuously regenerate and realize their network of processes (relations) that produced them; and (2) constitute it (the

Copyright © 2006, Idea Group Inc. Copying or distributing in print or electronic forms without written permission of Idea Group Inc. is prohibited.

machine) as a concrete unity in space in which they exist by specifying the topological domain of just realization as such a network.

An autopoietic system produces itself. That is, unlike conventional systems theories that model change as a series of inputs and outputs (e.g., competition for resources and reproduction for living systems), Maturana and Varela see autopoietic systems as primarily engaged in the work of their self-organization. This is in contradistinction to what they term allopoietic systems that are organizationally "open."

Although this has proven suggestive for both human social life and intelligent systems, Maturana and Varela would tend to confine autopoiesis to living systems like the nervous system or single cells. AI, for example, wouldn't exist without the intercession of a programmer at some point along the way. However, autopoiesis theorists like Niklas Luhmann—updating early communication theorists like Claude Shannon and Warren Weaver—have suggested that communication might be considered autopoietic, especially in terms of what Maturana and Varela term "structural coupling" (Luhmann, 1989).

Whether metaphor for human and machine interaction, or, via Luhmann, applicable to communication and media, autopoiesis is nevertheless descriptive—at least metaphorically—of characteristics common to both living- and non-living systems and, moreover, suggests possibilities for studying similarities and differences between them.

Specifically, several characteristics of autopoietic systems are suggestive for research:

1. *Structure and organization*: Maturana and Varela differentiate between organization, which "consists of the relations among components and the necessary properties of the components that characterize or define the unity in general as belonging to a particular type or class" (14), while "structure" is the actual, shifting constitution of the organization. "Structure," according to this definition, undergoes continuous change during the process of structural coupling, but this change, rather than being functional (maximizing outputs) or teleological (directed), is part of the continuous structural coupling of the system with the environment. That is, the system is functional only with regard to the system's components.

2. *Structural coupling*: As Winthrop-Young (2000, p. 400) explains:

Copyright © 2006, Idea Group Inc. Copying or distributing in print or electronic forms without written permission of Idea Group Inc. is prohibited.

Structural coupling refers to the ongoing developing engagement between a structure-determined system and its environment or to the recurring interactions between two (or more) structure-determining systems. A child learning and an adult continuing to walk are examples of a system coupling with its environments, while a child talking and continuing to talk with its parents is an example of a system interacting with other systems.

The idea of "structural coupling" denies that systems "adapt" to the outside, focusing attention instead on the elaboration of internal structure.

Accordingly, there are multiple opportunities for research here, including:

1.   The applicability of autopoiesis to living- and non-living systems;
2.   The social and cultural characteristics of machine-human interfaces (i.e., cyborg anthropology);
3.   The question of the observer and the importance of "emic" (insider) understandings;
4.   The reflexive analysis of the institute team as a system that displays characteristics common to autopoietic and allopoietic systems; and
5.   The possibilities and limitations in applying cybernetic understandings to social analyses.

Initializing the Process

As educators in higher education or elsewhere, we encounter diversity on daily basis, in all the senses of the word. We can easily identify issues and challenges that need to be met in our IT classrooms. An experienced educator knows that he or she needs to embrace all the aspects of diversity in order to guarantee a successful classroom experience.

Just by being us, living in diverse societies, we have encountered diversity in one way or another, and have had our own, diverse experiences. When working with people, our and their experiences are transfused, thus contributing towards the discovery of (yet another side) of the rich tapestry of life. The

Copyright © 2006, Idea Group Inc. Copying or distributing in print or electronic forms without written permission of Idea Group Inc. is prohibited.

learning in the classroom does not happen in the direction "from" the instructor "towards" the student(s) in our classrooms, whether we want to admit it or not: Not only that our students learn from us, but also that we learn from them. There is a constant transfusion of diversity. Most instructors already infuse diversity issues in their IT classrooms without realizing it or labeling it as such.

This chapter focuses on our solution for training our peers for diversity infusion in the IT curriculum. We have been conducting a number of workshops in the past four years following this general pattern. To assume that diversity issues can be infused via one training session only is too far a stretch. It simply—we think – cannot be done. What we can do instead is help our peers start thinking about a systematic infusion of these topics throughout their teaching process.

Diversity Workbook

The diversity workbook that we use in our training is given in Figures 1-15. In the gray, explosion-like objects there are numbers that will be used to refer to the activity being done with that particular space.

In the space in Figure 1 denoted as 1.1, participants are asked to write in their names, affiliation, e-mail and URL. This is the initiation activity that is happening while the participants go around the table and introduce themselves. They may use the space in box 1.2. to scribble down names of the other people in the room, as that would facilitate better communication and possibly discussion in

Figure 1. The cover page of the Diversity Workbook

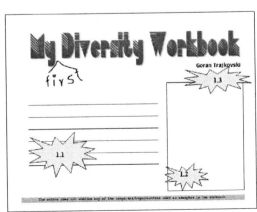

Copyright © 2006, Idea Group Inc. Copying or distributing in print or electronic forms without written permission of Idea Group Inc. is prohibited.

the room. Participants usually create a seating chart of the room. Alternatively, this box may be used by the participants to illustrate, with a simple drawing, what diversity represents to them. At these initial stages, the drawings we get almost always contain the (overused) globe with a number of people holding hands and making a circle around it. We attribute this to the overuse of those objects in a vast number of logos related to diversity and multiculturalism.

The training facilitator is the one in charge of the contents in box 1.3. That is the space where he or she shares as much of his or her information as they feel comfortable with. It is this box that, after the training has started, usually becomes the sample for contents in box 1.1. In the past, we have stated, for example, the word welcome in English and several other languages.

During the workshop, especially when giving examples, registered names or names of companies will inevitably be mentioned. The facilitator should state a disclaimer that he or she does not endorse any of them personally, and that their names are used purely in the context of giving examples. The line across the bottom of the cover page is a disclaimer that this indeed was the facilitator's intention.

During the workshop, there are normally two introspective modules. We usually use one in the beginning and one at the very end of the training, and make the participants contrast them to see if there has been a significant attitude change. That may easily be done by contrasting what the faculty wrote on the activity sheets in Figures 2 and 15 of the Diversity Workbook.

Figure 2. The introspection activity at the beginning of the training

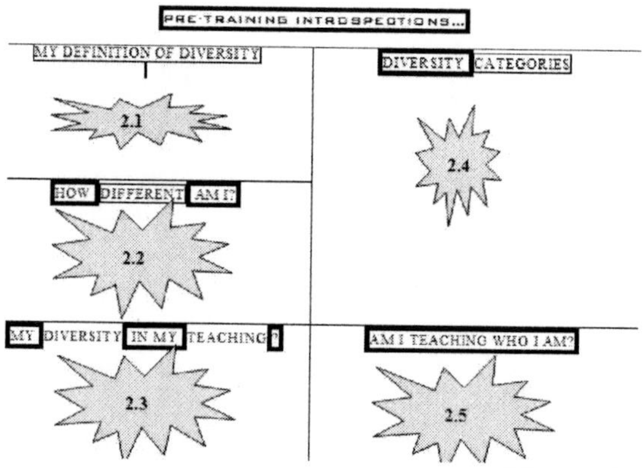

Copyright © 2006, Idea Group Inc. Copying or distributing in print or electronic forms without written permission of Idea Group Inc. is prohibited.

Figure 3. The Comparison of Search Engines activity sheet

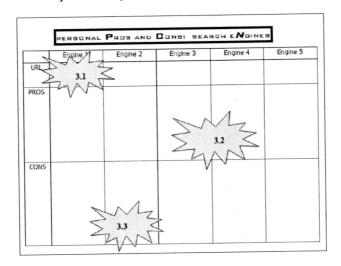

As there is no widely agreed upon definition of diversity, participants are asked to provide their own in box 2.1, Figure 2. We normally write the definitions out on a board. By the time all participants and/or groups have shared theirs, together with the categories listed in box 2.4, we get a fairly comprehensive, axiomatic definition of the term. There have been some great definitions of diversity over the years, but the author's personal all-time favorite is "Not me," meaning that diversity is everything that they are not.

In box 2.2. participants are encouraged to write down ways that they perceive themselves as significantly different from the other people they know. This introspective part should not be shared unless the participants want to. Participants in the past have felt comfortable sharing their national origins, languages they speak, places they have been, sexual orientation, etc.

"Where do you see diversity being introduced in your teaching?" is the question that participants answer in box 2.3. At the early stage of the training, the answers are wide ranging. Participants usually share modules from their courses that focus on the societal and legal issues that they teach. The answers and comments vary greatly here.

The answers in box 2.4, together with those from 2.1, give a definition to what diversity represents to the congregated group, and they compose the working definition for the term in that micro-society.

Copyright © 2006, Idea Group Inc. Copying or distributing in print or electronic forms without written permission of Idea Group Inc. is prohibited.

Figure 4. Domains around the world activity sheet

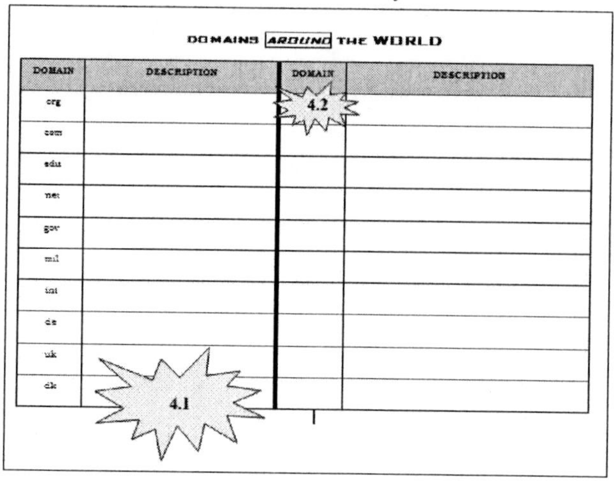

As we are teaching who we are—and cannot get away from it—box 2.5. is a reflexive, and in most cases a rhetorical, box placed in that space to initialize the introspective process in the participants, important for the paradigmatic shift expected to be initialized with this training module.

We not only become aware that we are all different when discussing and sharing introspective pieces from the boxes in Figure 2, but also we can use the exercise in Figure 3, "The Personal Pros and Cons on Search Engines," to make the point.

This activity makes the point on a near-trivial, discipline-neutral example. It consists in asking the group to state up to five search engines and what they like and do not like about all of them. There is a wealth of search engines stated, and the list of likes and dislikes varies. Most of the comments so far have been on different aspects on the interfaces and the format of the hits, which is not surprising, as the interface is the product to the user (Raskin, 2000). After being exposed to some search engines that they might have never used, the participants achieve another goal—they now have a list of search engines to consider and use when compiling their own diversity resources database. So on this page, in the row 3.1, they state up to five URLs of search engines and then write down their personal likes and dislikes in the rows 3.2 and 3.3. At the bottom of the page they are requested to write down their personal favorite one.

In the *Domains around the World* activity (Figure 4), the participants experience another, international, dimension of diversity. They talk about the

Copyright © 2006, Idea Group Inc. Copying or distributing in print or electronic forms without written permission of Idea Group Inc. is prohibited.

Figure 5. A suggested format for building a personal diversity resources repository

EVALUATION OF **MY** DIVERSITY RESOURCES ON THE WEB

URL	Type of Information Provided	Personal Star Rating
		☆☆☆☆☆
		☆☆☆☆☆
	5	☆☆☆☆☆
		☆☆☆☆☆
		☆☆☆☆☆
		☆☆☆☆☆
		☆☆☆☆☆
		☆☆☆☆☆

Figure 6. Page six of the workbook: Activities I-1 and I-2

PRÊTE À PORTER IDEAS 1
$TOCK MARKET$

I-1

PRÊTE À PORTER IDEAS 2
CURRENT WORLD ISSUES

I-2

domain solutions in the United States and around the world, the parallels and differences between the ".edu-.com" and ".ac-.co" systems, as well as the introduction of the variety of new domain names to make up for the overused, older ones (for example, .tv, .kids, .adult, .info, etc.). In the boxes 4.2 they state

Copyright © 2006, Idea Group Inc. Copying or distributing in print or electronic forms without written permission of Idea Group Inc. is prohibited.

Figure 7. Page seven of the workbook: Activities I-3 and I-4

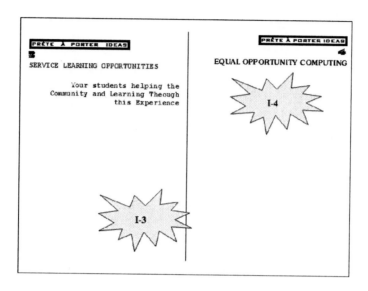

domains that they are familiar with and they could share some of those with the group.

The *Evaluation of My Diversity Resources on the Web* (Figure 5) is a suggestion of a page that a participant may choose to place in his or her diversity scrapbook, or replicate electronically. This activity is the initiation of the building of a personal online resources repository, linking to pages with relevant information. When preparing for their classes, the participants will be using it as a source of information and inspiration for the micro- and macro-infusion of topics in their courses. They state the URL of pages that they have used, a brief description and a personal star rating. The initial contents of this activity sheet will consist of resources used by the attendees, and this resource is expected to grow over time with experience.

The ten "I" parts of the workbook (Figures 6-10) have been designed to present the participants with ten "Prête-à-porter" (Ready-to-Wear) ideas that may be used in the process of designing contents for the courses that would initiate diversity-related conversations in the classroom.

Have you ever tried to ask your students if they can name more than one stock exchange? We have hardly ever gotten an answer to that question apart from the New York Stock Exchange. The rich stock exchange landscape (finix.ac) provides a venue for multinational issues to be infused in the curriculum, helpful

Copyright © 2006, Idea Group Inc. Copying or distributing in print or electronic forms without written permission of Idea Group Inc. is prohibited.

Figure 8. Ready to wear ideas: Bar codes and number systems, currencies, calendars and time

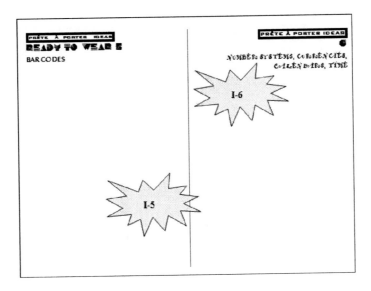

Figure 9. World geography and men's studies

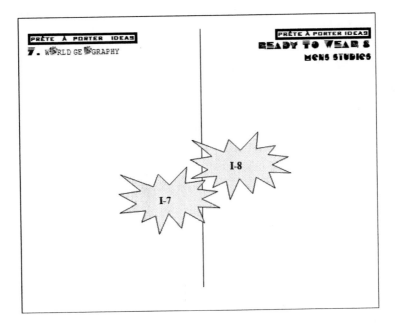

Copyright © 2006, Idea Group Inc. Copying or distributing in print or electronic forms without written permission of Idea Group Inc. is prohibited.

Figure 10. E-business and personal research interests as sources of topics for consideration for infusion in the courses taught

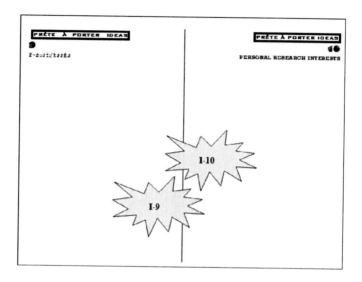

for courses in e-Commerce; for example, I-1 gives a space to collect some notes on the stock markets around the world. The conversation on the stock markets may be incorporated across the curriculum, starting from modules when we are teaching the students how to use tables in Excel, to upper level courses that discuss doing business internationally online.

Most of us—educators or not—try to stay atop of the news. Current world issues can provide interesting approaches to monologues when introducing a topic in the classroom (Part I-2, Figure 6). The recent tsunami catastrophe, for example (npr.org), may be used in a variety of courses where relevant statistics may be presented and used in a variety of ways.

The incorporation of service learning components (the new wave in "trendy" terminology suggests the use of the "hotter" term, "civic engagement") (Figure 7, I-3) to IT courses may be beneficial to the student from the diversity standpoint. Most of our experience with service learning has been in developing applications to be used in group homes with behaviorally-challenged clients. By working with the staff in the group homes and overseeing agencies, and interacting with people with disabilities, students develop their views or modify their existing stereotyped attitudes on the issues that people with a variety of disabilities face.

Copyright © 2006, Idea Group Inc. Copying or distributing in print or electronic forms without written permission of Idea Group Inc. is prohibited.

Figure 11. Brainstorming in groups

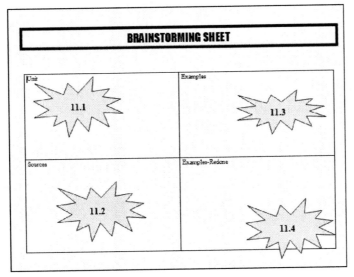

Figure 12. Micro- and macroinfusion of topics in the curriculum

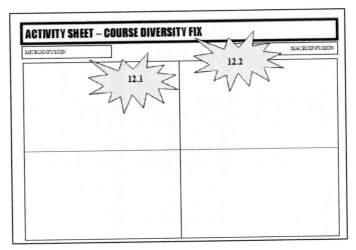

In the sense of the previous Ready-To-Wear snippet, talking about Equal Opportunity Computing whenever possible is another venue of introducing topics in disabilities and gender differences in the cognitive process (Figure 7, part I-4).

Bring a product to the classroom and start talking about the UPC code, or a code that the United States Postal Service has put on a recent letter that you

Copyright © 2006, Idea Group Inc. Copying or distributing in print or electronic forms without written permission of Idea Group Inc. is prohibited.

have received. The codes (Figure 8, part I-5) can provide information on the country of origin of a product, for example, and much more, or the 5+4 zip code of the receiver of the letter. By extending the information to ISBN and ISSN, we create an opportunity to present students with relevant publications in the very core area of the course.

In the sense of the codes, further discussion may be led by using topics such as number systems, currencies and various ways time has been measured throughout history (Figure 8, part I-6). The topics within the number systems would comprise positional and nonpositional number systems, while a discussion on calendars would cover the Julian, Gregorian, Mayan and other calendars that are currently used or have been used by different civilizations in the past, as well as alternative solutions to measuring time that have been proposed in the past, but never "picked up."

Topics such as the Bulgarian virus phenomenon (Bennahum, online), the quantity of computer viruses that were "exported" from Bulgaria in the beginning of the 1990s, can introduce geography related, international topics in parallel to the IT-related topics that we would be teaching when using these examples (Figure 9, part I-7). Not only that, some of these activities would make students aware of, say, the geographical position of a country and some of its national issues, and also provide a venue for the foreign students to share personal experiences and views on the same issues in their country of origin.

As a counterpart to Women's studies, a large number of courses on which are available across campuses nationwide, the area of men's studies seems to be still in its inception. This emerging field studies the problems of men, fatherhood, gender relations, men's health, etc. We have experienced the emergence of several journals in this area (see, for example, Mensstudies.com) (Figure 9, part I-9).

E-business/E-commerce case studies may also account for a rich source of diversity-related topics as candidates for infusion in the curriculum of virtually every IT-related course. Topics can be found on a wealth of companies worldwide, companies run by, or with, predominantly female workers, or focused on serving the female customer. Alternatively, students could be given projects to write their own case studies on, say, companies that are focused on the gay customer (Figure 10, Part I-9).

We believe that we teach who we are and what we know (Figure 10, Part I-10). Personal interest and personal research interest in one way or another find their place in our classrooms.

Copyright © 2006, Idea Group Inc. Copying or distributing in print or electronic forms without written permission of Idea Group Inc. is prohibited.

Figure 13. Group activity sheet

Figure 14. Introspection after the workshop: Part 1

After going over these (all, selected or modified) ideas that are put in the workbook to initialize the thinking of possible implementable topics, the participants, alone or in small teams, start working on the activity on page 11 in the workbook (Figure 11). The objective of this activity is experiencing the process of microinfusion of topics in the curriculum. The easiest way to start,

Copyright © 2006, Idea Group Inc. Copying or distributing in print or electronic forms without written permission of Idea Group Inc. is prohibited.

Figure 15. Introspection after the workshop: Part 2

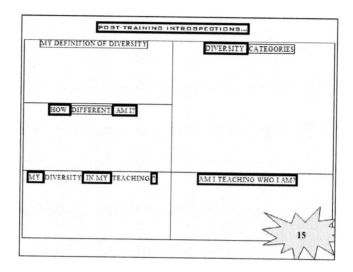

at least, is by reworking the examples provided with the course literature, or providing alternative, diversity-spiced examples in place of the offered, more sterile ones. On this activity sheet the instructors identify a unit (box 11.1) in which to transform an example (box 11.3) that they usually use, by using possible sources of information from the diversity scrapbook, or the resource sheets (11.2), to state the transformed example in box 11.4.

Thinking about the microinfusion leads to more elaborate discussions on global changes of courses that may be introduced into the course planning process and syllabus writing (12.2). In this context we usually discuss reworking the policies on the project that can account for more open-ended projects, or projects on diversity-related aspects of the topics being covered.

On page 13 (Figure 13), small team participants discuss ideas for rewording parts of their syllabi, to make sure they are compliant with the institution's policies on non-discrimination (this varies from one institution to another).

The last two activities are retrospective in nature, and do not necessarily have to be a part of the on-ground activities (Figures 14 and 15).

Copyright © 2006, Idea Group Inc. Copying or distributing in print or electronic forms without written permission of Idea Group Inc. is prohibited.

Figure 16. An excerpt from a resource list used at a training session.

EDUCATIONAL CYBERPLAYGROUND
http://www.edu-cyberpg.com/culdesac/bhm/bhm.html
Featuring, among other, Black History Month All Year Long.

ASSOCIATION OF WOMEN IN SCIENCE
http://www.awis.org/
AWIS is dedicated to achieving equity and full participation for women in science, mathematics, engineering and technology.

ASSOCIATION FOR WOMEN IN COMPUTING
http://www.awc-hq.org/
Promoting the advancement of women in the computing professions.

GENDER, SCIENCE AND TECHNOLOGY: INTERNATIONAL POLICY ISSUES
http://www.ifias.ca/GSD/GSDinfo.html
Links to information on GSD and its collaborators.

The DIVERSE e-group is designed to serve as a meeting cyber-place where we can exchange ideas and experiences from our efforts to incorporate different diversity concepts and views in their curriculum. To subscribe to the list, please visit XXX.

The Basic Components of the Workshop

The training consists of four general modules and uses trainer's short introductory comments, and the participants work, individually or in small teams. The global agenda is as follows:

1. *Getting Hooked*: How I Infuse Diversity in My Classes
2. *Getting Inspired (from the Outside)*: Diversity in IT
3. *Getting Inspired (from the Inside)*: How Different Are You?
4. Introduction of the Online Community

The first module's goal is to give examples and thus expose the participants to a variety of ways that various topics may be introduced while teaching an IT-related course. The second module talks about some of the resources available to the participants for consideration for infusion in the curriculum. The third part is introspective. As we all teach basically who we are, looking into ourselves and our experiences can give us inspiration for transformations of modules in

Copyright © 2006, Idea Group Inc. Copying or distributing in print or electronic forms without written permission of Idea Group Inc. is prohibited.

the courses we are teaching. As the goal of the workshop is far-reaching and cannot be achieved—but only initialized—at the training itself, the fourth part introduces a solution for an online community created to facilitate the exchange of experiences between the participants of the workshop.

Getting Hooked: Motivating Examples from My Classroom

In order to achieve a certain level of dynamics at the training session, I normally offer tidbits on how I do the diversity topics infusion in some of the courses that I have taught in the past or I am currently teaching.

The CS0-level course (COSC 111) is a course where we introduce basic concepts of Computer Science, IS and IT to the students. The example from this class that I give is from Figures 3 and 4 . I also state that I give a variety of topics for the individual homework assignments and projects that the students are expected to do in this class. An excerpt of the list of topics for an individual research project consists of topics such as Portraying a Woman in Science (for a project when wrapping up the coverage of the word processor), Women in Congress around the World (spreadsheets) and Tracking currency exchange rates (databases) etc. When working on the Women in Sciences (or Women in Computing) project, the students are expected to identify and write a short biography and summary of achievements of a prominent female figure that has made a contribution in the field. For the spreadsheet project, students are expected to collect data on the actual numbers and/or percentages of women in governmental structures comparable to the U.S. senate in various countries around the world, or of a particular region, and compare them with the US statistics. A particularly interesting region is the Scandinavian countries, where the number of women in congress surpasses significantly the number of men. In the database project, students learn about different countries and their currencies, and work on a simple database application and interface that serves as an exchange calculator.

In my e-Commerce course, I normally talk about the business traditions and behaviors in different cultures. The transfer protocols vary from one country to another. Different countries have varying levels of technological infrastructure for doing business online. What is ethical in one culture, even business-wise, might not be in another.

Copyright © 2006, Idea Group Inc. Copying or distributing in print or electronic forms without written permission of Idea Group Inc. is prohibited.

Courses like Human-Computer Interaction are a wonderful foundation for introducing topics on "equal opportunity computing" (see discussion on Figure 7, part I-7). Topics where more elaboration has been found useful are accessibility for people with a range of disabilities, such as speech synthesizers, keyboard alternatives, computer talk, magnification and translation of text into Braille, etc.

There are existing alternatives to the hardware and software interfaces that we are accustomed to use. The design of interfaces teaches us that many times better designs (ergonomically and cognition-wise) have been proposed, but due to the economic predominance of certain corporations, we have grown "attached" to some that might be seriously flawed.

In courses that have focused on computer security, apart from the cultural dimensions when discussing privacy, ethics, and legal issues, we always have a nice discussion on the global perspectives of computer security, and, in that context, we mention the Bulgarian phenomenon. We analyze the geographical origin of malicious code and the efforts of different members of the international community to fight (and penalize) these attacks. Software piracy, with its cultural and geographical dimensions, also emerges as a natural topic for discussion in these courses.

Figure 17. The scheduled dynamics of the workshop

On-Ground Session 1
Hour 1: The Multicultural Classroom. Teaching Who You Are.
Hour 2: Learning about yourself and teammates. Stereotypes. Intercultural Hooks that Block Communication. Assumptions about Appearance.
Hour 3: On with the Groups. Diversity Resources – An Intro
Hours 4-6: Movie "Legally Blonde." Discussion.

Online Intersession 1 (online activities)

OnGround Session 2
Hour 1: Transforming the Syllabi.
Hours 2-3: Subtle changes to the Lecture Goals.

Online Intersession 2 (online activities)

On-Ground Session 3
Hour 1: Civic Engagement and the Curriculum. Using the Internet to cater to Civic Engagement Projects.
Hours 2-3: Discussion and preparations for the Civic Engagement.
Hours 4-6: Movie: "Legally Blonde 2: Red, White and Blonde," and discussion.

Online Intersession 3 (online activities)

On-Ground Session 4

Hours 1-3: Civic Engagement Project

Copyright © 2006, Idea Group Inc. Copying or distributing in print or electronic forms without written permission of Idea Group Inc. is prohibited.

Getting Inspired on the Outside

The second module of the workshop tends to introduce the participants to the available resources they can use in the diversity reexamination of the courses they teach. Depending on the structure of the participants, we usually try to provide an appropriate reading list that can be distributed even prior to the workshop, or left to be read after the meetings. An excerpt of a handout given at a workshop may be seen in Figure 16.

Getting Inspired from the Inside: How Different Are You?

With activities focusing on introspection, we engage the participants in thinking about how different they are and how they might want to consider incorporating that knowledge in their classrooms.

Introduction of the Online Community

The on-ground workshop is usually the place where the thinking of diversity in its teaching would be initiated. The process is significantly faster if there is a supporting community of people with similar needs and ideas, where participants could share experiences from successful and unsuccessful classroom experiments. For those purposes, we usually create an online e-group with Yahoo! Groups or Google (in Figure 16, we call the e-Group DIVERSE), and give directions to the participants on how to sign up for the service. It has been our experience that the participants need a little bit of initiative in the beginning in order to start feeling comfortable sharing with the others in the group. But, we as facilitators do intervene in the beginning by sharing our experiences. Soon, the participants will see that there are no experiences that are unworthy of sharing, no experiences too small or insignificant and that we learn from.

Copyright © 2006, Idea Group Inc. Copying or distributing in print or electronic forms without written permission of Idea Group Inc. is prohibited.

Suggested Structure for the Workshop

This section of the chapter discusses a suggested structure for a workshop, the on-ground component of which spans over two weeks.

This session is designed specifically for the teachers and leaders in the IT field, where additional stress in put on civic engagement. Via short lecture sessions, hands-on activities and discussions (with two light movies to kick them off), the participants will understand and plan the implementation of diversity inclusion in the activities they have been involved in, as well as investigate the possibilities for civic awareness and civic engagement as a part of the teaching process.

At the first session, the trainers assemble diverse teams of 3-4 teachers and community leaders. After initial lectures by the trainer (and possibly guest speakers) showcasing the infusion of diversity in different disciplines, the participants will begin self-designed curriculum modification projects of a course that they teach or activity they engage communities in.

Participants will present project ideas and goals to the whole group. During the second meeting, they will present the curriculum modifications (micro- and macro-level) that they have managed to achieve with the help of their team-mates.

During the third and fourth meetings, they explore alternative media for civic engagement in the curriculum, and explore the possibilities of engaging civically with their communities.

The goals of the workshop are:

1. Address the importance of diversity infusion across disciplines;

2. Provide the participants with a framework for such interventions;

3. Provide examples and procedures of diversity topics infusion across a variety of disciplines;

4. Give the participants an opportunity to exchange their views with peers;

5. Understand that a vibrant democracy requires engaged citizens; and

6. Explore the possibilities of civic awareness and civic engagement across the curriculum.

The workshop activities can be categorized as on-ground and online. As we are focusing on autopoiesis in this community of educators, we have tried to

Copyright © 2006, Idea Group Inc. Copying or distributing in print or electronic forms without written permission of Idea Group Inc. is prohibited.

Figure 18. The reader

-- "Multiculturalism", available online at http://www.essaybank.co.uk/free_coursework/1410.htm

-- "From Multiculturalism to Diversity Management," available online at:
http://www.fhsu.edu/~jkerriga/ids350frommulti.html

Caplan, M. "Evolution of the Theory of Multiculturalism," available online at:
http://www.sonoma.edu/depts/amcs/upstream/theory.html

James, E. "The Multivisions of Multiculturalism," available online at:
http://wwww.bu.edu/wcp/Papers/Poli/PoliJame.htm

McTighe-Musil, C. "Educating for Citizenship," peer review, Spring 2003.

Sleeter, C. *Culture, Difference and Power*, Teachers College Press, 2001.

Sleeter and Grant. "Multicultural Education," from *Making Choices for Multicultural Education*, Merrill, 1994.

Tiedt & Tiedt, "Learning about Ourselves," from *Multicultural Teaching*, Allyn and Bacon, 1998.

Tiedt & Tiedt, "Infusing Multicultural Concepts across the Curriculum," from *Multicultural Teaching*, Allyn and Bacon, 1998.

Parks & Wiseman, *Maryland: Unity in Diversity*, Kendall/Hunt, 1990.

UNESCO, "Multiculturalism: A Policy Response to Diversity," available at:
http://www.unesco.org/most/sydpaper.htm

minimize the structured activities to the bare minimum necessary to focus and facilitate the work of the teams.

1.   On-Ground Information Sessions and Workshops
2.   Online Activities
  a.   Establishing and using a global online learning community
  b.   Communication within the groups

The on-ground component of the workshop spans over two weeks. After the first two on-ground meetings, the teams continue to work collaboratively on their projects. The results and experiences are shared after the projects have been experimented with in the classroom/ community, using the online community that is be created to facilitate the information interchange past the end of the on-ground component of the workshop.

The details on the activities are included in Figure 17.

Copyright © 2006, Idea Group Inc. Copying or distributing in print or electronic forms without written permission of Idea Group Inc. is prohibited.

Figure 19. Diverse classroom on-ground and online workshop structure

The Workshop. These sessions have been designed to introduce you to the extraordinary efforts that US educators are undertaking towards incorporating diversity topice in the everyday classroom, weather it is on ground, or online. The participants will work on a production of resource page on a diversity topic, syllabus development, lecture plan development, and lecture enchancement with a variety of topics mainly focused on multiculturalism. They will be introduced to new and modern approaches in teaching in order to serve the diverse student population, such as the Multiple Intelligence theories, and the active learning paradigms.

The Schedule.

Time	Topic
	SESSION 1: WHAT IS MULTICULTURALISM
1 hour	The Multicultural Classroom: US perspective
1 hour	Diversity Case: Maryland life, Culture and Statistics
1 hour	Teaching Who You Are: Diversity in the Curriculum
	SESSION 2: CELEBRATING DIVERSITY ONLINE
1 hour	Web Page Design: How to be Successful
1 hour	Web Page Enhancement: Making it Fun
1 hour	Cases of Successful Resource Pages: Make Your Own
	SESSION 3: TEACHING DIVERSITY ONLINE
1 hour	Creating Multimedia on a Budget of $5 a year:
1 hour	Distance Education: Why?
1 hour	Success with Online Courses: How?
	SESSION 4: TEACHING FOR DIVERSE STUDENTS
1 hour	Online Discussions: When?
1 hour	Multiple Intelligences: Who?
1 hour	Active Learning in the Classroom: Where?

Catalog of Activities

The Multicultural Classroom. The new demographics. What is diversity? Diversity and representation. Exploring diversity. Encountering difference. Identity. Mobilizing for social justice. Culturally relevant pedagogy. Multicultural curriculum.

Teaching Who You Are. Examples of diversity infusion in the curriculum—a panel discussion with 2-3 panelists.

Learning About Yourself and Teammates. The "Me" collage. How does it feel to be different? Stereotypes. Group activities, team building.

On with the Groups. Groups share the basics of the courses/activities that they have decided to work on, and identify units in each one of the courses in the team for the lower-level infusion exercises.

Copyright © 2006, Idea Group Inc. Copying or distributing in print or electronic forms without written permission of Idea Group Inc. is prohibited.

Figure 20. Participants' reactions to a training session in teaching diversity. In part a) are the acquired benefits from the training and in part b), comments on the teaching methods.

a) The workshop has provided us with much information on dealing with diversity in the classroom. The lectures were not solely based on theory, but included a great deal of practice.
I thought it would be more formal. Great atmosphere...
It helped me better understand diversity in every segment of society.
The experience was learning through fun.
We had excellent introduction of theoretical and practical concepts. We learned a lot from each other.
It was designed for teachers; we were doing something really useful. The teaching tricks, the movies, the reader were all great.
We came to see and hear many things for the first time.
We got good materials, gained knowledge about some cultural diversity in USA, used our experience, and gained some computer skills.

b) The teacher's methods were great. The structure of the presentation was new and interesting.
Interactive, fun and well-designed.
It has been more fun than expected.
The facilitator was excellent, willing to help and teach... He really prepared lots of materials for us which would be more than useful. I learned that we can learn from films and games. If we didn't show a decent level of ability, interest or knowledge, that was definitely due to the fact that the workshop was late at night and nothing else... It would have been better to have these workshops during the day.
He was well prepared, creative and had understanding for our way of learning. He shared his ideas with us, organized great activities, motivated us, and socialized during the break and after the sessions, which was very important in bringing the group together.

Diversity Resources – An Intro. Overview of some of the diversity resources available online. Distribution of the reading packages. Overview of the package contents.

Movie Session 1: "Legally Blonde." The movie that has been chosen, "*Legally Blonde,*" is a comedy that deals with breaking the stereotypes about blondes and other socially distinguished categories. The discussion after the movie will help wrap-up the session.

Online Intersession 1. Groups work together in online brainstorming sessions on the unit plan and syllabus diversification.

Copyright © 2006, Idea Group Inc. Copying or distributing in print or electronic forms without written permission of Idea Group Inc. is prohibited.

Transforming the Syllabi, Subtle changes to the Lecture Goals. The participants are wrapping up on-ground the work done online and share their findings and ideas with the other participants, autopoietically.

Online Intersession 2. Participants prepare for implementing the changes in the syllabi. They document the preparation and the experiences from the classroom. They design questionnaires on attitude change using quantitative measurement.

Civic Engagement and the Curriculum. Educating for citizenship. Community service and service learning. Creating integrative environments and projects on the levels of the neighborhood through global initiatives. Integration of the diversity movement, the civic engagement movement and the movement to create more student-centric institutions. Adapting to changes and change management. Student-centered pedagogies. Engaged, participatory learning; Dialogue and collaboration. Faces of citizenship (exclusionary, oblivious, naïve, charitable, reciprocal, generative).

Using the Internet to Cater to Civic Engagement Projects. Modalities of use. Sample sites. Using synchronous and asynchronous channels for advertising a cause.

Discussions, Preparations for the Civic Engagement Project. Teams of 3-4 teachers discuss an implementable project for their home schools/organizations, plan it and devise a plan of implementation.

Movie: "Legally Blonde 2: Red, White and Blonde." Discussion on civic engagement.

This comedy illustrates a legislative initiative being pushed trough the legal system.

Conclusions: Experiences from the Experiments. Participants meet and discuss the expected outcomes of the implementations of the changes in their institutions.

The Reader

Figure 17 presents the chosen readings for the participants, distributed during the third hour of the first on-ground meeting.

Copyright © 2006, Idea Group Inc. Copying or distributing in print or electronic forms without written permission of Idea Group Inc. is prohibited.

The Diverse Classroom On-Ground and Online: Another Workshop Example

In this section we give another example of a workshop that we have held on diversity infusion in the curriculum in general. For the group activities, we paired a participant from the "hard" sciences and a participant from the social sciences. The participants were high-school teachers from South and Eastern Europe that participated in an exchange program funded by the U.S. State Department and the Open Society Institute. The brief on the four-day workshop is given in Figure 19.

Comments from the Workshop Participants

In order to gather information for calibrating the future workshops, at the end of each training session we distribute evaluation sheets where the participants share their insights on the training. In this section (Figure 20), we present some of the participants' opinions on the training on teaching diversity.

Conclusion: The Training Must Go On...

In this chapter, we gave an overview of diversity training components that we have used over the years when working with IT faculty or faculty in general. Based on the need, and the time allotted, the components and activities can be arranged in an appropriate fashion.

The training must go on past the on-ground workshop. In order to continue the processes of building the faculty, the participants would reflect and share their experiences from their experiments in the classroom online.

Copyright © 2006, Idea Group Inc. Copying or distributing in print or electronic forms without written permission of Idea Group Inc. is prohibited.

References

Abraham, I. (2000). Postcolonial science, big science, and landscape. In R. Reid & S. Traweek (Eds.), *Doing science and culture* (pp. 49-70). New York: Routledge.

Bennahum, D. (1997, November). Heart of darkness. *Wired.*

Coleman, S. (1999). *Japanese science.* New York: Routledge.

Downey, G., & Dumit, J. (1999). *Cyborgs and citadels.* Sante Fe, NM: SAR Press.

Downey, G. L., & Lucena, J. (1997). Engineering selves: Hiring in to a contested field of education. In G. L. Downey & J. Dumit (Eds.), *Cyborgs and citadels.* Santa Fe, NM: School of American Research Press.

Exchange Links. (n.d.). Retrieved March 7, 2005, from http://www.finix.at/fin/selinks.html

Helmreich, S. (1998). *Silicon second nature.* Berkeley: University of California Press.

Hess, D. (1995). *Science and technology in a multicultural world.* New York: Columbia University Press.

Knorr-Cetina, K. (1981). *The manufacture of knowledge.* New York: Pergamon.

Luhmann, N. (1989). *Ecological communication.* Cambridge: Polity Press.

Maturana, H., & Varela, F. (Eds.). (1980). *Autopoiesis and cognition.* Dordrecht: Reidel.

Mead, M. (1964). *Continuities in cultural evolution.* New Haven: Yale University Press.

Men's Studies Press. (n.d.). Retrieved March 1, 2005, from http://www.mensstudies.com

Raskin, J. (2000). *The humane interface: New directions for designing interactive systems.* Boston: Addison Wesley Professional.

Tsunami (n.d.). Retrieved March 7, 2005, from http://www.npr.org

Varela, F. (1979). *Principles of biological autonomy.* New York: Elsevier.

Winthrop-Young, G. (2000). Silicon sociology, or two kings on Hegel's throne. *The Yale Journal of Criticism, 13*(2), 391-420.

Copyright © 2006, Idea Group Inc. Copying or distributing in print or electronic forms without written permission of Idea Group Inc. is prohibited.

About the Authors

Goran P. Trajkovski is assistant professor of computer and information sciences and director of the Cognitive Agency and Robotics Laboratory at Towson University (USA). He chaired the 2004 Multicultural Conference, "Defining Dimensions of Diversity," at Towson University. He is a member of the University System of Maryland (USM) Faculty Diversity Initiative Task Force and sits on the organizing committees of the USM Diversity Conferences. He has organized a number of panels of diversity infusion in the Information Technology curriculum. He is a member of numerous program committees of international conferences, and a reviewer for professional journals, including ACM Reviews and CHOICE. He has published over 120 items, including three previous books.

* * * * * *

Ali Akbari is a professor of economics at California Lutheran University (CLU) (USA). He has been active professionally—publishing articles, presenting papers, serving on professional programs and consulting. He has co-authored two textbooks in economics: *Explorations in Macroeconomics* and *The Economic Way of Thinking*. Dr. Akbari is director of the CLU Center for Economic Research. His latest project was the development of an economic and business forecasting model that provides quarterly forecasts of economic activities in the major cities of Ventura County.

Copyright © 2006, Idea Group Inc. Copying or distributing in print or electronic forms without written permission of Idea Group Inc. is prohibited.

Virginia Johnson Anderson is a professor of biological sciences at Towson University (USA). She is a classroom assessment activist. Having worked with faculty in all disciplines at over 100 colleges/universities, she brings national perspectives to very local concerns—grading and assessment! Dr. Anderson has directed two major Towson University urban science education NSF initiatives, published numerous articles and book chapters and is best known for her work with Barbara Walvoord in coauthoring *Effective Grading: A Tool for Learning and Assessment* (Jossey-Bass, 1998). She has served as a consultant for the American Society for Microbiology, Ecological Society of America, Woodrow Wilson Foundation, the United States Peace Corps, National Science Teachers Association and both state and national Writing Across the Curriculum projects.

Madhumita Bhattacharya completed her PhD while working as a faculty member at the Indian Institute of Technology. She did her postdoctoral research at the Tokyo Institute of Technology. She has 18 years of research and teaching experience at universities in India, UK, Japan, Singapore, Australia, Estonia and New Zealand. Madhumita is a senior lecturer at Massey University (New Zealand) and a visiting professor at the University of Tartu. Madhumita's specialization and research interest is in science education, multicultural issues and learning design and technologies. She is a recipient of several research grants. She is the author and co-author of more than 80 publications.

Samuel G. Collins is an associate professor of at the Department of Sociology, Anthropology and Criminal Justice at Towson University (USA) and a co-director of the Cultural Studies Program, an area devoted to applying methods and theories across disciplines. His research includes the cultural organization of knowledge in information society, emergent cultures and social structures and the application of qualitative methodologies to cyber-environments.

John R. Dakers lectures at the University of Glasgow in the Department of Educational Studies. His research interests include technology education, the philosophy of technology, technological literacy and creating communities of learners in technology education. He has written extensively on these subjects, delivered presentations at various conferences around the world and acts as a guest lecturer on these topics to several universities around Europe. He has acted as principle consultant to the European Commission for the past two

Copyright © 2006, Idea Group Inc. Copying or distributing in print or electronic forms without written permission of Idea Group Inc. is prohibited.

years on matters relating to increasing recruitment of science, mathematics and technology subjects. He recently acted as director for a major conference on "Pupils Attitudes Towards Technology" (PATT), held in Glasgow recently and co-edited the peer-reviewed conference book with Marc J. de Vries from The Netherlands. His latest book *Defining Technological Literacy: Towards an Epistemological Framework*, is due to be published in the USA by Palgrave Macmillan later this year.

Jamshid Damooei is a professor of economics and co-director of The Center for Leadership and Values at California Lutheran University (USA). Before joining the faculty at CLU in 1987, he taught at California State University, Northridge. Dr. Damooei was director general of the Bureau of Economic Studies and Policies of the Ministry of Economic Affairs and Finance of Iran. He also served as a senior economist for the United Nations Development Program (UNDP). He currently consults for the United Nations and is most recognized for his expertise on economic and institutional capacity building in East Africa and the Middle East.

Mats Daniels is a senior lecturer in computer science at Uppsala University, Sweden, where as well as teaching undergraduate courses, he is also director of undergraduate education. He has used Open Ended Group Projects in courses involving collaboration with industry and has been part of developing, running and studying courses with international student collaboration based on OEGP methods. Mats has been active internationally in the computer science education area for over 10 years and chaired the European ACM SIGCSE Innovation and Technology in Computer Science Education conference when it was held in Uppsala in 1997.

Alfreda Dudley-Sponaugle is a lecturer in the Department of Computer and Information Sciences at Towson University (USA). She currently teaches the computer ethics courses in the curriculum. Her research focus is technology, ethics and culture. Her interests include: information technology, systems analysis, management information systems, databases and computer educa- tion. Professor Dudley-Sponaugle presented and published at the following conferences: Proceedings of the Eighth Annual Consortium for Computing Sciences in Colleges- Northeastern Conference, IEEE 2002 International Symposium on Technology and Society (Social Implications of Information

Copyright © 2006, Idea Group Inc. Copying or distributing in print or electronic forms without written permission of Idea Group Inc. is prohibited.

and Communication Technology), and the Forty-first ACM Southeast Regional Conference. She is Co-Advisor to the National Black Science and Engineering chapter at Towson. She serves on the Business and Education Steering Committee on a proposed NSF grant entitled, "The Grace Hopper Scholars Program in Mathematics and Computer Science." Professor Dudley-Sponaugle has participated as a faculty representative/participant at The Howard County Public School System: Mathematics, Science, and Technology Fair.

Xristine Faulkner is a reader in human computer interaction education development at London South Bank University where she teaches computer studies and business information technology courses to undergraduates. She has made extensive use of group work over her 30 years in teaching and has used the Open Ended Group Project to work with large classes on one project. She is the author of *Essence of HCI* and *Usability Engineering* and has published a number of papers with co-authors Ian Newman and Mats Daniels on the subject of the OEGP.

Lone Jorgensen is a senior lecturer at Massey University College of Education, New Zealand. She lectures in pedagogical studies and the teaching of science, biology, physics and technology. Her current research interests are in comparative school systems in Denmark and New Zealand and how these affect the retention of students in the science areas, as well as the philosophical implications of values education. After many years in secondary schools teaching the sciences, life-skills and health to adolescents, she left to complete a PhD in environmental technology. She has a personal interest in philosophy and environmental issues.

Mary Kirk is an assistant professor in the Individualized, Interdisciplinary and Lifelong Learning Department at Metropolitan State University (USA), where she also teaches in the Women's Studies Program. She has convened panels on women in science and technology at conferences such as the Grace Hopper Celebration of Women in Computing, National Women's Studies Association and Conference on Computing in Small Colleges. She has published on women in science and technology in the *Journal of Computing in Small Colleges* and the *NWSA Journal*. Kirk earned her PhD in women's studies/women in computing from Union Institute and University.

Copyright © 2006, Idea Group Inc. Copying or distributing in print or electronic forms without written permission of Idea Group Inc. is prohibited.

Blaise W. Liffick is a professor of computer science at Millersville University of Pennsylvania (USA), where he has been on the faculty for some 25 years. His specialty is human-computer interaction, with an emphasis on adaptive technology for the disabled. He holds a PhD in computer and information science from Temple University, MS and BS degrees in computer science (University of Pittsburgh and Purdue University), and specialist certificates in assistive technology applications from California State University at Northridge and accessible information technology from the University of Southern Maine and EASI. Additional information about his Adaptive Computing Lab can be found at cs.millersville.edu/~liffick.

Luz Mangurian, PhD, is currently the director of The Center for Faculty Excellence at Towson University (USA). She has organized several conferences on teaching/learning for college and university faculty, given numerous keynote and plenary addresses, teaching/learning workshops and serves as a reviewer for the *Journal of Excellence in College Teaching* and the *Journal of Microbiology Education*. Dr. Mangurian, a professor of biology at Towson University, is also an affiliate professor of the Women Studies Program, The Center for Science and Mathematics Education and the founding director of the Women in Science program at Towson University. Mangurian's research uses neuroanatomical methods to investigate the role of prolactin and other lactogenic hormones in modulating maternal behavior. Her publications include numerous articles and peer-reviewed presentations in anatomy, neuroendocrinology, science pedagogy and two Spanish-language textbooks on human anatomy.

Peter McKenna is a senior lecturer in computing at Manchester Metropolitan University, UK. He teaches introductory programming and multimedia authoring and is active in multimedia learning pedagogy research and development, as well as research into gender and computing.

Gabriele Meiselwitz is a visiting assistant professor in the Department of Computer and Information Sciences at Towson University. She has worked for over 12 years as a computer engineer in industry in Europe and the US and has been teaching at Towson University since 1998. She is teaching introductory computer and creativity courses involving artwork, animation, dynamic story telling, computer music, Web publishing and computer games. Her research

Copyright © 2006, Idea Group Inc. Copying or distributing in print or electronic forms without written permission of Idea Group Inc. is prohibited.

interests are computer science introduction courses for majors and non-majors, creative computing and non-traditional teaching methods.

Tracy Miller is the director of university retention at Towson University (USA), where she has worked for more than 25 years. She advises undergraduate students and coordinates a domestic exchange program.

After graduating in physics and obtaining a PhD in theoretical physics, **Ian Newman** has been working with computers in universities for nearly 40 years, more than 30 of which have been spent in the Department of Computer Science at Loughborough University. Ian has researched in, and taught courses covering, many different subjects (from operating systems to distributed databases and systems analysis to formal methods) but usually concentrates on trying to get students to develop problem-solving techniques using open ended group projects, since this is a skill which can be applied to any area both within academia and, subsequently, in the outside world.

Reza Sarhangi is the graduate program director for mathematics education at Towson University (USA). Apart from working with teachers, he has been teaching geometry courses at different class levels. Most of his research focuses on the interdisciplinary approaches in mathematics, and the use of technology in the classroom. He is the director and the proceedings editor of the International Conference of Bridges: Mathematical Connections in Art, Music, and Science. The Bridges Conference is a gathering of science and mathematics educators, visual artists and computer scientists from several schools and countries. The purpose of the conference is to explore the links among disciplines through mathematical properties of objects and matter.

Shirish Shah is an adjunct faculty member in the Department of Chemistry at Towson University (USA) and at Villa Julie College. He has taught at the College of Notre Dame of Maryland and at several community colleges. He chaired the Computer Science Department at the Community College of Baltimore, where he developed courses for the Baltimore City Department of Public Works. He has served on several review teams for the Middle States Association of Colleges and Universities.

Copyright © 2006, Idea Group Inc. Copying or distributing in print or electronic forms without written permission of Idea Group Inc. is prohibited.

Russell Stockard is an assistant professor of communication at California Lutheran University (USA). He does research on globalization and communication, information technology and underserved communities, information and communication technologies (ICTs), NGOs and social movements, cultural studies and Latin American and Caribbean studies. He also has taught electronic media management and marketing at California State University, Northridge. He has served as a member of the International Advisory Board of Radio for Peace International, Colon, Costa Rica and has done broadcast journalism at the same station. He is the author of the *African American Consumer Handbook*.

Copyright © 2006, Idea Group Inc. Copying or distributing in print or electronic forms without written permission of Idea Group Inc. is prohibited.

Index

Copyright © 2006, Idea Group Inc. Copying or distributing in print or electronic forms without written permission of Idea Group Inc. is prohibited.

Copyright © 2006, Idea Group Inc. Copying or distributing in print or electronic forms without written
permission of Idea Group Inc. is prohibited.

Copyright © 2006, Idea Group Inc. Copying or distributing in print or electronic forms without written
permission of Idea Group Inc. is prohibited.

Experience the latest full-text research in the fields
of Information Science, Technology & Management

InfoSci-Online

InfoSci-Online is available to libraries to help keep students,
faculty and researchers up-to-date with the latest research in
the ever-growing field of information science, technology, and
management.

The InfoSci-Online collection includes:
- Scholarly and scientific book chapters
- Peer-reviewed journal articles
- Comprehensive teaching cases
- Conference proceeding papers
- All entries have abstracts and citation information
- The full text of every entry is downloadable in .pdf format

Some topics covered:
- Business Management
- Computer Science
- Education Technologies
- Electronic Commerce
- Environmental IS
- Healthcare Information Systems
- Information Systems
- Library Science
- Multimedia Information Systems
- Public Information Systems
- Social Science and Technologies

InfoSci-Online features:
- Easy-to-use
- 6,000+ full-text entries
- Aggregated
- Multi-user access

"...The theoretical bent of many of the titles covered, and the ease of adding chapters to reading lists, makes it particularly good for institutions with strong information science curricula."
— Issues in Science and Technology Librarianship

To receive your free 30-day trial access subscription contact:
Andrew Bundy
Email: abundy@idea-group.com • Phone: 717/533-8845 x29
Web Address: www.infosci-online.com

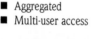

InfoSci Online
Full Text · Cutting Edge · Easy Access

A PRODUCT OF **Idea Group Inc.**
Publishers of Idea Group Publishing, Information Science Publishing, CyberTech Publishing, and IRM Press

infosci-online.com

Single Journal Articles and Case Studies Are Now Right at Your Fingertips!

Purchase any single journal article or teaching case for only $18.00!

Idea Group Publishing offers an extensive collection of research articles and teaching cases that are available for electronic purchase by visiting www.idea-group.com/articles. You will find over **980** journal articles and over **275** case studies from over 20 journals available for only $18.00. The website also offers a new capability of searching journal articles and case studies by category. To take advantage of this new feature, please use the link above to search within these available categories:

- ◆ Business Process Reengineering
- ◆ Distance Learning
- ◆ Emerging and Innovative Technologies
- ◆ Healthcare
- ◆ Information Resource Management
- ◆ IS/IT Planning
- ◆ IT Management
- ◆ Organization Politics and Culture
- ◆ Systems Planning
- ◆ Telecommunication and Networking
- ◆ Client Server Technology

- ◆ Data and Database Management
- ◆ E-commerce
- ◆ End User Computing
- ◆ Human Side of IT
- ◆ Internet-Based Technologies
- ◆ IT Education
- ◆ Knowledge Management
- ◆ Software Engineering Tools
- ◆ Decision Support Systems
- ◆ Virtual Offices
- ◆ Strategic Information Systems Design, Implementation

You can now view the table of contents for each journal so it is easier to locate and purchase one specific article from the journal of your choice.

Case studies are also available through XanEdu, to start building your perfect coursepack, please visit www.xanedu.com.

For more information, contact cust@idea-group.com or 717-533-8845 ext. 10.

www.idea-group.com

IDEA GROUP INC.

Design and Implementation of Web-Enabled Teaching Tools

Mary Hricko
Kent State University, USA

As the multifaceted environment of the Internet continues to evolve, web accessibility has become a major issue in terms of providing effective communication to the public. Although web accessibility guidelines exist, there are some academic institutions and areas of industry that have not developed guidelines to ensure that web documents are accessible. The primary objective of *Design and Implementation of Web-Enabled Teaching Tools* is to explore the myriad of issues regarding web accessibility, specifically focusing on those areas that cover the design and implementation of web-enabled teaching tools.

ISBN 1-59140-107-0(h/c); eISBN 1-59140-115-1: US$79.95 • 284 pages • Copyright © 2003

"We all realize that the force of the World Wide Web can be amazing and that it has yet to reach its potential, but the Web can only become more powerful and go beyond its limitations only if we always remember to advocate ways to make it completely accessible."
–Mary Hricko, Kent State University, USA

It's Easy to Order! Order online at www.idea-group.com or call 1-717-533-8845x10!
Mon-Fri 8:30 am-5:00 pm (est) or fax 24 hours a day 717/533-8661

Information Science Publishing

Hershey • London • Melbourne • Singapore • Beijing

An excellent addition to your library